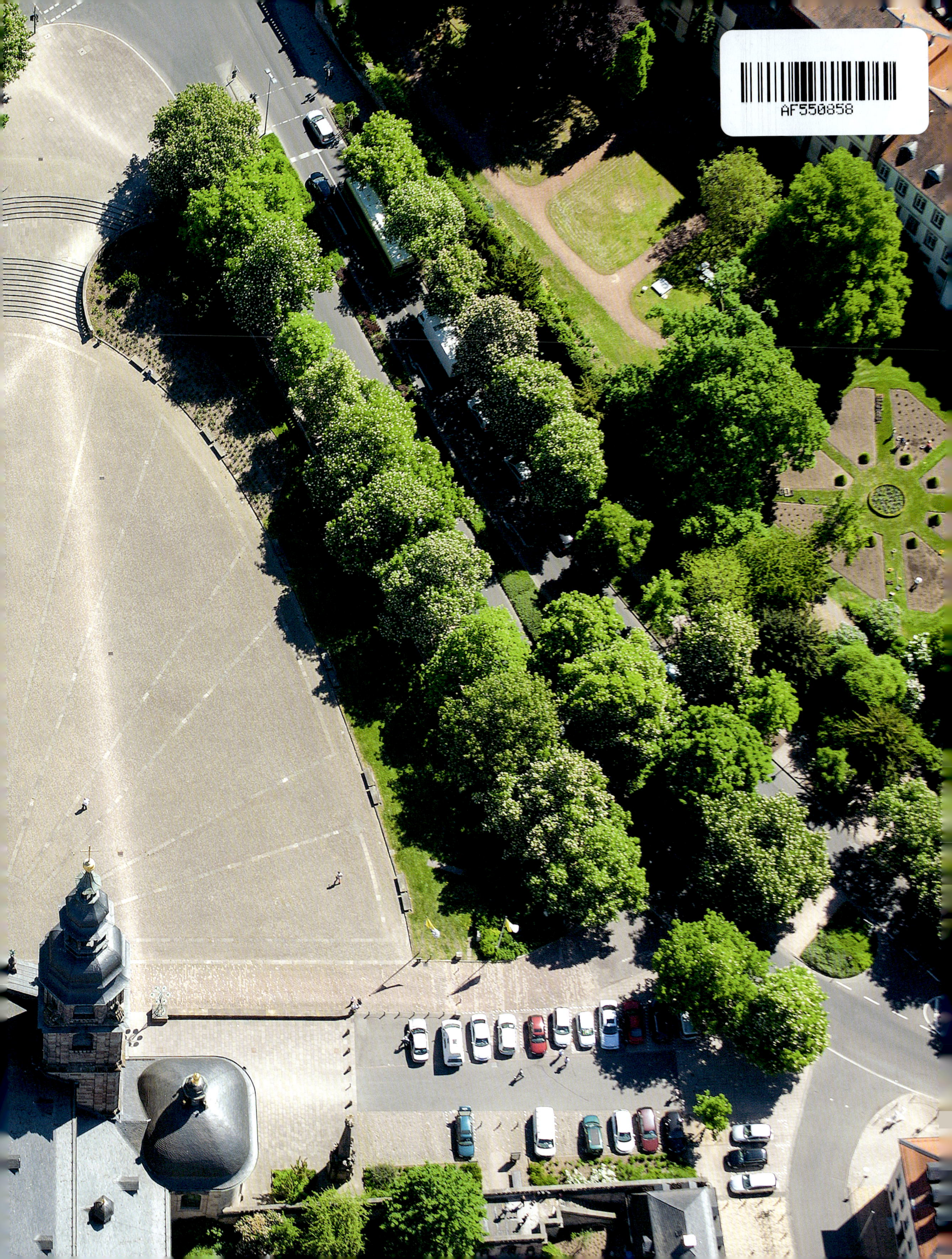

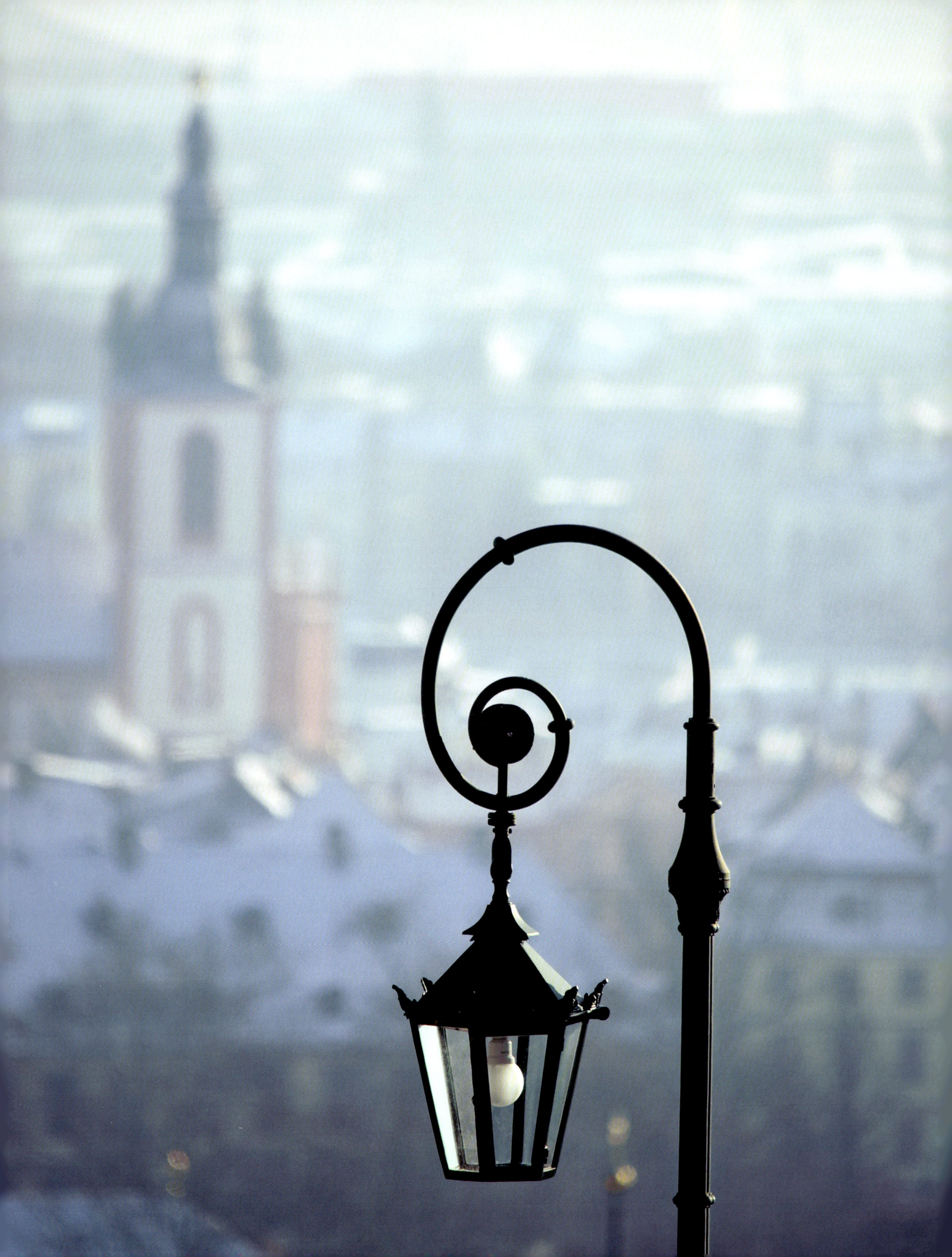

TEXT: JOHANNES HELLER
FOTOGRAFIE: CHRISTIAN TECH

Fulda

EIN BILDERBOGEN AUS DER BAROCKSTADT

A PHOTO PORTRAIT OF THE BAROQUE CITY

MICHAEL IMHOF VERLAG

INHALT

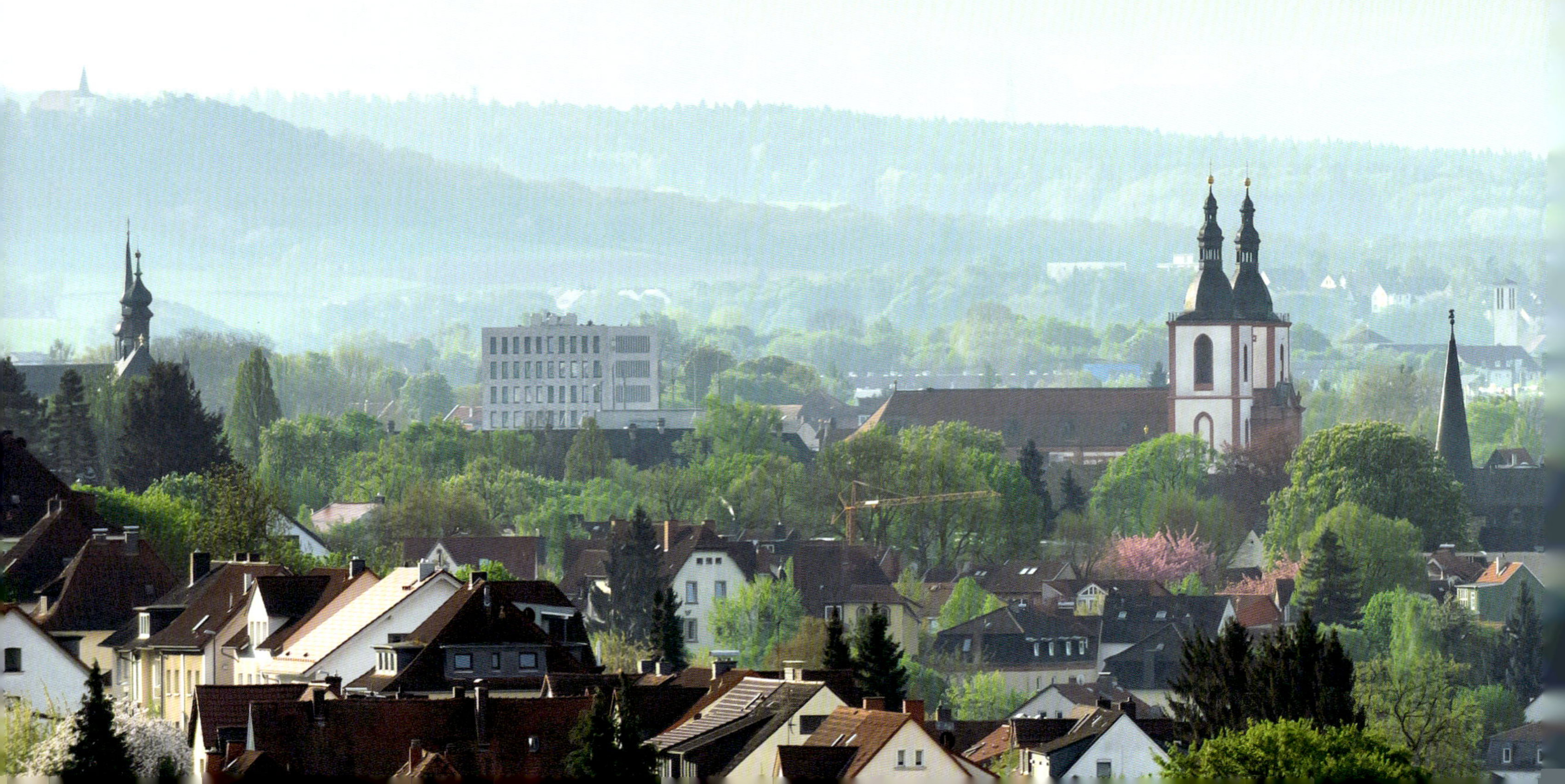

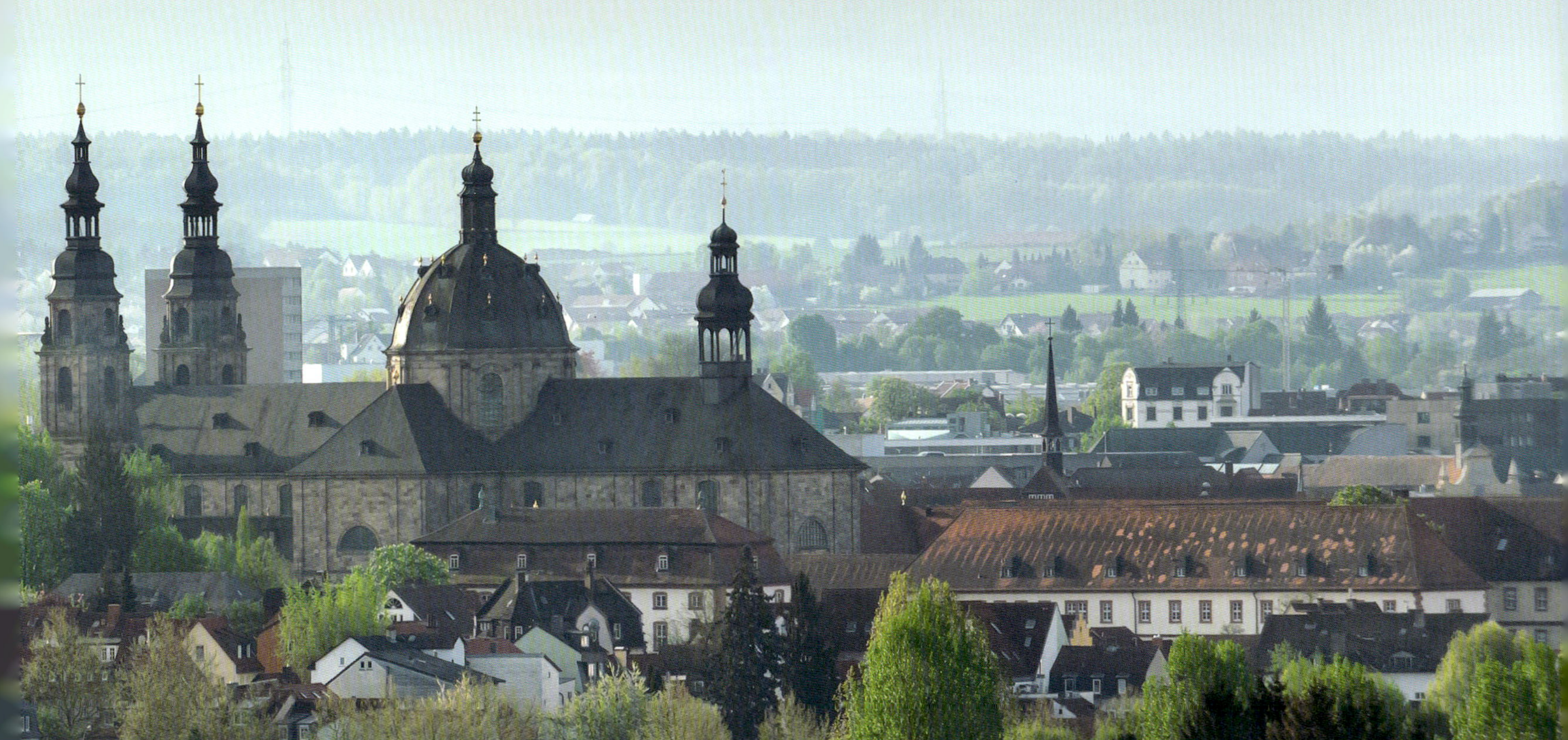

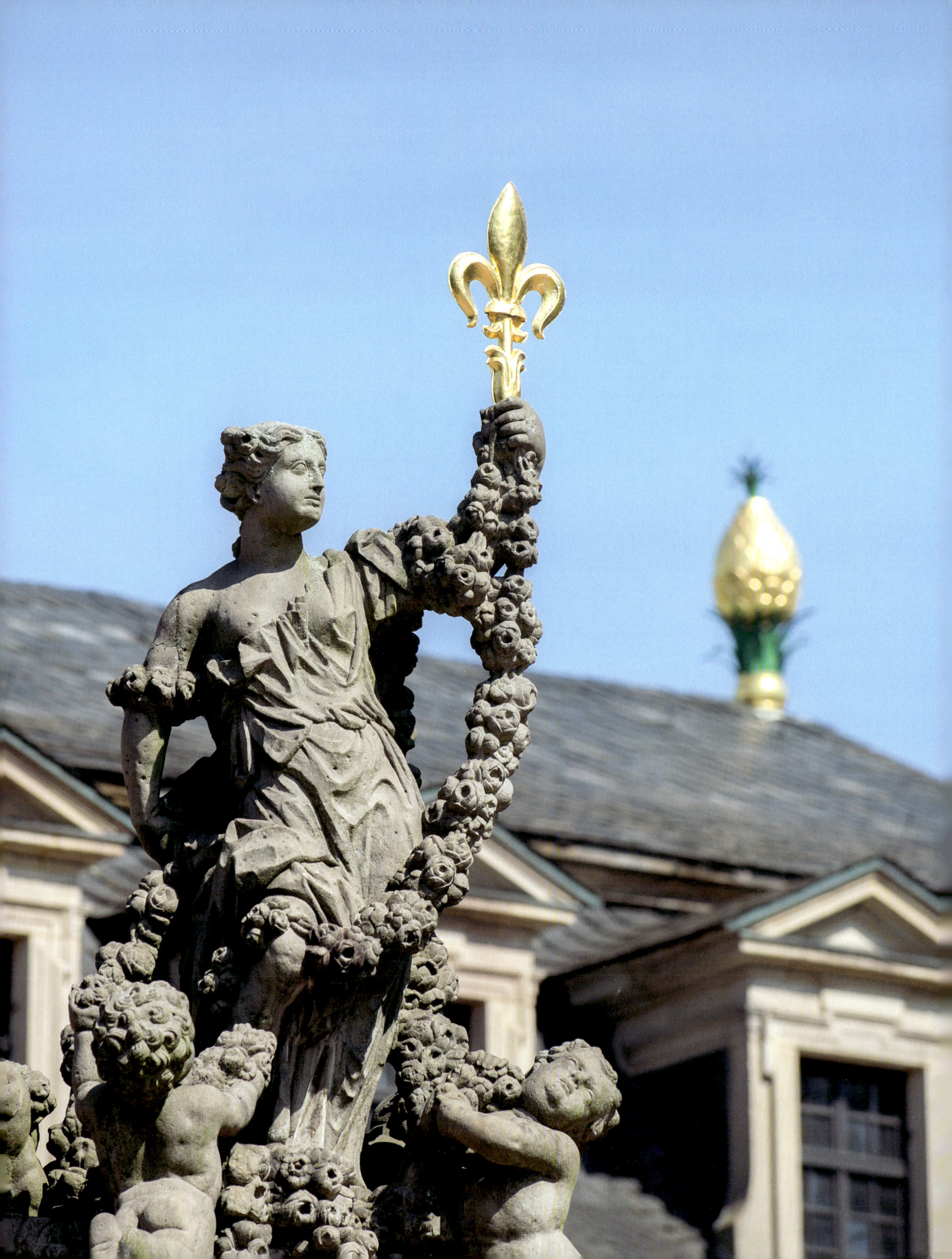

EIN SPAZIERGANG DURCH FULDA

Vorwort

„Wenn man einige Zeit in Fuld gewohnt hat, ohne weiter gekommen zu seyn, als etwa auf Würzburg und Bamberg, so weiß man freylich nicht, was man aus Fuld zu machen hat. Sobald man aber entferntere Gegenden durchreiset hat, und alsdann zu Fuld auf dem Frauenberg oder mitten in der Stadt auf dem höchstem Thurme die Gegend betrachtet, wird man sie schön, und sehr schön finden. Es sind vielleicht in ganz Europa wenige Gegenden, welche schöner sind."
MELCHIOR ADAM WEIKARD (1742–1803)

Gewiss, man darf dem Autor dieser Zeilen eine gehörige Portion Lokalpatriotismus unterstellen, schließlich wurde der Arzt und Philosoph Melchior Adam Weikard im Südteil des Fürstbistums Fulda geboren und lebte und wirkte viele Jahre als Leibarzt des Fürstbischofs Heinrich von Bibra am fuldischen Hof. Doch er hatte durchaus etwas von der Welt gesehen: Er verbrachte mehrere Jahre am Hofe der russischen Zarin Katharina II. in St. Petersburg, später wirkte er in Mainz, Mannheim und Heilbronn. Sein wohlmeinendes Urteil über die Stadt Fulda hat also durchaus Gewicht – und interessanterweise geht es noch heute vielen so, die in jungen Jahren die Stadt verließen, um irgendwo sonst in Deutschland und Europa zu lernen oder zu studieren: Mit der Zeit kehren sie zurück, schlendern durch die bunt bevölkerte Altstadt, setzen sich bei einem kühlen Getränk in die Sonne vor ihre Lieblingskneipe, bummeln durch die Geschäftsstraßen oder steigen wieder einmal hinauf zum Frauenberg, genießen den Ausblick – und sehen ihre Heimatstadt auf einmal mit ganz anderen Augen. Nämlich mit ganz ähnlichen wie die jährlich vielen Tausend Gäste unserer Stadt, die sich schon beim ersten Besuch in die barocke Pracht und die mittelalterlichen Gassen, die fast mediterrane Lebensfreude und angenehme Atmosphäre auf den Straßen und Plätzen, den liebevollen Blumenschmuck und die gepflegten Grünanlagen, die gelungene Mischung aus historischem

Die verspielte Floravase bildet den Blickfang zwischen Orangerie und Schlossgarten – gekrönt von einer goldenen Fuldaer Lilie.

Crowned by a golden fleur-de-lys, the Flora Vase, in between the Residence garden and the Orangerie, is a real eye-catcher.

"When you have lived in Fulda for some time without ever going further than Würzburg or Bamberg, you cannot really decide what to make of Fulda. However, when you have ventured further afield and then, on returning to Fulda, you enjoy the views of the area from Frauenberg or the highest city towers you will find it beautiful, most beautiful. There are perhaps only a few places in the whole of Europe that are more beautiful."
MELCHIOR ADAM WEIKARD (1742–1803)

A Walk Through Fulda

Introduction

It really cannot be denied that the author of these lines exhibits a certain, not unsubstantial, local pride. This is hardly surprising as the doctor and philosopher Adam Weikard was born in the south of the Fulda prince-bishopric and lived and worked at the Fulda court for many years as the personal physician of the prince-bishop Heinrich von Bibra.
However, he did see something of the world: he spent several years at the court of the Russian Tsarina Katherina II in St Petersburg, and later worked in Mainz, Mannheim and Heilbronn. His somewhat biased opinion of Fulda therefore does carry some weight. It is interesting to note that , even today, young people who leave the city to train or study in some other part of Germany or Europe often follow Weikard's example: after a time they return, stroll through the multicultural old town, take a seat in front of their favourite pub for a cool drink, wander down the shopping streets, or once again walk up the Frauenberg to enjoy the view – and suddenly see their hometown with completely fresh eyes: with similar eyes to those of the many thousands of guests who visit our city every year, for many of whom it is love at first sight – enchanted by the Baroque elegance and the medieval passageways, the almost Mediterranean feeling, the pleasant atmosphere in the streets and squares, the lovingly

Erbe und moderner Urbanität verlieben. Dieser Bildband will Sie mitnehmen auf einen Spaziergang durch die Stadt Fulda – zu den Sehenswürdigkeiten aus der 1275-jährigen Geschichte, die kein Tourist verpassen darf, aber auch zu den versteckten Schönheiten und Besonderheiten, die sich selbst den Einheimischen vielleicht erst auf den zweiten oder dritten Blick erschließen, die aber erst ein spannendes und authentisches Gesamtbild einer lebendigen und lebenswerten Stadt entstehen lassen.

Ausgangspunkt dieses Spaziergangs sind die uralte Michaelskirche und – wie könnte es anders sein – der Dom. Er steht an jener Stelle, an der laut der Überlieferung der Mönch Sturmius am 12. März 744 im Auftrag des Missionars Winfried-Bonifatius das Kloster Fulda gründete. Es bildete die Keimzelle der Stadt, auch wenn Ausgrabungen belegt haben, dass der flache Hügel nahe des Flusses Fulda schon vorher zeitweise besiedelt war.

Bonifatius und Fulda – bis heute eine besondere Liebesbeziehung

Das Benediktinerkloster im damals abgelegenen Buchonien und der angelsächsische Missionar Bonifatius – das war eine ganz besondere Liebesbeziehung. Der „Apostel der Deutschen" wählte das Kloster zu seiner Begräbnisstätte und legte damit den Grundstock dafür, dass Fulda als Ziel frommer Pilger auf Jahrhunderte hinaus eine besondere Stellung erhielt. Wie heißt es doch so schön in einer der vielen Strophen des Bonifatiusliedes, der heimlichen Hymne der Fuldaer, im pathetischen Tonfall des 19. Jahrhunderts:

arranged flowers and the well-kept parks. This all goes into producing our city's successful blend of historical heritage and modern urban life. This photo book will take you on a walk through Fulda to the sights which have come into being during the course of its 1,275-year-old history. The walk takes you to the classic sights, but also includes some hidden beauties and unusual features nooks and crannies which even local people may have some difficulty identifying. This combination helps to create an interesting, authentic impression of this lively, charming city.

The walk starts at the ancient Michaelskirche and – where else? – the cathedral. The cathedral is located in the place where, according to the records, the monk St. Sturmius was instructed to found the Fulda Monastery by the English missionary Winfried-Boniface on 12th March 744. The foundation of the monastery was the real starting point for the development of the city, although archaeological excavations have revealed that this low hill near the River Fulda had been used as a settlement for some time prior to 744. The Anglo-Saxon missionary St. Boniface had a particular love for this Benedictine monastery in the wilds of Buchonia. The "Apostle of the Germans" chose the monastery as his burial place, thus establishing the basis for the monastery's centuries-long tradition as an important place of pilgrimage. To quote from one of the many verses of the Bonifatius Song (Fulda's secret anthem) which carries all the pathos of the 19th century: "Mainz and Utrecht make all preparations to bury you finely, but no, you want Fulda to have you and your mortal remains." For some people from Fulda this proud self -perception still echoes quietly in their identity …

Leaving the cathedral we pass through the Baroque quarter with its fine buildings (never a postcard without

Der Blick vom Schlossturm: Das Ensemble aus Dom, Orangerie und Frauenberg fasziniert jeden Beuscher.

The view from the Residence tower: the ensemble formed by the cathedral, the Orangerie and Frauenberg never fails to delight visitors.

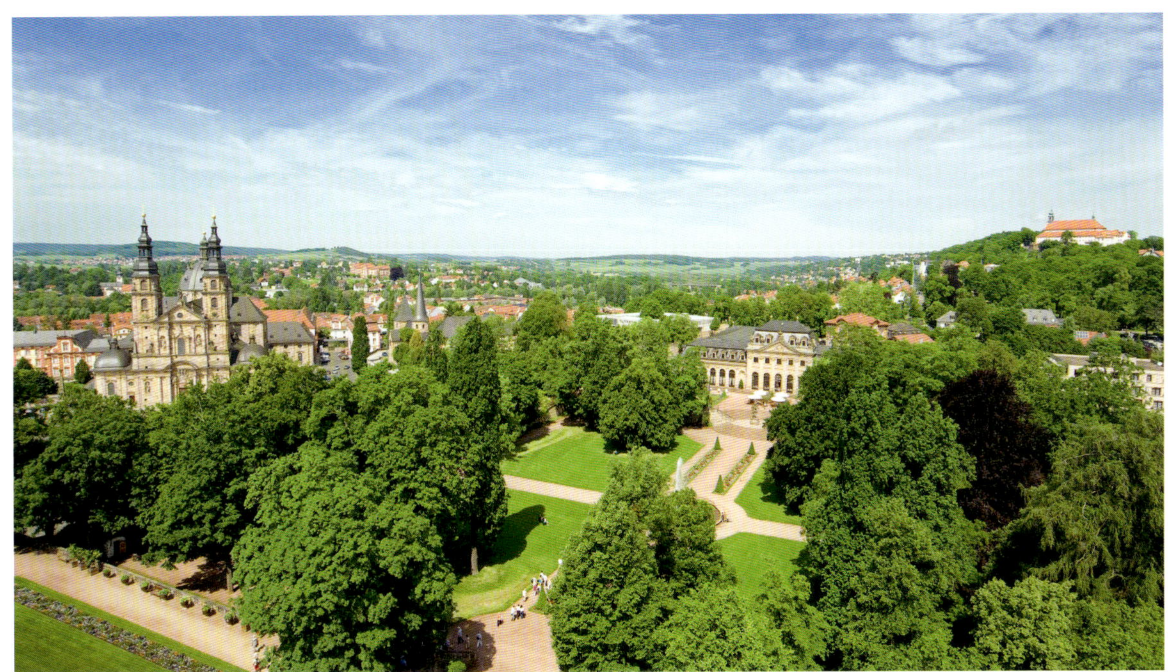

„Zwar Mainz und Utrecht rüsten sich, dich herrlich zu begraben, doch nein, Du willst, nur Fuld soll Dich und Deinen Leichnam haben." So mancher Fuldaer zehrt noch heute ein wenig von diesem stolzen Selbstverständnis …

Vom Dom aus durchstreifen wir das Barockviertel mit seinen schmucken Gebäuden, die auf keiner Panoramapostkarte fehlen dürfen, bevor wir uns in die mittelalterliche, einst von Handwerk und Handel geprägte Altstadt begeben und von dort aus auch die jüngeren Stadtviertel und das Umland erkunden. Lassen Sie sich mitnehmen und genießen Sie die Impressionen aus einer Stadt, die in Geschichte und Gegenwart gleichermaßen interessante Facetten zu bieten hat und die spätestens seit der deutschen Wiedervereinigung 1990 wieder dort liegt, wo Bonifatius sie einst verortet hat: mitten in Deutschland und Europa.

these gems!) and then continue into the medieval old town which was a centre for craftwork and trading. We then discover the more recent parts of the city and the surrounding area. Come on this walk and enjoy the impressions of a city which, both in the past and present, has many interesting facets and which, at the latest, since German reunification in 1990 lies where St. Boniface once situated it: in the middle of Germany and Europe.

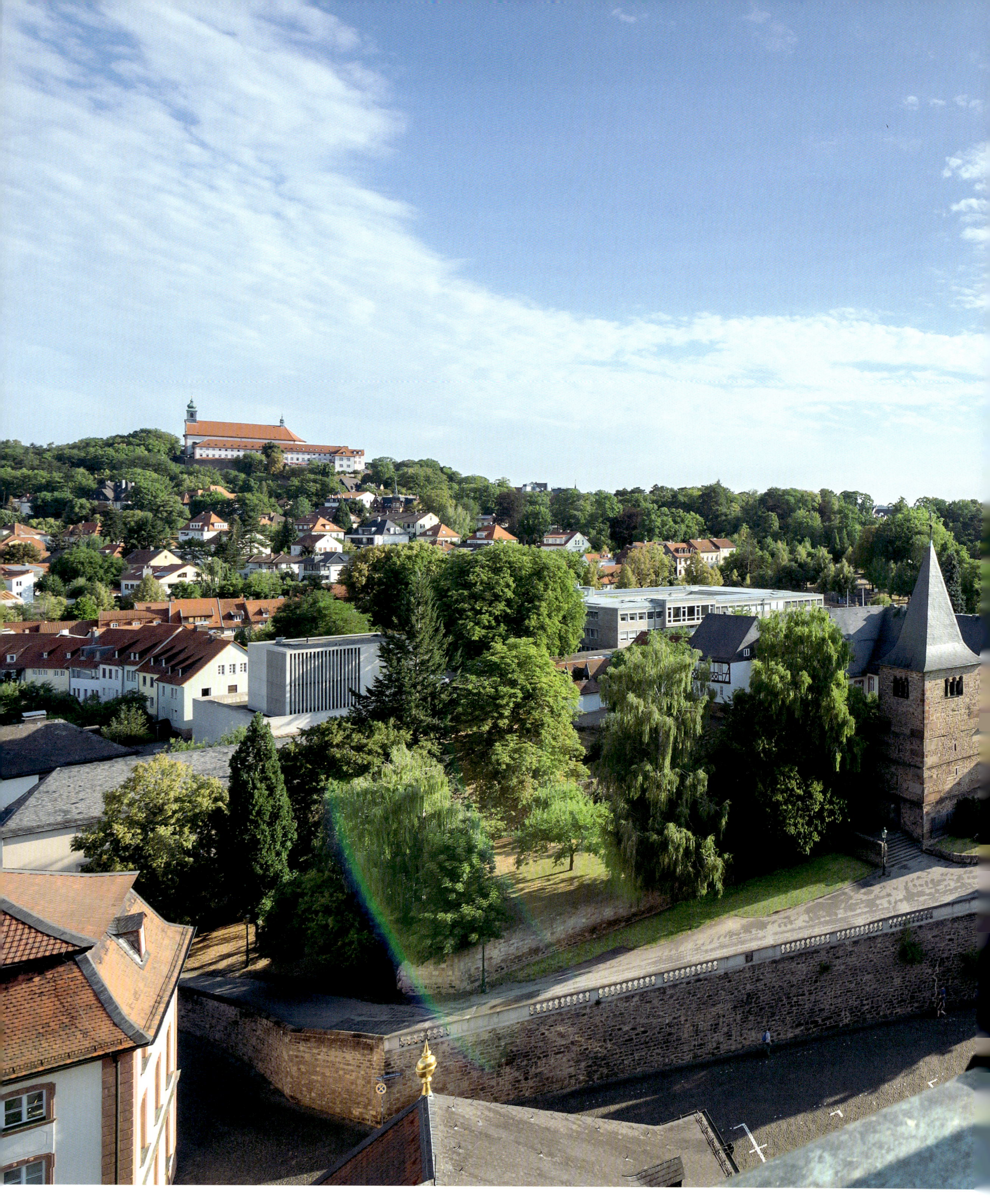

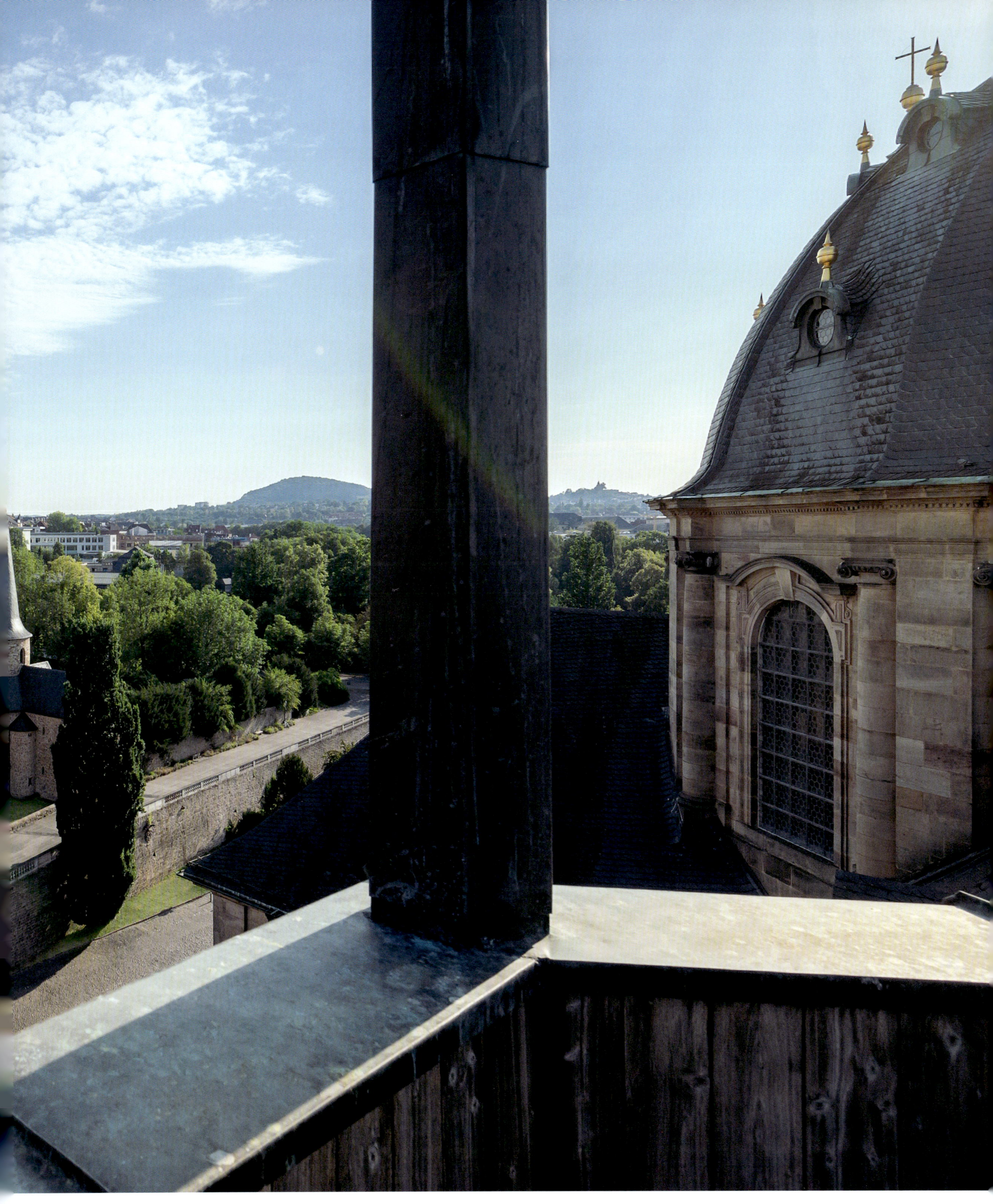

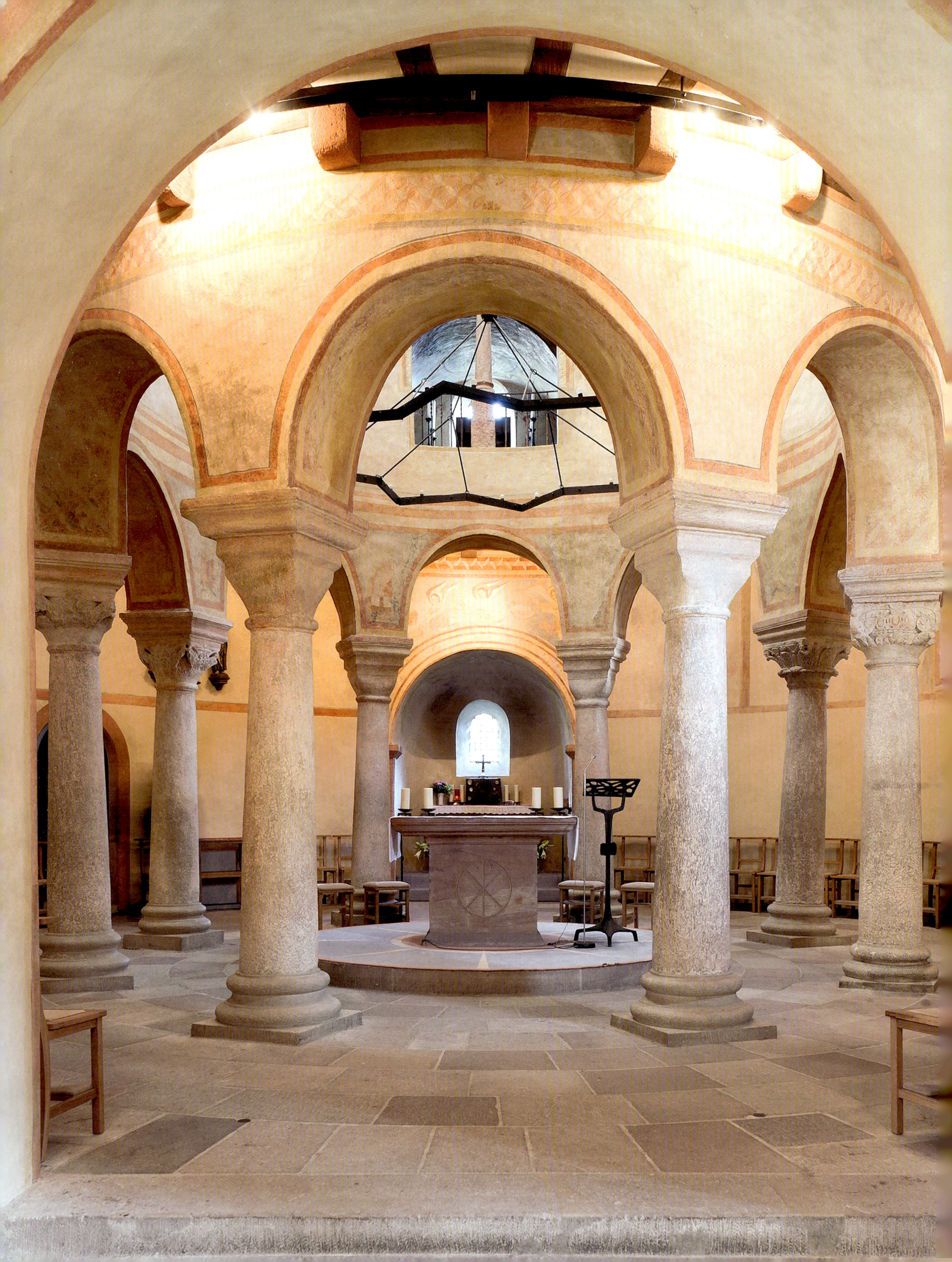

EINE SÄULE, AUF DER ALLES RUHT

Die Michaelskirche – das älteste Bauwerk der Stadt

Der Abstieg in Fuldas Ursprünge ist eng und alles andere als barrierefrei. Aber wer die Steintreppe zur Krypta der Michaelskirche hinabgestiegen ist, der wird mit einer einzigartigen Atmosphäre belohnt: Hier liegen die ältesten erhaltenen baulichen Wurzeln der Stadt. Die Michaelskirche wurde 818–822, also noch in karolingischer Zeit, erbaut, vermutlich als Grabeskirche. Und die archaisch anmutende Krypta stammt wohl noch weitgehend unverfälscht aus dieser Epoche. Eine einzige, schlicht verzierte Säule trägt die Decke der Krypta und damit das Fundament des Kirchenbaus – ein ebenso starkes wie eingängiges Symbol für Christus, auf den sich die christliche Kirche gründet.

Der kreisrunde, nach oben in Richtung Turm geöffnete Altarraum befindet sich direkt über der Krypta, der Kranz der acht Säulen lenkt die Blicke und die Aufmerksamkeit des Betrachters auf das Zentrum. Ein Raum, der auf besondere Weise zur Besinnung und Kontemplation einlädt – zumal er weit weniger Besucherströme anlockt als der barocke Dom nebenan.

Die Fresken sind nicht so gut erhalten wie in den beiden anderen frühmittelalterlichen Gotteshäusern in der Nachbarschaft – der Grabeskirche der hl. Lioba auf dem Petersberg und der Krypta der Andreaskirche in Neuenberg. Gleichwohl entfalten die dezente Wandbemalung und die strenge Geometrie des Kirchenraums eine Wirkung, welche durchaus die klösterliche Atmosphäre zur Zeit der Äbte Ratger und Eigil erahnen lassen – und in einem spannenden Kontrast zu den vielen, zum Teil opulenten Barockbauten in der unmittelbaren Umgebung stehen.

One Column on which Everything Rests

Michaelskirche - the oldest building in the city

The descent to Fulda's origins is narrow and far from barrier-free, but should you go down the stone steps to the Michaelskirche crypt, you are rewarded by experiencing a unique atmosphere: here you find the oldest surviving architectural roots of the city. The Michaelskirche was built as a funeral church from 818 to 822 during the Carolingian period, and the scarcely changed, ancient crypt originates from that period. Just one simply carved stone column holds the ceiling of the crypt and therefore the foundations of the church – a powerful, striking symbol for Christ who forms the fundament of the Christian church.

The circular chancel, which ascends to the tower, is directly above the crypt. The ring of eight columns draws one's attention to the centre of the chancel. It is a space which, in a very special way, lends itself to reflection and contemplation – particularly because, unlike the cathedral just opposite, it does not attract throngs of visitors. The frescoes are not as well preserved as in the two other early medieval churches in the vicinity – the burial church of St. Lioba on Petersberg and the crypt of the Andreaskirche in Neuenberg. Nevertheless, the beautiful simplicity of the frescoes and the strict geometry of the church interior produce a monastic atmosphere which evokes a feeling of the period of the abbots Ratger and Eigil. The strong contrast to the many opulent Baroque buildings nearby could not be greater.

Die besondere Atmosphäre des runden Altarraums der Michaelskirche lässt sich in einem Foto kaum einfangen – man muss sie vor Ort erleben.

The undefinable atmosphere of the round chancel of the St. Michaelskirche cannot be captured in a photograph – you simply have to experience it.

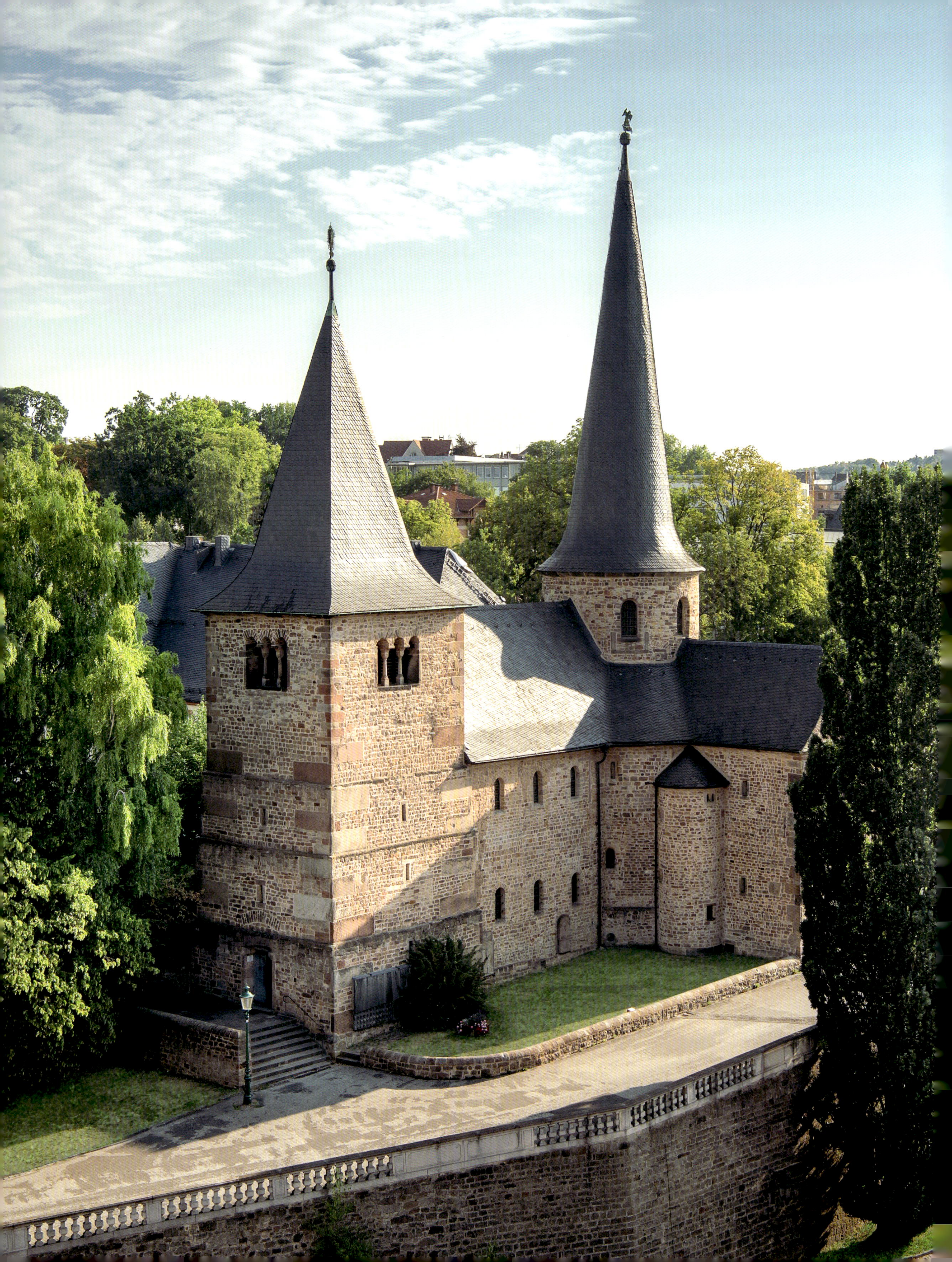

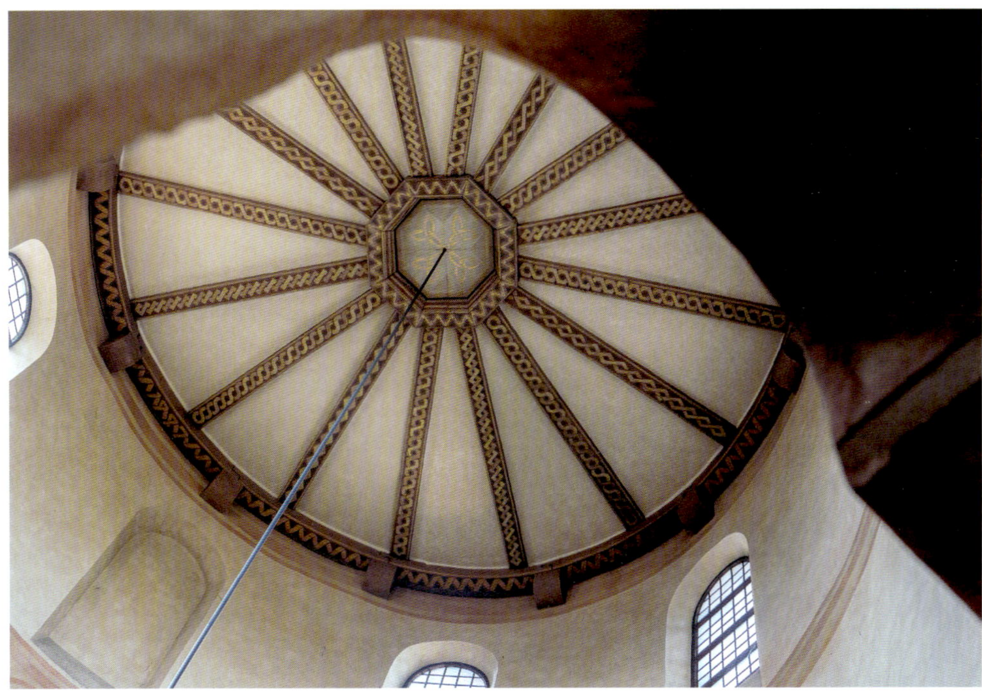

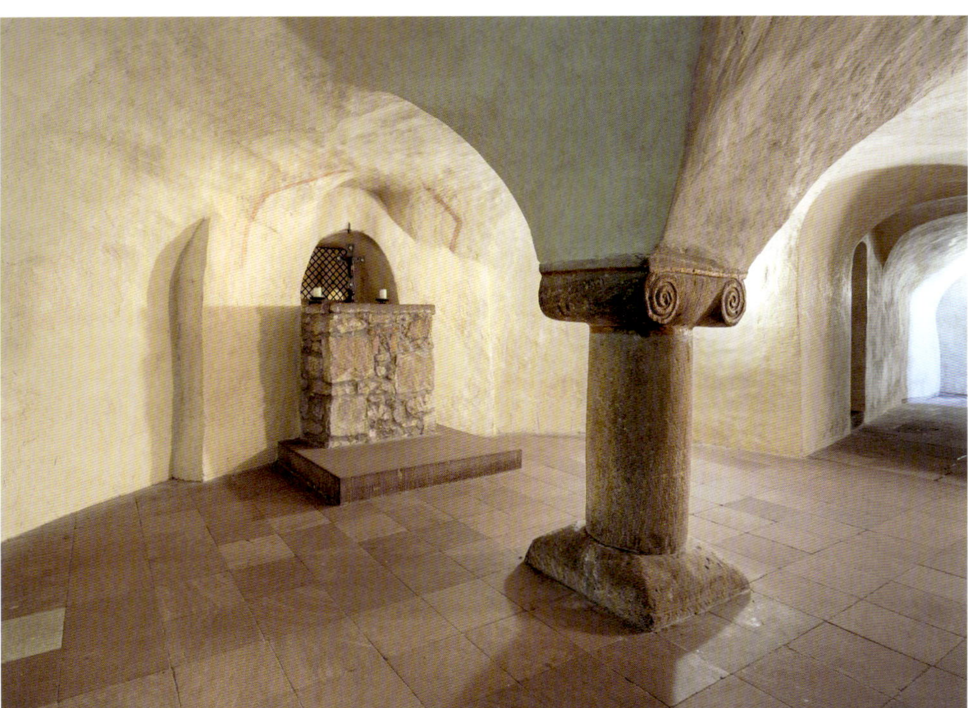

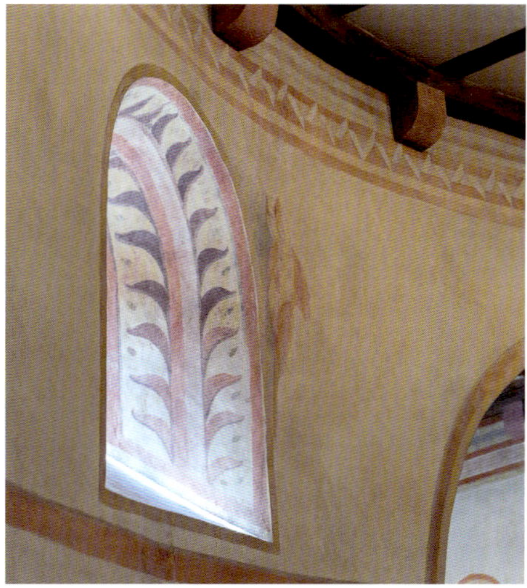

Die Michaelskirche gehört zu den architekturgeschichtlich wichtigsten Bauten Fuldas. Mit ihrer uralten Krypta (und zentralen tragenden Säule im Zentrum) ist sie ein in Fulda einzigartiges Zeugnis der karolingisch-romanischen Epoche.

Architecturally, the Michaelskirche is one of most important buildings in Fulda. The ancient crypt with its central, load-bearing column is an exceptional example of a structure from the Carolingian-Romanesque period and is unique in Fulda.

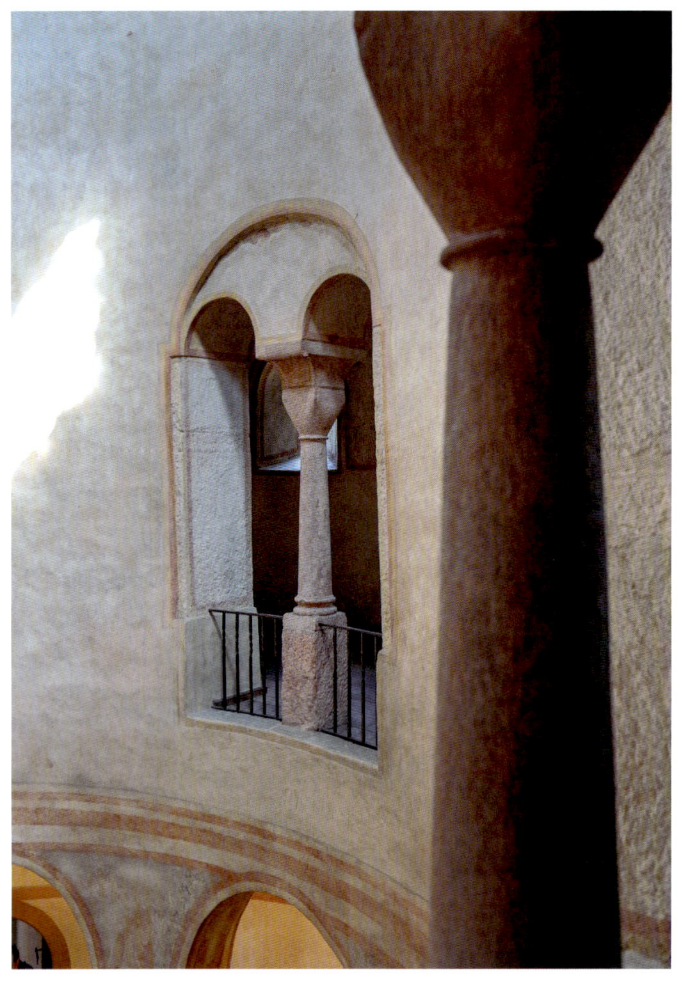

Die Rotunde des Altarraums setzt sich im Obergeschoss, das über eine weiteren Altar verfügt, in Richtung Turm fort, und die in der Renaissancezeit eingebauten Turmfenster lassen vergleichsweise viel Licht in das Gebäude.

The chancel rotunda continues up to the upper floor where there is an additional altar. The windows in the tower, which were added in the Renaissance period, allow a relatively large amount of light into the building.

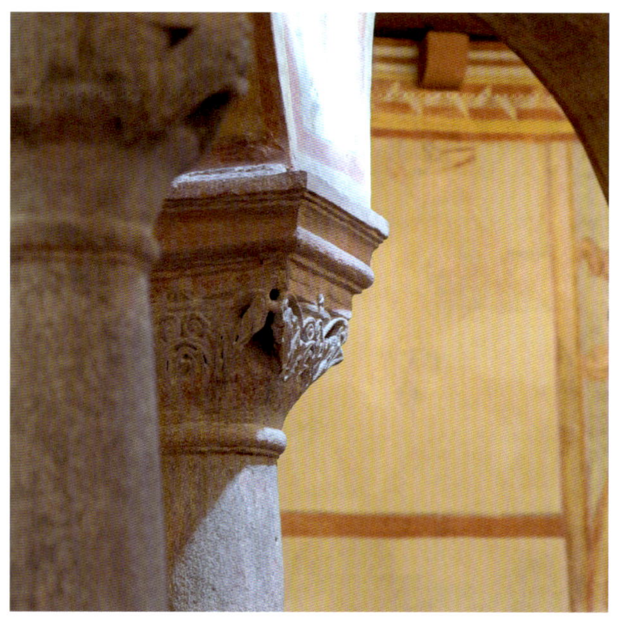

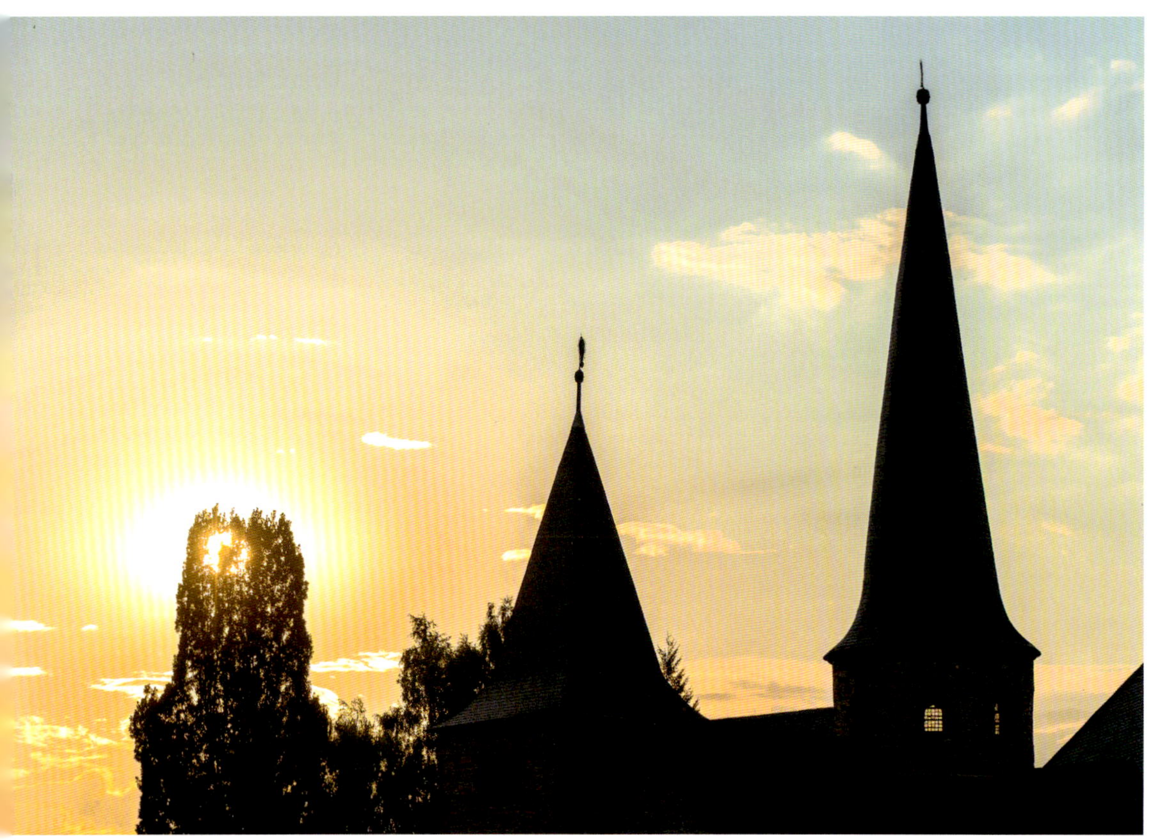

Die Michaelskirche steht auf einer natürlichen Erhebung, dem Michaelsberg, und bildete im Hochmittelalter das Zentrum der gleichnamigen Propstei.

The Michaelskirche lies on a small hill, the Michaelsberg. During the Middle Ages it formed the central point of the collegiate church ("Propstei") of the same name.

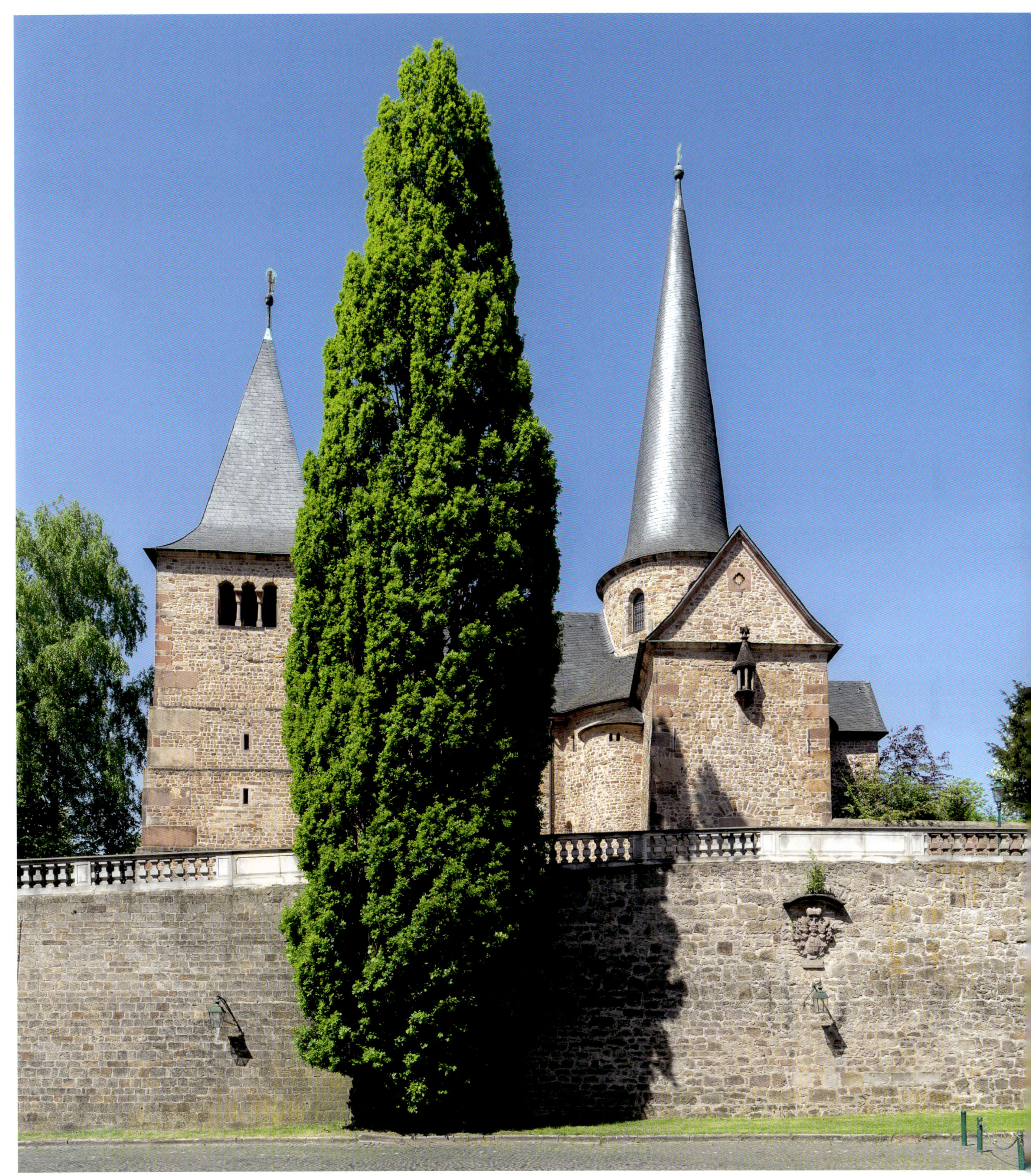

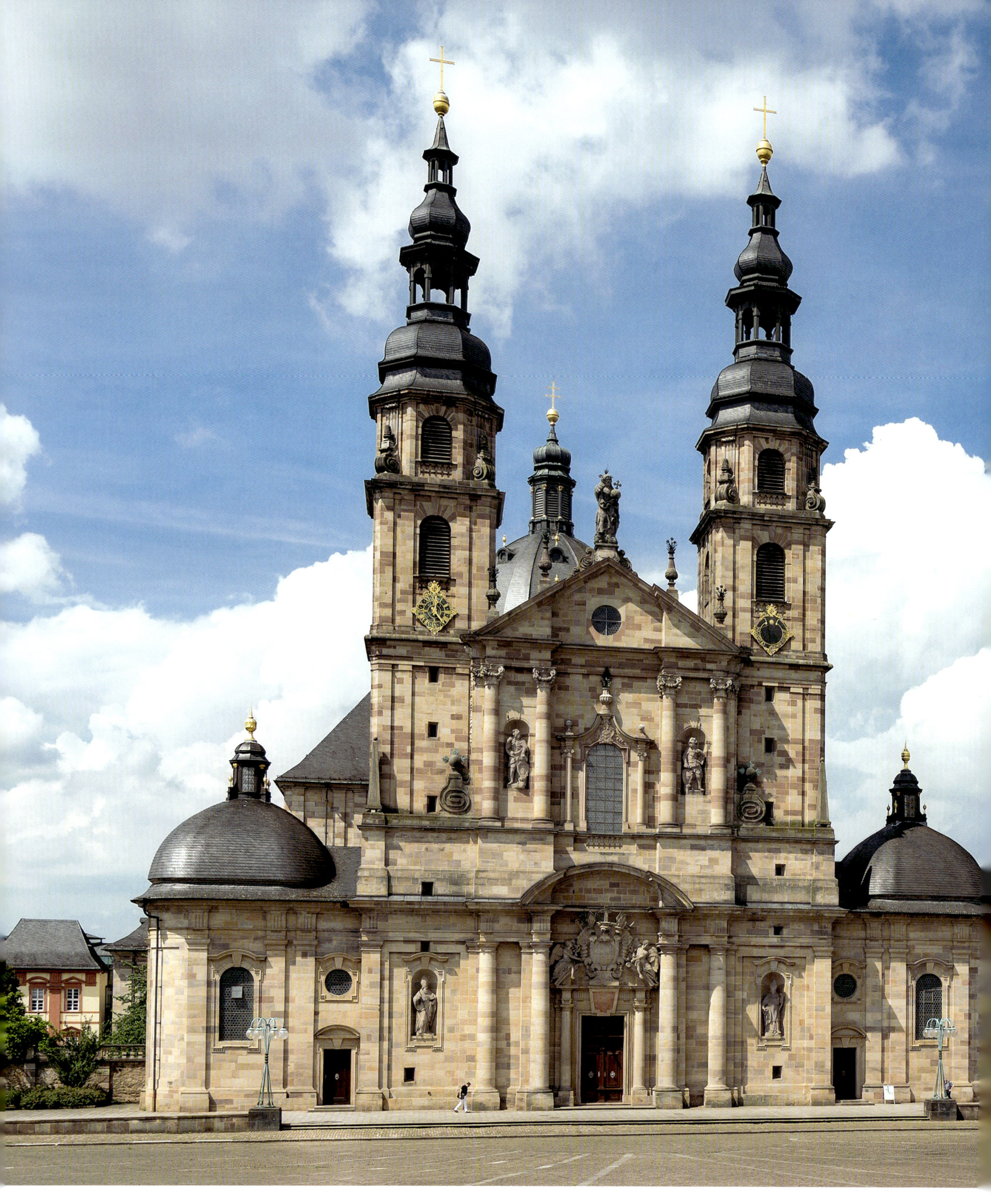

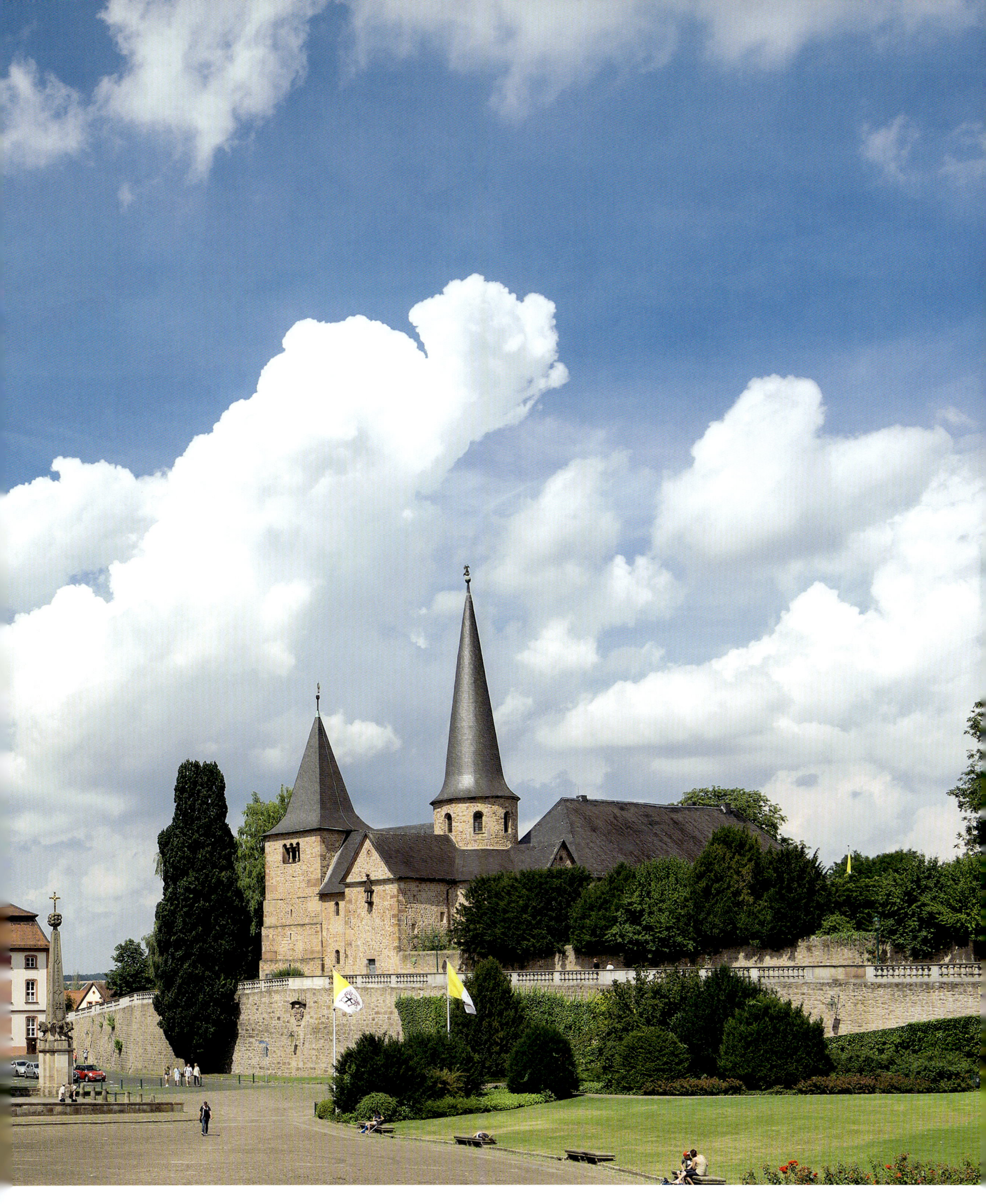

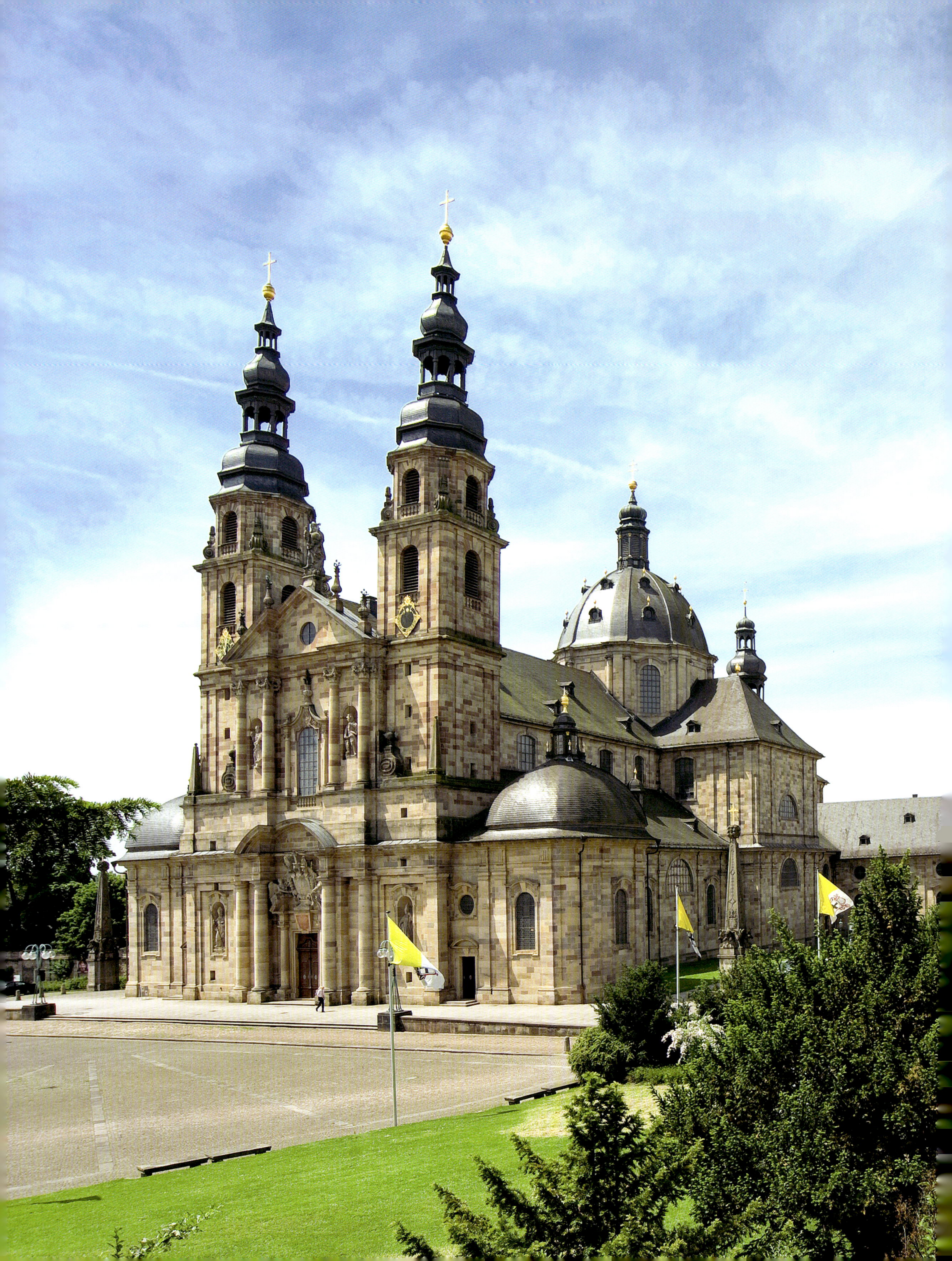

EIN WAHRZEICHEN, DAS IDENTITÄT STIFTET

Der barocke Dom steht an der Stelle der mittelalterlichen Ratgerbasilika

Was wäre wenn? Diese bei Historikern eigentlich verpönte Fragestellung sei mit Blick auf den Fuldaer Dom einmal erlaubt: Was wäre heute, wenn die romanische Ratgerbasilika nicht dem Zeitgeschmack der Barockzeit hätte weichen müssen? Wenn dieser einst so bedeutende Sakralbau, der Vorbild war für viele Klosterkirchen nördlich der Alpen, heute noch an seinem Platz stünde? Sicher wäre Fulda dann nicht so ohne Weiteres unter der Rubrik „Barockstadt" zu fassen, sondern stünde mit einem solch gewaltigen Bau mit karolingischen Wurzeln sicher in einer Reihe mit den UNESCO-Welterbe-Städten Aachen, Speyer oder Hildesheim.

Der Bau der Ratgerbasilika, der sich von 791 bis 819 hinzog, wurde übrigens zur echten Belastungsprobe für das noch junge Kloster, die schließlich sogar in der Absetzung des namensgebenden Abts Ratger (oder auch Ratgar) 817 gipfelte. Ungeachtet der Querelen um ihren Bau war die Basilika, die zum Zeitpunkt ihrer größten Ausdehnung noch weite Teile des heutigen Domplatzes umfasste, eine würdige Pilgerstätte für den heiligen Bonifatius, dessen Grab sich auch schon in der Vorgängerkirche, dem sogenannten Sturmiusbau befunden hatte. Als Patron hatte die Ratgerbasilika aber nicht den „Apostel der Deutschen", sondern sie wurde – wie später auch der Dom – St. Salvator, also Christus, dem Erlöser, geweiht.

Von der Ratgerbasilika ist leider nicht viel Sichtbares erhalten. So sind zum Beispiel im Innern der eckigen Domtürme noch die runden Türme der Basilika erhalten geblieben. Auch einzelne Reliefs und Säulenfragmente sind heute noch zu bewundern, Teile der Basilika-Einrichtung – wie etwa die Kanzel – wurden in anderen Kirchen „zweitverwertet". Säulenteile sollen Handwerker der Dombauzeit auch in ihren Privathäusern am „Eichsfeld" verbaut haben.

Ansonsten ist die Ratgerbasilika, von der es nur wenige Abbildungen gibt, längst Geschichte. Sie ist der Mode der Zeit zum Opfer gefallen, obwohl die Bausubstanz Anfang des 18. Jahrhunderts durchaus noch

A Landmark that Symbolises Fulda

The Baroque cathedral stands on the site of the Ratger Basilica

What if…? This is a line of questioning which is normally frowned upon by historians, but should be allowed, just once, when considering Fulda cathedral. What would it be like if the Romanesque Ratger Basilica had not fallen victim to Baroque tastes? What if this, once so significant, church building, the model for so many monastery churches north of the Alps, still stood today?

Certainly, Fulda could not then simply be dubbed a "Baroque City", but would take its place in the list of UNESCO World Heritage sites along with the cities of Aachen, Speyer and Hildesheim. At this point it is worth noting that the building of the Ratger Basilica from 791 to 819 became an endurance test for the young monastery, a situation which came to a head when Abbot Ratger (after whom the church was named) was relieved from office in 817. Unconcerned by the conflict surrounding its construction the basilica grew to cover a large part of today' s cathedral square; a worthy place of pilgrimage for St. Boniface whose grave had, until then, lain in the preceding church, known as the Sturmiusbau. However, the patron of the Ratger Basilica was not to be the "Apostle of the Germans", but – like the later cathedral – was dedicated to St. Salvator, Christ Our Saviour.

Unfortunately, little is left to see of the Ratger Basilica, but you can still see the round towers of the ancient building in the interior of the cathedral's square towers. Some fragments of columns and a few reliefs can still be seen, while several parts of the interior decoration of the basilica found new homes in other churches. Interestingly, craftsmen who worked on the Baroque cathedral apparently integrated parts of columns in their private houses in the nearby street "Eichsfeld". Otherwise the Ratger Basilica, of which there are only a few illustrations, has long been history. The early monastery fell victim to the tastes of the time, although

Dombaumeister Johann Dientzenhofer (1663–1726) nahm sich den römischen Barock zum Vorbild und schuf für Fulda ein steinernes Zeugnis des wiedererstarkten Katholizismus zu Beginn des 18. Jahrhunderts.

The cathedral architect, Johann Dientzenhofer (1663-1726), took the Roman baroque style as his model and created a stone monument which expressed the regained strength of Catholicism at the beginning of the 18th century.

zu retten gewesen wäre. Zwei Dinge spielten bei den Plänen zum Bau des barocken Domes eine wichtige Rolle. Zum einen das Wiedererstarken des Katholizismus in der zweiten Hälfte des 17. Jahrhunderts nach den Wirren des Dreißigjährigen Krieges – der Dom im Stil der entsprechenden Vorbilder in Rom sollte auch die enge Verbundenheit zum Papsttum demonstrieren; zum anderen das liebe Geld: Der Neubau unter Fürstabt Adalbert von Schleiffras (Regentschaft: 1700–1714) war nur deshalb möglich, weil sein knausriger Vorgänger Placidus von Droste (1668–1700) während seiner langen Amtszeit die Finanzen streng geordnet und einen wahren Schatz angehäuft hatte, der erst nach seinem Tod entdeckt wurde. Fürstabt Adalbert konnte also aus dem Vollen schöpfen, holte den bekannten Baumeister Dientzenhofer nach Fulda und ließ den Dom in seiner heutigen Form erbauen. Im Zuge der Arbeiten wandelte sich auch das gesamte Erscheinungsbild des Domumfelds. Hatte die alte Stiftskirche noch optisch auf einer Anhöhe gestanden, so wurde jetzt der Waidesbach in einen Tunnel verlegt und das Tal aufgefüllt. So rückte der Dom eher in eine Senke, was dem Gebäude etwas an Wucht nimmt. Gleichwohl hat es sich zum beliebtesten Fotomotiv der gesamten Stadt entwickelt, zum Identität stiftenden Wahrzeichen, das es inzwischen sogar als Bauklötzchen-Satz zum Nachbauen gibt.

it would probably still have been possible to save it at the beginning of the 18th century. Two factors played an important role in the planning of the Baroque cathedral: one was the regained strength of Catholicism after the turmoil of the Thirty Years' War – a cathedral built following the design of churches in Rome was intended to demonstrate a close connection to Rome. The other factor was good old money! The new building constructed under the rule of Prince-abbot Adalbert von Schleiffras (1700–1714) was only made possible by his penny-pinching predecessor, Placidus von Droste (1668–1700) who kept his finances strictly in order during his long rule and therefore amassed a veritable fortune – something that was only discovered after his death. Being able to draw on these abundant resources, Prince-abbot Adalbert brought the well-established architect Johann Dientzenhofer to Fulda and had the cathedral built as it stands today. During the course of the work the whole area around the cathedral changed in appearance: the old monastery church appeared to be on raised ground, but now the stream in front of it, the Waidesbach, was routed through a tunnel and the valley was filled in. This is the reason that the cathedral seems to be in a slight hollow – something that reduces the massive impact of the building. The cathedral has, nevertheless, become the most popular photo motif in the whole city. It is, indeed, such an iconic landmark that meanwhile there are even building-block sets to build your own.

Strahlendes Weiß dominiert im Innern des Doms und lässt die aufwendigen Stuckarbeiten besonders plastisch wirken.

Radiant white dominates the cathedral's interior and makes the stucco work look particularly vivid.

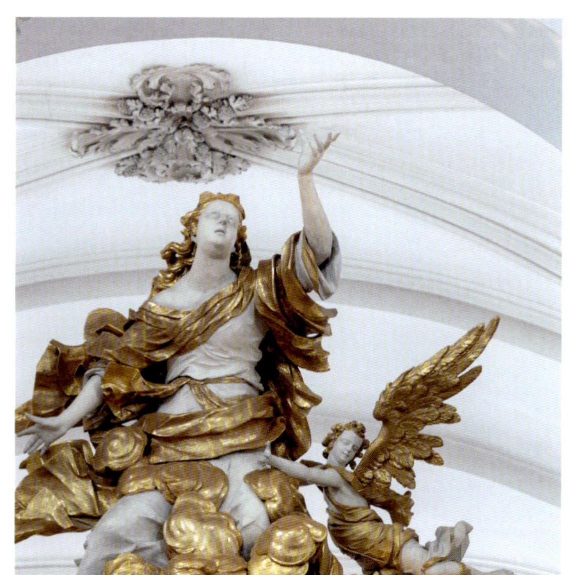

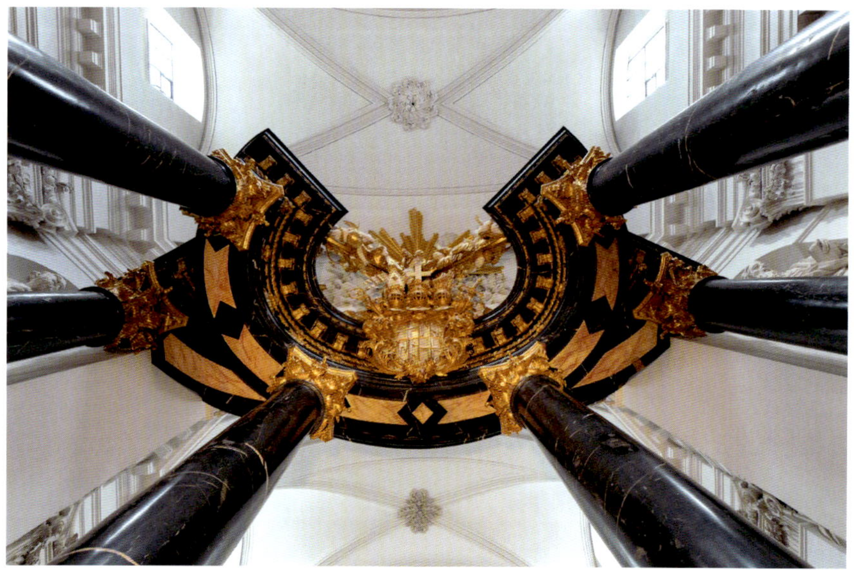

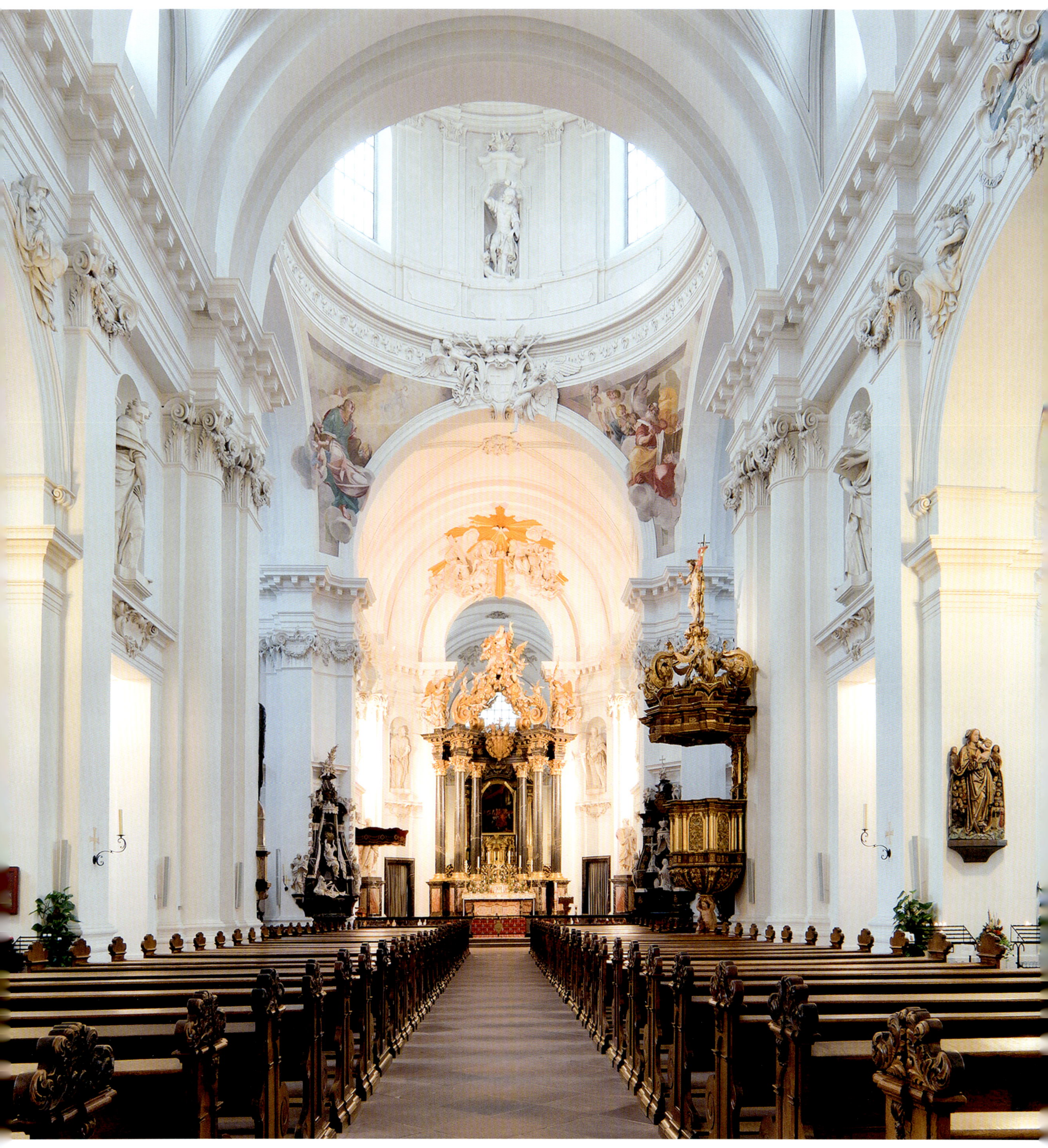

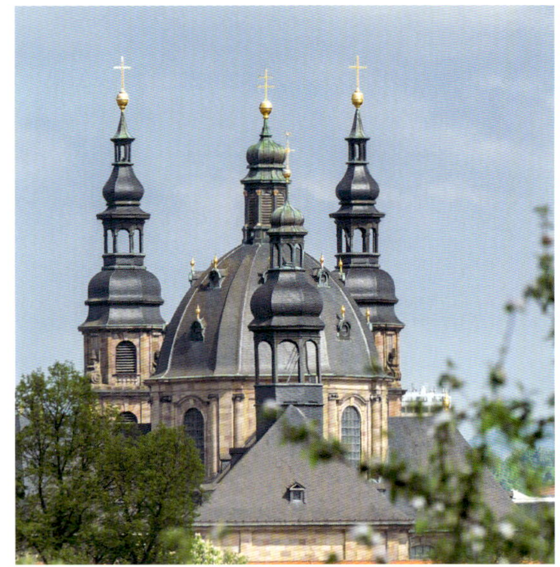

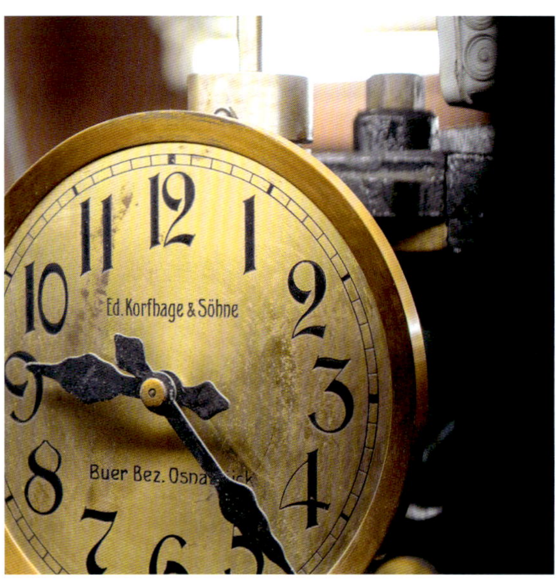

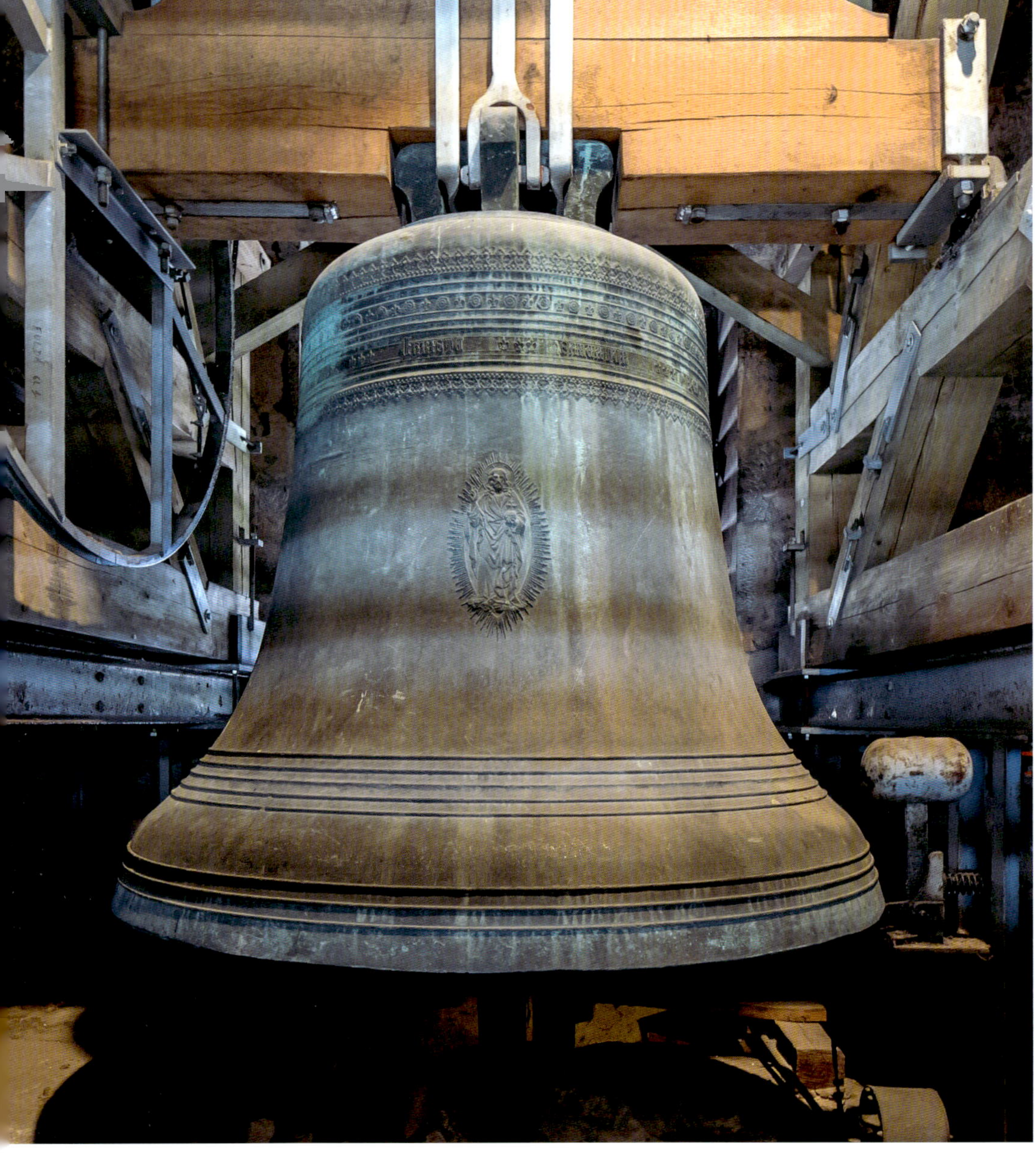

Im Nordturm des Domes hängen die drei größten Glocken des Domgeläuts – hier die fast drei Tonnen schwere Salvatorglocke aus dem Jahr 1897. Noch größer und vom Schlagton tiefer ist die „Osanna", die mehr als 5,8 Tonnen auf die Waage bringt.

The three largest cathedral bells hang in the north tower of the cathedral – here the nearly 3-ton Salvatorglocke from 1897. The larger and deeper "Osanna" weighs in at more than 5.8 tons.

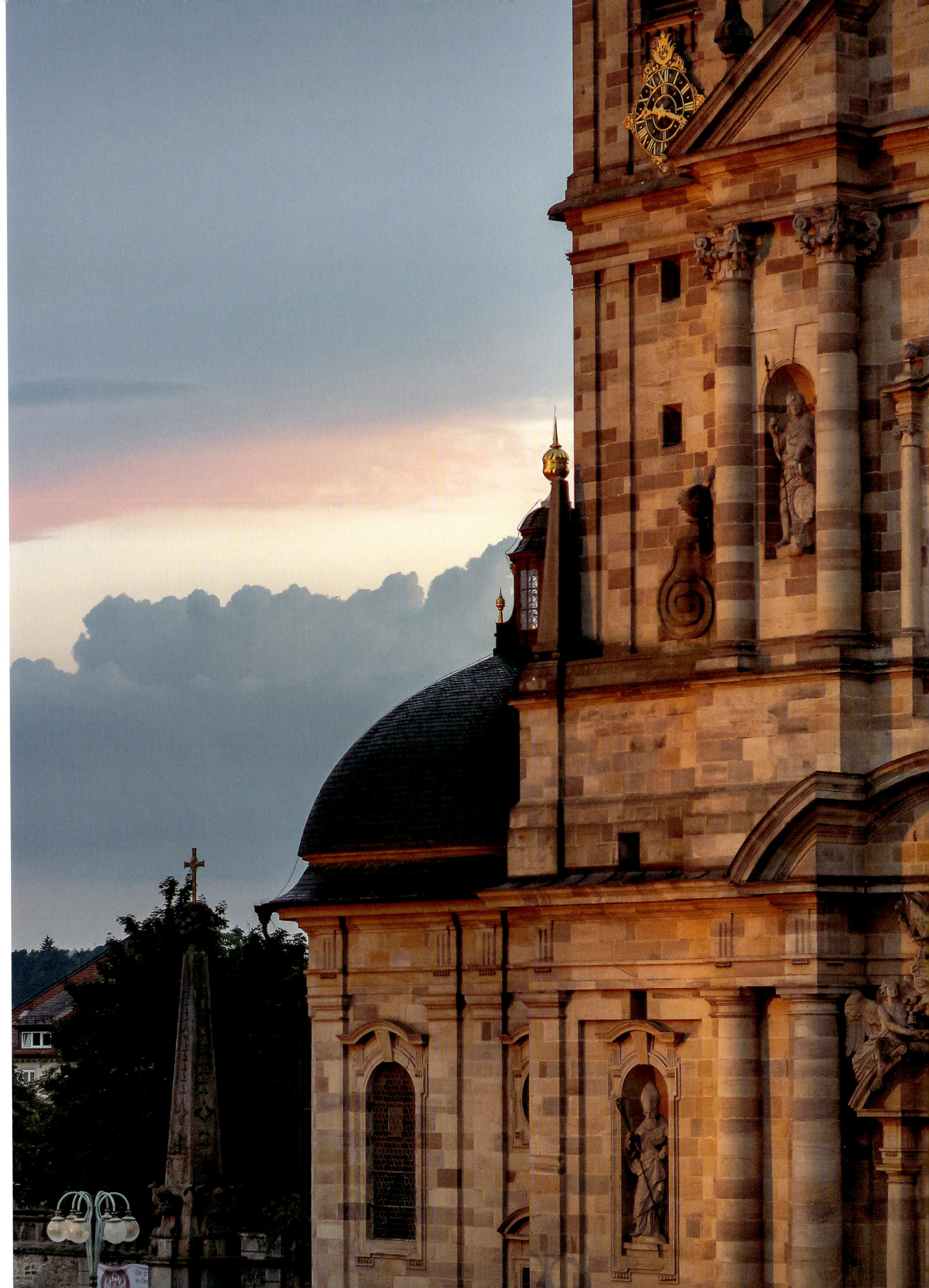

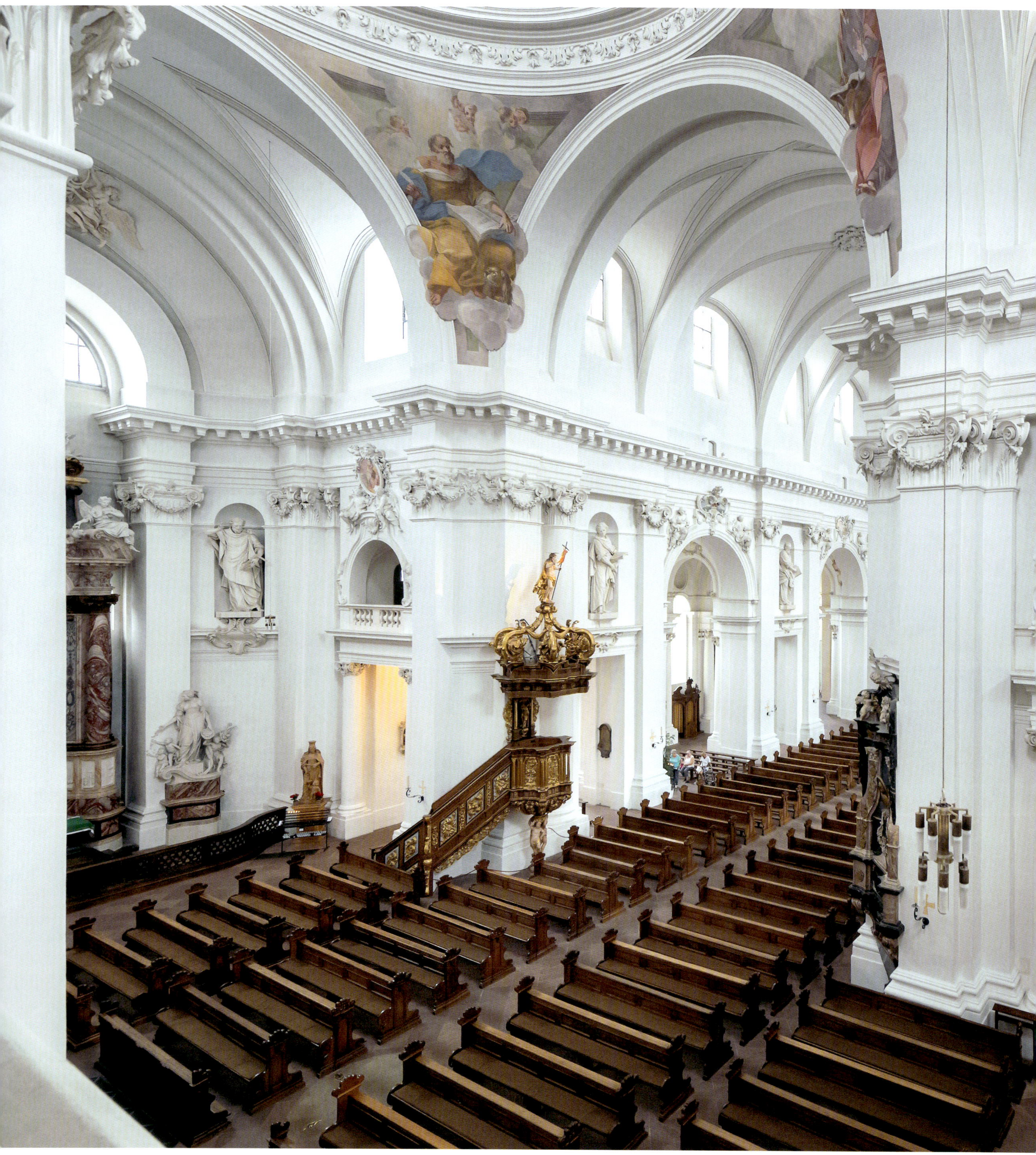

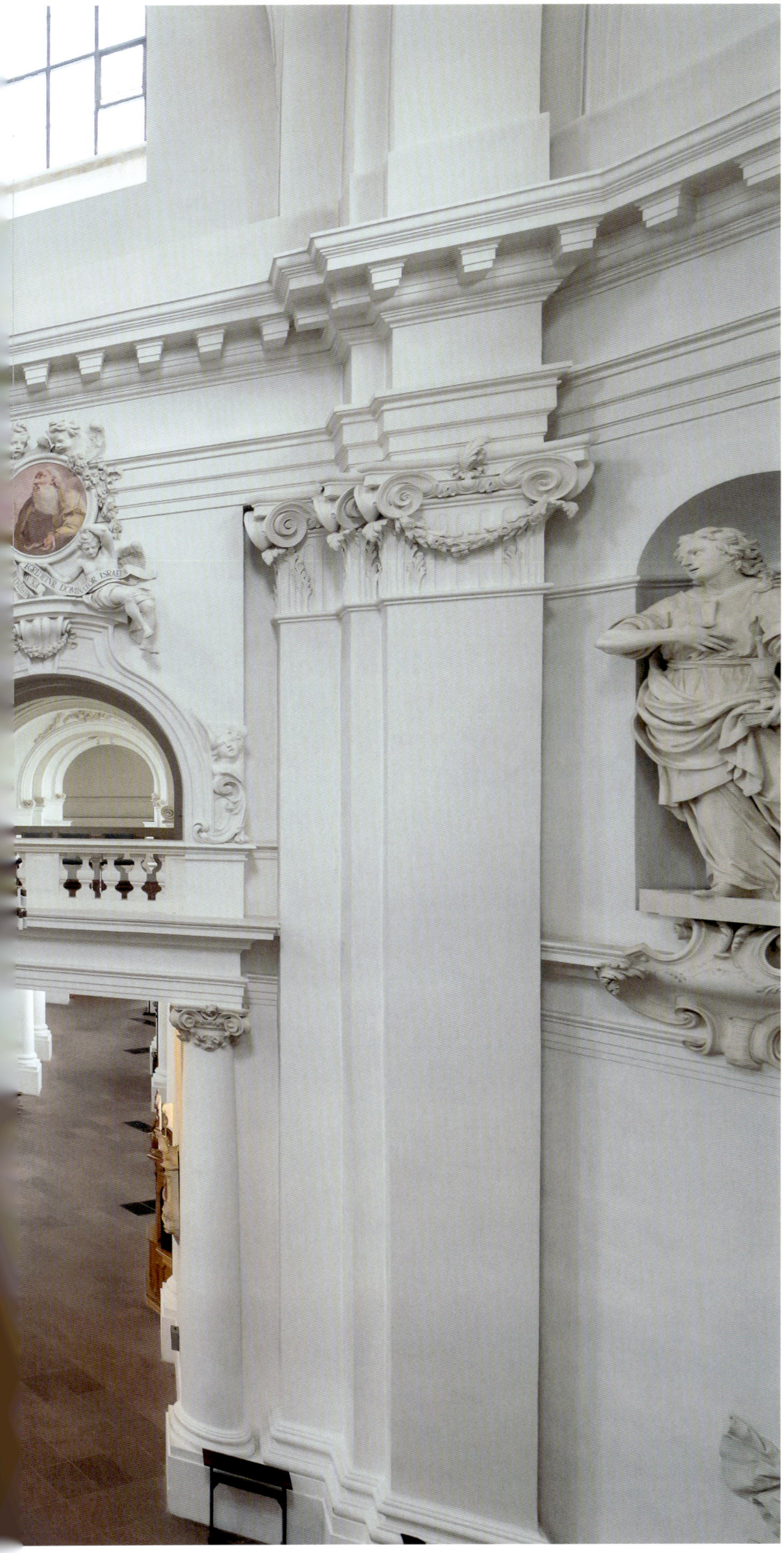

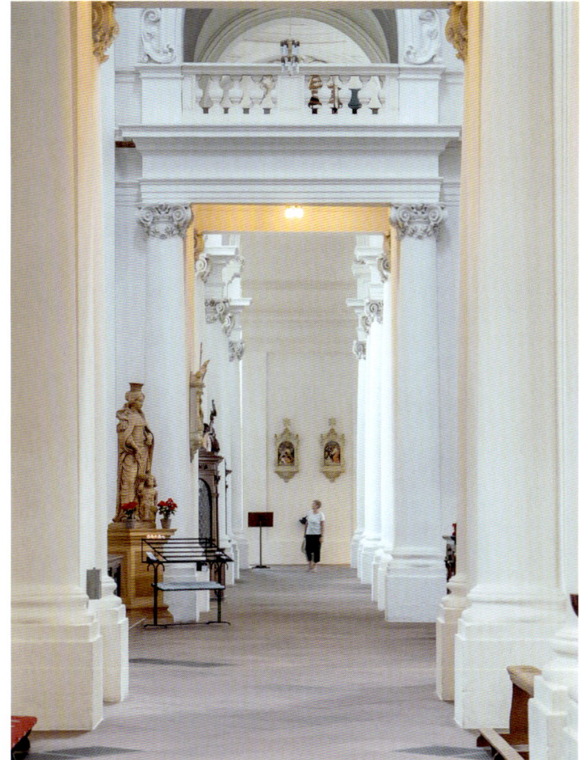

Dombaumeister Dientzenhofer orientierte sich auch bei Gestaltung des Dom-Inneren an Vorbildern aus Rom. Für die zentrale Kuppel etwa nahm er Anleihen bei der barocken Jesuitenkirche „Il Gesù", die europaweit Baumeister inspirierte.

The architect Johann Dientzenhofer based the interior design of the building on the interiors of churches in Rome. For the central dome, for example, he was inspired by the Baroque Jesuit church "Il Gesù" which was the source of inspiration for architects all over Europe.

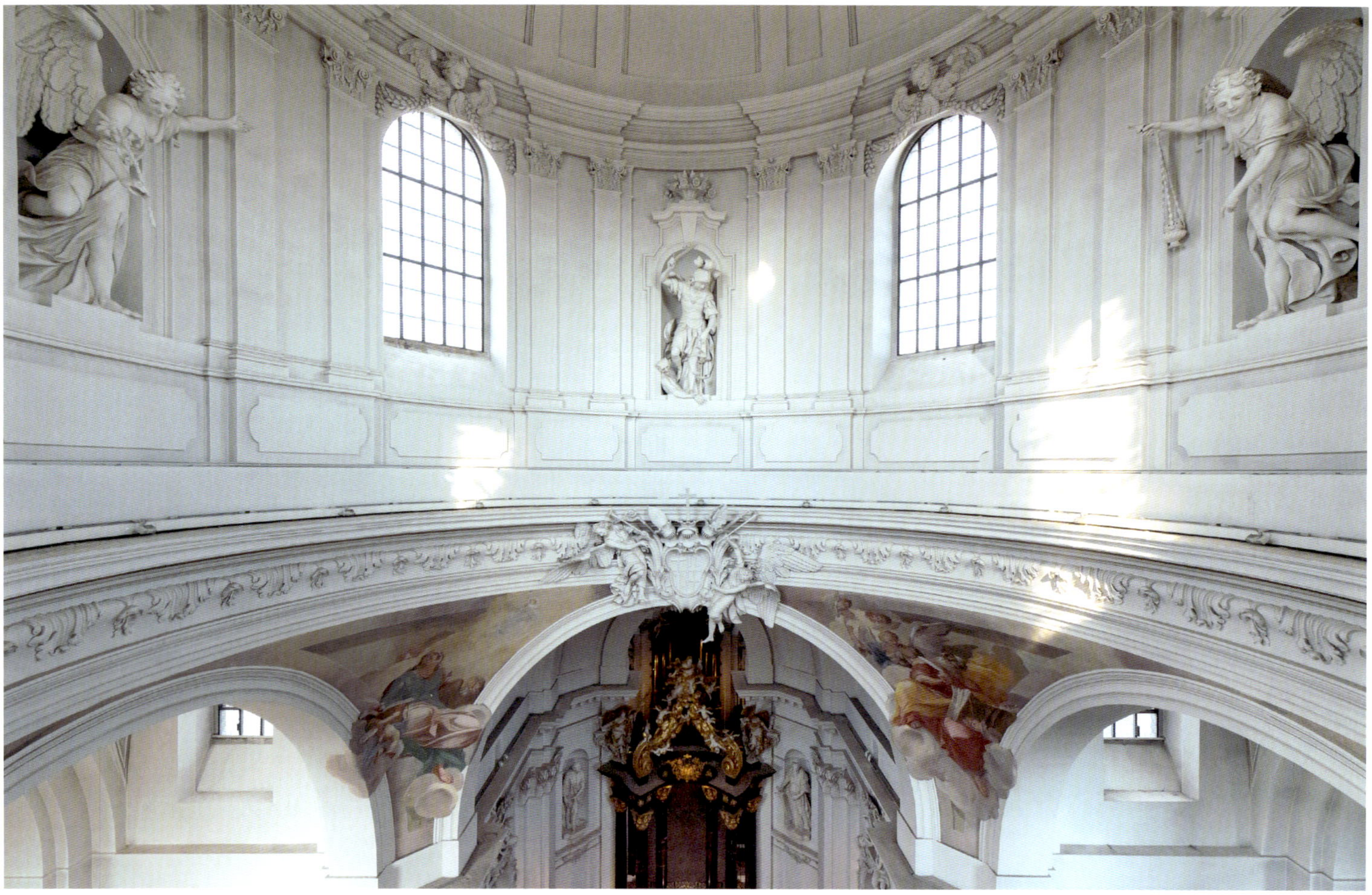

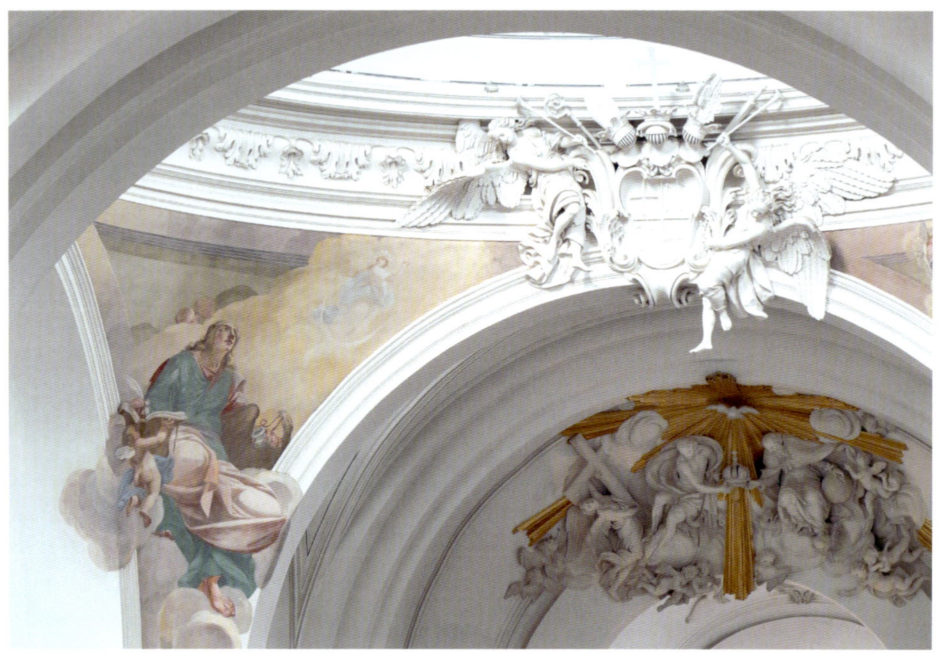

Zahlreiche bedeutende Künstler wurden für die Innenausstattung engagiert, so zum Beispiel der Maler Luca Antonio Colomba, der die Gemälde der vier Evangelisten in den Zwickeln unterhalb der Kuppel schuf – und dabei durch optische Tricks und das Anfügen plastischer Teile (wie etwa eines Fußes) in die dreidimensionale Darstellung vorstieß.

Many significant artists were commissioned for the interior decoration, for example, the painter Luca Antonio Colomba who did the paintings of the Evangelists in the spandrels below the dome, using optical illusions and the addition of solid elements (such as a foot) to create a 3D effect.

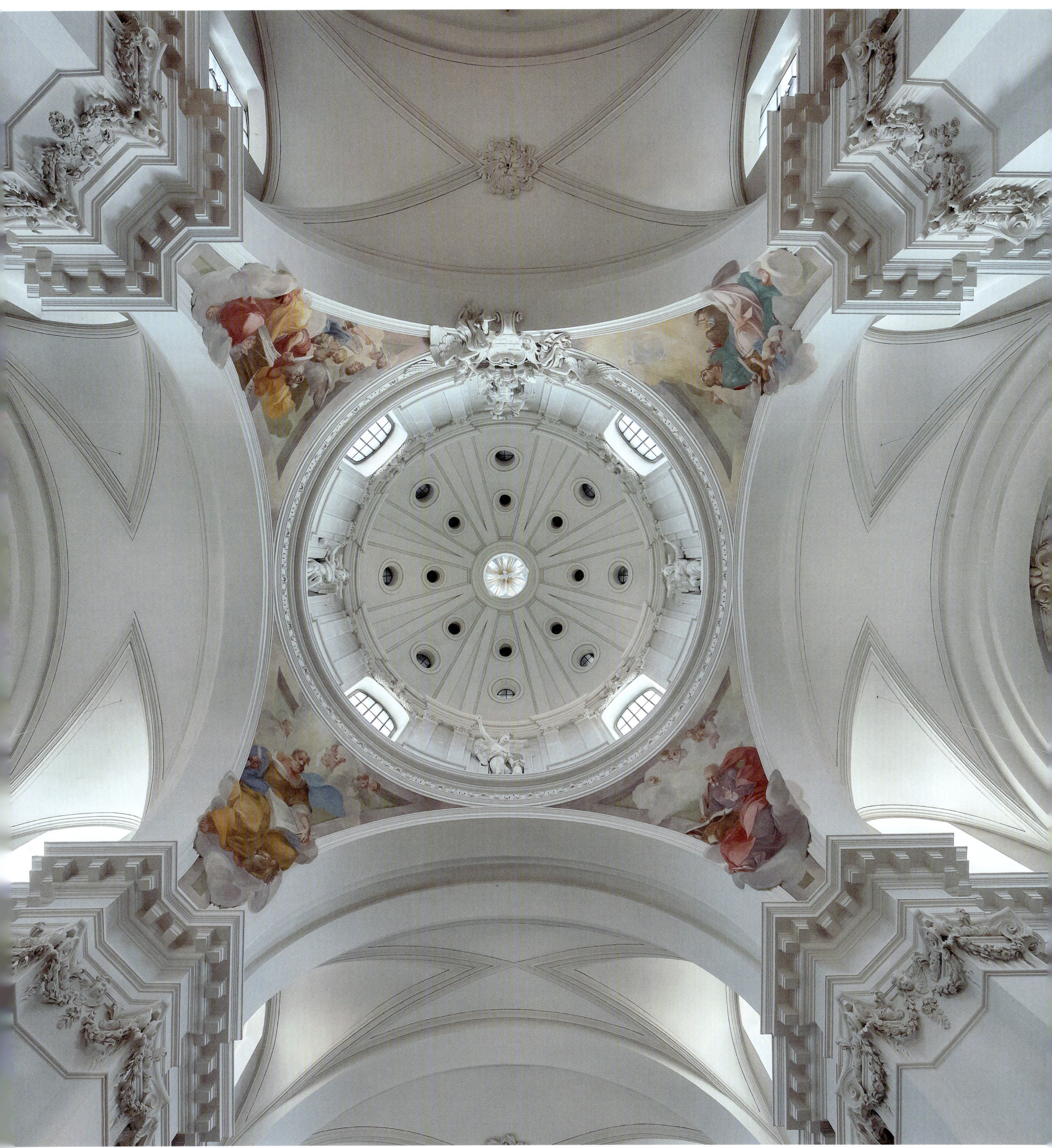

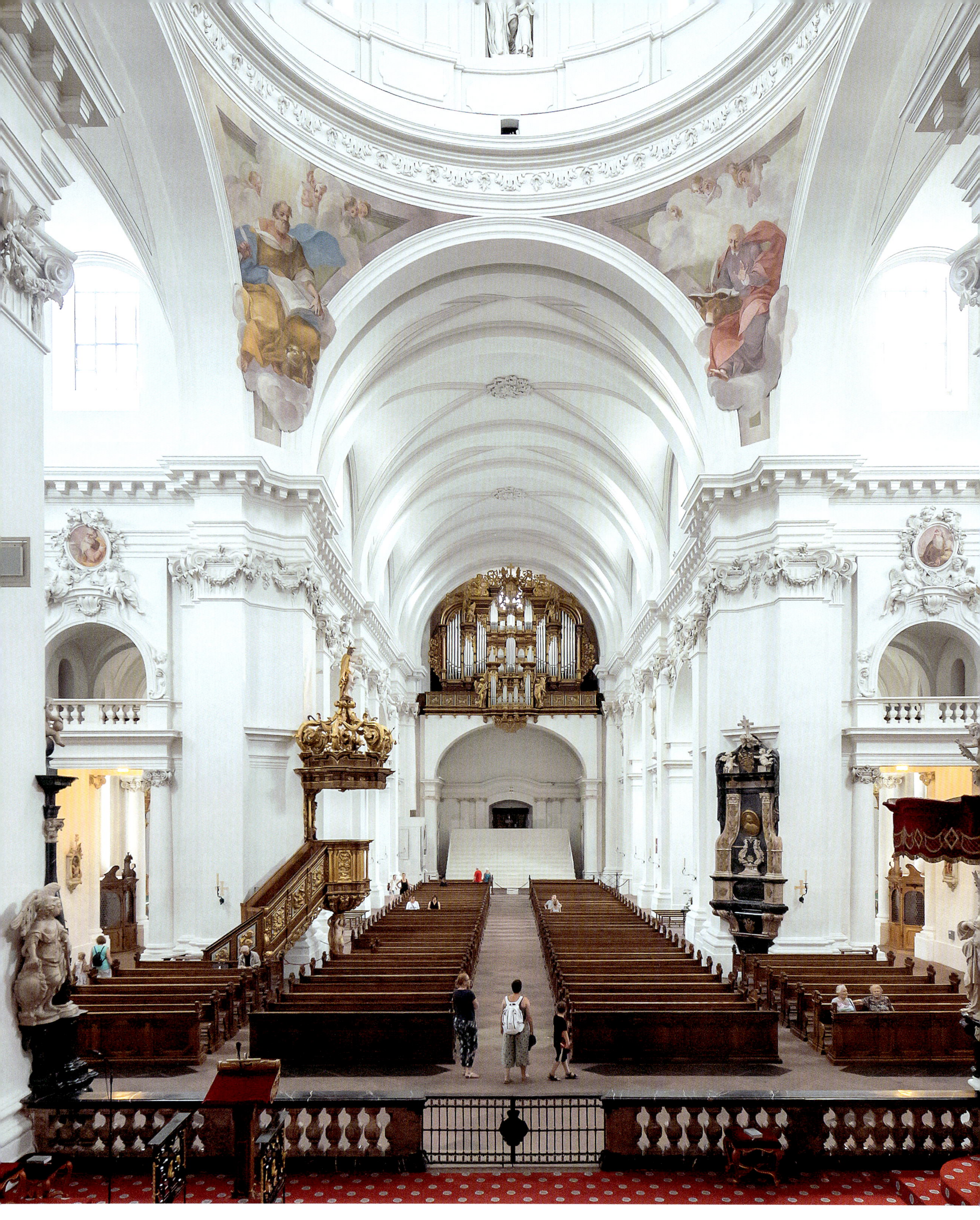

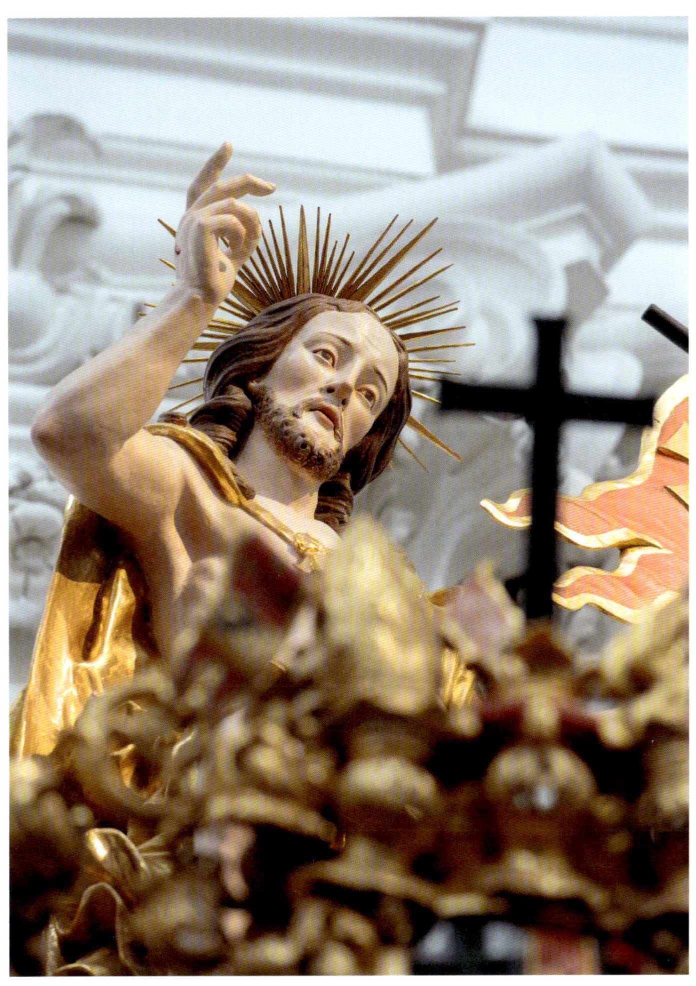

Giovanni Battista Artari gilt als der Meister des Figurenschmucks im Dom, Andreas Schwarzmann schuf viele der reichen Stuckarbeiten. Das Steinrelief in der Bonifatiusgruft wiederum gilt als ein Meisterwerk Johann Neudeckers d. Ä.

Giovanni Battista Artari is regarded as the master craftsman responsible for the statues in the cathedral, while Andreas Schwarzmann created the fine stucco work and Johann Neudecker the Elder sculpted the stone relief for the tomb of St. Boniface.

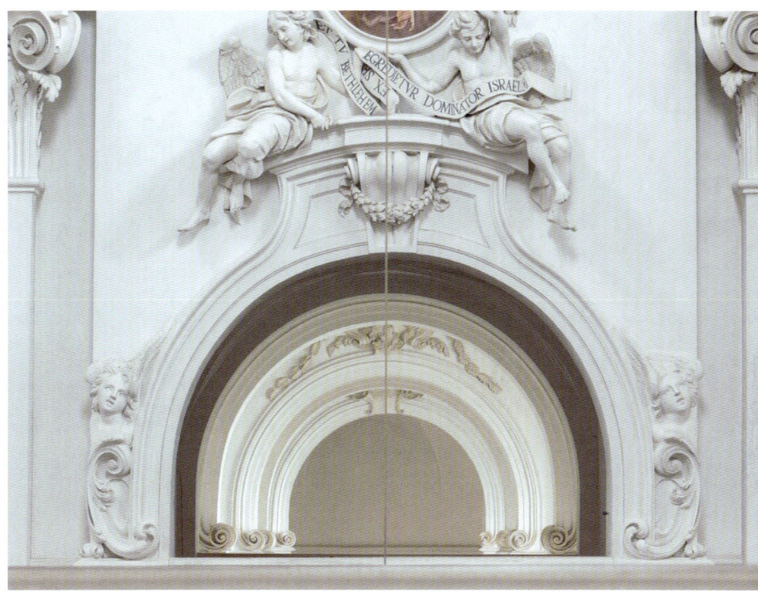

Das Orgelgehäuse mit seinen aufwendigen Schnitzarbeiten stammt noch aus der Entstehungszeit des Domes. Das Klangbild jedoch prägen spätere Jahrhunderte: Gut zwei Dutzend Register stammen noch aus der in Fulda legendären Sauer-Orgel von 1876/77, die meisten anderen wurden während der Restaurierung 1995/96 von der Firma Rieger (Vorarlberg) eingebaut.

The organ front with its intricate wooden carvings originates from the time of construction of the cathedral. The sound of the organ, however, is produced by organ pipes which were installed much later: more than two dozen registers are from the legendary "Sauer Organ" from 1876/77 while the rest were added during the restoration work carried out by Rieger Orgelbau (Voralberg) in 1995/96.

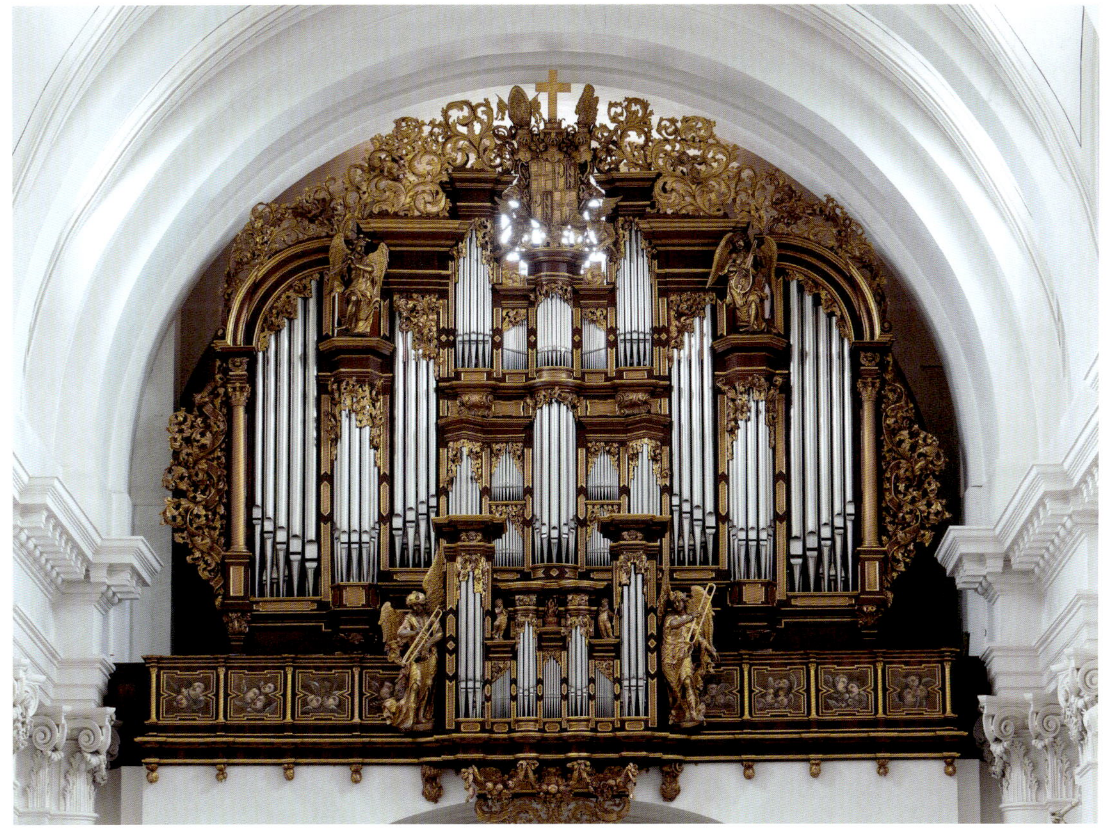

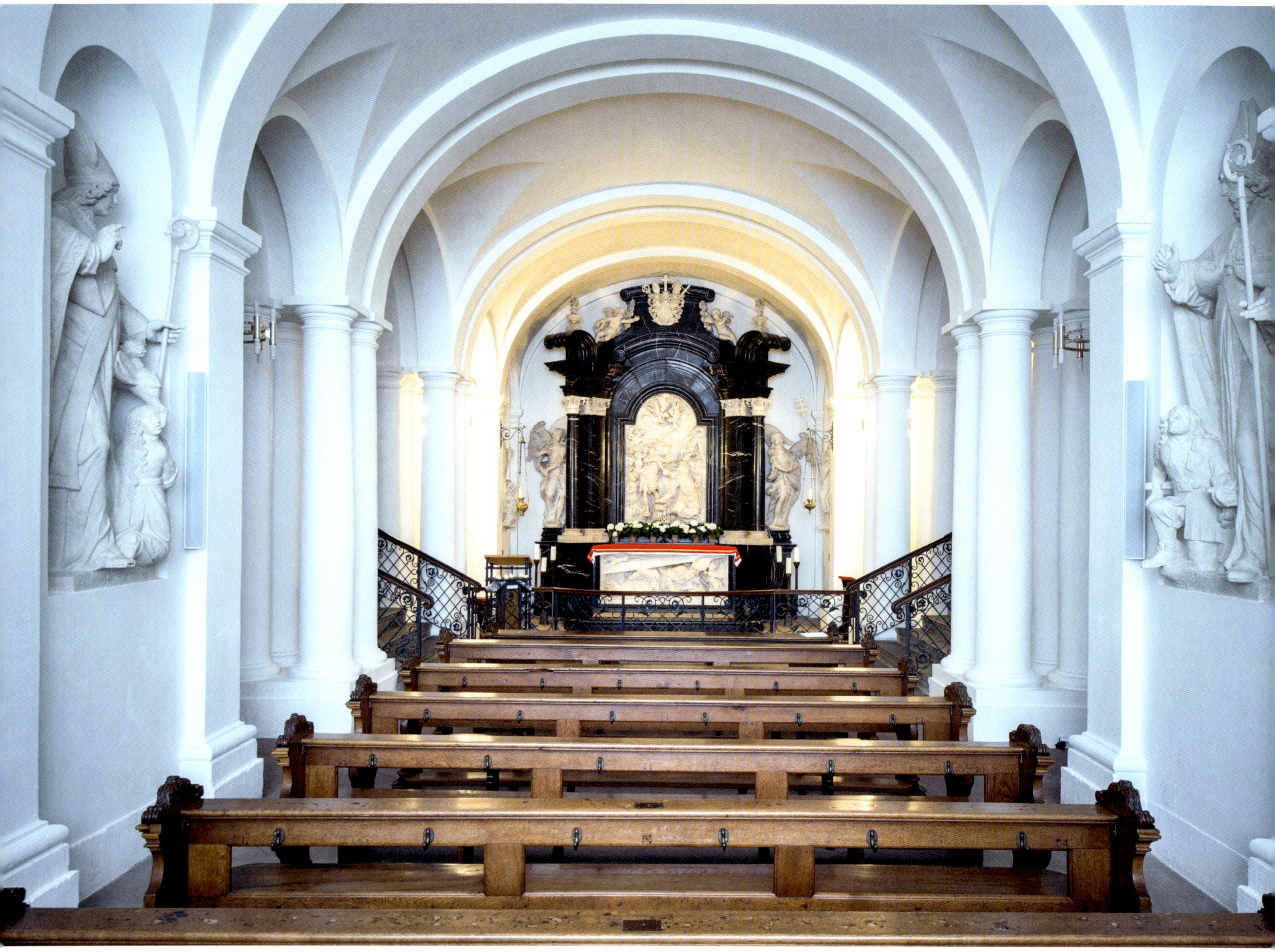

Unter dem Hochchor des Domes befindet sich die Bonifatiusgruft. Der Überlieferung nach ist hier der hl. Bonifatius bestattet. Als die Gruft einmal geöffnet wurde, fand man die sterblichen Überreste eines etwa 1,85 bis 1,90 Meter großen Mannes – für die damalige Zeit eine wirklich außergewöhnlich stattliche Größe.

The Boniface tomb is located under the choir. According to the records, St. Boniface is buried here. Once, when the tomb was opened, the mortal remains of a man of about 1.85 – 1.90 metres were found – for that time an exceptionally imposing height.

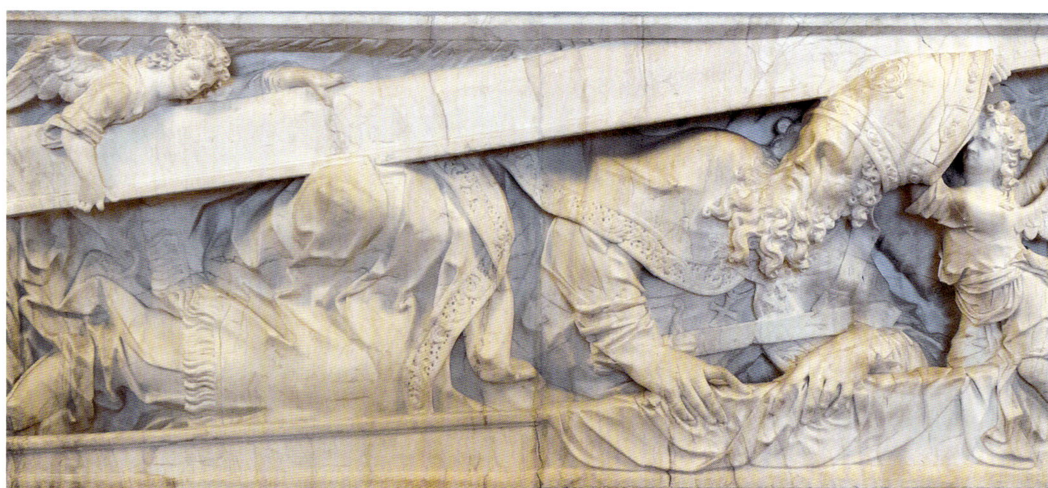

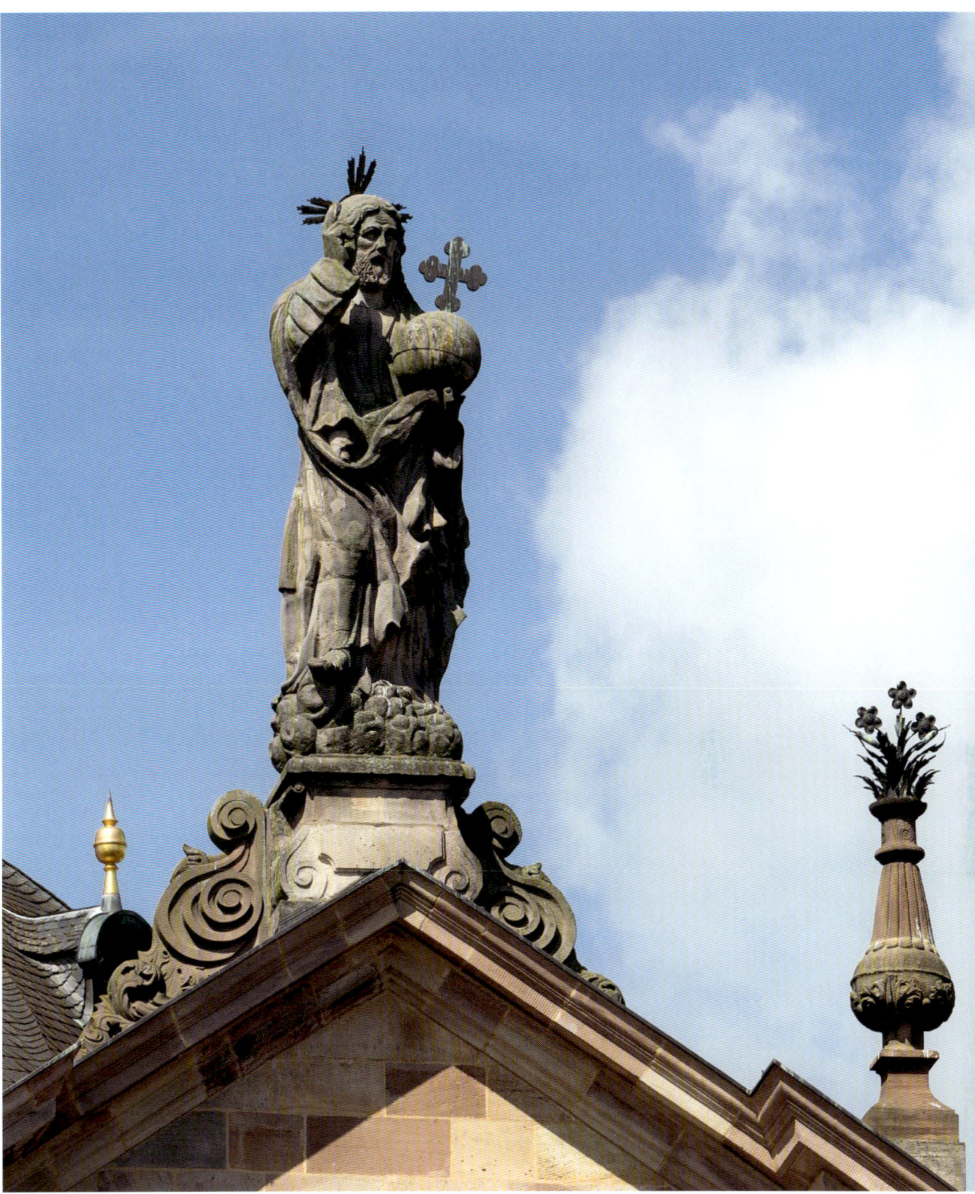

Eine Christus-Erlöser-Statue – St. Salvator ist schließlich auch Patron des Kirchenbaus – bildet den krönenden Abschluss der Hauptfassade im Osten.

A statue of Christ the Saviour – to whom the church was dedicated – forms the crowning finish of the main East front.

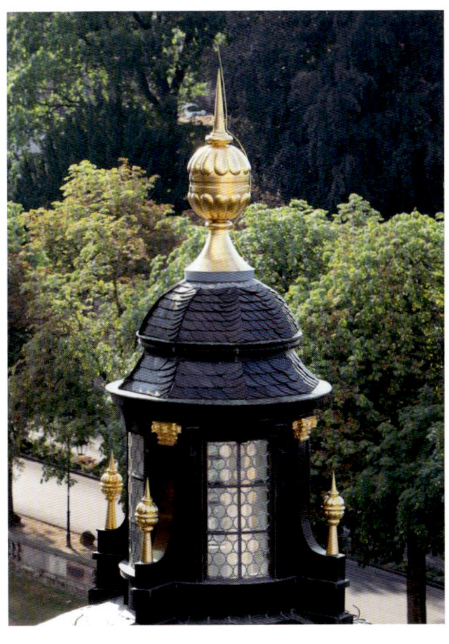

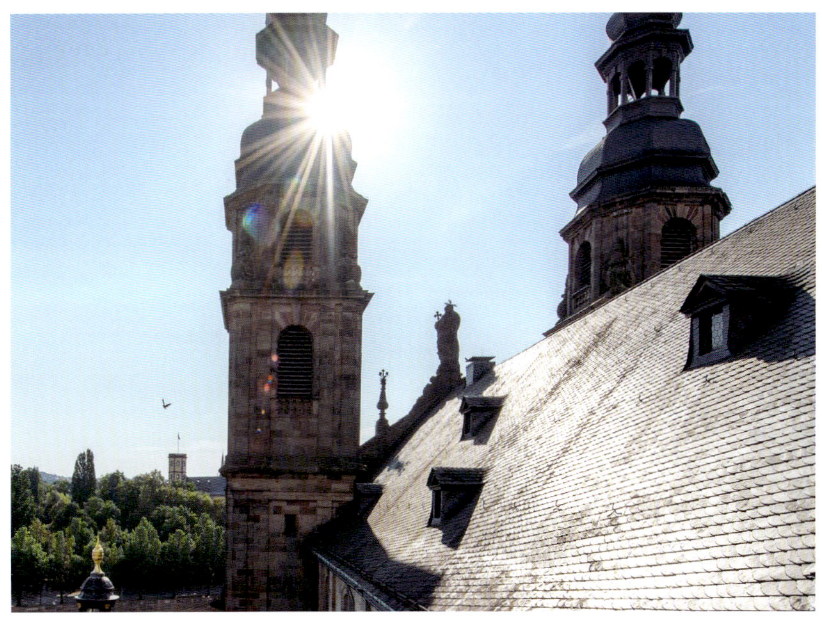

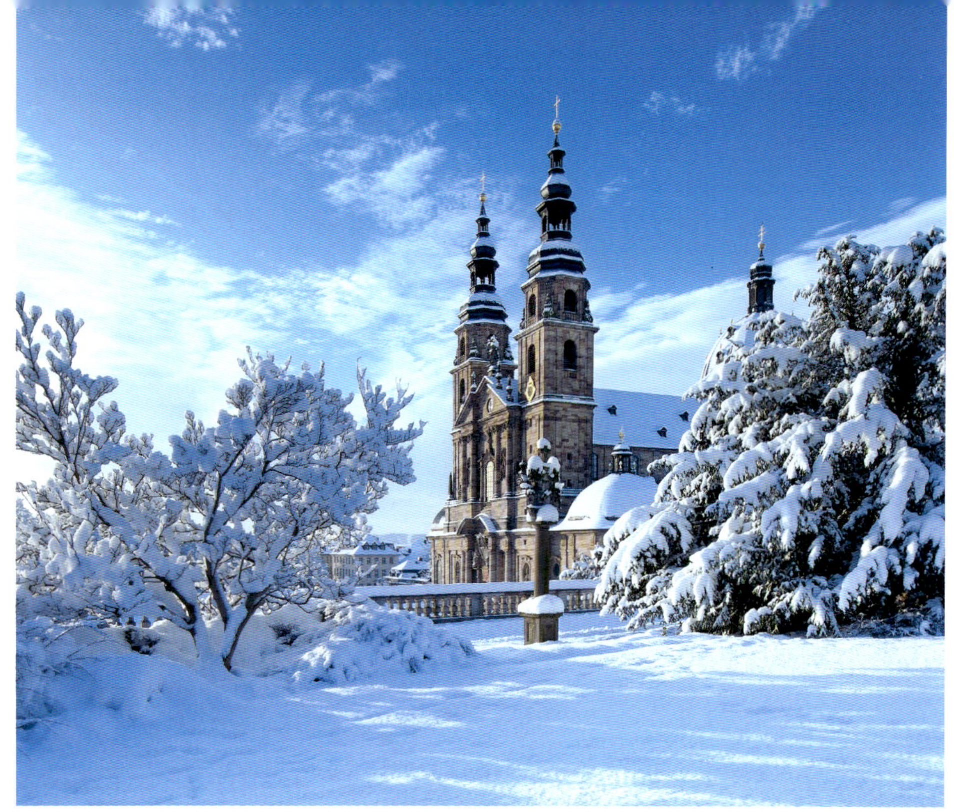

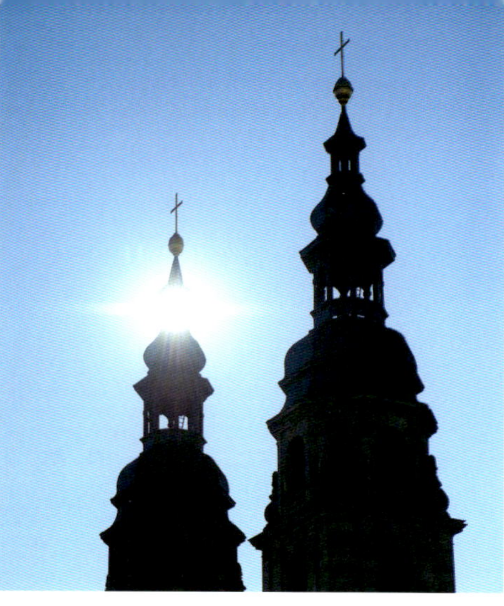

Zu allen Jahreszeiten und aus allen Blickwinkeln bildet der Dom eine Identität stiftende Bezugsgröße für Fuldaer und Gäste.

In all seasons and from all angles, the cathedral is an indivisible part of Fulda's identity for both local people and guests.

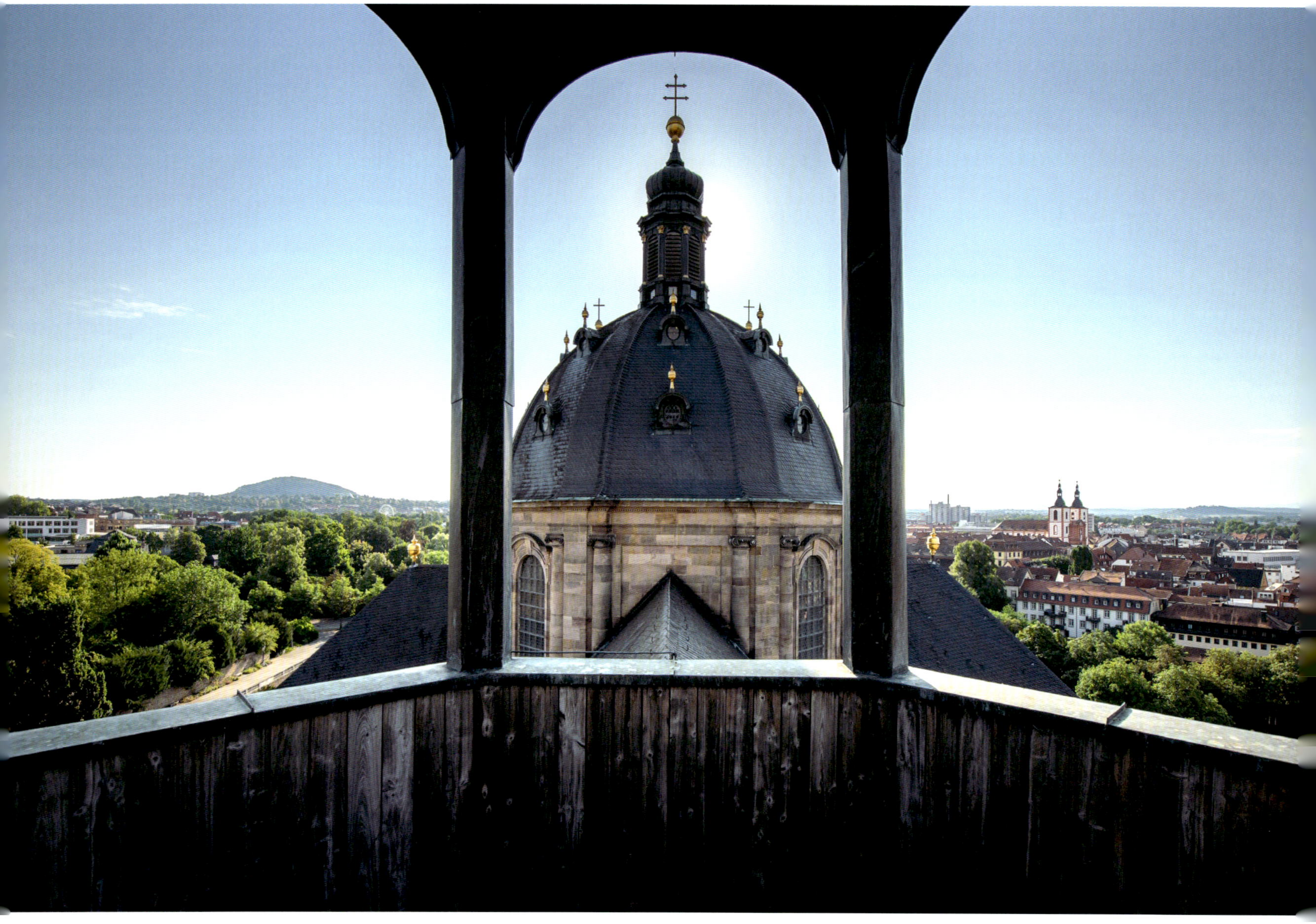

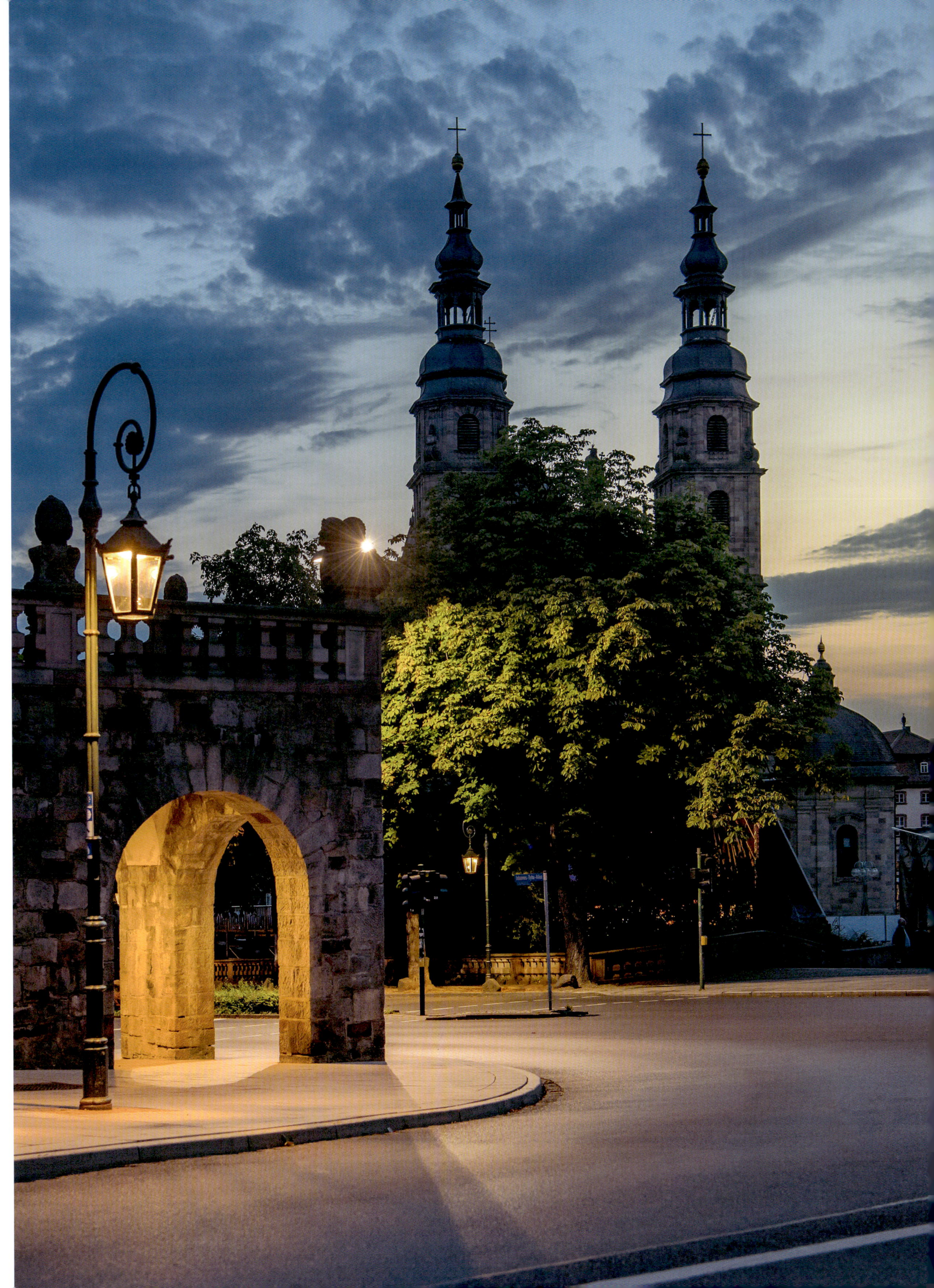

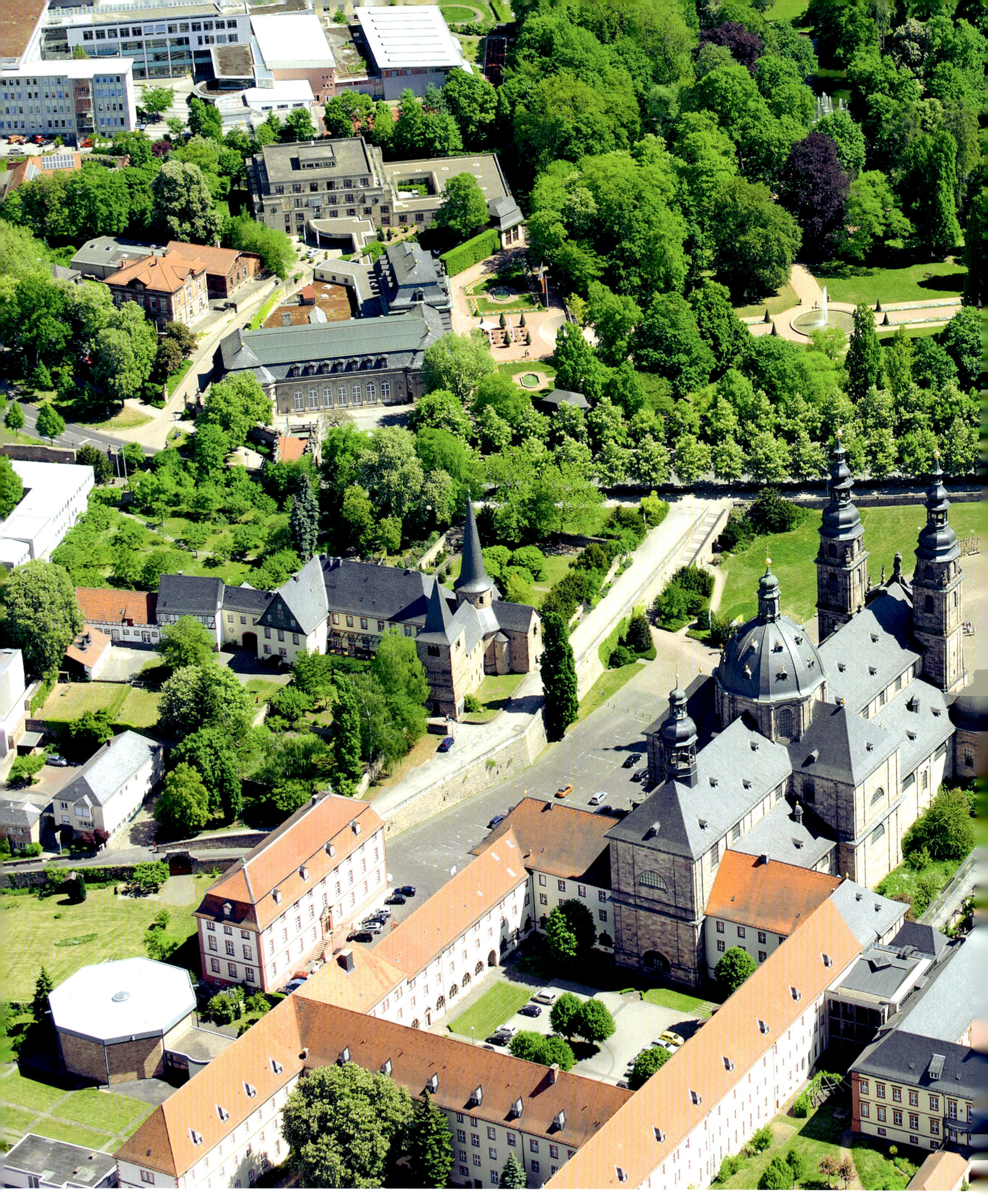

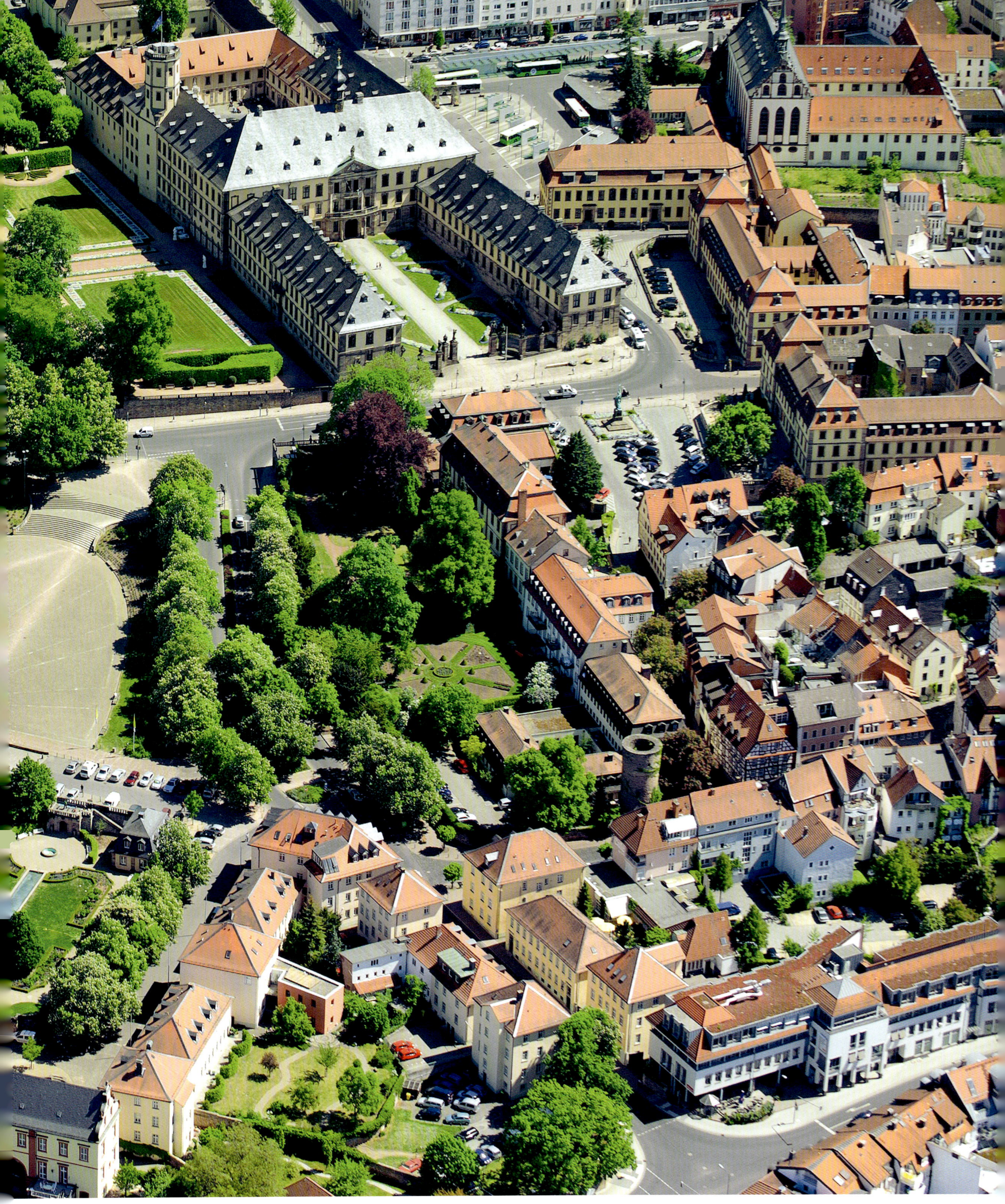

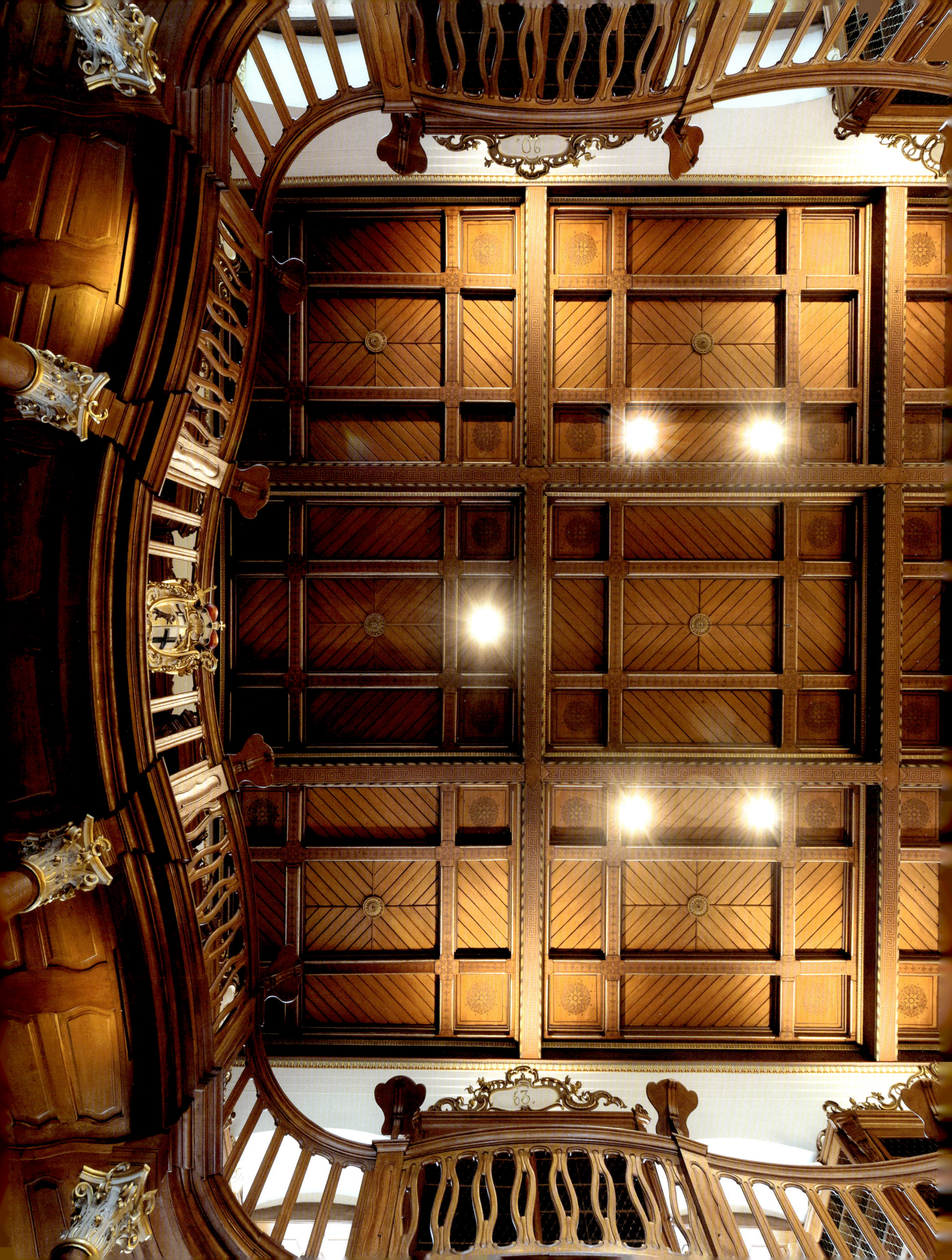
63

ENTDECKUNGEN RUND UM DEN DOM

Von der Bibliothek der Theologischen Fakultät zum Dechaneigarten

Etwas versteckt im Schatten von Dom und Michaelskirche liegt ein Gebäude, das nur eingeschränkt öffentlich zugänglich ist, aber eine nähere Betrachtung unbedingt verdient: In dem 1771–78 von Bauinspektor Karl Philipp Arnd unter der Ägide des „Reform-Fürstbischofs" Heinrich von Bibra errichteten Gebäude befindet sich heute die Theologische Fakultät Fulda. Hier werden die Priesteramtskandidaten, aber unter anderem auch die Pastoralreferentinnen und -referenten für das Bistum Fulda ausgebildet. Das Prunkstück im Innern des Baus ist die Bibliothek. Die Holzschnitzereien und Vertäfelungen sowie die alten, ledergebundenen Bände nehmen den Besucher sofort gefangen. Unter Fürstbischof von Bibra war der Raum jedoch nicht nur optisch, sondern auch inhaltlich eine echte Neuerung für die Stadt: Es war die erste öffentliche Bibliothek, und sie steht für die vielseitigen Bemühungen des aufgeklärten Regenten um die Bildung seiner Landeskinder.

Bücher und Fulda – das war schon im Mittelalter eine fruchtbare Kombination. Unter dem berühmten Abt Rabanus Maurus, der zuvor Leiter der Fuldaer Klosterschule war, erblühte die Schreibkunst im Kloster, bedeutende Schriften und kunstfertige Illustrationen entstanden. Leider befinden sich heute noch nur die

Discovering the Area around the Cathedral

From the Library of the Theological Faculty to the Deanery Garden

Somewhat hidden in the shadow of the cathedral and Michaelskirche there is a building (with restricted public access) which is, nevertheless, worth our closer attention: the Fulda Theological Faculty, which was built in the years 1771–78 by the inspector of construction Karl Philip Arnd under the aegis of the "Reformer Prince-bishop" Heinrich von Bibra. Here seminarists are prepared for the priesthood and curates are trained for the Fulda diocese. A magnificent library forms the centre of this building. The wooden carvings and panelling, and the historic, leather-bound books instantly captivate the visitor. During the time of Heinrich von Bibra this room not only represented an innovation in design, but also regarding its contents – it was the first public library and serves as an example of one of the many reformatory measures the prince-bishop took to bring education to the people of Fulda. Books and Fulda – this has been a fruitful combination since the Middle Ages. Under the abbot Rabanus Maurus, who had previously been the headmaster of the monastery school, the art of creating illuminated manuscripts flourished in the monastery.

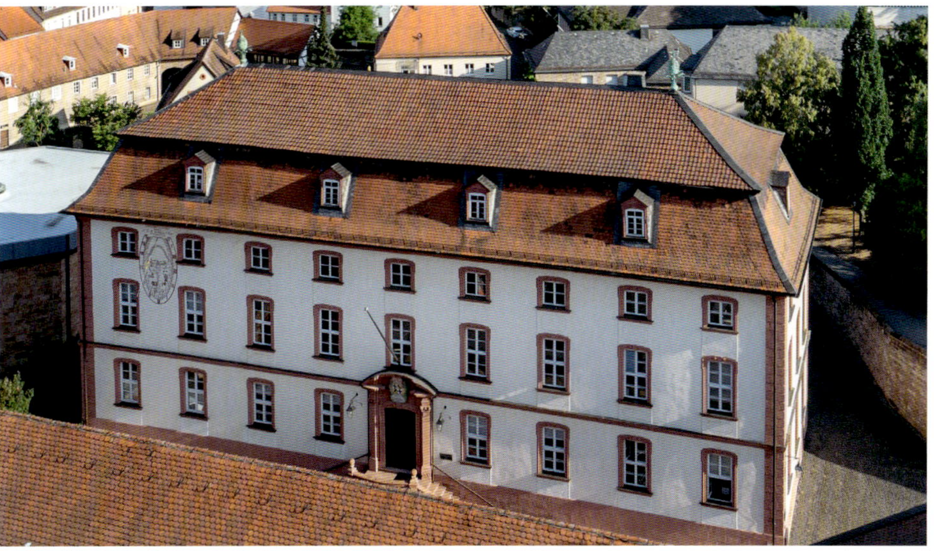

Das Fakultätsgebäude am Eduard-Schick-Platz neben dem Dom beherbergt im Obergeschoss unter anderem den eindrucksvollen Bibliothekssaal, der auch als Auditorium maximum der Theologischen Fakultät dient.

The impressive library of the theological faculty on Eduard-Schick-Platz (next to the cathedral) also serves as its main lecture hall.

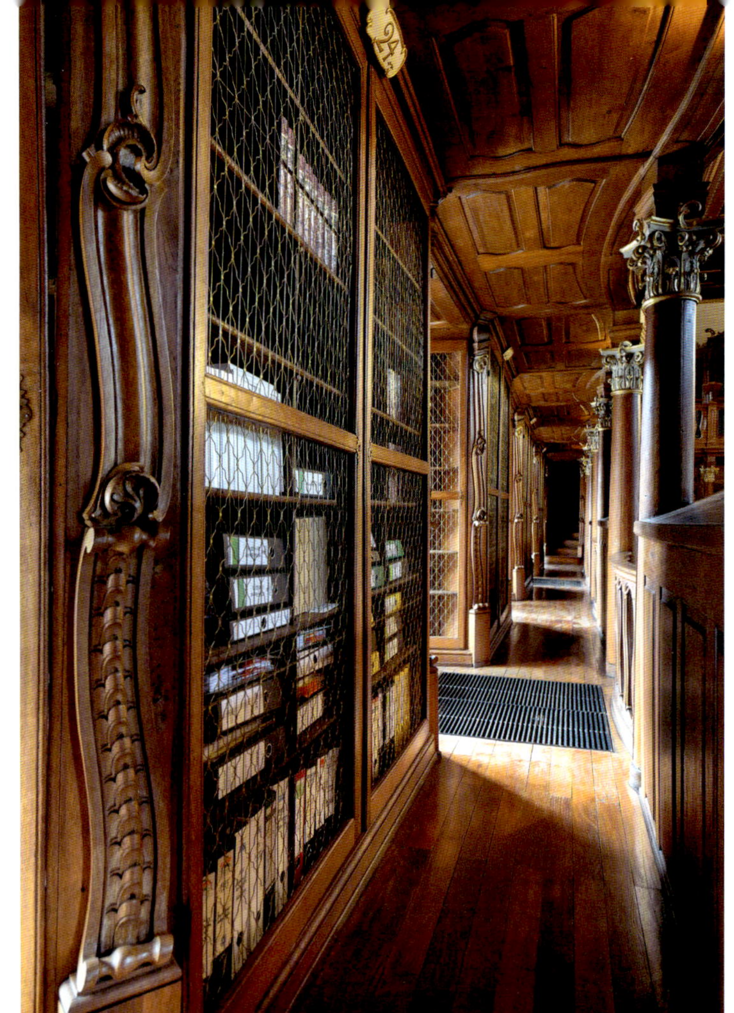

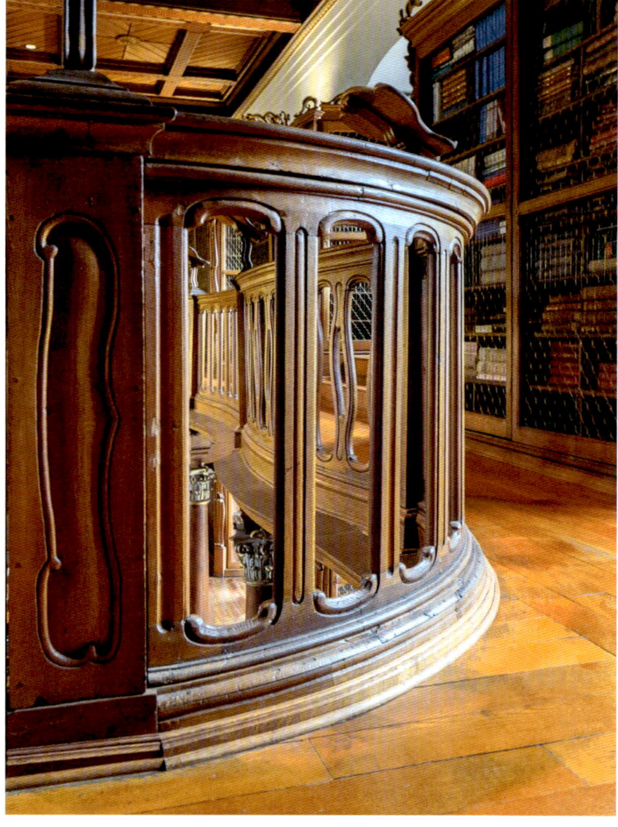

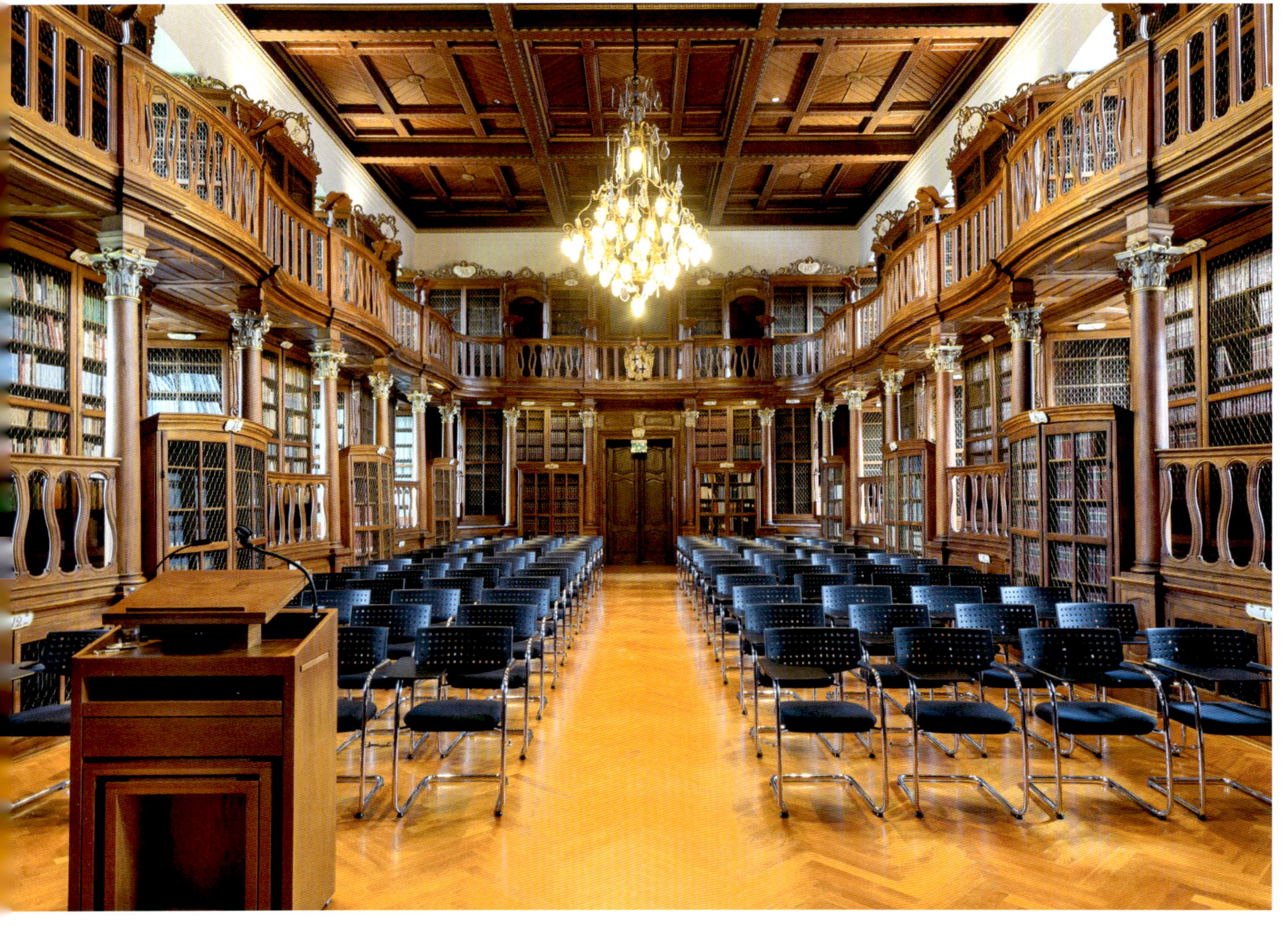

Das Brunnenhaus im Innenhof des Priester-seminars (siehe rechte Seite) ist ein Zeugnis der ursprünglichen benediktinischen Klosteranlage.

The well house in the courtyard of the seminary (on the right) is a remnant of the original Benedictine monastery.

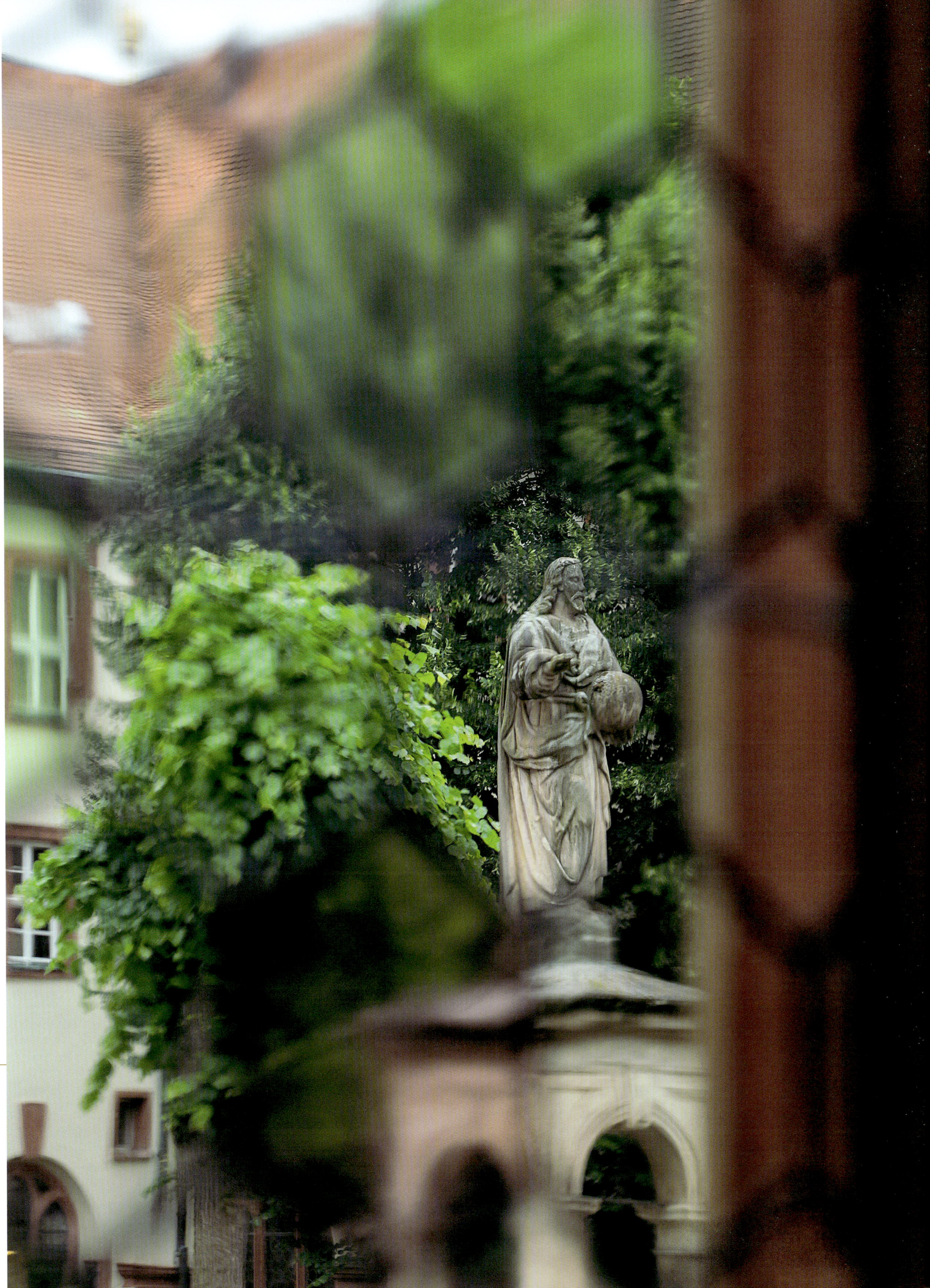

Das reich verzierte Portal des Priesterseminars schuf Johann Philipp Preuß 1668. Im Innern finden sich derweil auch Ornamente der klassizistischen Epoche.

The richly decorated doorway to the seminary was made by Johann Philipp Preuss in 1668. In the interior you can now see examples of Neo-classical ornamentation.

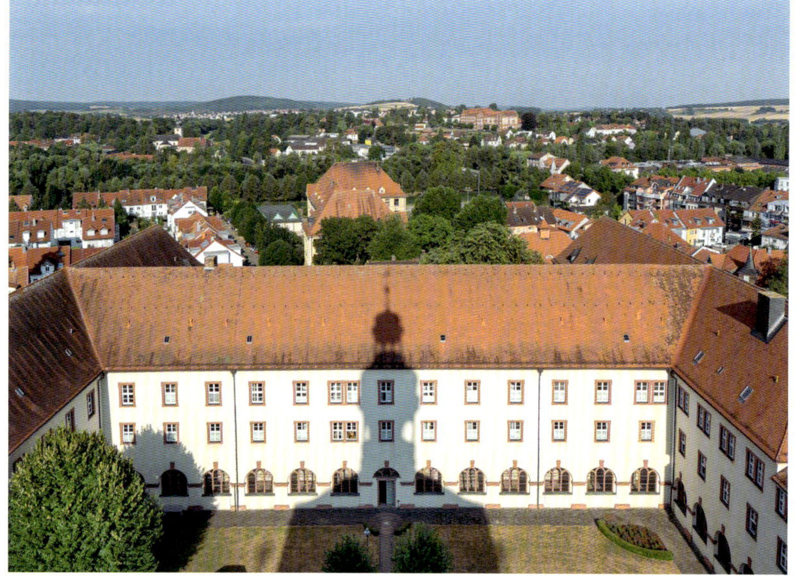

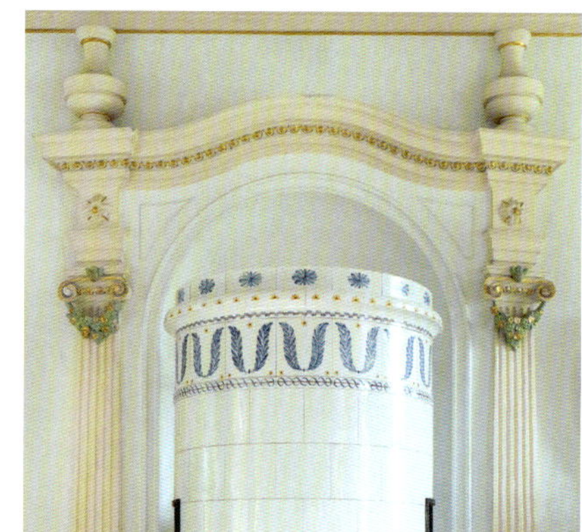

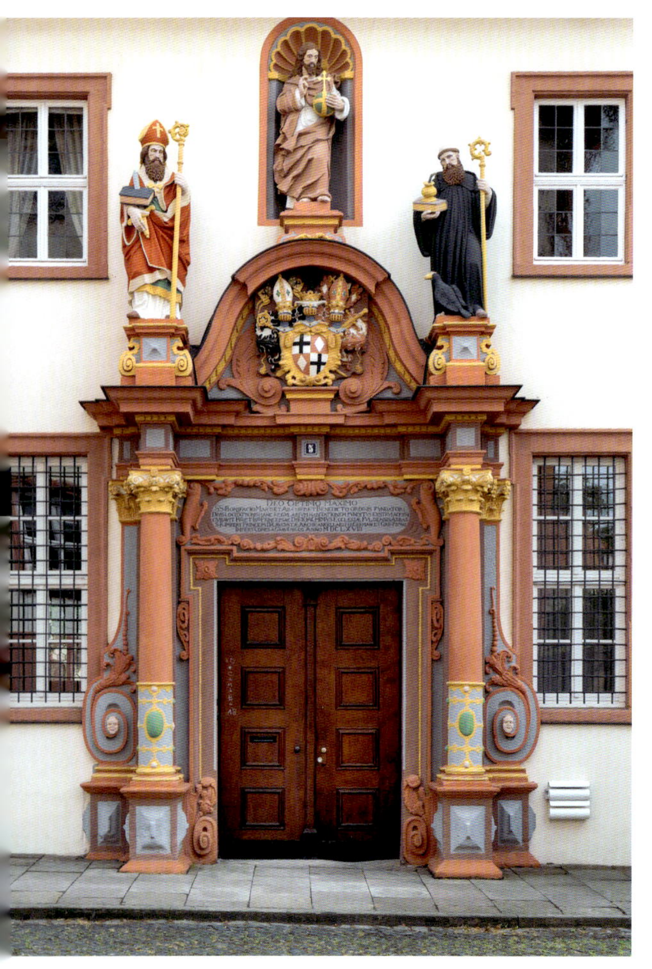

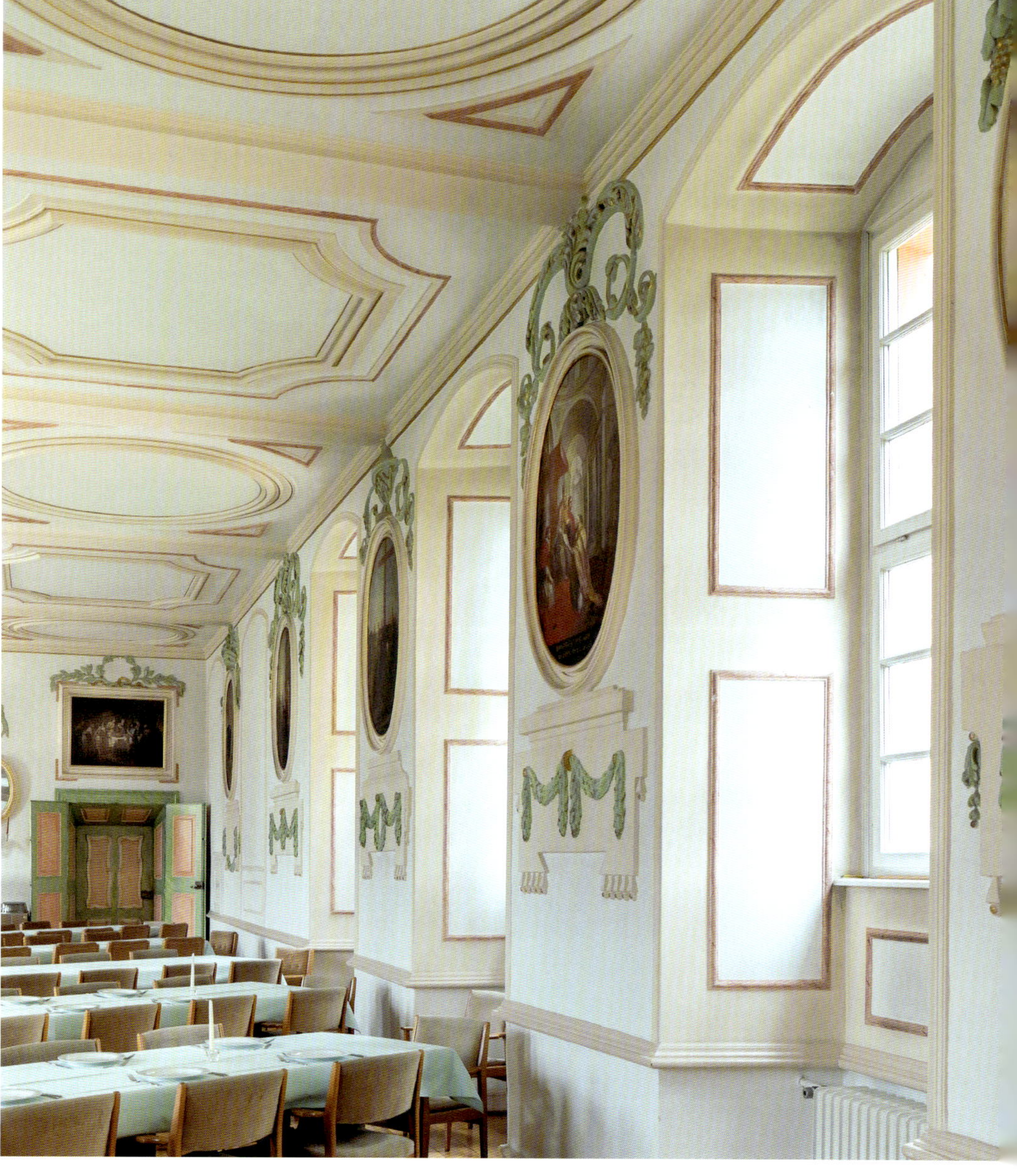

wenigsten dieser Werke in Fulda. Immerhin kümmert sich das der Theologischen Fakultät angegliederte Institut Bibliotheca Fuldensis um die Erforschung und Rekonstruktion dieses gewaltigen Schatzes.

Gleich gegenüber dem Bibliotheksgebäude befindet sich der Eingang zum Priesterseminar. Dass schmucke Portal aus dem Jahr 1668 zierte ursprünglich den Eingang zum Benediktinerkloster, das sich an die Stiftskirche beziehungsweise den Dom in westlicher Richtung anschloss. Noch heute ist die ursprüngliche Klosteranlage mit Kreuzgang, Innenhof und den verschiedenen Schlaf, Ess- und Studierräumen der Mönche erkennbar.

Einen markanten architektonischen Akzent inmitten der barocken Umgebung nördlich des Doms setzt die moderne Kapelle des Priesterseminars: Der Architekt Sep Ruf (1908–1982) schuf damit 1968 einen seiner bedeutendsten Sakralbauten.

Auf der sonnigen Südseite des Doms dagegen ist im Zuge der Landesgartenschau 1994 ein besonderes Refugium entstanden: der Domdechaneigarten. Hier lässt sich wunderbar verweilen, während die Wasserspiele eine beschauliche Geräuschkulisse bilden. Der Garten bildet zugleich den Zugang zum Dommuseum, wo die wertvollsten Stücke des Domschatzes aufbewahrt werden.

Unfortunately, only very few of these texts have remained in Fulda. However, the Bibliotheca Fuldaensis institute, which is affiliated to the Theological Faculty, is dedicated to reconstructing and conducting research into this vast treasure. Just opposite the library building you come to the entrance to the priests' seminary. The ornate doorway from 1668 originally embellished the entrance to the Benedictine monastery, which lay to the west of the monastery church (later the cathedral church). Still today you can identify the original layout of the monastery with its cloister, courtyard and the monks' various dormitories, refectories and studies. Lying right in the middle of the Baroque ensemble north of the cathedral, a striking architectural accent is set by the seminary's modern chapel, designed by the architect Sep Ruf (1908–1982) in 1968; one his most important religious buildings. On the sunny south side of the cathedral there is a place of tranquillity which was created during the preparations for the Hesse Garden Show in 1994: the Deanery Garden. This is a wonderful place to sit back, relax and listen to the calming sound of gurgling fountains. The garden also leads you to the entrance of the Cathedral Museum, where the most valuable of the cathedral's treasures are kept.

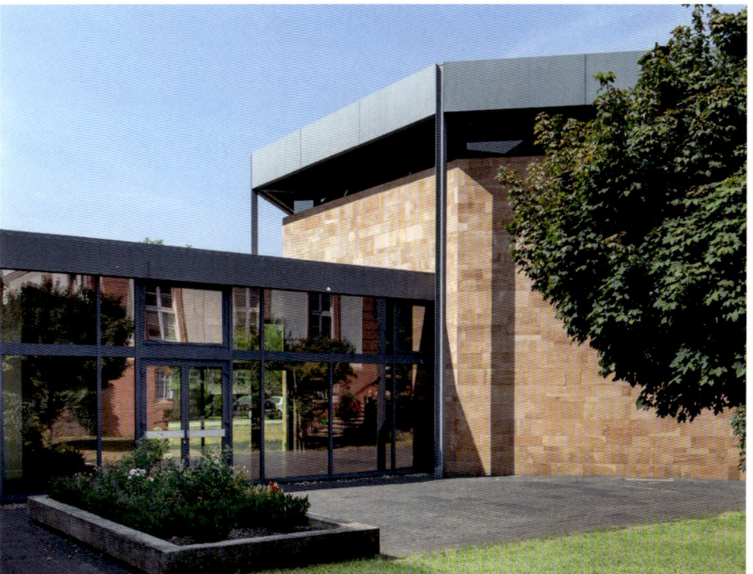

Einen interessanten Kontrast zu den historischen Bauten der Umgebung bildet die moderne Seminarkapelle Zur Heiligen Dreifaltigkeit (siehe auch folgende Doppelseite), die Sep Ruf 1968 schuf.

The modern seminary chapel designed by Sep Ruf in 1968 creates an interesting contrast to the historical buildings around it (see also double-page spread overleaf).

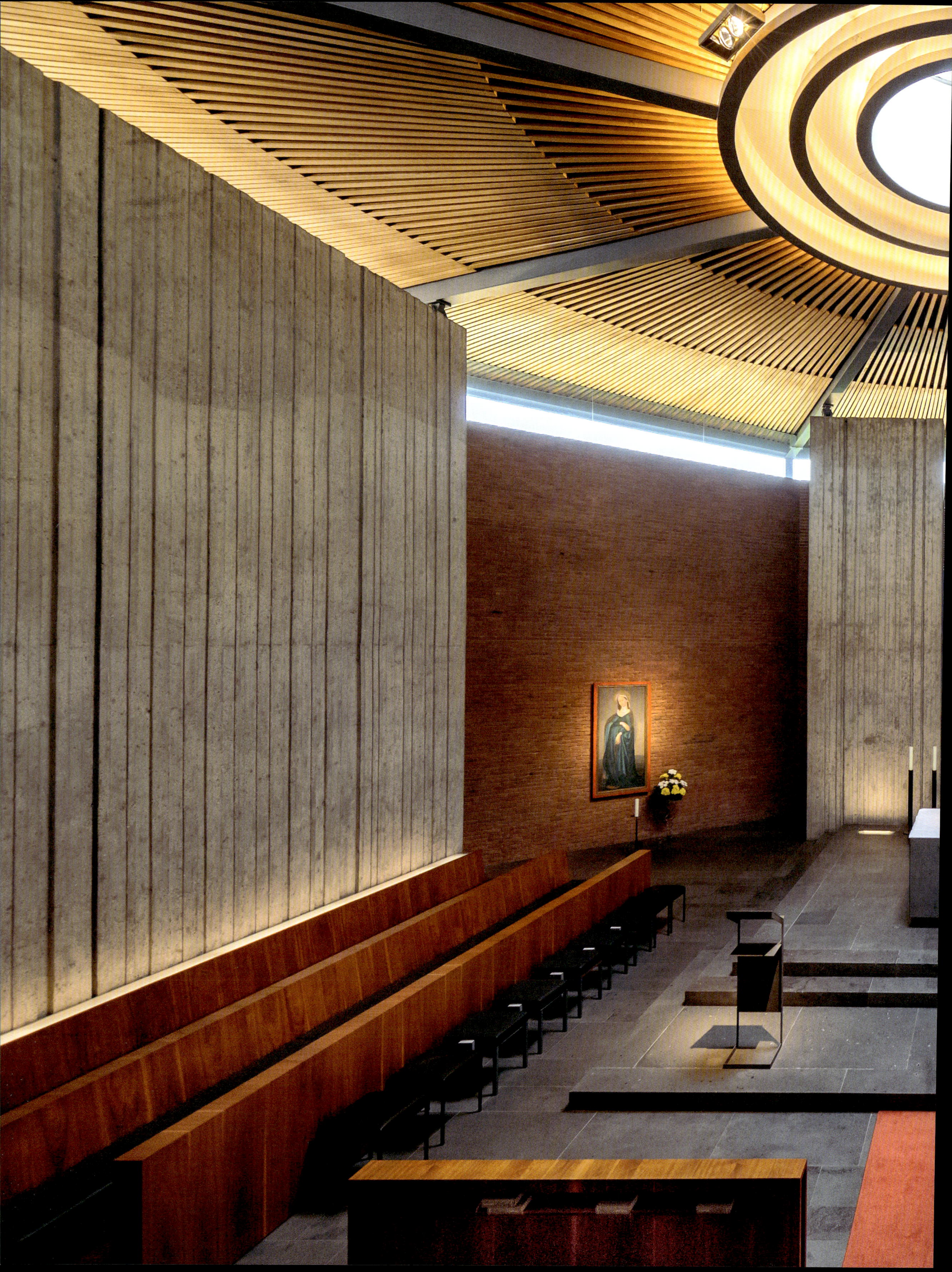

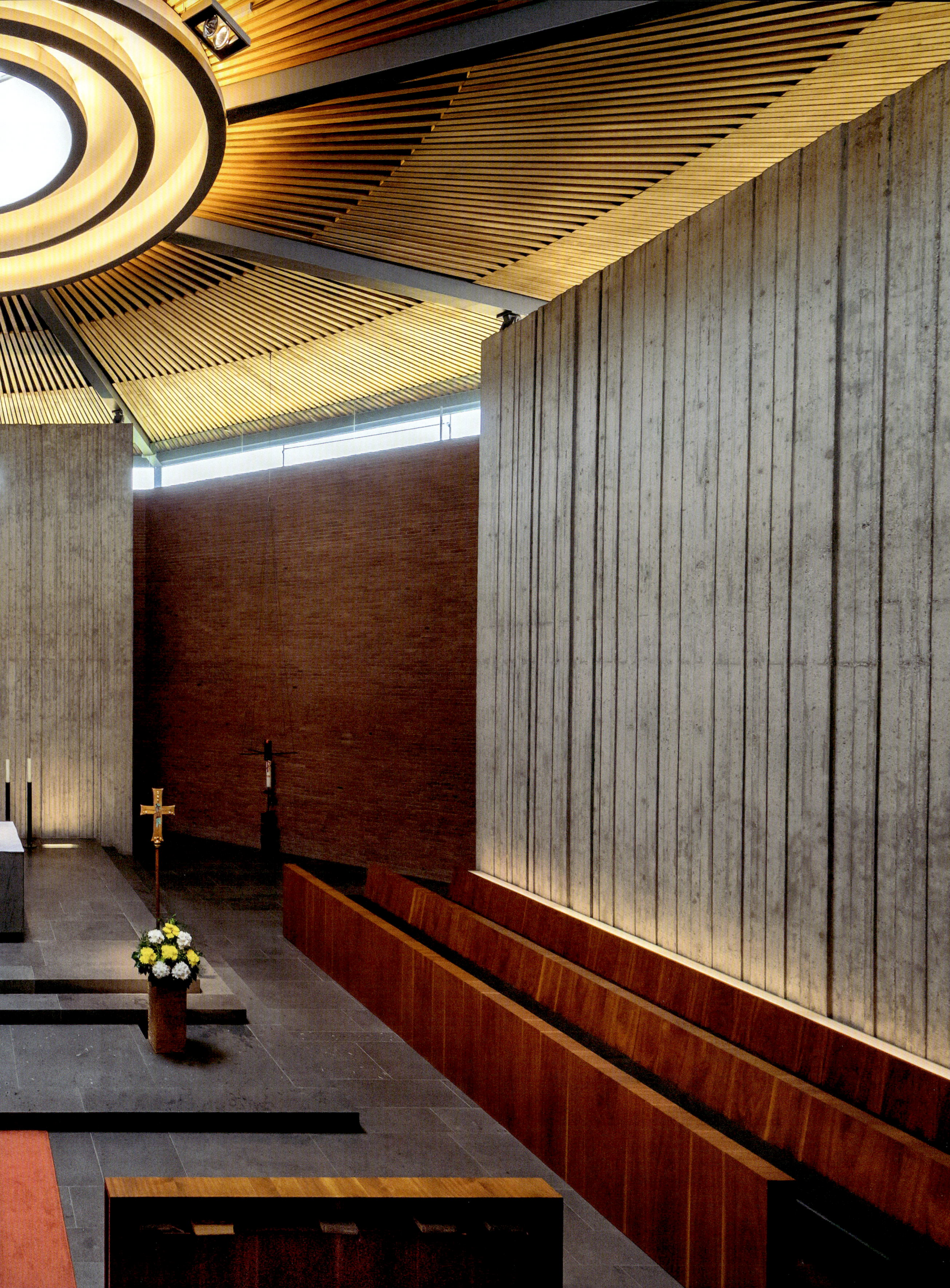

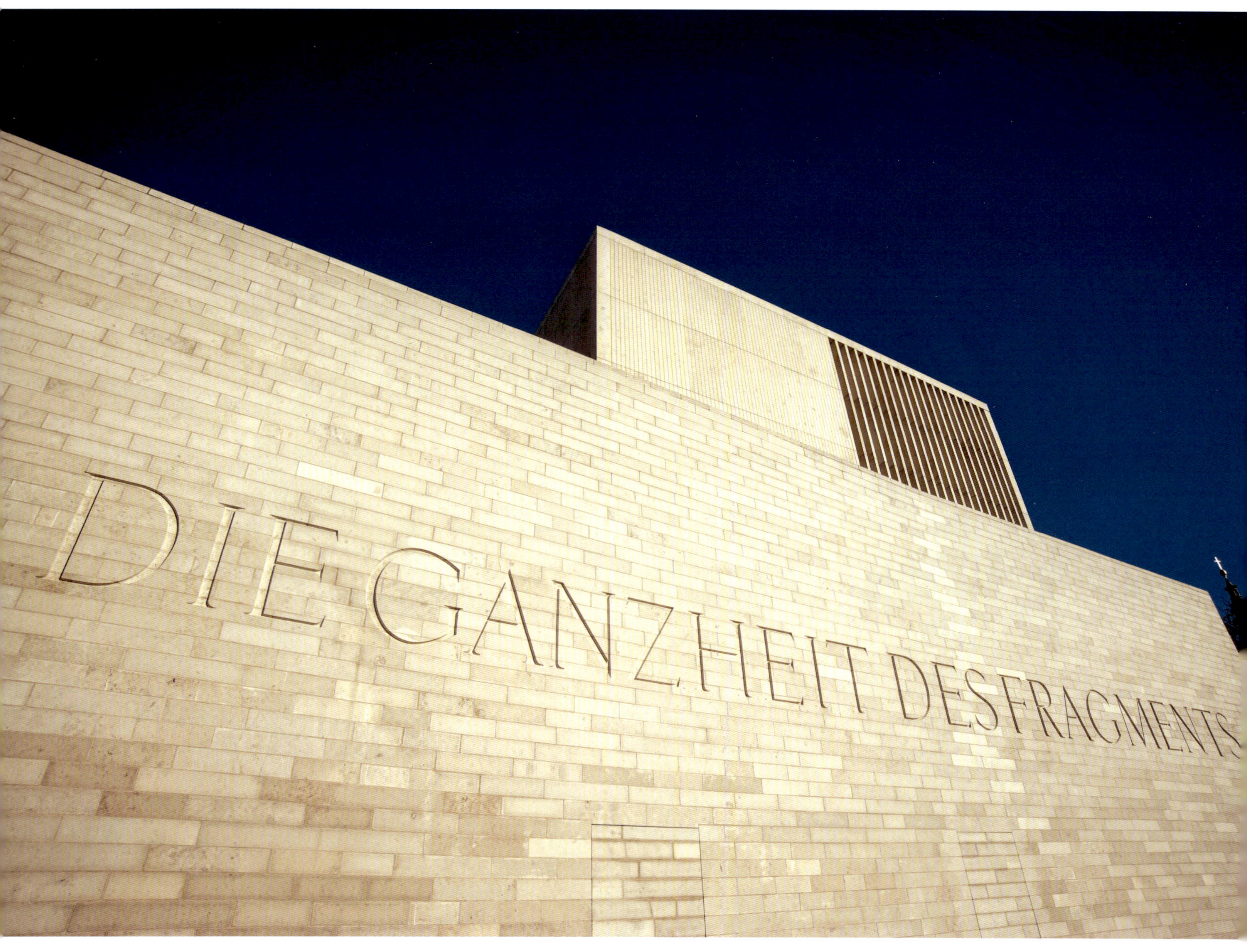

Einen weiteren Akzent mit Blick auf die zeitgenössische Architektur setzt das Gebäude des Bistumsarchivs (2005 entworfen von den Fuldaer Architekten Peter Sichau und Hartmut Walter), das etwas versteckt zwischen Michaelskirche, Generalvikariat und Dompfarrzentrum liegt. Eine Besonderheit ist die Inschrift „Die Ganzheit des Fragments", die von dem international renommierten Künstler und Biennale-Preisträger 2017, Prof. Franz Erhard Walther, 2007 eigens für dieses Gebäude geschaffen wurde.
Walther, der 1939 in Fulda geboren wurde, hat auch an anderen Stellen seine künstlerischen Spuren im Stadtbild hinterlassen, zum Beispiel bei den „Raumformen für Fulda" (1994), die in der Nähe des Doms und des Schlosses zu finden sind.

Another striking example of contemporary architecture is the building that houses the diocesan archive (designed by the Fulda architects Peter Sichau and Hartmut Walter). This building lies somewhat tucked away between the Michaelskirche, the diocesan office and the cathedral parish centre. A special feature of this building is the inscription "Die Ganzheit des Fragments" ("The Wholeness of the Fragment") which was conceived specially for the archive by Prof. Franz Erhard Walther in 2007. This internationally renowned artist, who won a Golden Lion at the Biennale in 2017, was born in Fulda in 1939 and has left artistic traces in other places in the city, for example, the "Raumformen für Fulda" ("Space Forms for Fulda", 1994) which can be seen near the cathedral and the Residence.

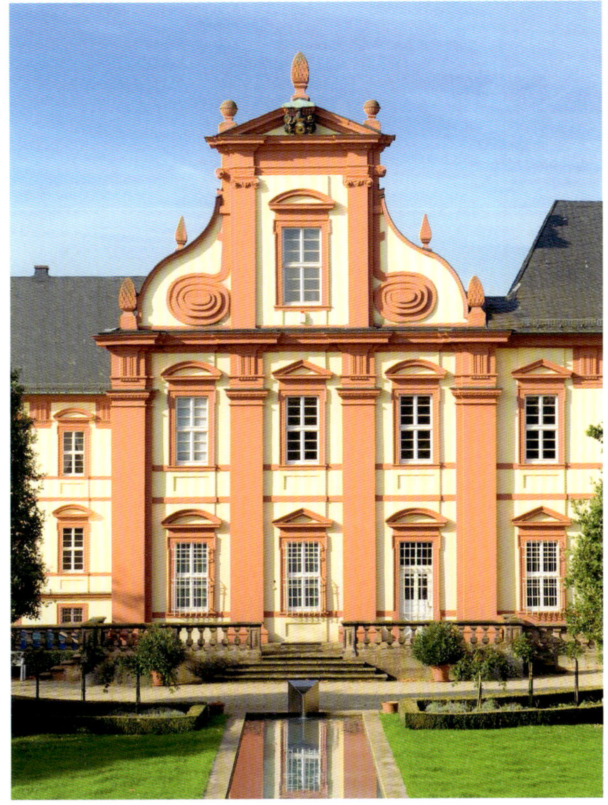

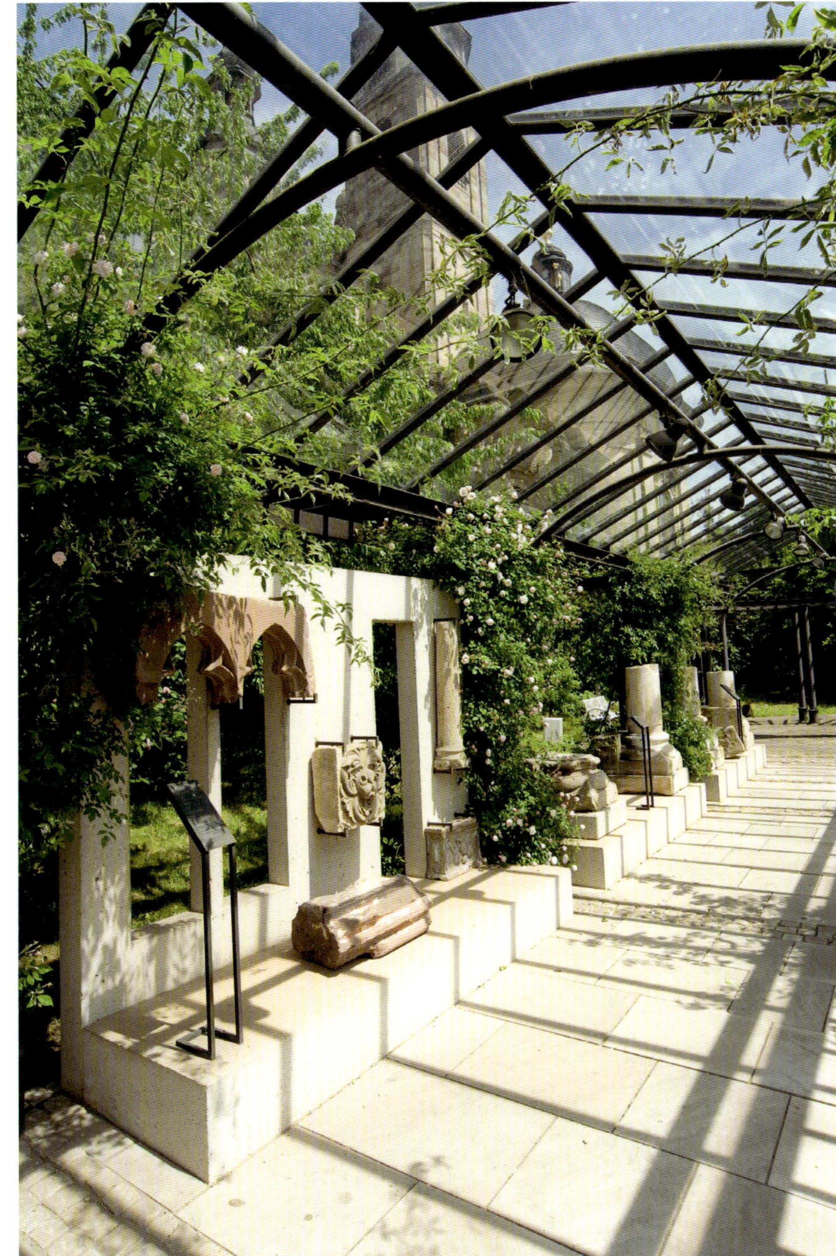

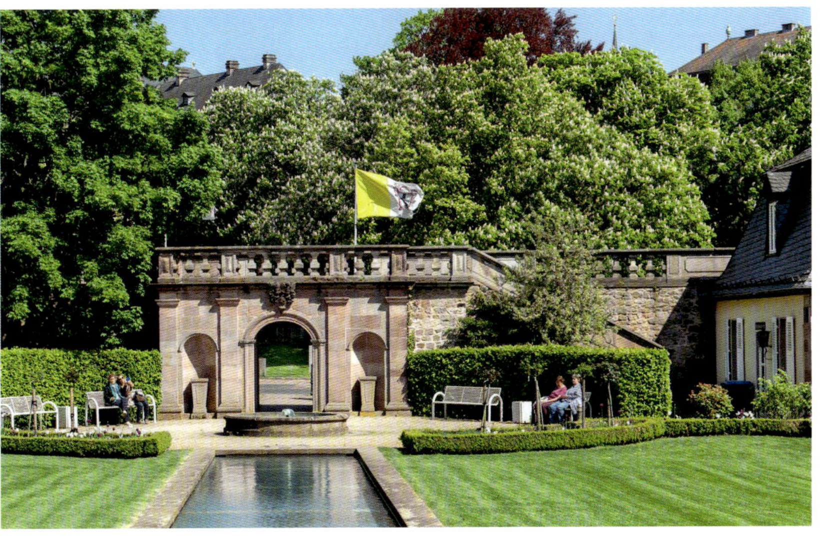

Eine Oase der Ruhe: der Domdechaneigarten mit dem zur Landesgartenschau 1994 geschaffenen Wasserlauf. Der Eingang zum Dechaneigarten bildet zugleich den Zugang zum Dommuseum. Im Außenbereich werden Fragmente aus der Ratgerbasilika aufbewahrt.

An oasis of peace: the Deanery Garden with its tranquil watercourse created for the Hesse State Garden Show in 1994. The entrance to the Deanery Garden also serves as the entrance to cathedral museum. The outdoor area is also used for displaying stone fragments from the Ratger Basilica.

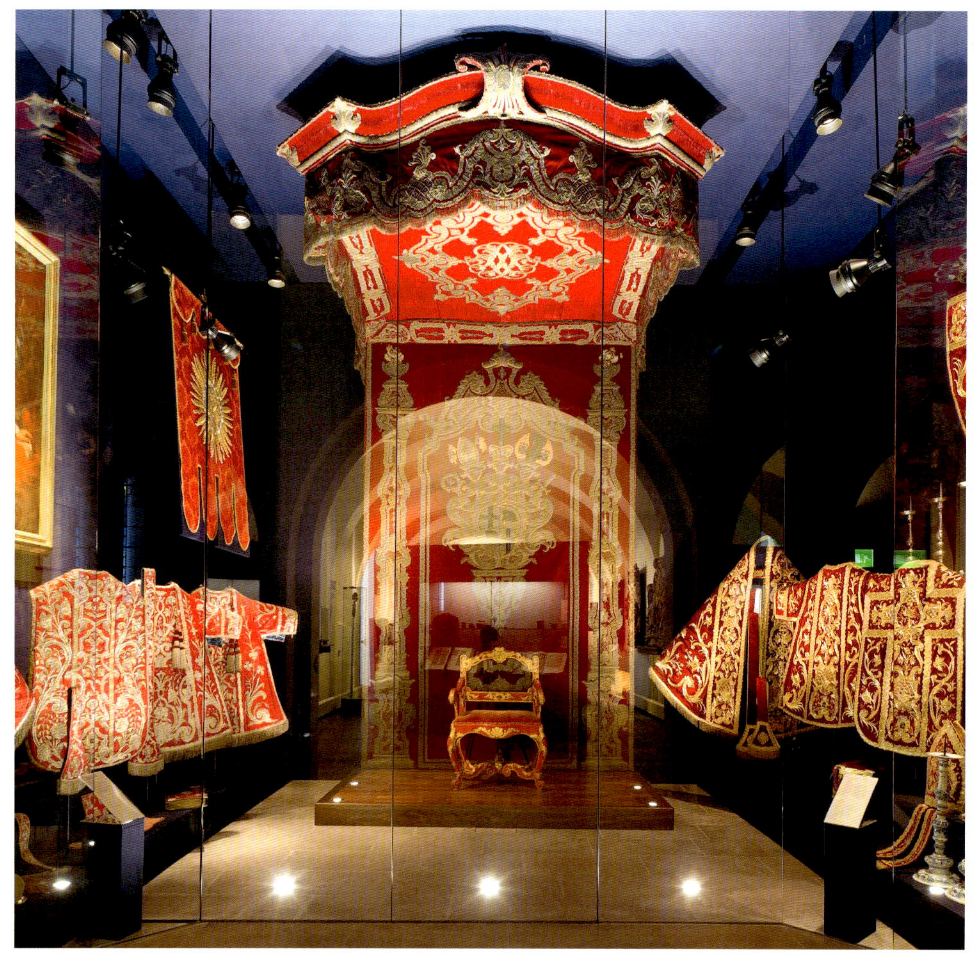

Das Dommuseum beherbergt eine Vielzahl an Kostbarkeiten, von reich bestickten liturgischen Gewändern bis hin zu wertvollen Gemälden (etwa ein Cranach von 1512), Handschriften und Reliquien. Zum Domschatz gehört auch der sogenannte Bonifatiusstab, der auch im Logo des Museums auftaucht, sowie der sagenumwobene Codex Ragyndrudis (Foto rechts), den Bonifatius angeblich während seines Märtyrertodes in Friesland schützend über den Kopf gehalten hat.

The cathedral museum holds many precious exhibits: from richly embroidered liturgical vestments to valuable paintings (e.g. a Cranach from 1512), manuscripts and relics.
The cathedral treasures also include the "Boniface Crozier", which is shown in the museum's logo, and the fabled Codex Ragyndrudis (see right-hand photo), which St. Boniface is supposed to have held above his head to protect himself against the murderous blows that led to his martyr's death in Frisia.

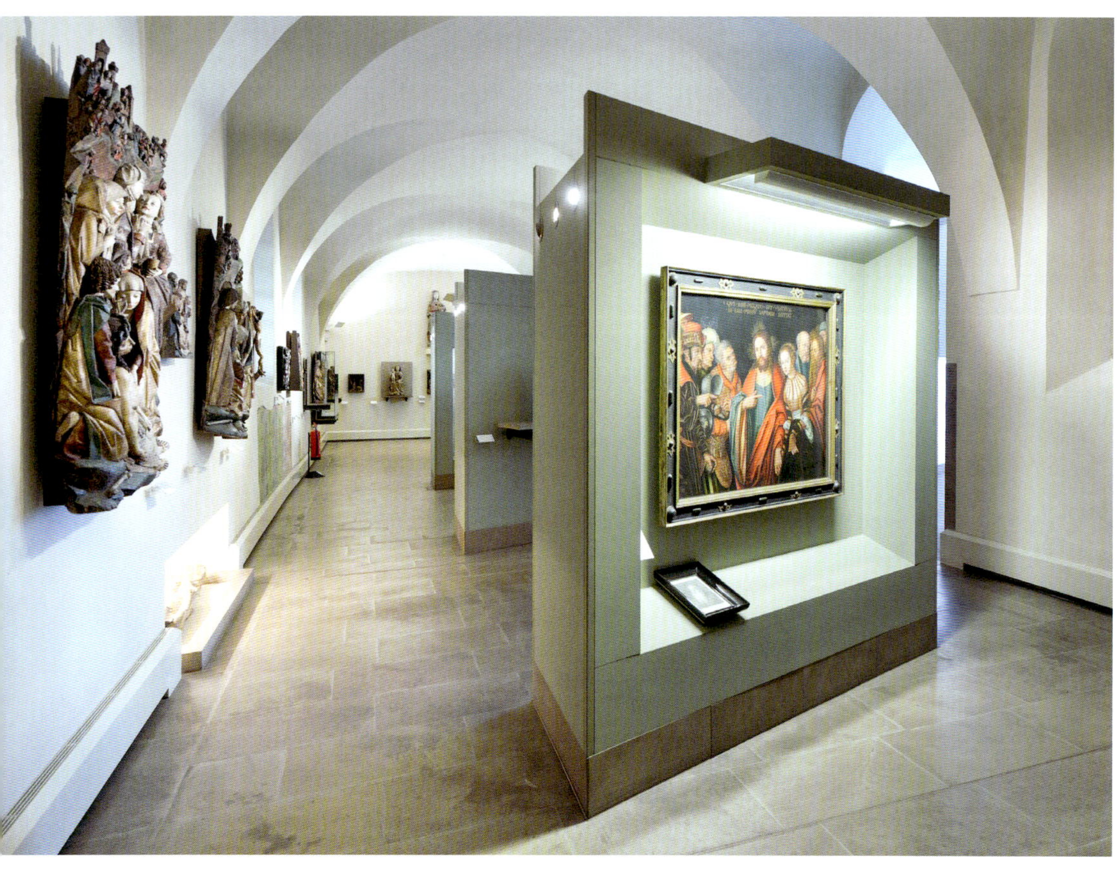

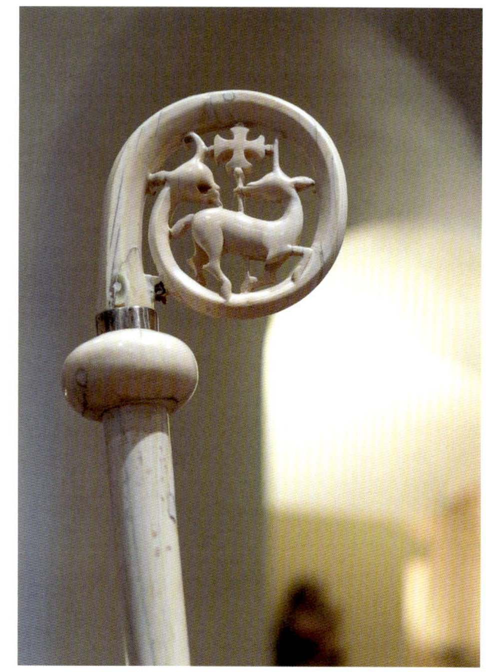

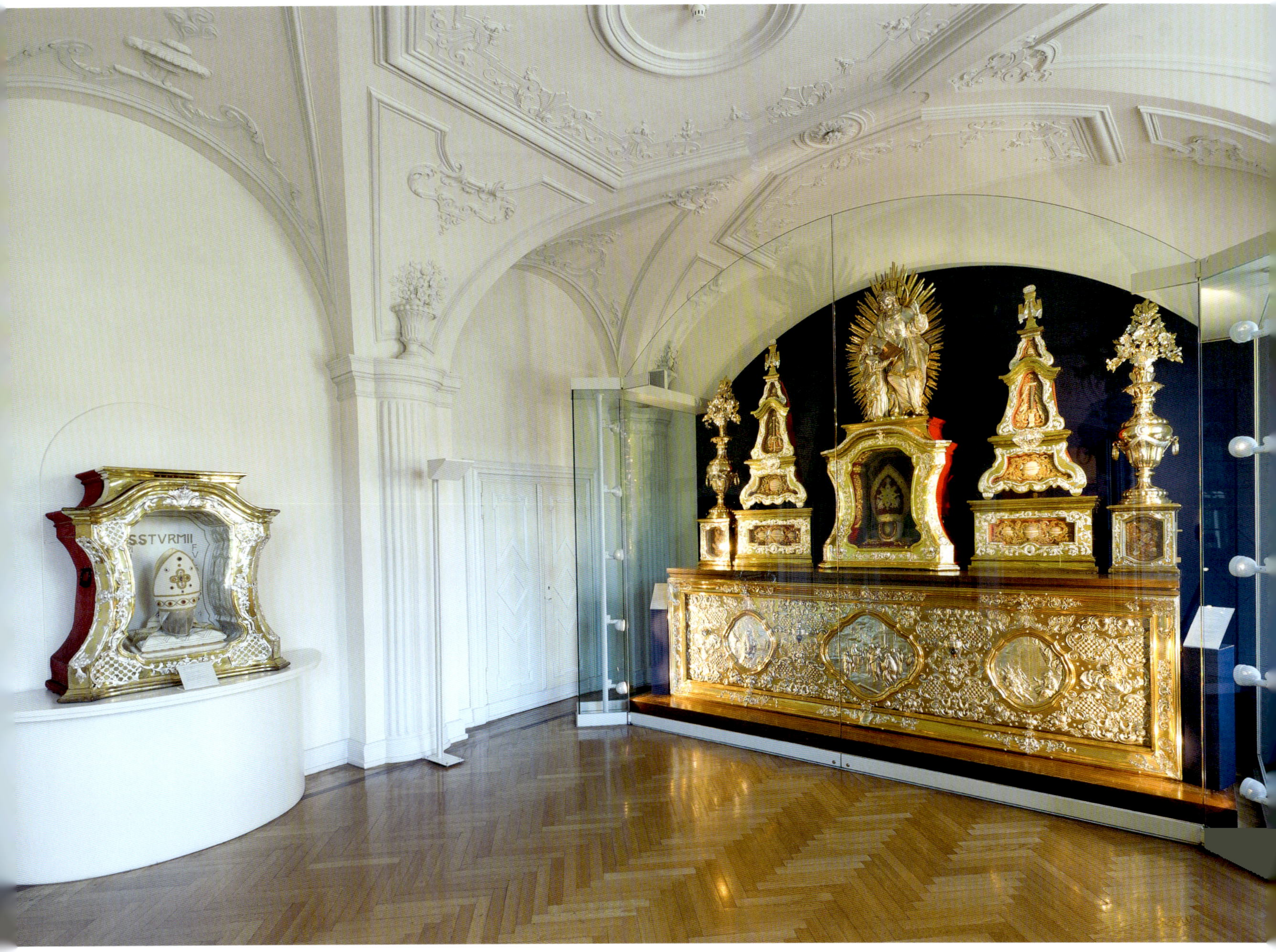

Der silberne Festaltar aus dem 18. Jahrhundert enthält unter anderem die Hauptreliquien des hl. Bonifatius und des hl. Sturmius und wird an hohen Festtagen oder auch während der jährlichen Herbsttagung der Deutschen Bischofskonferenz im Dom aufgebaut.

This silver altar from the 18th century contains, among other things, the main relics of St. Boniface and St. Sturmius. It is erected in the cathedral on important holy days and during the annual autumn meeting of the German Bishops' Conference.

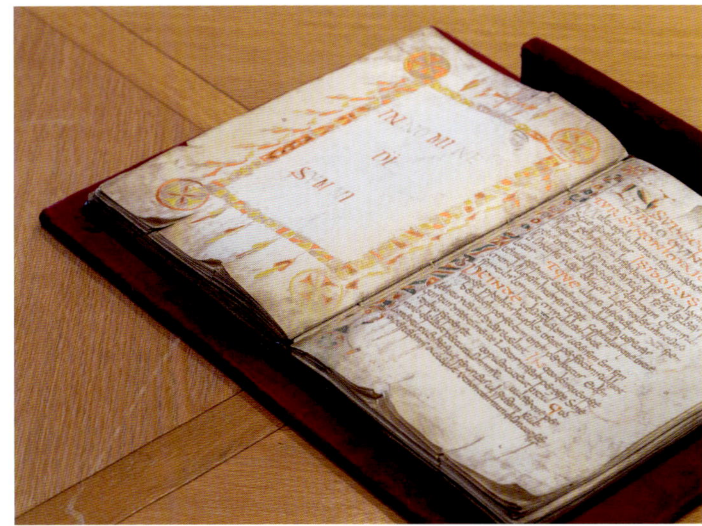

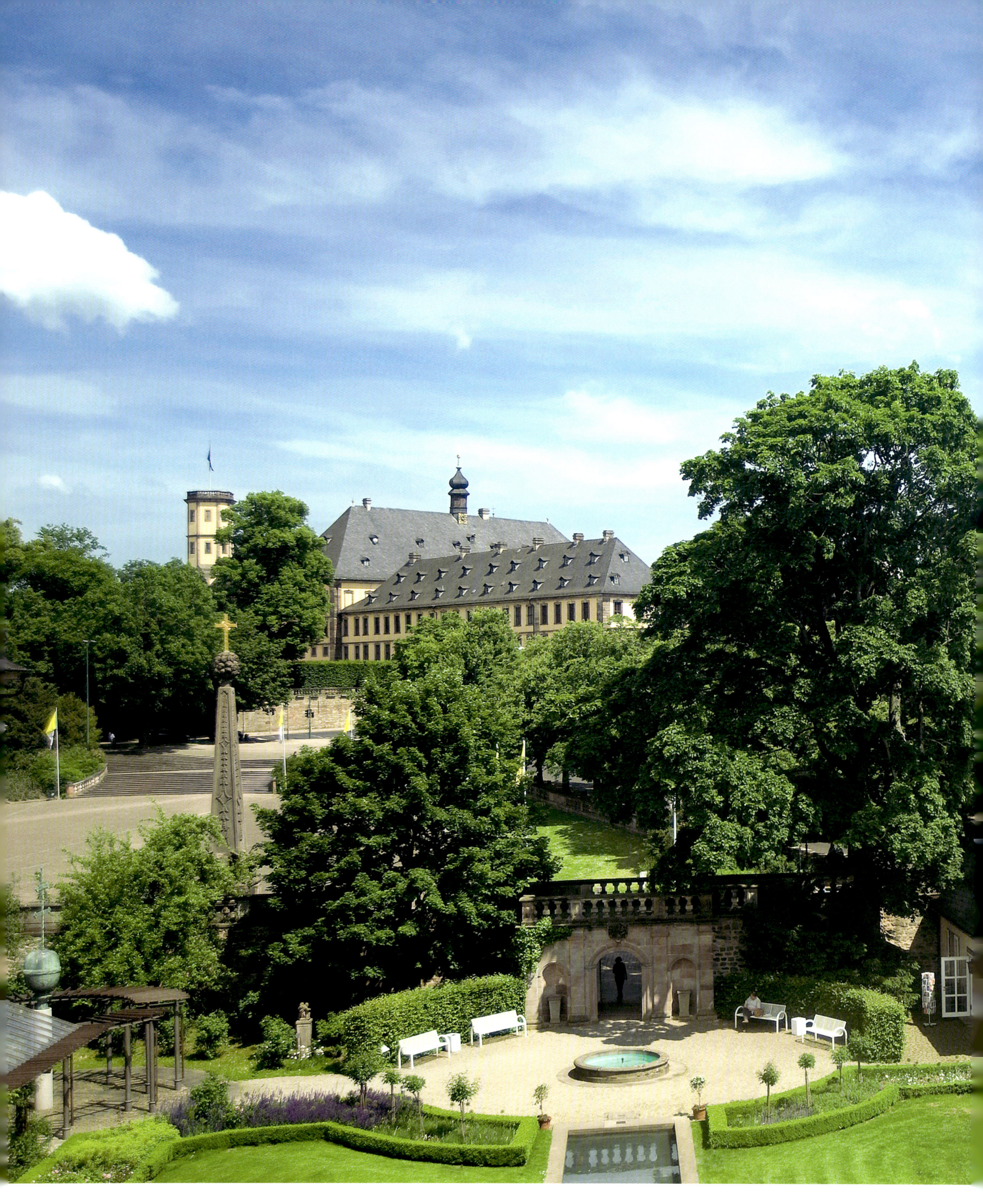

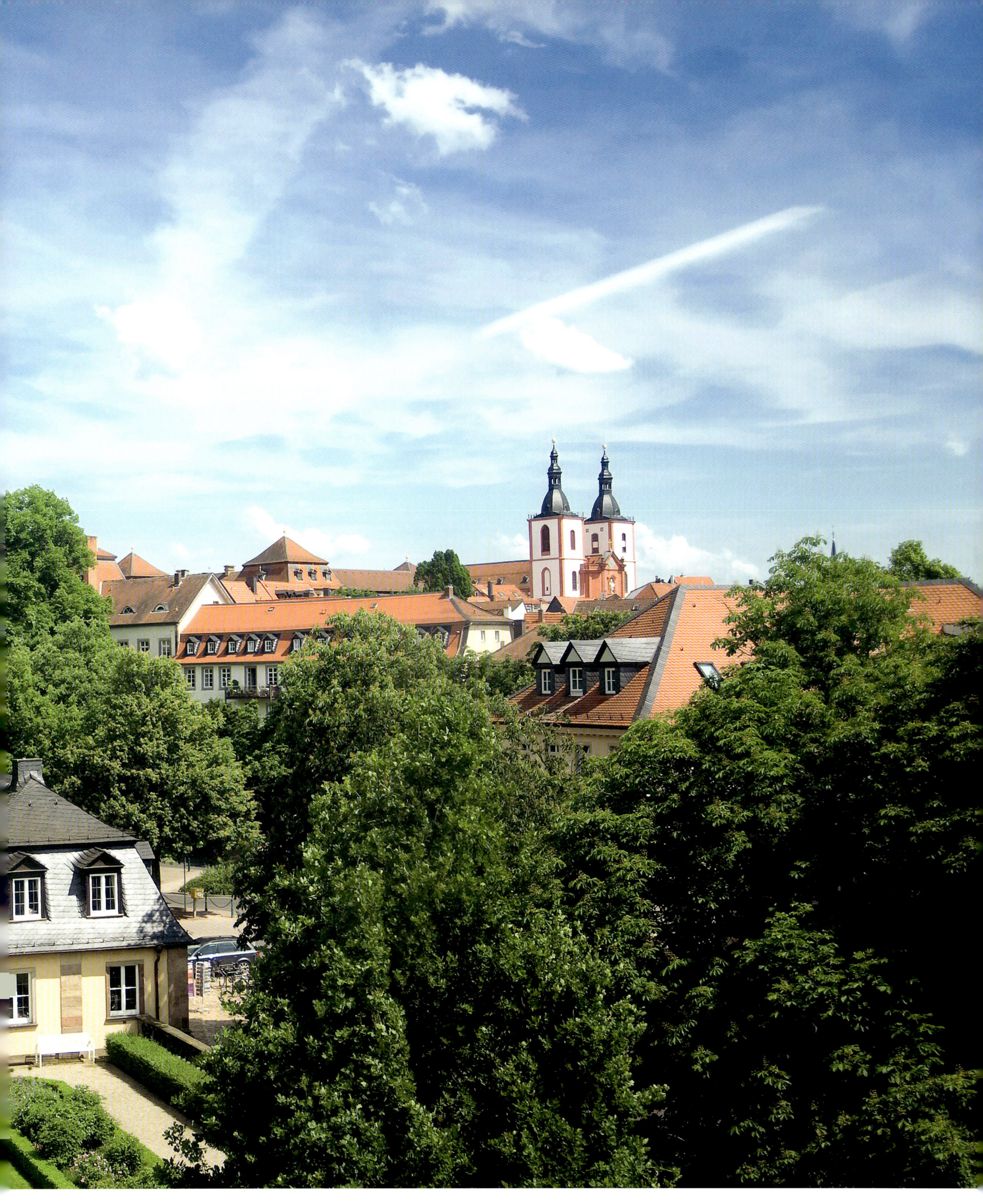

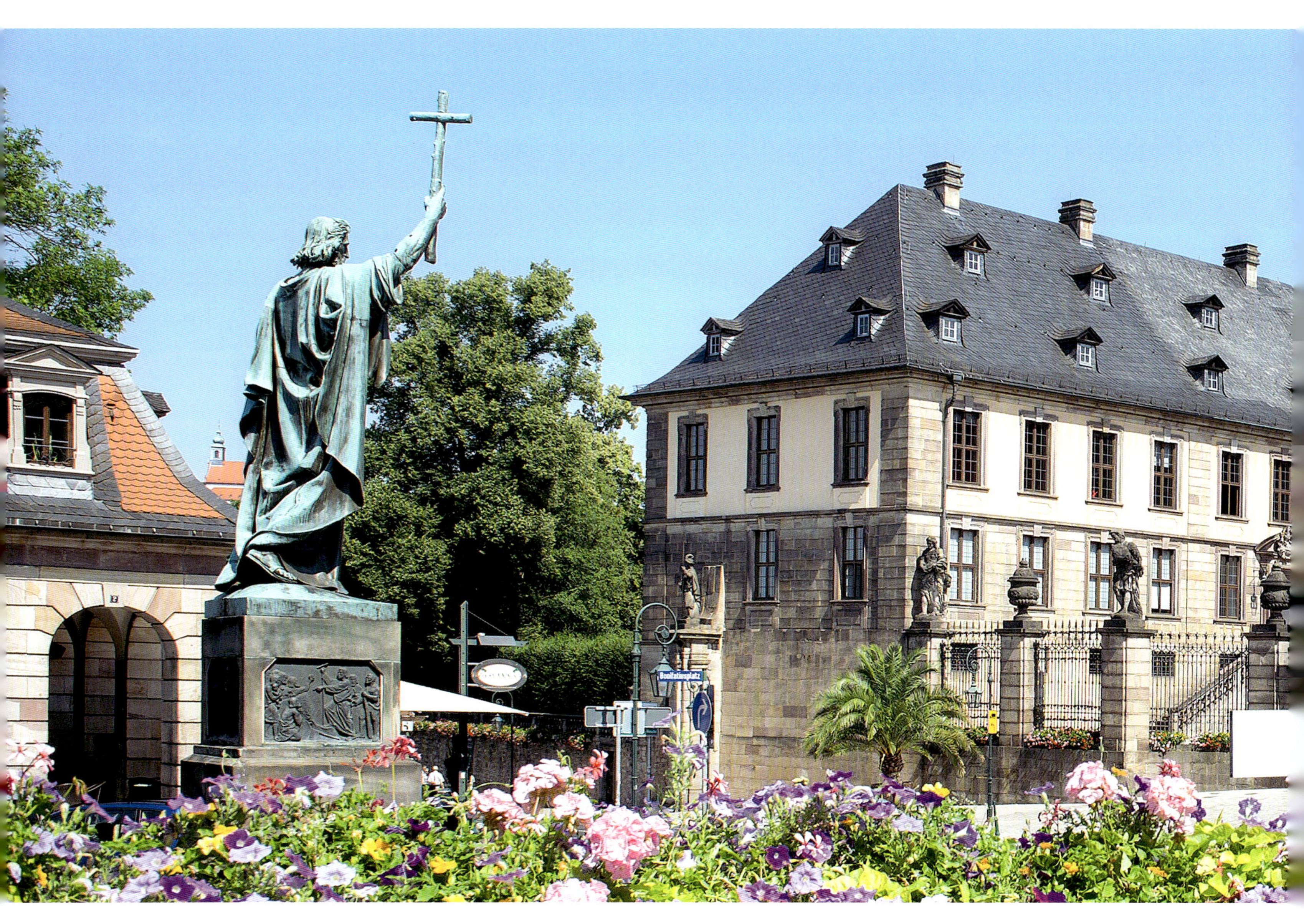
Bonifatiusplatz

EIN RATHAUS IM GEWAND EINES SCHLOSSES

Das Stadtschloss war einst der Regierungssitz der Fürstbischöfe – und beherbergt heute die Stadtverwaltung

Als 1953 die Produktionsfirma Filmaufbau GmbH einen Schauplatz für die Verfilmung des Thomas-Mann-Romans „Königliche Hoheit“ suchte, wurde sie in Fulda fündig: Das Barockviertel war im Zweiten Weltkrieg glimpflich davongekommen, die meisten Schäden waren inzwischen repariert – und so bot die Stadt die geeignete Kulisse, um die Residenz des fiktiven Großherzogtums Grimmburg zu mimen.

"A Town Hall Dressed as a Palace"

The Residence was once the seat of government of the prince-bishops – it now houses the city council

When, in 1953, the production company Filmaufbau GmbH was looking for a location for the film adaptation of Thomas Mann's novel "Royal Highness", Fulda was the best candidate: the Baroque quarter had survived World War II largely unscathed and most

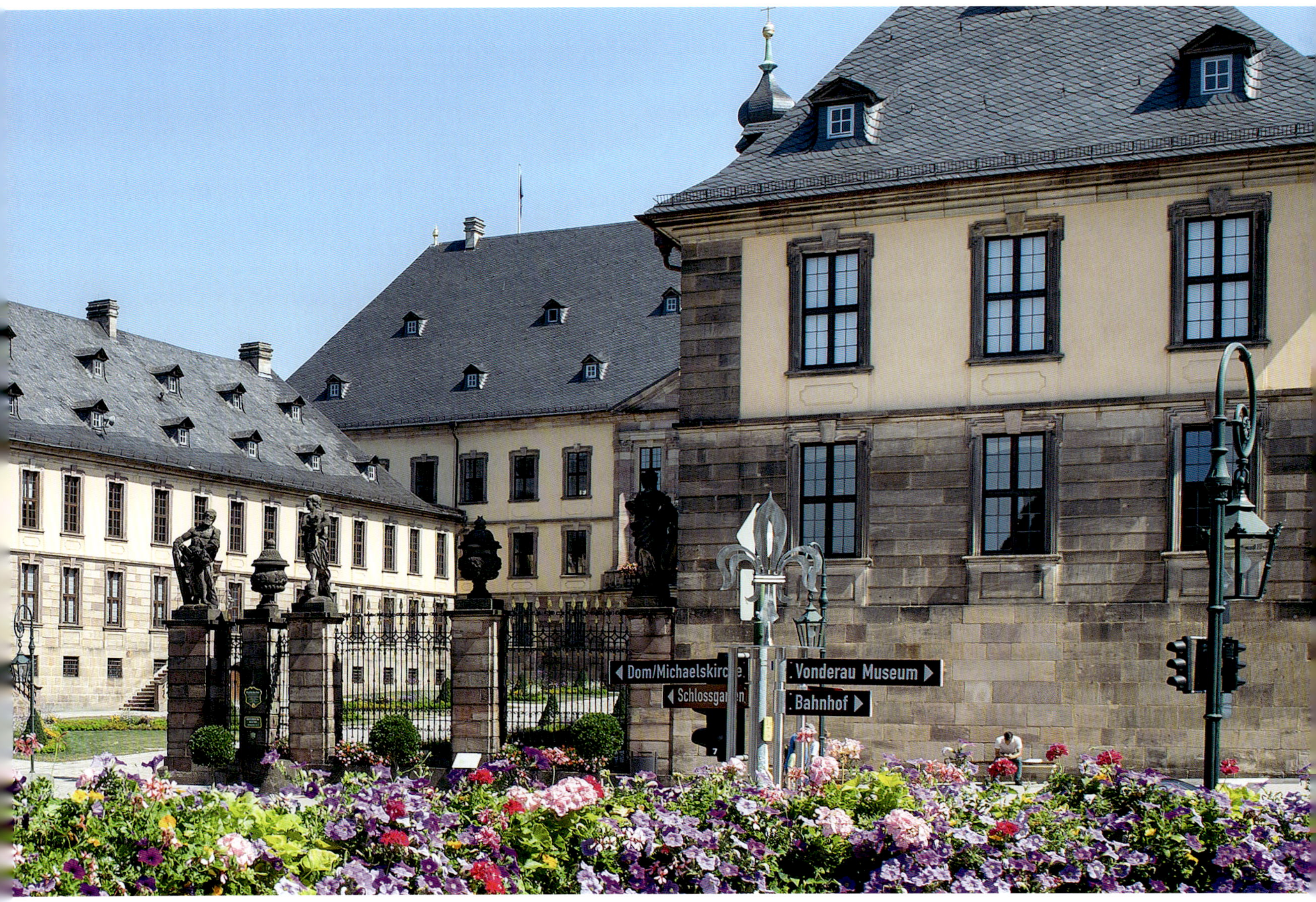

Eine zentrale Rolle spielte dabei für die Außenaufnahmen das Stadtschloss als Amtssitz von Prinz Klaus Heinrich, etwas ungelenk verkörpert vom Schauspieler Dieter Borsche.

Dass das Schloss dabei für einen authentischen Dreh so gut geeignet war, hat einen einfachen Grund: Es war selbst einmal die Residenz der Landesherren eines kleinen Territoriums gewesen, auch wenn es sich bei den Regenten natürlich nicht um Großherzöge, sondern um die fuldischen Fürstäbte beziehungsweise seit 1752 Fürstbischöfe handelte. Faktisch waren die Fuldaer Äbte bereits fast von Beginn der Klostergeschichte an durch ihre besonderen Privilegien sowie die beachtlichen Ländereien in der Position eines weltlichen Landesherrn. Offiziell wurde der Titel Fürstabt dann 1220. Etwa zur gleichen Zeit verstärkten sich Bestrebungen, den geistlichen und den weltlichen Part der Herrschaft in Fulda auch baulich zu trennen. So entstand im Grenzbereich zwischen Klosterbezirk und Bürgerstadt eine Burg, die als weltlicher Amtssitz des Fürstabts diente. 1294 bis 1312 ließ Fürstabt Heinrich von Weilnau diese sogenannte Abtsburg errichten. Deren älteste Teile sind im Fuß des heutigen Schlossturms erhalten und wurden im Zuge von Sanierungsarbeiten 2017/18 dokumentiert. Aus dieser Keimzelle heraus entstand 1606–1622 ein erster Schlossbau, dessen Formen noch in der Gestalt des Turms nachklingen. Gleichwohl glich dieses Renaissancegebäude noch eher einer Burg als einem Schloss.

Das änderte sich erst im „Bauboom" des Barock, als die Innenstadt binnen weniger Jahrzehnte durch die Ideen der Baumeister Johann Dientzenhofer und Andreas Gallasini eine komplett neue Gestalt erhielt. Noch während der Bau des Doms mitten im Gang war, initiierte Fürstabt Adalbert von Schleiffras die nächste Großbaustelle: Er beauftragte Dientzenhofer mit der barocken Umgestaltung des Schlosses, die sich dann über gut zwei Jahrzehnte bis zur Fertigstellung hinzog. Durch den Anbau eines Nord- und Südflügels schuf Dientzenhofer einen Ehrenhof, der bis heute das eindrucksvolle Entree bildet. So ganz verlor das Gebäude seinen burgartigen Charakter jedoch nicht, verglichen mit der verspielten Orangerie wirkt es eher wuchtig. Gleichwohl entstanden im Innern im Geschmack der Zeit die reich dekorierten

of the damage had already been repaired. Fulda, therefore, provided the best backdrop for the story that surrounded the fictional Duchy of Grimmburg. The Residence was particularly important for the outdoor scenes of the palace of Prince Klaus Heinrich, somewhat awkwardly portrayed by Dieter Borsche.

There was a simple reason why the Residence was so authentic as the location: it had once actually been the residence of the rulers of a small territory, although the rulers had not been grand dukes, but rather Fulda prince-abbots and (later on) prince-bishops. In fact, the Fulda abbots attained the position of secular rulers due to the special privileges they enjoyed right from the beginning of the history of the monastery and the substantial territories they ruled over. The title "prince- abbot" then became official in 1220. At approximately the same time efforts were made to also separate the religious and secular domains architecturally. Thus a castle was built between the monastery area and the city which then served as the prince-abbot's secular seat of government. The so-called "Abtsburg" was built by Prince-abbot Heinrich von Weilnau between 1294 and 1312. The oldest parts of this castle still form the base of today's Residence tower and were surveyed during restoration work in 2017/18. This castle was the basis for the first palace building (constructed between 1606 and 1622), whose forms can still be seen reflected in the design of the tower. The Renaissance building, however, still resembled a castle more than a palace.

Then everything changed when, within very few decades, the Baroque "building boom" totally transformed the inner city. While work was still in progress on the cathedral, Prince-abbot Adalbert von Schleiffras initiated the next large building project: he commissioned the architect Johann Dientzenhofer to redesign the Residence in Baroque style – a project that would take over two decades to complete. By constructing the north and south wings Dietzenhofer created a superb courtyard which still today provides an impressive entrance area to the Residence. Even after these changes, however, the Residence did not really lose its castle-like appearance and appears decidedly bulky compared to the light playfulness of the Orangery design. During the same period richly decorated and exquisitely furnished rooms were created according to contemporary tastes.

Fuldas „gute Stube": Der Fürstensaal war einst Festsaal des Fuldaer Hofs, die Porträts sämtlicher fuldischer Fürstäbte und Fürstbischöfe zwischen 1606 und 1802 schmücken den Raum. Inzwischen wird er als Konzert- und Veranstaltungsraum genutzt, auch die Stadtverordnetenversammlung tagt hier im barocken Ambiente.

Fulda's "front parlour": the Princes' Hall was once the banquet hall of the Fulda court. The portraits of all the prince-abbots and prince-bishops from 1606 to 1802 dominate the hall, which is now used as a concert and event venue. The city council meets here in this Baroque ambience.

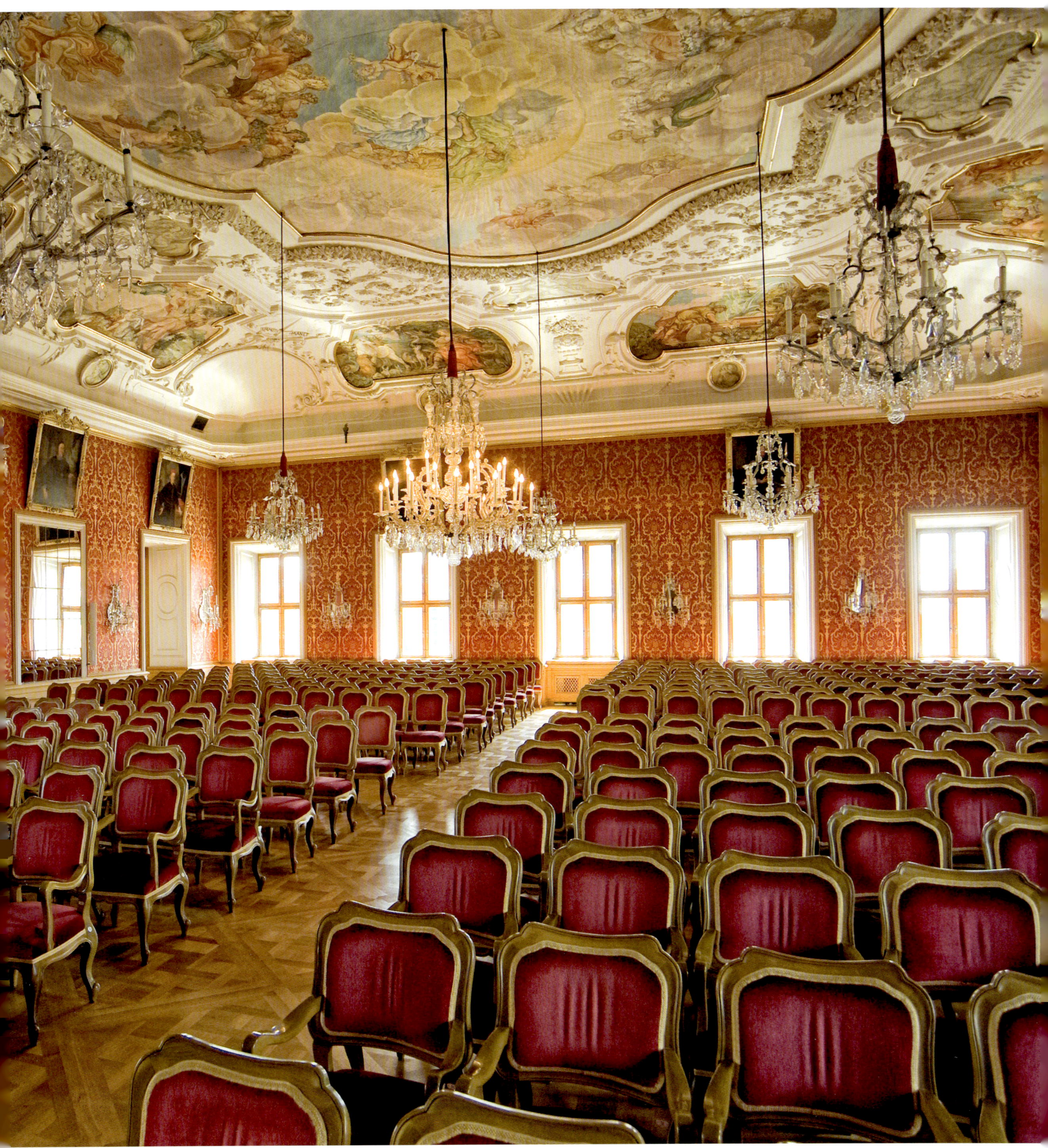

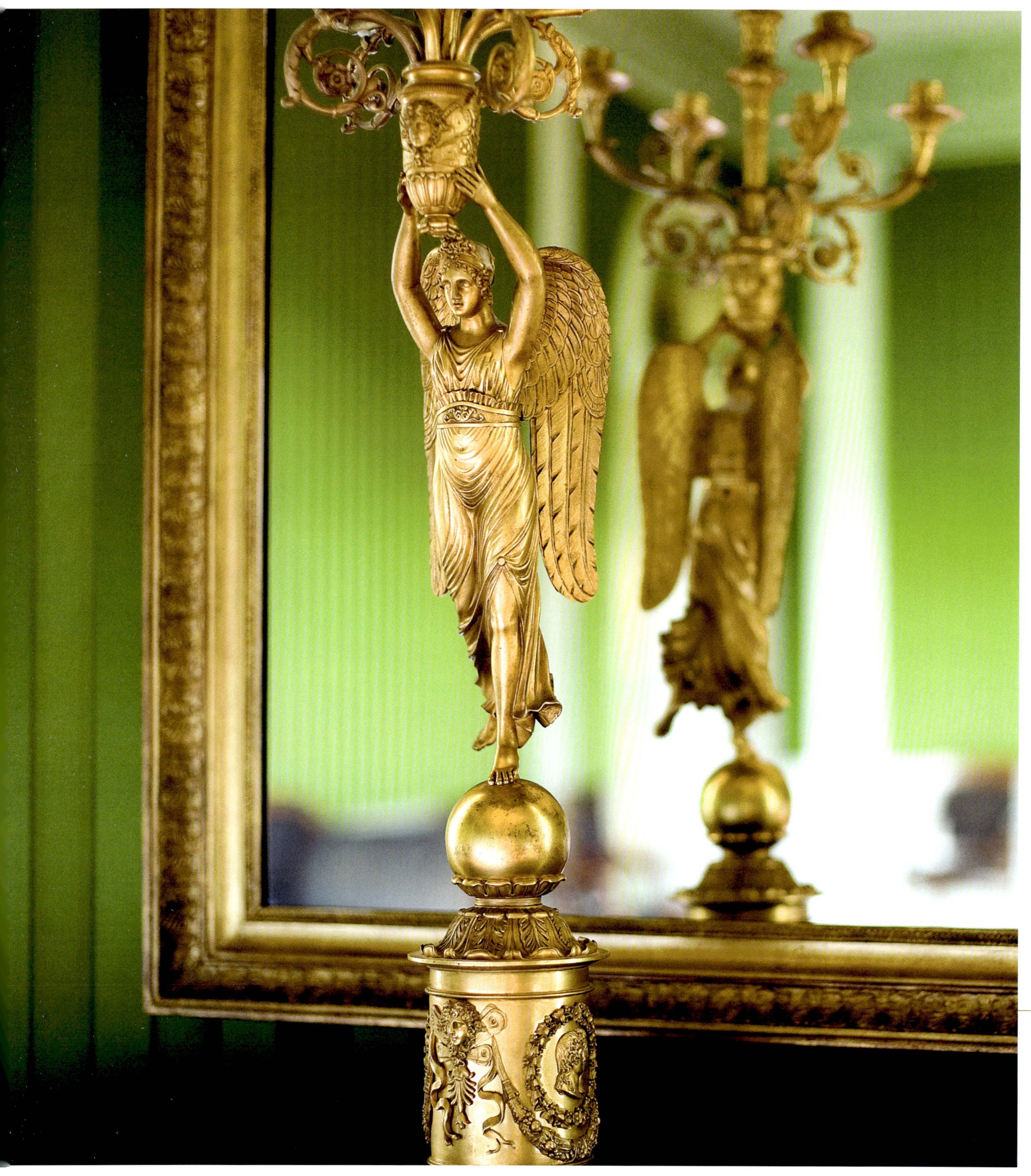

und edel ausgestatteten Wohn- und Repräsentationsräume der Fürstäbte in der damals üblichen, streng festgelegten Abfolge von Zimmern (Enfilade). Diese Räume mit dem Prunkstück des Spiegelkabinetts im Südflügel bilden heute das Herzstück des Schlossmuseums.

„Regiert" wird freilich im Stadtschloss immer noch: Denn hier hat seit 1894 die Stadtverwaltung ihren Sitz. Es ist seither gewissermaßen ein Rathaus im Gewand eines Schlosses. Und im Innern geben sich mitunter Touristen auf Besichtigungstour und Bürger auf dem Weg zum Einwohnermeldeamt oder zur Bauaufsicht die Klinke in die Hand.

The prince-abbots both lived and conducted their official duties in these rooms and so they were therefore laid out in a strictly defined sequence, the "enfilade". This series of rooms, which includes the magnificent mirror cabinet, now forms the centrepiece of the Residence Museum. Government still takes place in the Residence as Fulda city council has been located here since 1894. From this time on, the Residence has been "a town hall dressed as a palace". Inside the building, tourists on guided tours and local people on the way to council offices frequently cross paths.

Nord- und Südflügel sowie der zentrale Trakt des Schlosses umschließen den Ehrenhof, über dem Eingang zur Hauptwache wachen antike Götterfiguren und Sandsteinvasen.

The north, south and central wings enclose the courtyard. The entrance is guarded by statues of gods and decorated with sandstone vases.

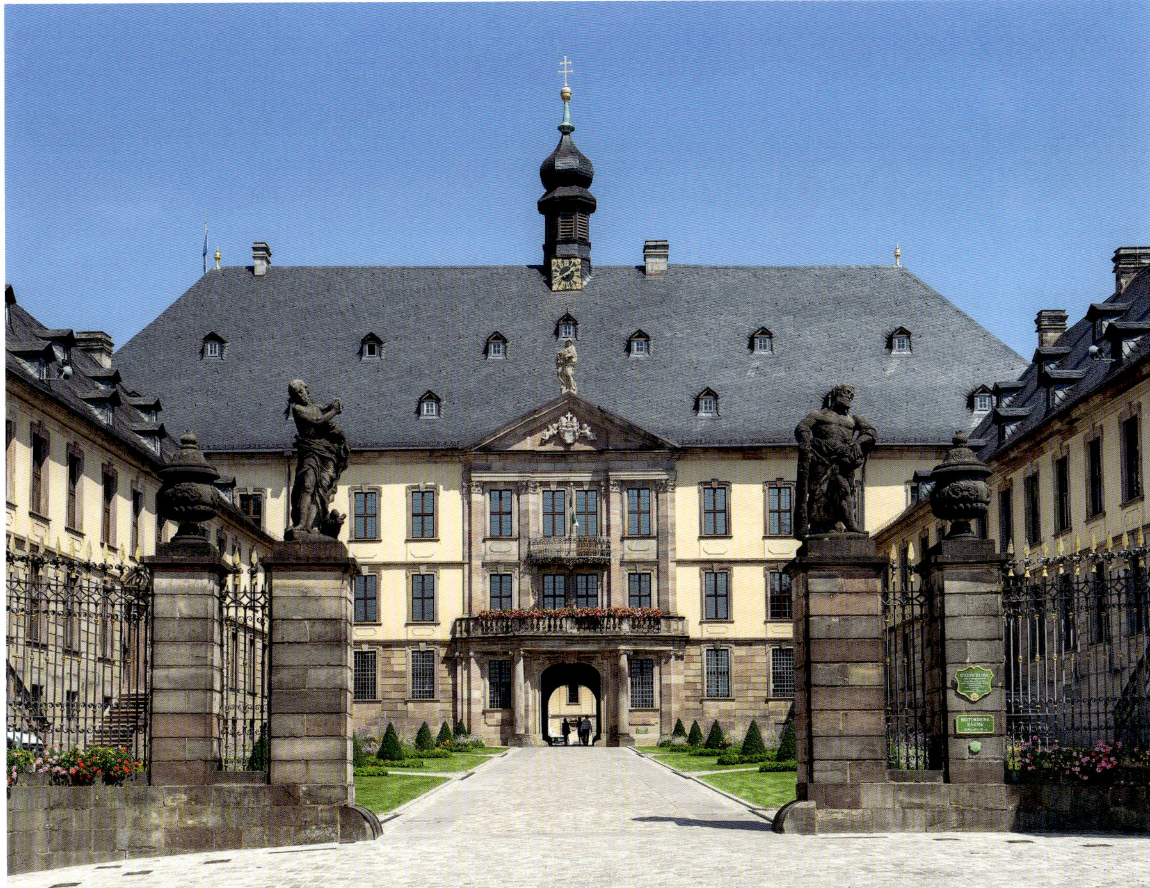

Das „Grüne Zimmer" (hier ein Leuchterdetail) wurde – wie auch der gesamte Nordflügel des Stadtschlosses – zu Beginn der kurhessischen Zeit (die von 1816 bis 1866 währte) im Stil des Spätklassizismus umgestaltet. Im Schloss residierte zu dieser Zeit der jeweilige Kurprinz von Hessen-Kassel.

The "Green Room" (here a detail of a chandelier) was – like the whole of the north wing – redesigned in the late classical style from 1816 to 1866. The princes of Hesse-Kassel lived in the Residence during this period.

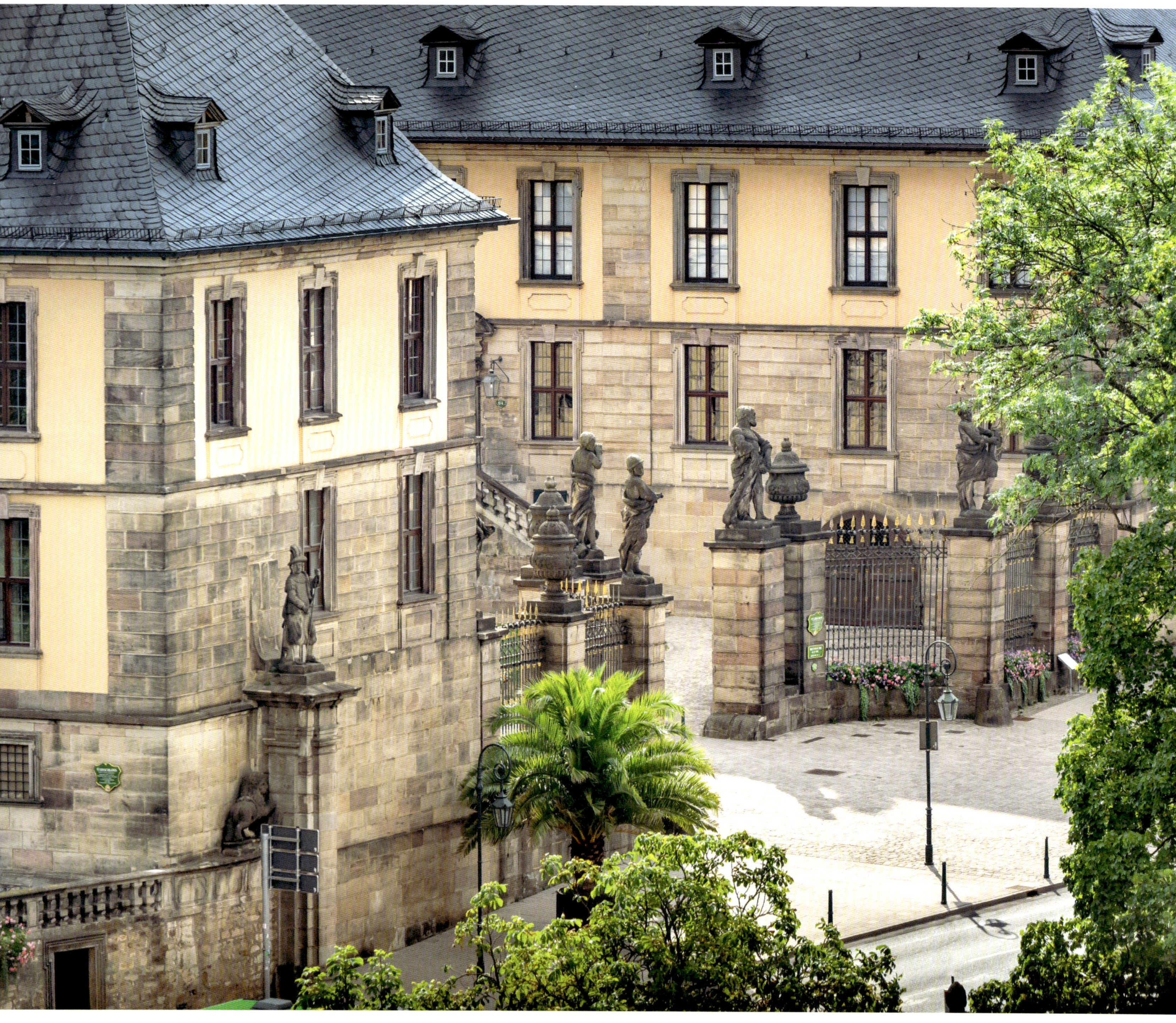

Diesen ungewöhnlichen Blickwinkel auf das Stadtschloss hat der Betrachter nur von den Türmen des Domes aus.

This unusual view of the palace is only possible from the cathedral towers.

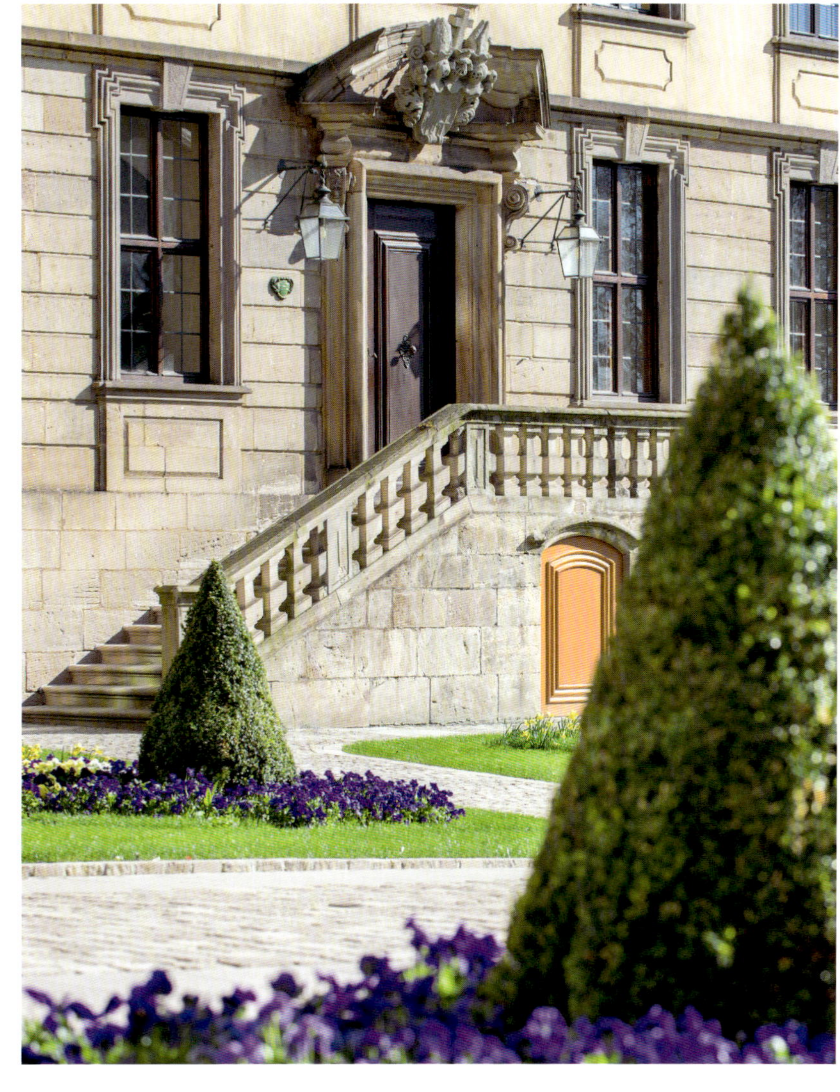
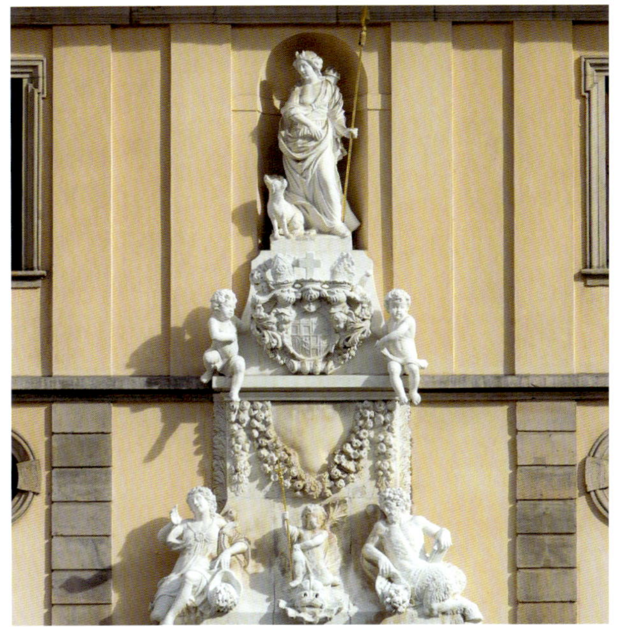
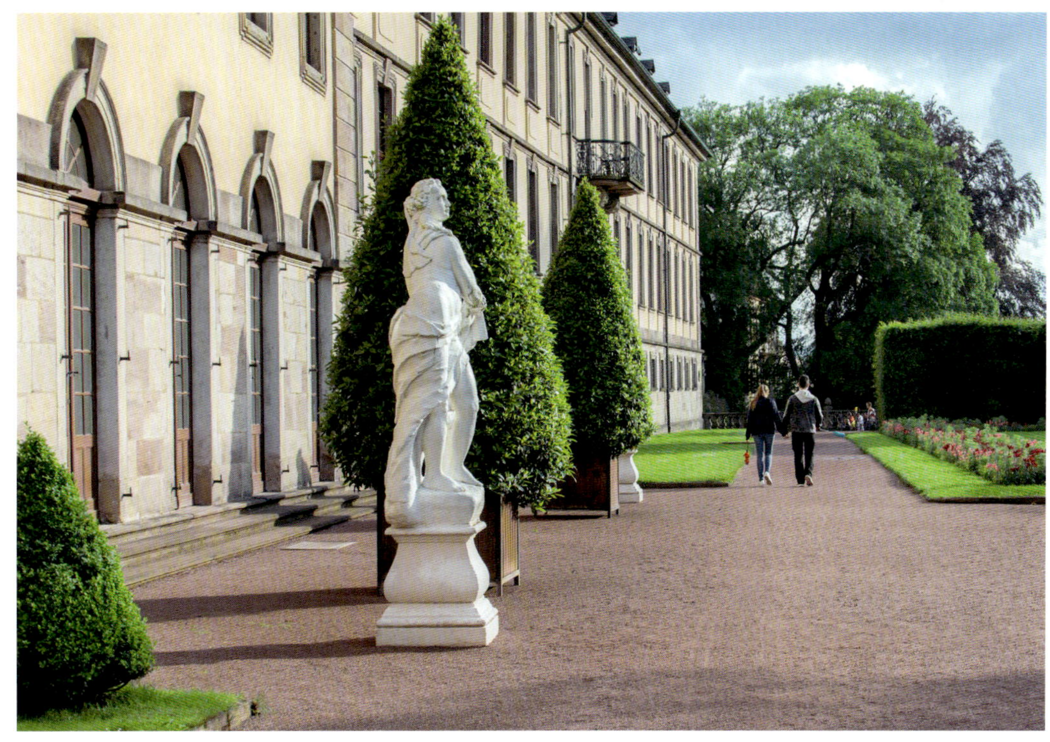

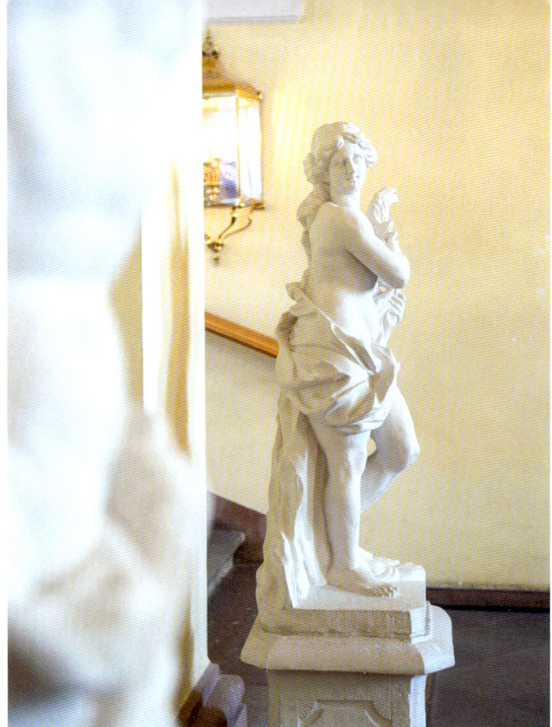

Fast 13 Jahre lang, von 1727 bis 1740, wurde am Kaisersaal gearbeitet, der als Gartensaal mit direktem Zugang zur Schlossgartenterrasse konzipiert war. Seinen Namen hat er von der Galerie mit Porträts habsburgischer Kaiser. Die Ausgestaltung ist eng mit den Namen der Künstler Maximilian von Welsch, Andreas Schwarzmann, Andreas Gallasini und Emanuel Wohlhaupter verknüpft.

It took almost thirteen years (1727–1740) to complete the work on the Kaisersaal, which was conceived as a garden room with direct access to the Residence garden terrace. The name of room refers to its gallery of portraits of the Habsburg emperors. The design of the room is closely associated with the names of the artists Maximilian von Welsch, Andreas Schwarzmann, Andreas Gallasini and Emanuel Wohlhaupter.

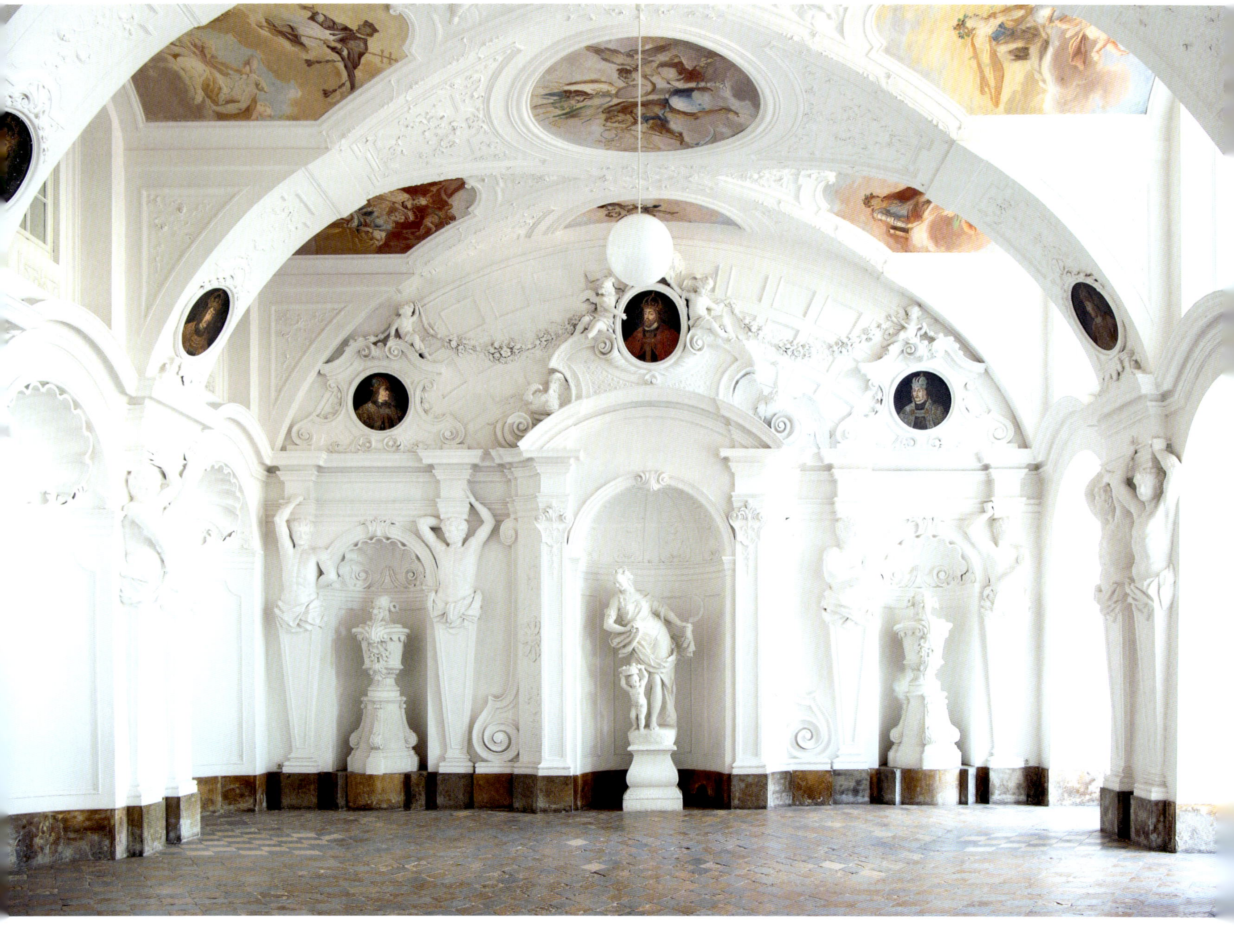

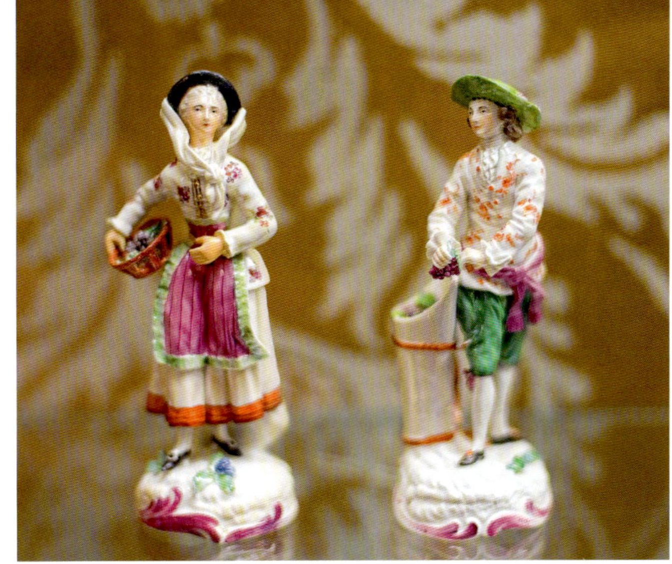

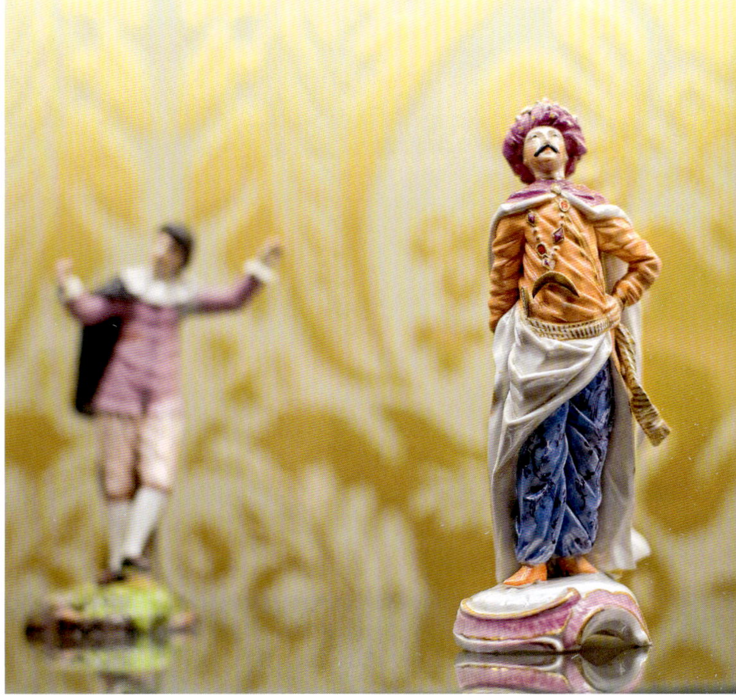

Das Schlossmuseum beherbergt eine umfangreiche Sammlung von wertvollen Stücken aus der Fuldaer Porzellan- und Fayencenmanufaktur. Die Werkstatt war zwar nur klein und bestand auch nur wenige Jahrzehnte, doch die Stücke genießen bis heute einen guten Ruf und erzielen auf Auktionen oft erstaunliche Summen.

The Residence museum holds a wide-ranging collection of valuable porcelain and faience pieces manufactured in Fulda. The small factory only operated for a few decades, but the faience ware produced there is still sought after today and attains astonishingly high prices at auction.

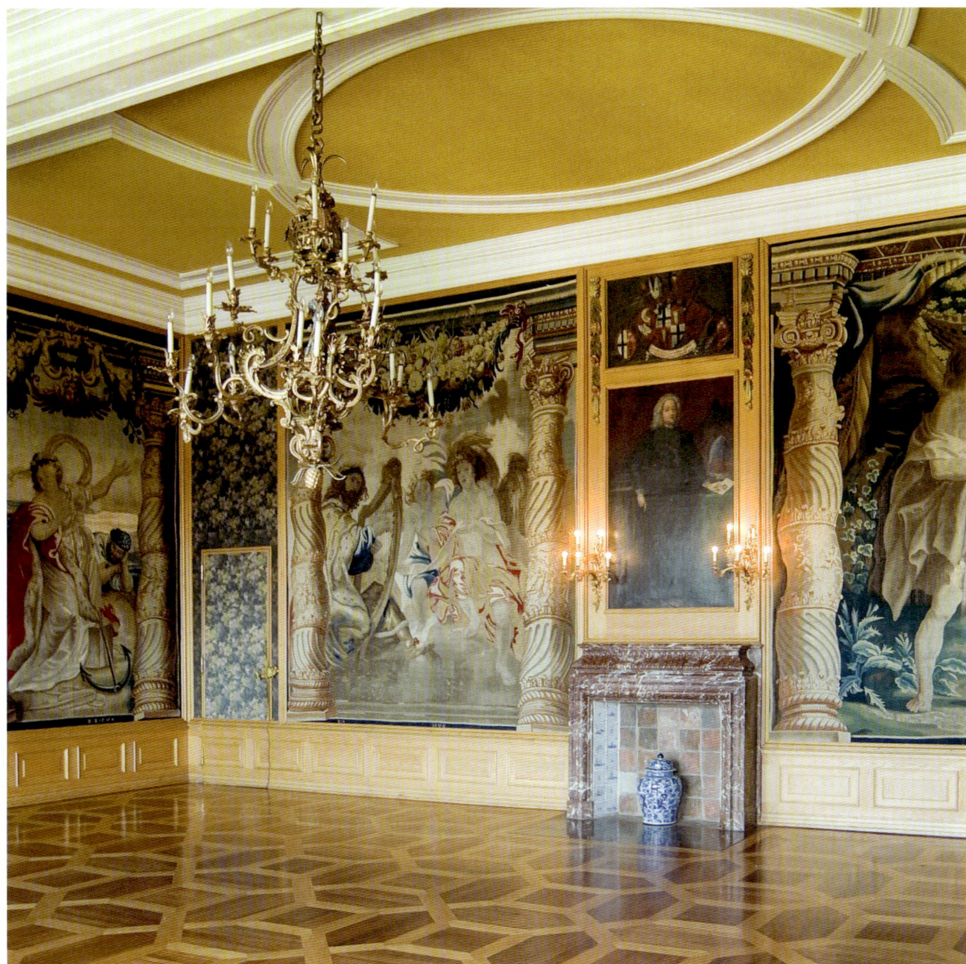

Die kunstvoll gestalteten Wandteppiche im sogenannten Gobelinzimmer stammen aus belgischer Produktion.

The intricately designed tapestries in the "Gobelinzimmer" were produced in Belgium.

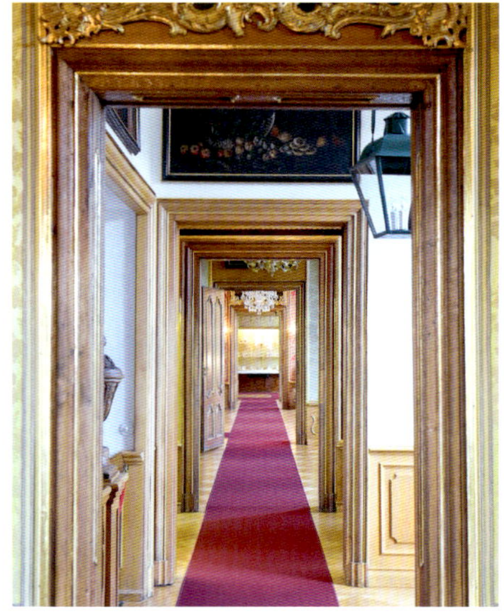

Im südlichen Ehrenhofflügel des Schlosses befinden sich die Räume noch zum Teil im barocken Originalzustand; darunter sind die Prunkstücke, der Dalbergsaal und das Spiegelkabinett.

In the south wing of the front courtyard the rooms are partly in their original Baroque state; the Dalbergsaal and the Mirror Cabinet are particularly impressive.

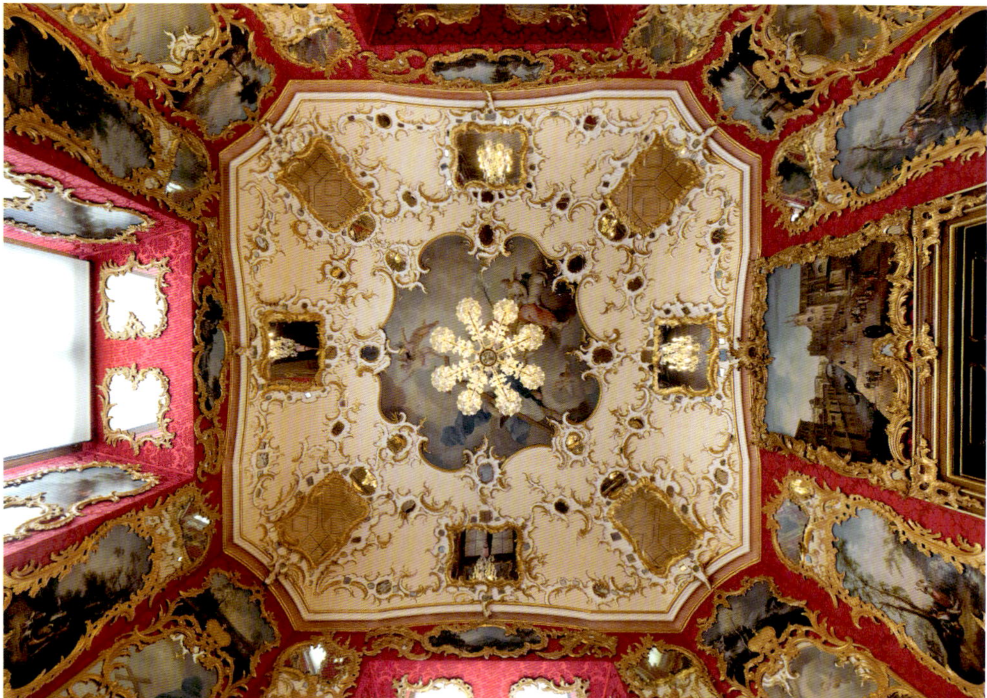

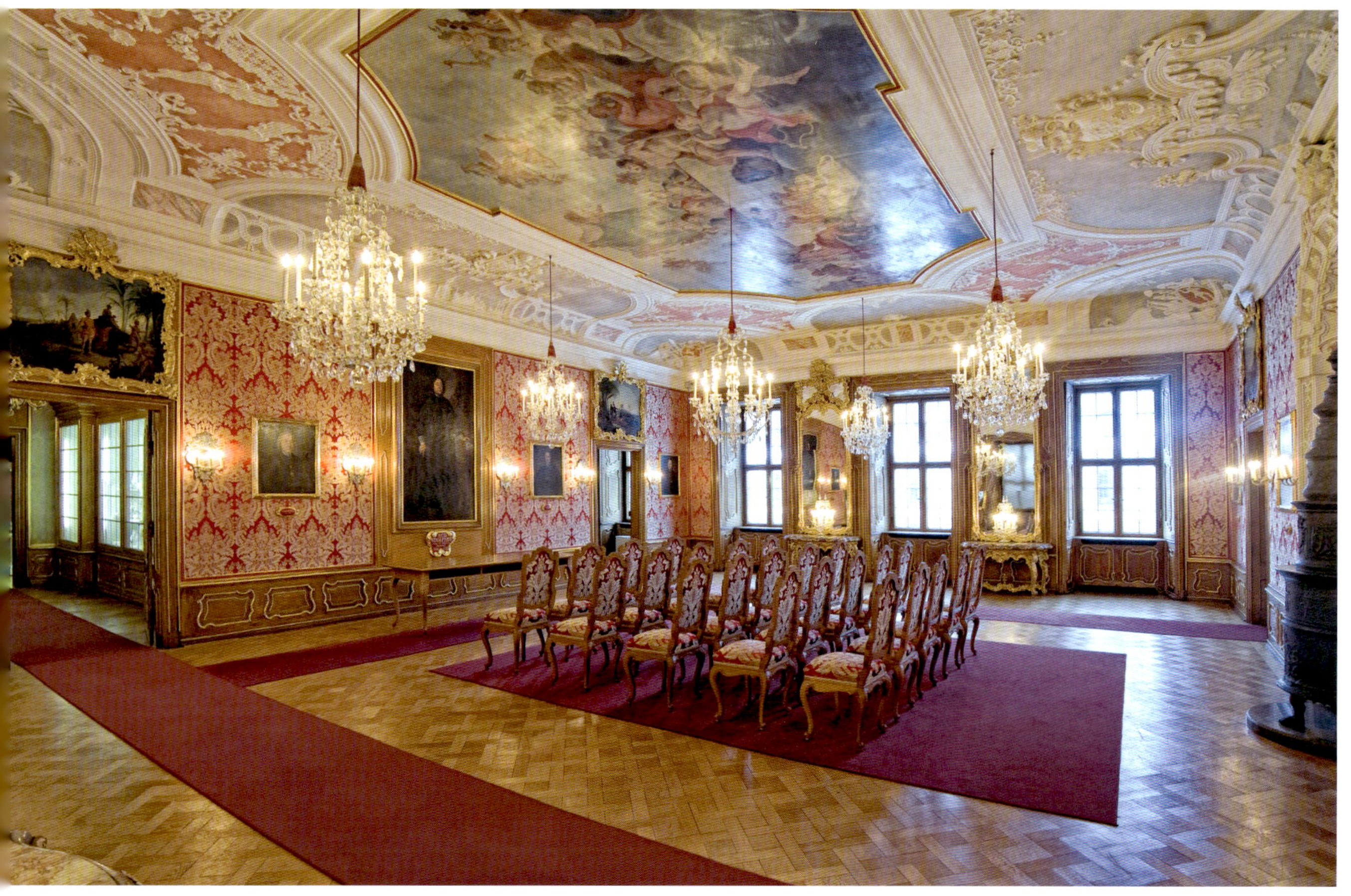

Fürstbischof Adalbert von Walderdorff regierte nur zwei Jahre (1757–59), hinterließ jedoch mit dem Spiegelkabinett ein Glanzstück des Fuldaer Barocks.

Prince-abbot Adalbert von Walderdorff only ruled for two years (1757–59), but left us the Mirror Cabinet, a magnificent example of Fulda baroque.

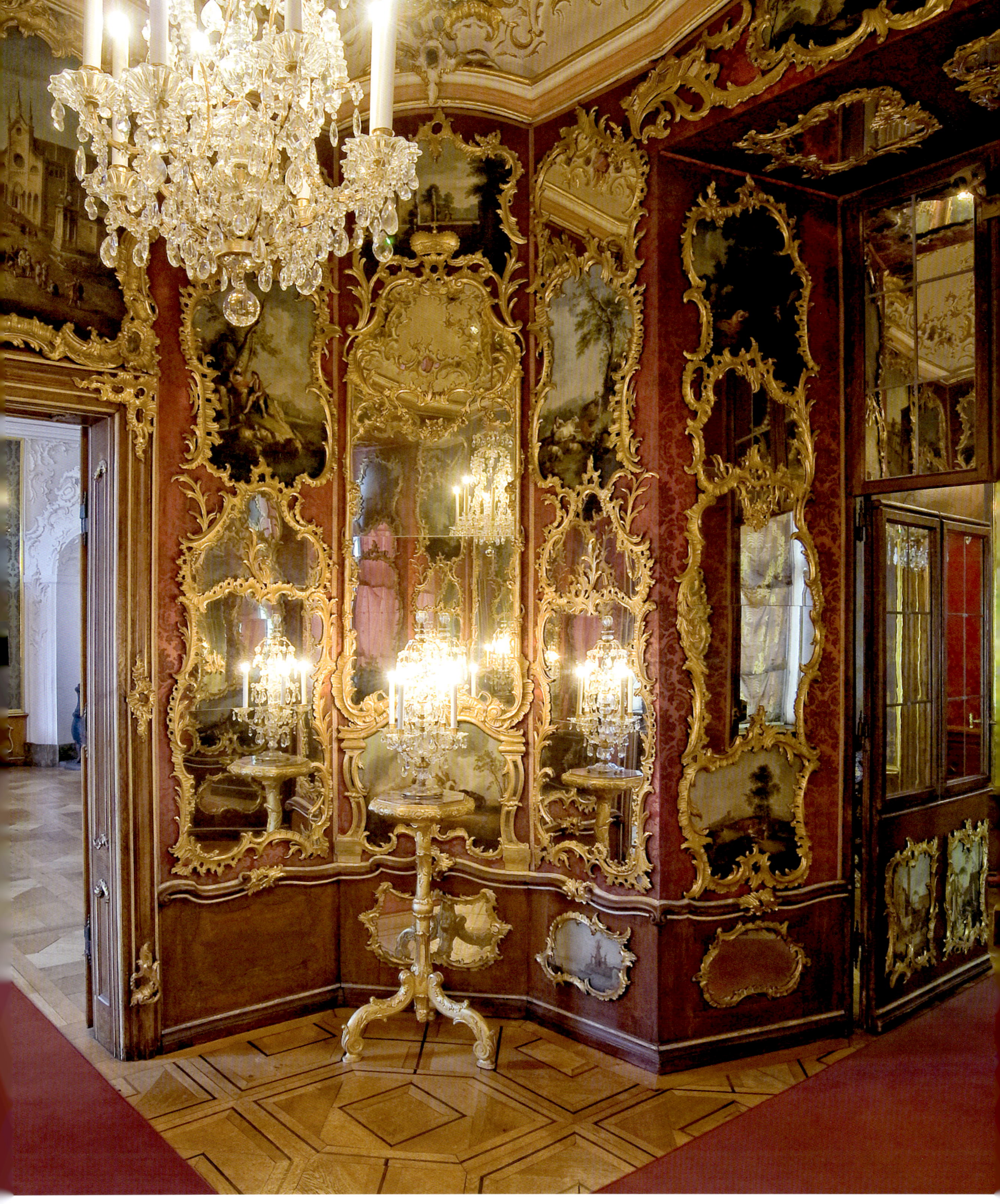

GRÜNE OASEN UND SCHMUCKE PALAIS

Der Schlossgarten bildet den blühenden Kontrapunkt zur steinernen Pracht des Barockviertels

Wer heute an einem sonnigen Nachmittag durch den Fuldaer Schlossgarten streift, vorbei an den akkurat angelegten und liebevoll gepflegten Blumenrabatten, an sorgfältig gestutzten Gehölzen und an Grünflächen, auf denen gleich scharenweise Menschen den Feierabend genießen, mit den Kindern Frisbee spielen oder verliebt und verträumt in die Gischt der Fontänen schauen, der wird sich kaum vorstellen können, dass dieser so bürgerfreundliche Park einst eine exklusive Fläche für den Fürstabt war, wo die höfische Gesellschaft in einem naturnahen, umzäunten Tiergarten der Jagdleidenschaft frönen konnte.

Doch in der Blütezeit des Fuldaer Barock wurde auch dieser Bereich ab 1715 massiv überformt: Das Tal des seinerzeit noch wildromantisch dahinplätschernden Waidesbachs wurde im vorderen Teil des Schlossgartens (wie auch im Bereich des Domplatzes) mit Hilfe gewaltiger Erdbewegungen eingeebnet und der Wasserlauf in einen Sandsteintunnel verbannt, der noch heute erhalten ist. Es entstanden – ganz im barocken Zeitgeschmack – zwei große Terrassen, die eine vor dem Nordflügel des Stadtschlosses, die andere vis-à-vis, wo dann ab 1721 unter Fürstabt Konstantin von Buttlar als Blickfang Richtung Frauenberg die Orangerie errichtet wurde. Angesichts des profanen Zwecks – nämlich des Überwinterns exotischer Pflanzen – ist dieser Bau innen wie außen wirklich außergewöhnlich schmuck ausgefallen. Zusammen mit der verspielten Floravase und den kühn geschwungenen Treppen markiert das Ensemble am Nordrand des Schlossgartens sicher einen Höhepunkt der fuldischen Baukunst. Flora, die römische Göttin der Pflanzenwelt, blickt heute auf ein ebenso üppiges wie klar gegliedertes Arrangement an Blumenbeeten, Brunnen, Hecken und Stauden, das seit der Landesgartenschau 1994 wieder die geometrischen Figuren, Blick- und Wegebeziehungen der Barockzeit aufnimmt. Denn im 19. Jahrhundert war der Schlosspark – damals sehr en vogue – in einen englischen Landschaftspark umgestaltet worden. Der hintere Teil des Schlossgartens

Green Oases and Ornate Palaces

The Residence garden forms a floral contrast to the stone elegance of the Baroque quarter.

When you wander through the Residence garden on a sunny afternoon, admiring the carefully laid-out and well-kept borders, shrubs and lawns which will soon be enlivened by people seeking peace and quiet after work or playing frisbee with the children, it is hard to believe that this very public park should once have been an area exclusively reserved for the prince-abbot, where he and his courtiers could enjoy hunting in an enclosed deer park. Today everyone can relax here, dreamily and contentedly contemplating the fountain spray.

The park was, however, to be dramatically changed at the peak of the Baroque era in Fulda: in 1715 this area was totally re-landscaped. The valley, through which the romantic, meandering stream – the Waidesbach – flowed, was flattened out by massive earth movements, both in the front part of the Residence garden and in the cathedral square area. The course of the Waidesbach was then re-directed through a sandstone tunnel which still exists today. In accordance with Baroque tastes, two large terraces were formed – one in front of the north wing of the Residence, the other directly opposite. On the latter terrace the Orangery was built in 1721 under Prince-abbot Konstantin von Buttlar as a special feature for the view towards the Frauenberg. Considering the rather mundane purpose of the building – wintertime protection for exotic plants – both the interior and exterior are unusually opulent.

Viewed together with the intricate Flora Vase and the extravagantly sweeping steps, this ensemble on the northern edge of the Residence garden surely represents a highlight in Fulda's architecture.

Flora, the Roman god of plant life, today looks down on a clearly arranged profusion of flower borders, fountains, hedges and shrubs. For the State Garden Show in 1994 the garden was returned to a Baroque lay-out with typical geometrical figures, visual axes and path patterns. Following the fashions in the 19th century, the garden

Der üppige Blumenschmuck ist längst zu einem Markenzeichen für Fulda geworden.

The profusion of flowers has long become a typical feature of Fulda.

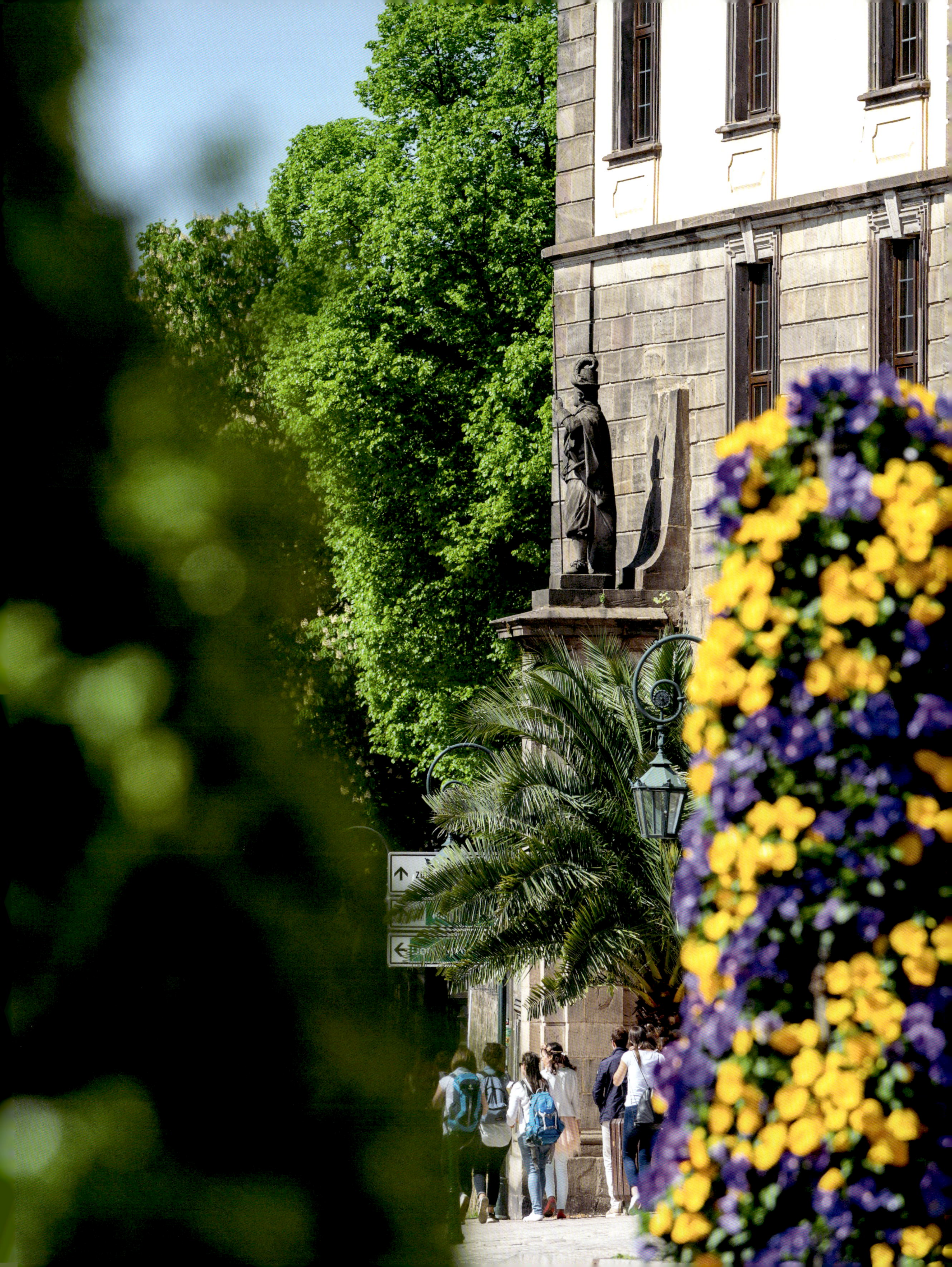

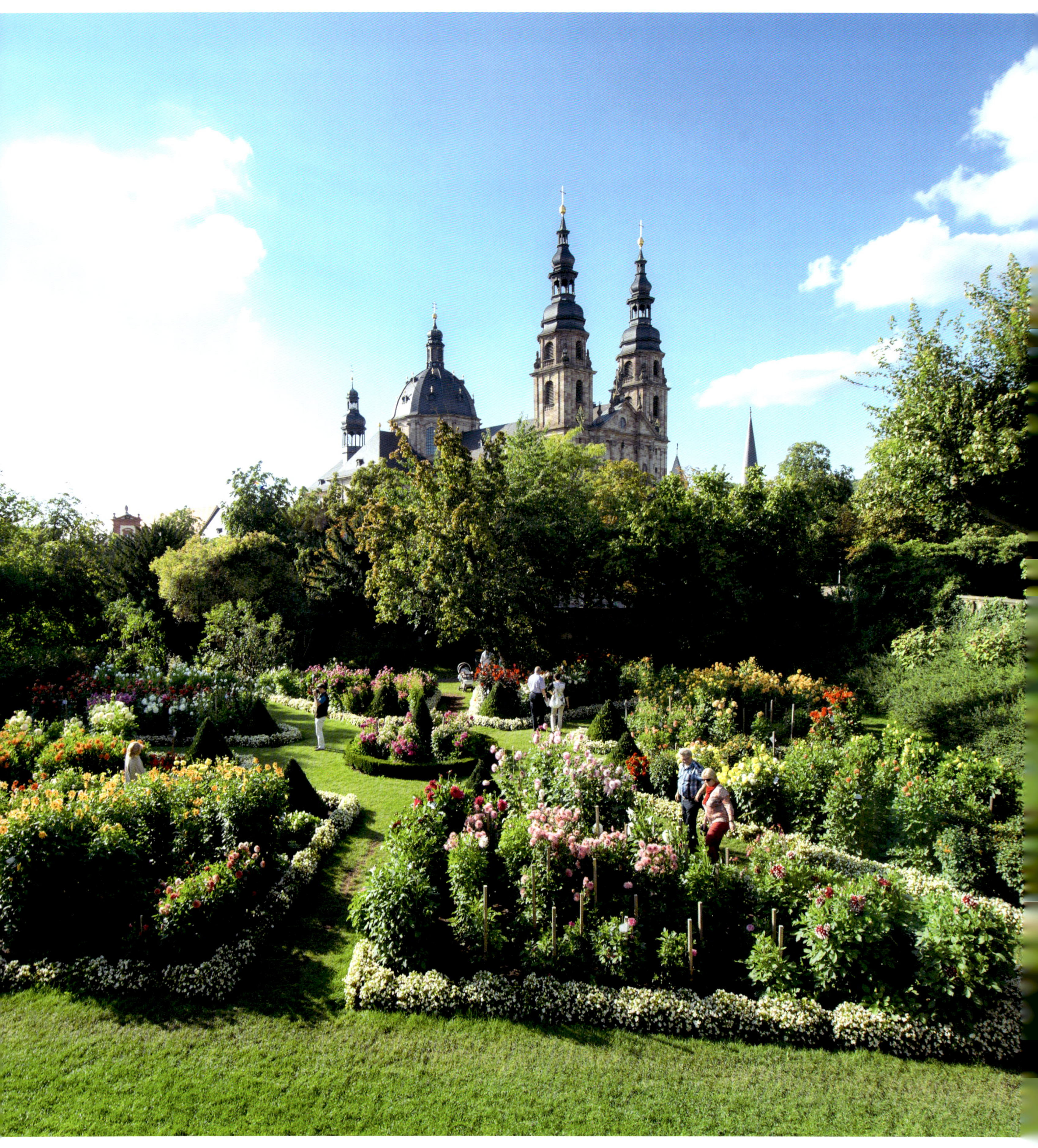

zeugt noch heute davon. Dass man in Fulda wirklich Blumen und Pflanzen liebt und sich die Stadt eine große Anzahl an Gärtnerinnen und Gärtnern leistet, welche die Pracht hegt und pflegt und sich immer neue Farb- und Sortenkombinationen einfallen lässt, dass ist längst nicht nur im Schlossgarten zu spüren: Überall in der Innenstadt stehen Pflanzkübel und Schalen mit saisonal wechselndem Blumenschmuck – häufig ein Fotomotiv begeisterter Touristen, während Einheimische meist achtlos vorrübergehen. Eine weitere beliebte grüne Oase bildet der versteckt liegende Dahliengarten. Hinter einer hohen Mauer an der Johannes-Dyba-Allee findet sich ein Refugium, das nicht nur Dahlienfreunde anlockt.

Die viele Natur bildet einen reizvollen Kontrast zur steinernen Pracht des Barockviertels. Den Charme desselben machen neben Dom, Schloss und Orangerie nicht zuletzt die vielen Adelspalais aus, die sich rund um den Bonifatiusplatz (früher „Dienstagsmarkt“) gruppieren: das Palais Altenstein mit seinem Kleinod, dem Rokokosaal; das Palais von der Tann, besser bekannt als Haus „Kurfürst“; das Palais Buttlar, das heute unter anderem die Tourist-Info beherbergt; oder das Palais Buseck, das als „Stift Wallenstein“ über viele Jahrzehnte hinweg evangelischen adeligen Damen einen Ruhesitz bot. Den besten Blick auf das geschlossene Barockensemble, dessen Gebäude sämtlich aus dem 18. Jahrhundert stammen, dürfte seit mehr als 175 Jahren der bronzene Bonifatius haben. Das vom Kasseler Bildhauer Werner Henschel mit dem heroischen Gestus jener Zeit geschaffene Denkmal, für das damals übrigens in ganz Deutschland die stolze Spendensumme von 12600 Gulden gesammelt wurde, bildet seit 1842 einen Fixpunkt im Barockviertel.

Der barocke Bauboom jener Jahre hatte übrigens längst nicht nur die adeligen Bauherren erfasst: Ein Blick in die breite Friedrichstraße und einige benachbarte Gassen zeigt, dass sich auch das wohlhabendere Bürgertum bei seinen Häusern Anleihen am barocken Formenschatz der Prachtbauten nahm. Zum Teil waren hier wie dort dieselben Handwerker im Einsatz, und die Markenzeichen der verschiedenen Hofbaumeister (beispielsweise die eckigen Fensterumrahmungen bei Dientzenhofer oder Gallasinis geschwungenes Fensterecken-Ornament) werden zum Teil noch Jahrzehnte später bei privaten Bauten zitiert.

had previously been converted into an “English” landscape garden, the horticultural style which can still be seen in the rear part of the garden. Not only in the Residence garden do you notice that the local people have a great love for flowers and plants. They are prepared to maintain a large team of gardeners who care for the plants and are always coming up with new combinations of colours and varieties. Throughout the city there are pots and troughs with seasonally changing flower arrangements – the flowers are a popular photo motif for tourists, but often busy locals hardly notice them. The dahlia garden, tucked away behind a high wall next to the Johannes-Dyba-Allee, is a peaceful urban refuge that attracts not only dahlia fans.

The many green areas provide a wonderful contrast to the stony opulence of the Baroque quarter. This area owes its charm not only to the cathedral, the Residence and the Orangery, but also to the nobles’ palaces grouped around the Bonifatiusplatz (formerly the Tuesday Market): Palais Altenstein with its jewel, the Rokokosaal; Palais von der Tann, better known as the “Kurfürst”; Palais Buttlar, which now houses the tourist information office, and Palais Buseck, which was owned by “Stift Wallenstein” for many decades and was used as a home for protestant noblewomen.

The bronze St. Boniface, who has stood in the centre of the square for last 175 years, has, no doubt, the best view of the entire Baroque ensemble! All the buildings in this ensemble originate from the 18th century. The monumental statue, showing the saint in a heroic posture typical of the 19th century, was cast by the sculptor Werner Henschel in Kassel. This spectacular figure, which was financed by donations from all over Germany to the proud tune of 12600 guilders, has been the centre point of the Baroque quarter since 1842.

It is interesting to note that the Baroque construction boom was not confined to noble property owners: if you take a close look in the broad Friedrichstrasse or some of the neighbouring alleys you can see that wealthy citizens also adopted Baroque elements used in the palaces for their own houses. Indeed, sometimes the same craftsmen even carried out the work. The characteristic styles of the different court architects (e.g. Dietzenhofer’s square window frames or Gallisini’s flowing window corner ornaments) can still be identified in private buildings sometimes constructed decades later.

Eine versteckte Idylle: Im Dahliengarten, ganz in der Nähe des Domes, kommen nicht nur Blumenfreunde auf ihre Kosten. Auf den Parkbänken kann man auch herrlich einen sonnigen, nahezu ungestörten Nachmittag mit einem guten Buch verbringen.

A hidden idyll: situated close to the cathedral this place is not just for flower fans! Sitting on a park bench you can enjoy a sunny (almost undisturbed!) afternoon reading a good book.

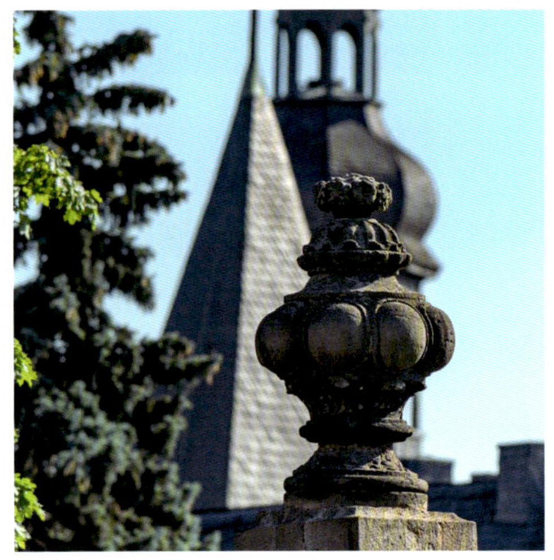

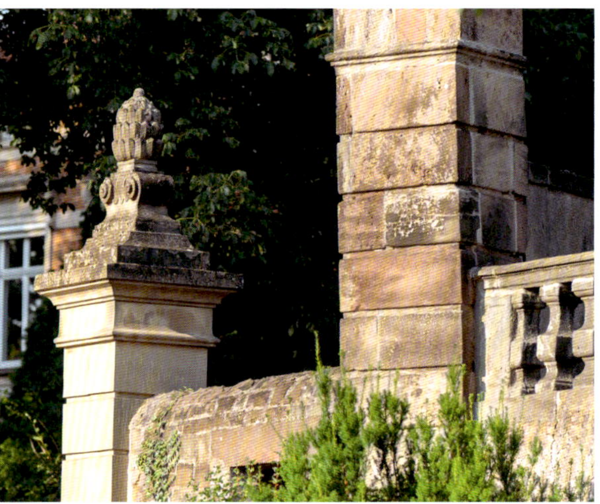

Mit der Orangerie erreichte der Fuldaer Barock eine besondere Blüte. 1721 nach Plänen von Maximilian von Welsch begonnen, wurde sie in den folgenden zwei Jahrzehnten unter Bauleitung von Andreas Gallasini und Friedrich Joachim Stengel fertiggestellt.

The Orangery represents a peak of perfection in Fulda Baroque. The building was begun according to plans by Maximilian von Welsch in 1721 and was completed in the next two decades under the supervision of Andreas Gallasini and Friedrich Joachim Stengel.

Der ursprüngliche Standort des 1710/11 geschaffenen Paulustors lag zwischen Hauptwache und Stadtschloss, also an der Grenze zwischen Bürgerstadt und Stiftsbezirk. 1771 wurde es an seinen jetzigen Standort versetzt.

The original position of the Paulustor (built 1710/11) was between the Hauptwache and the Residence, between the city and the monastery area. In 1771 it was moved to its current site.

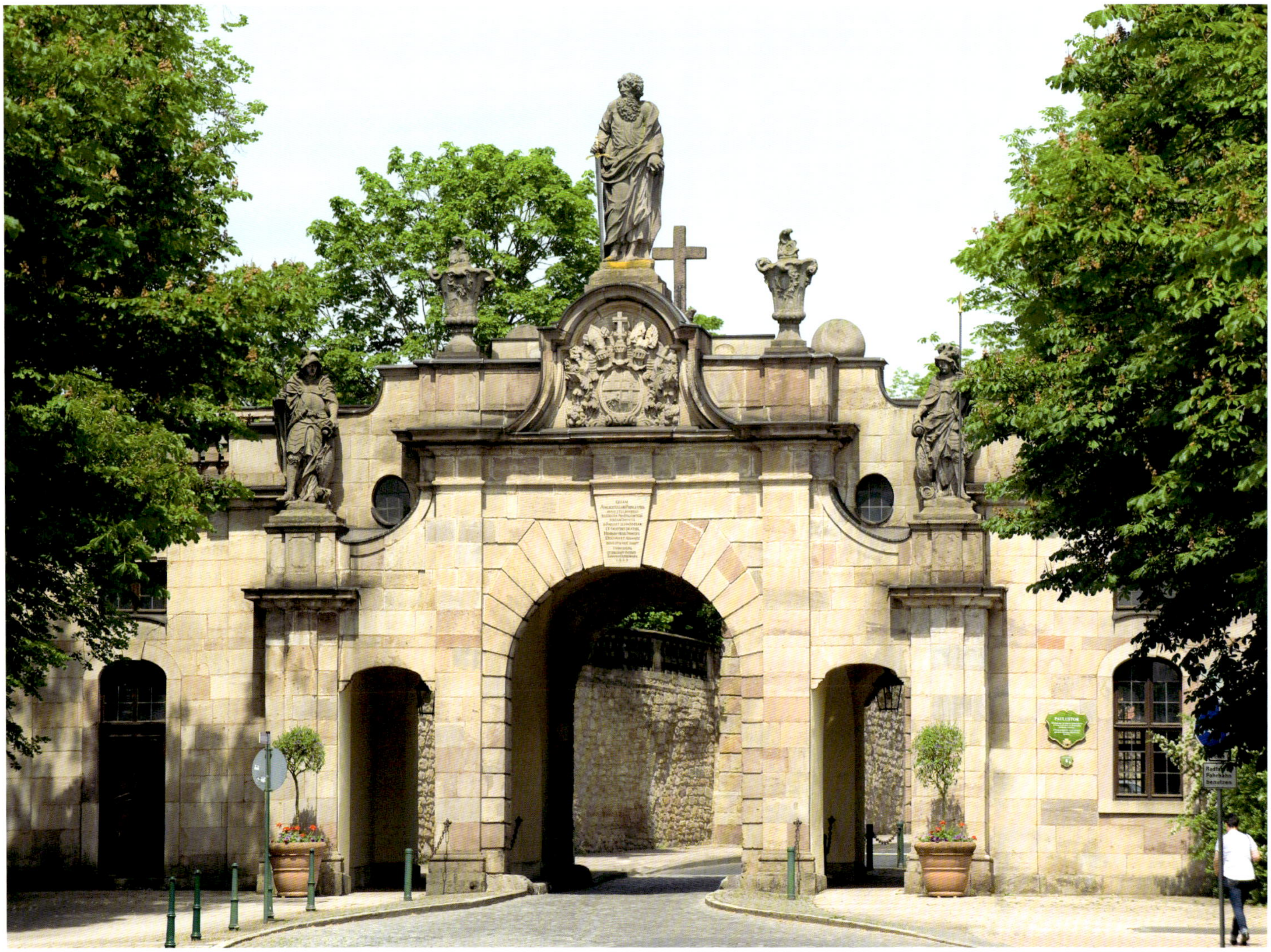

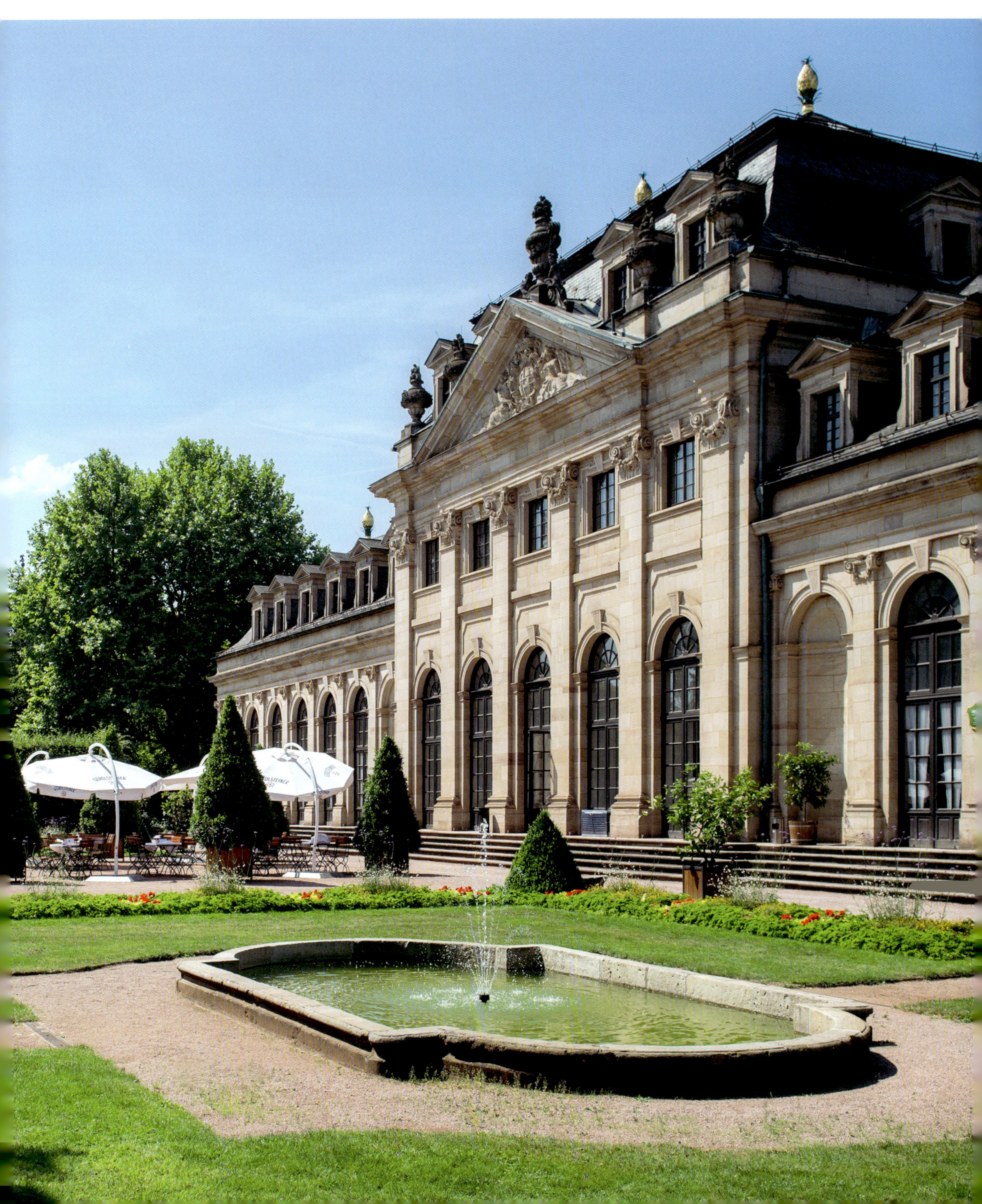

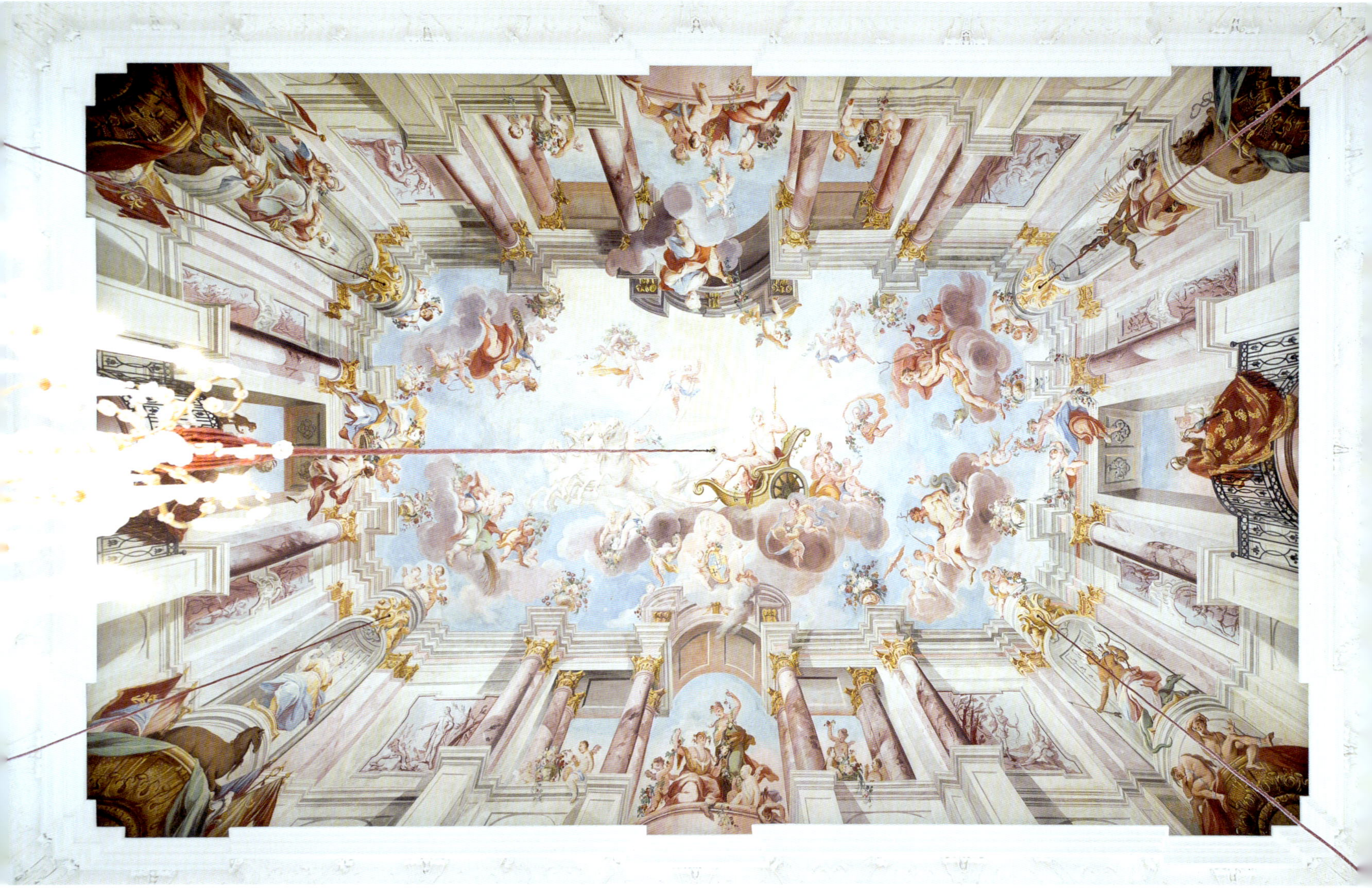

Das große Deckengemälde im Apollosaal der Orangerie schuf Hofmaler Emanuel Wohlhaupter. Genutzt wird der Saal heute als Frühstückssaal des angegliederten Hotels.

The large ceiling painting in the Apollosaal of the Orangery was executed by the court painter Emanuel Wohlhaupter. The room is used by the adjoining hotel as a breakfast room.

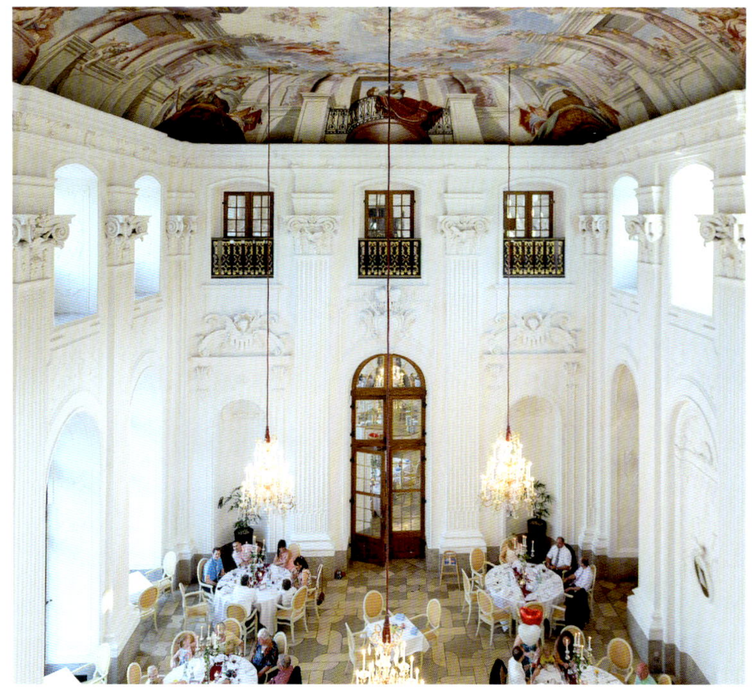

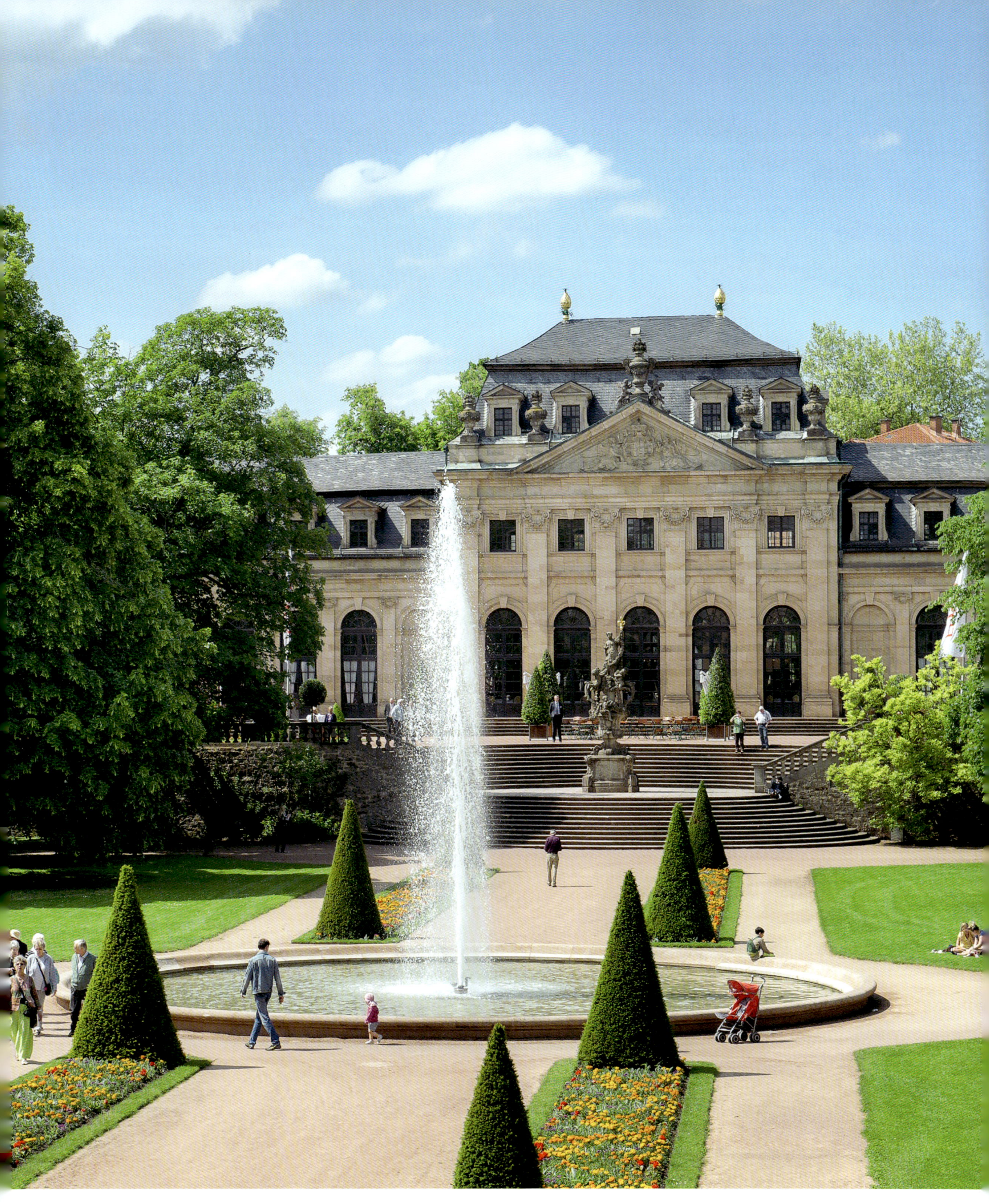

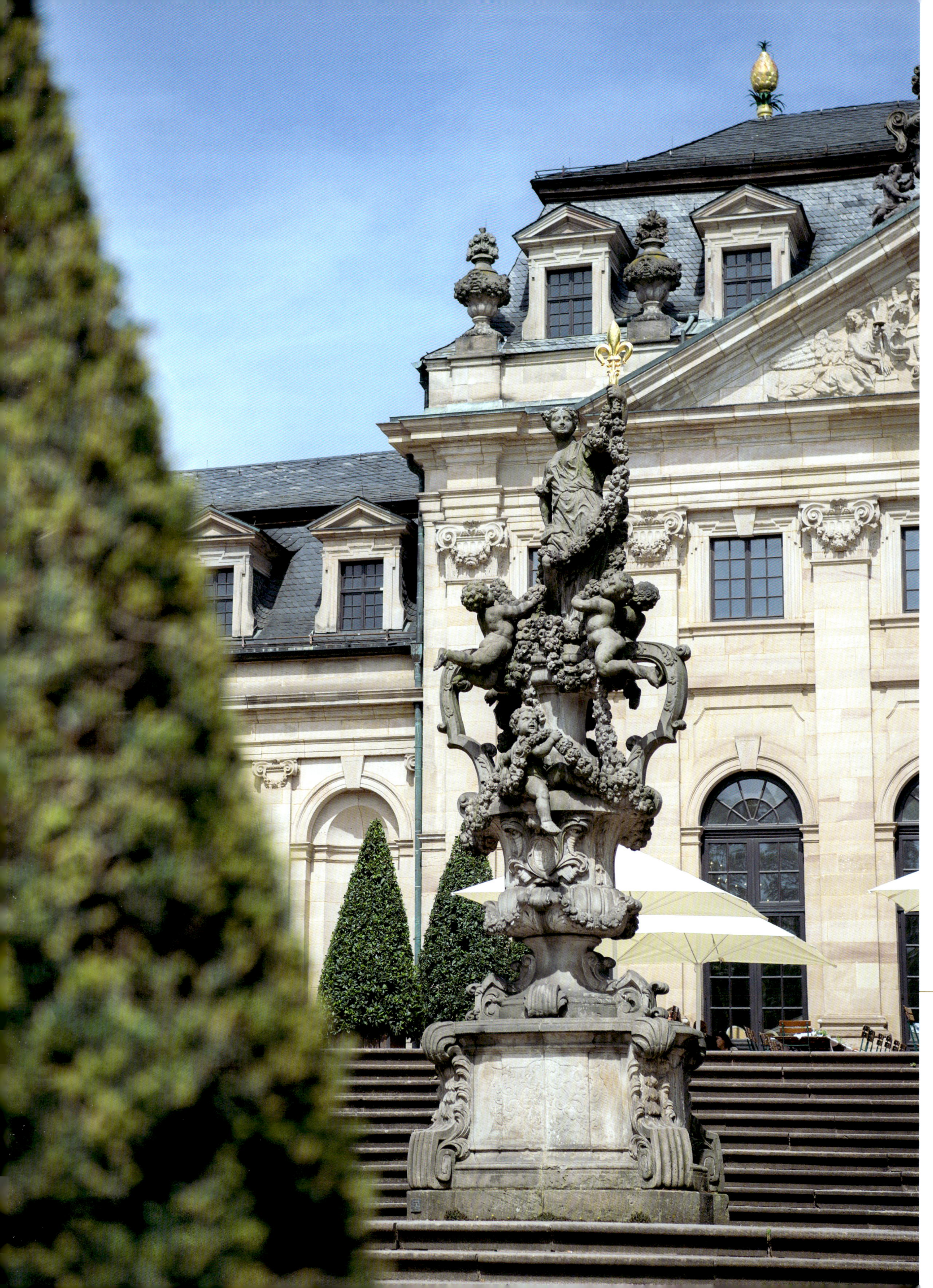

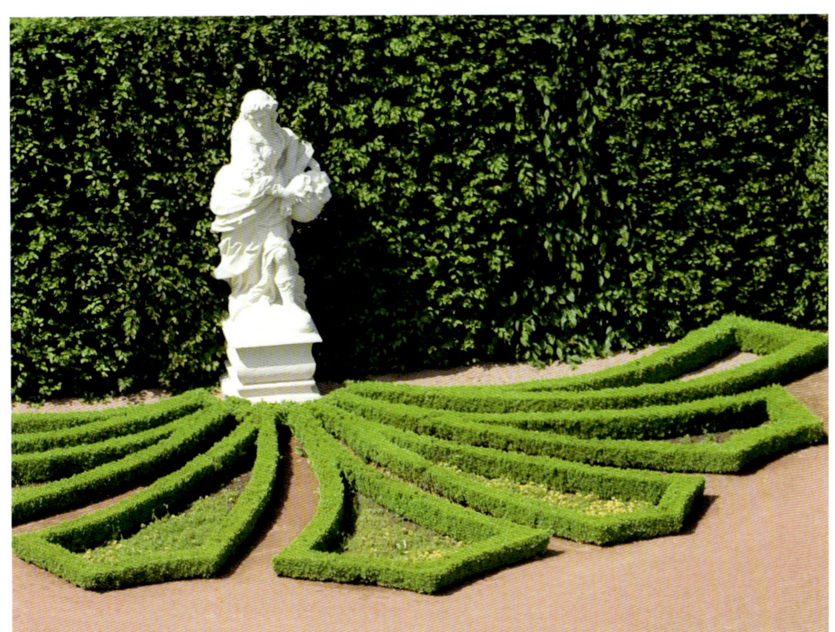

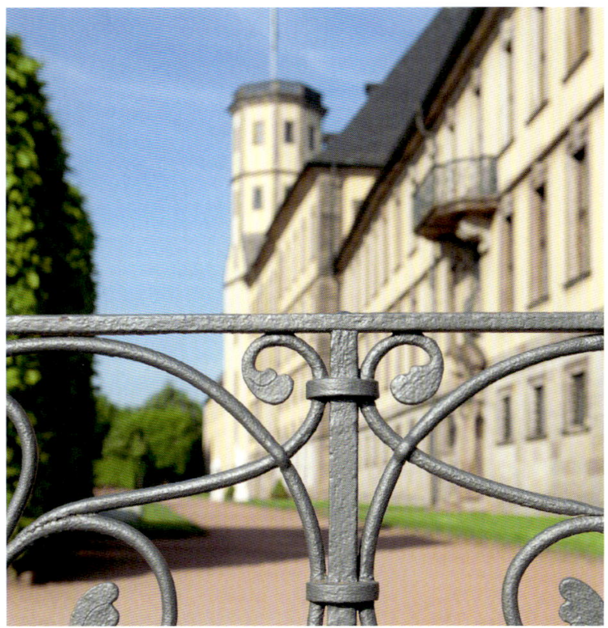

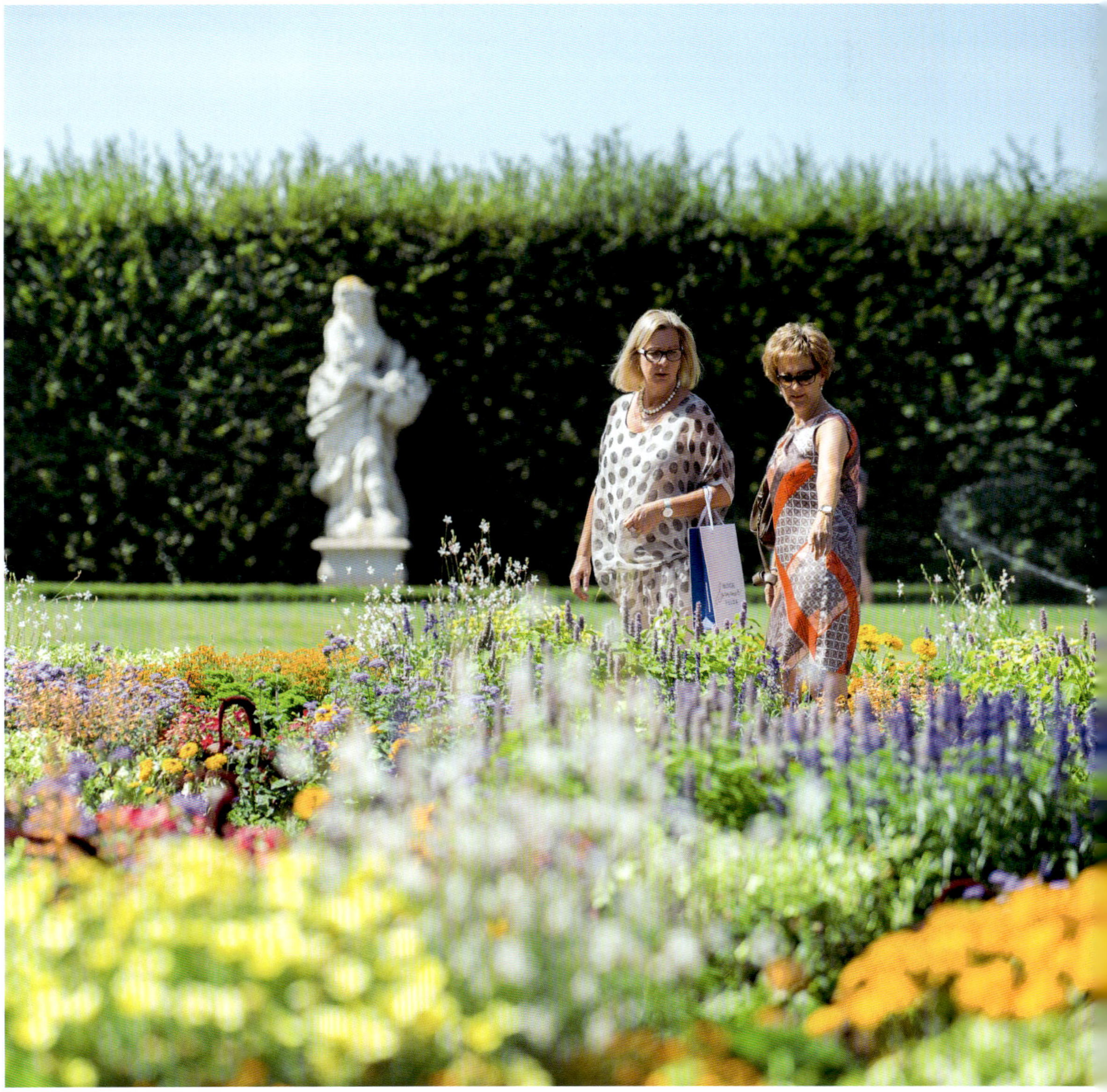

Die verspielte Floravase (1728) ist längst ein Sympathieträger für Fulda geworden, und die Lilie (die sowohl als Symbol der drei Stadtheiligen im Stadtwappen als auch im Wappen der Freiherren von Dalberg enthalten ist) nutzt die Stadtverwaltung als Logo.

The playful, lively spirit of the Floravase (1728) has long made this stone vase a popular Fulda feature. The fleur-de-lys, which is depicted in the coat-of-arms of the Freiherren von Dalberg, also appears three times in the city coat-of-arms, representing the city's three patron saints. Today the fleur-de-lys is used as the city logo.

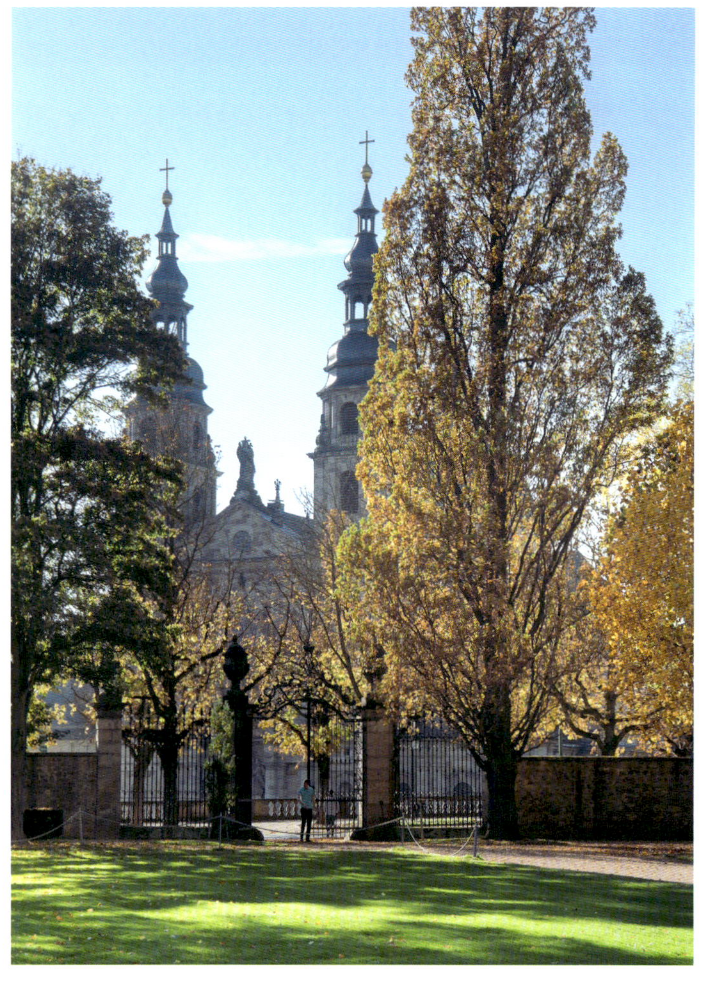

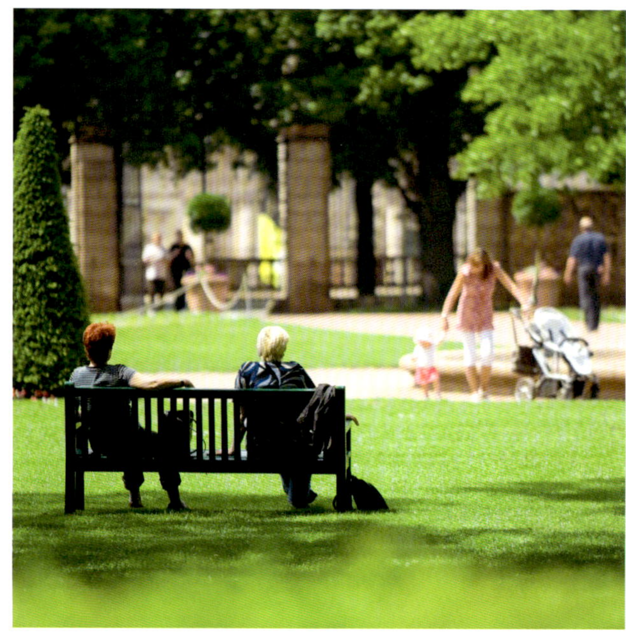

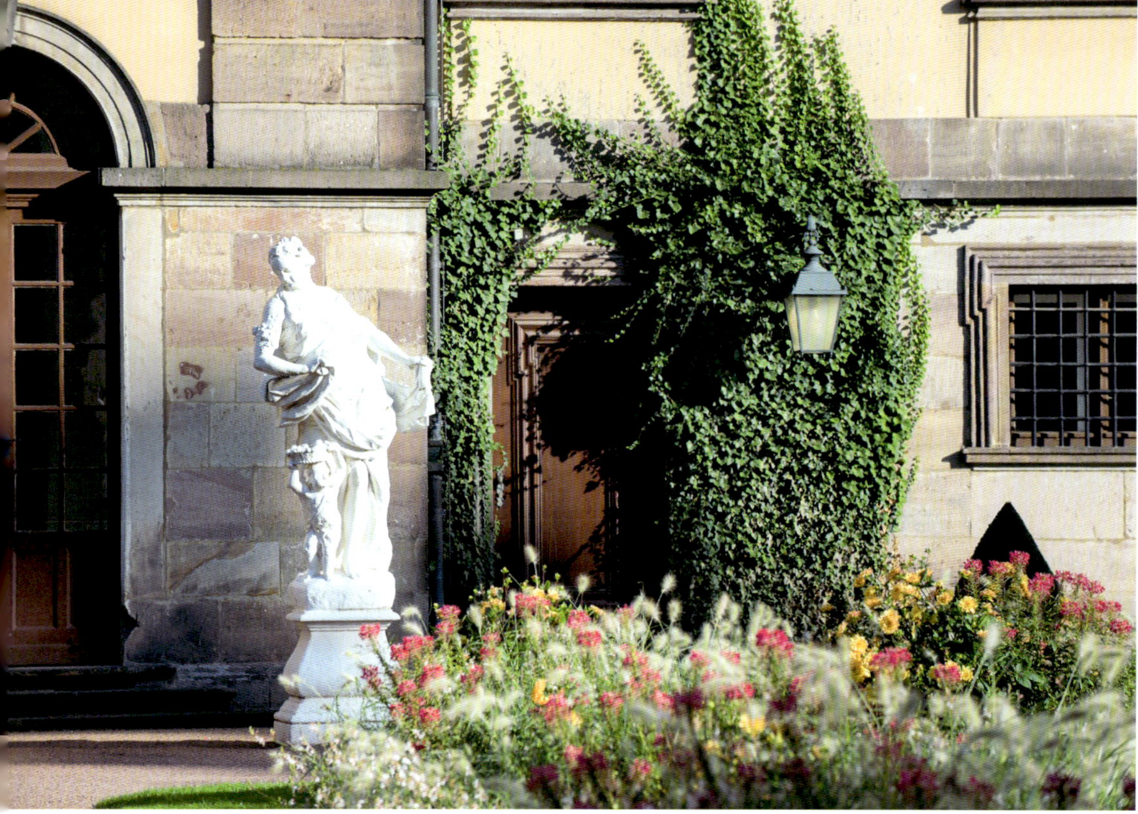

Der Schlossgarten ist nicht nur Touristenattraktion, sondern auch ein lebendiger Bürgerpark.

The Residence garden is not only a tourist attraction, but also a lively city park.

Brunnen und Wasserspiele verleihen dem Schlossgarten zusätzlich Charme – und bieten bei heißen Temperaturen willkommene Abkühlung.

Fountains and ornamental basins add to the charm of the Residence garden and provide a welcome cooling effect when the temperatures soar.

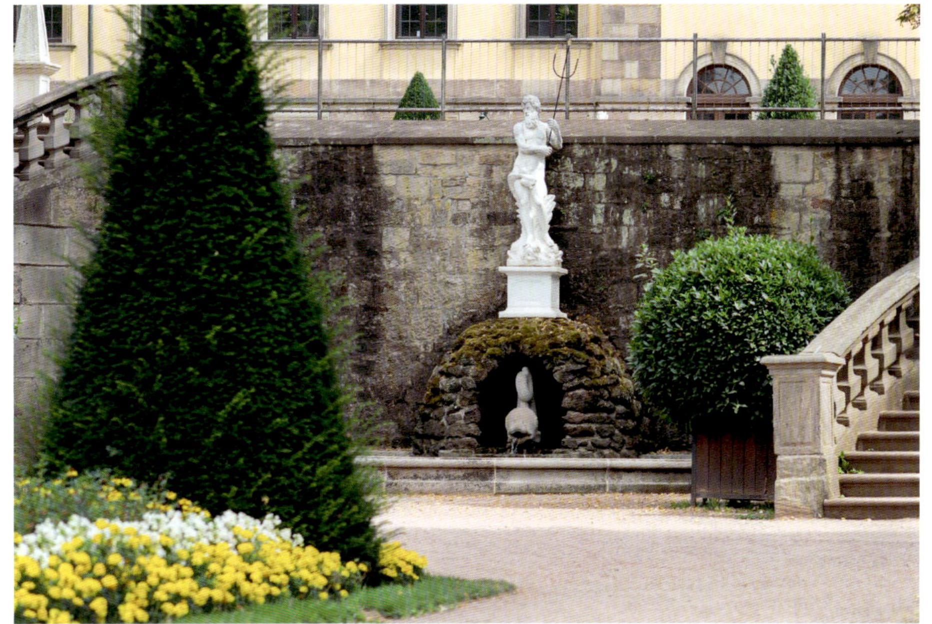

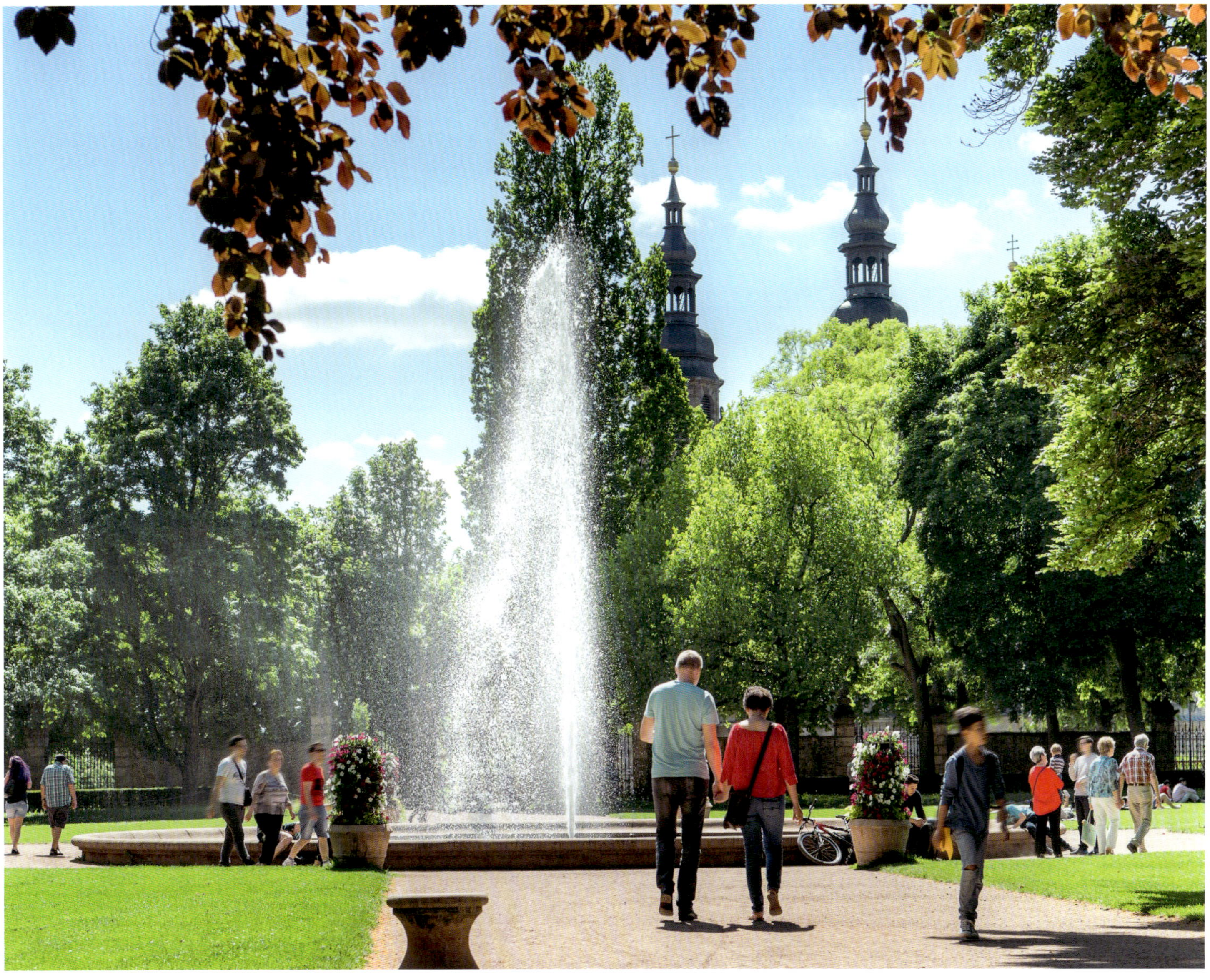

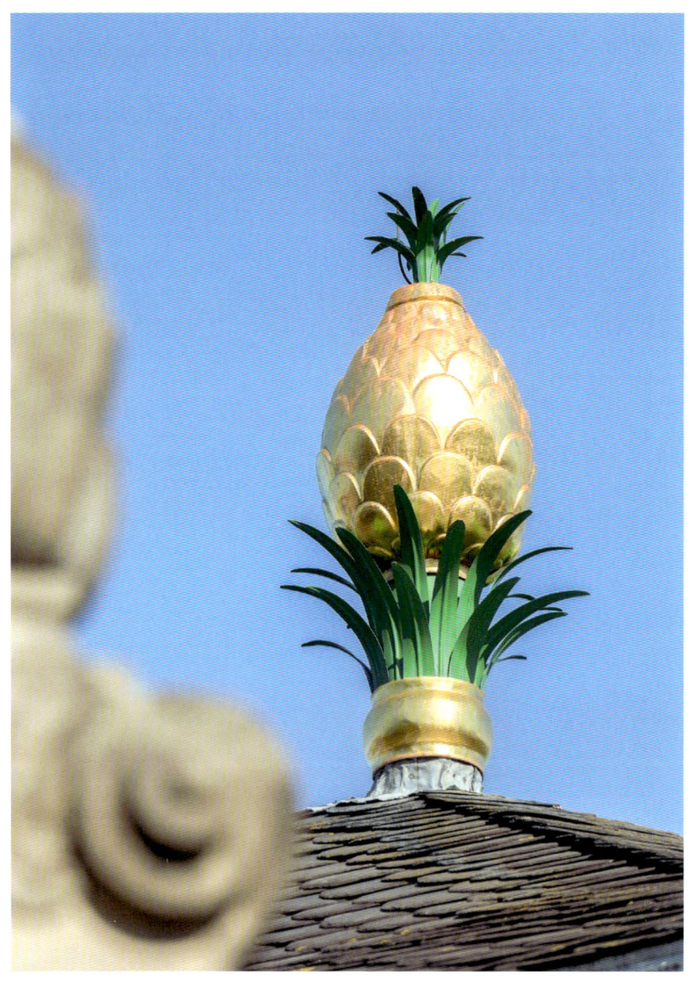

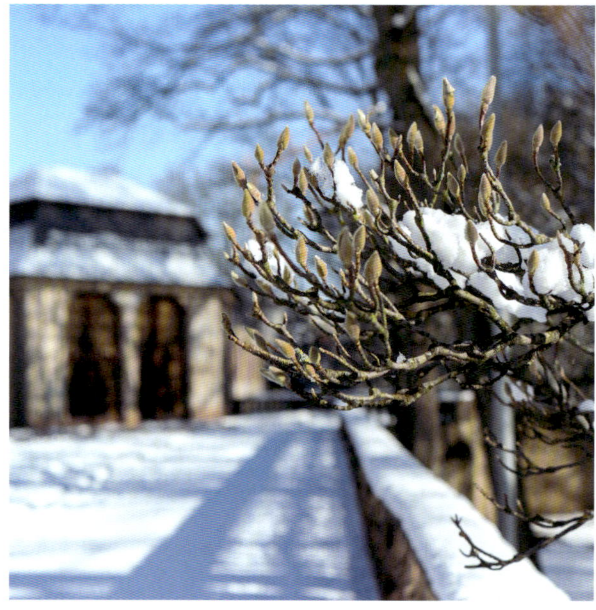

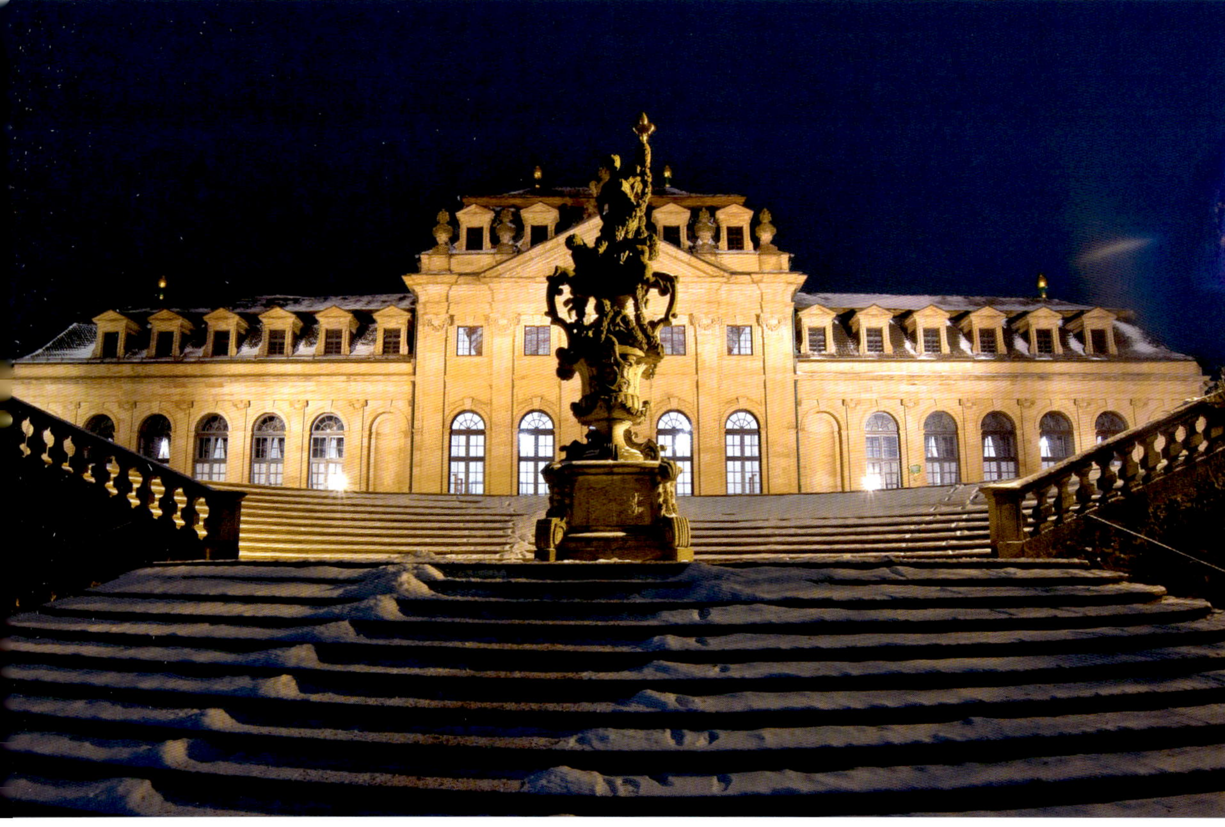

Auch im Winter entfaltet das barocke Ambiente an der Orangerietreppe seinen Reiz.

In winter the Baroque ambience around the Orangery steps also unfolds its charm.

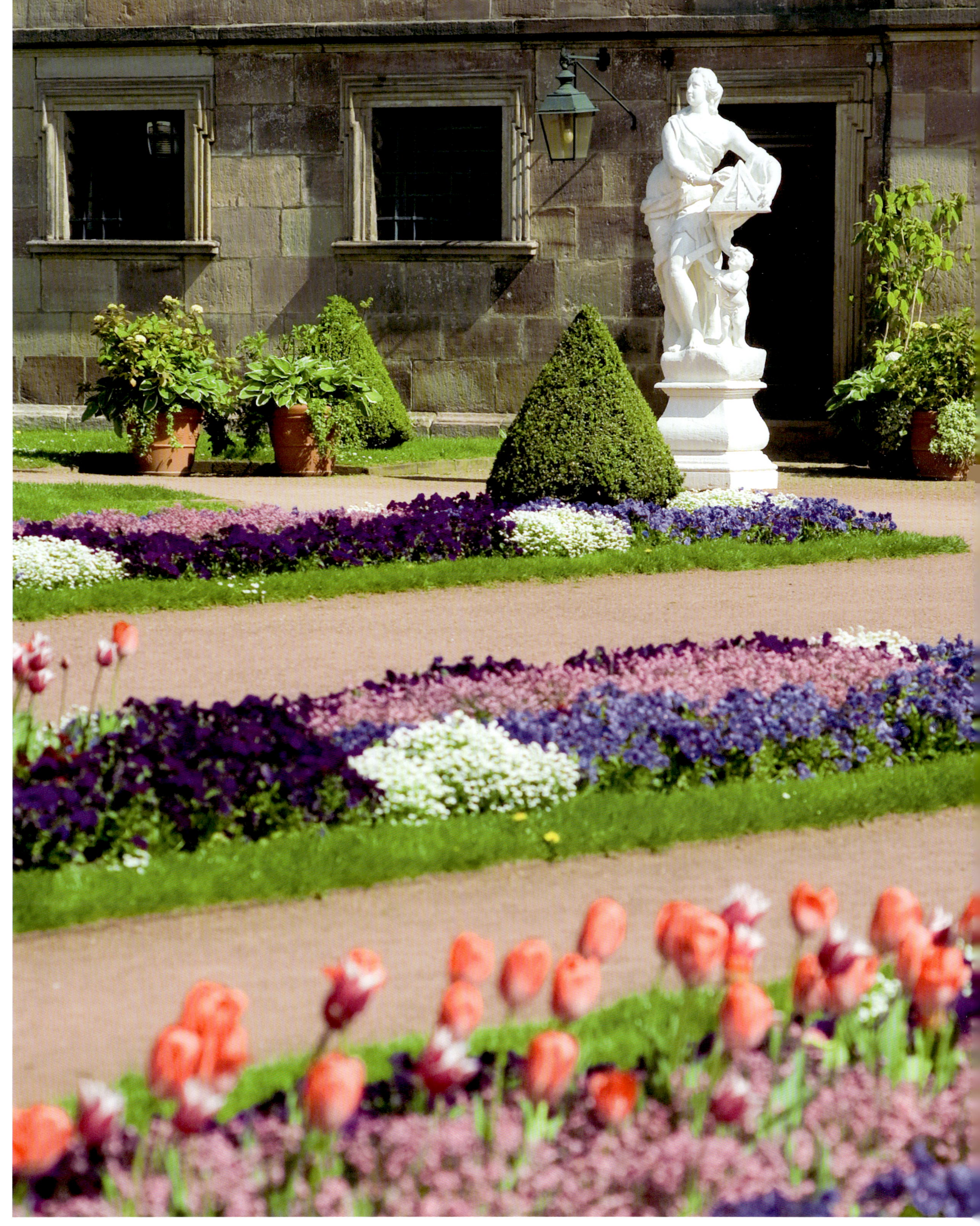

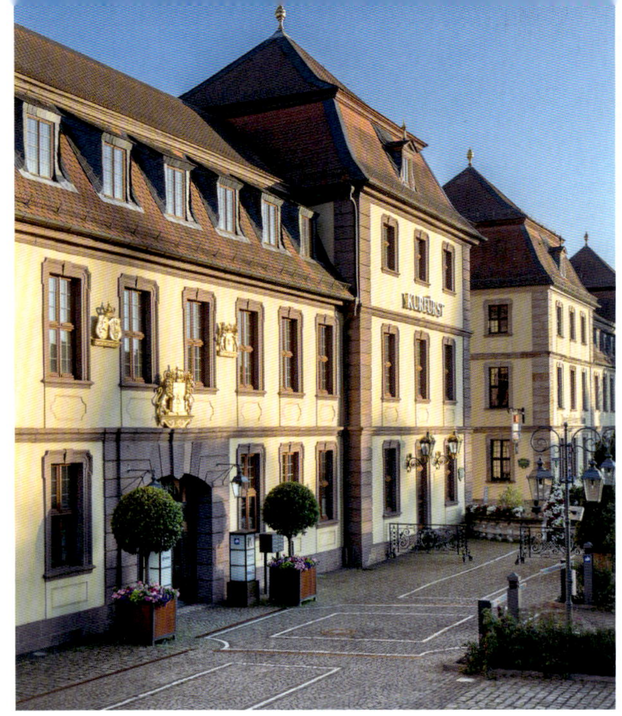

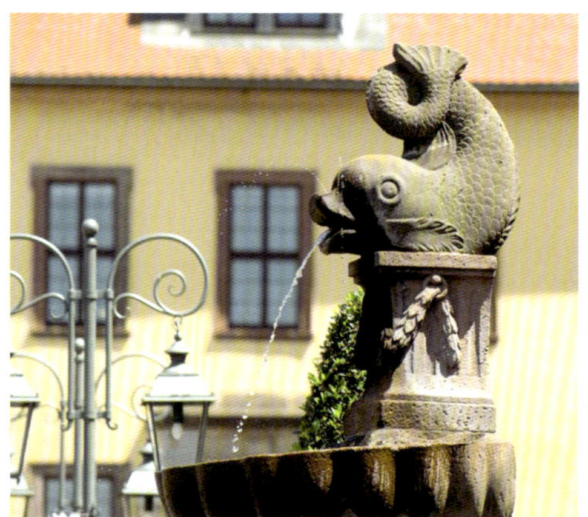

Rund um den Bonifatiusplatz gruppieren sich Adelspalais und barocke Bürgerhäuser, die das Barockviertel erst komplett machen.

The Baroque quarter is only complete with Baroque nobles' palaces and other houses of the same style which are grouped around the Bonifatiusplatz.

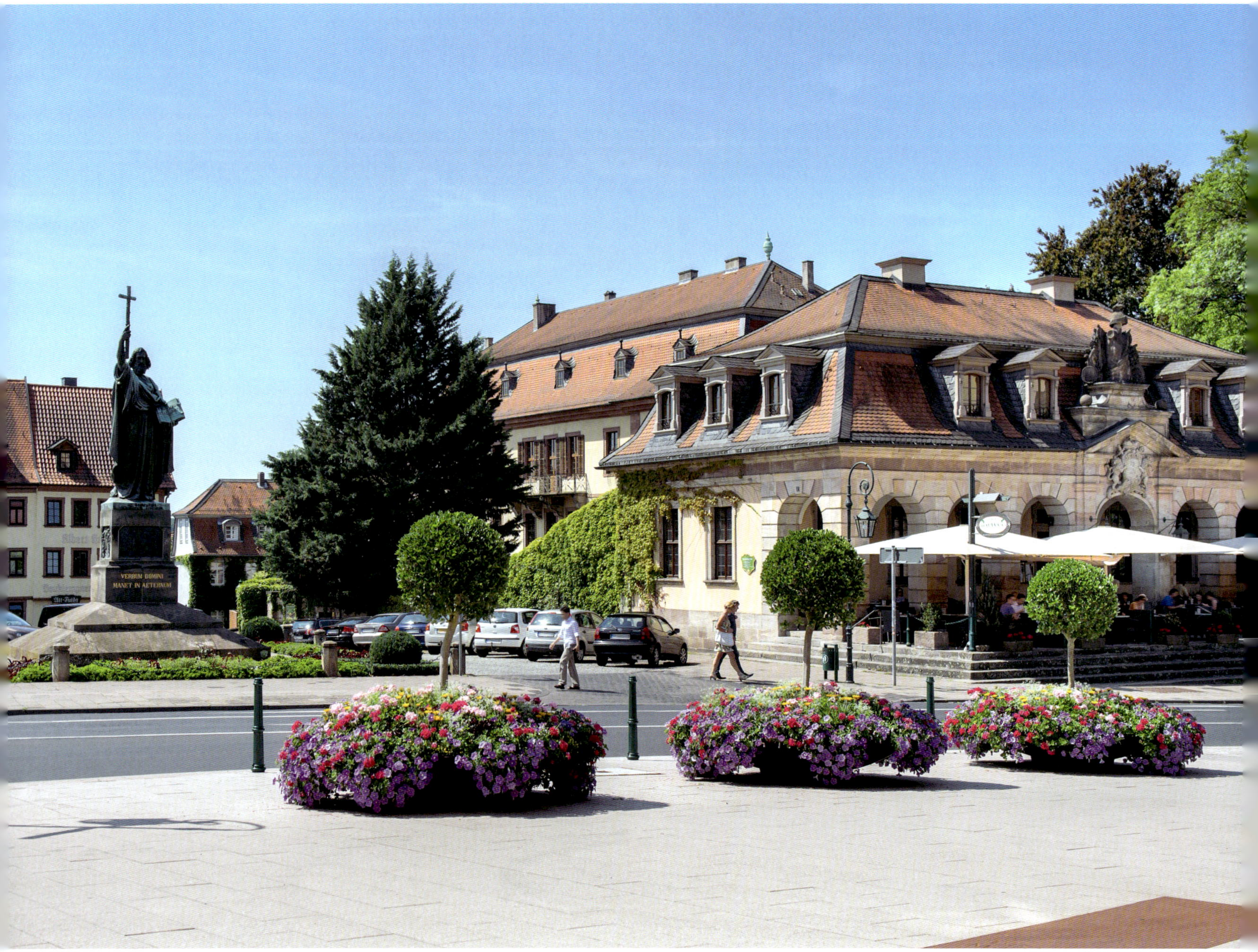

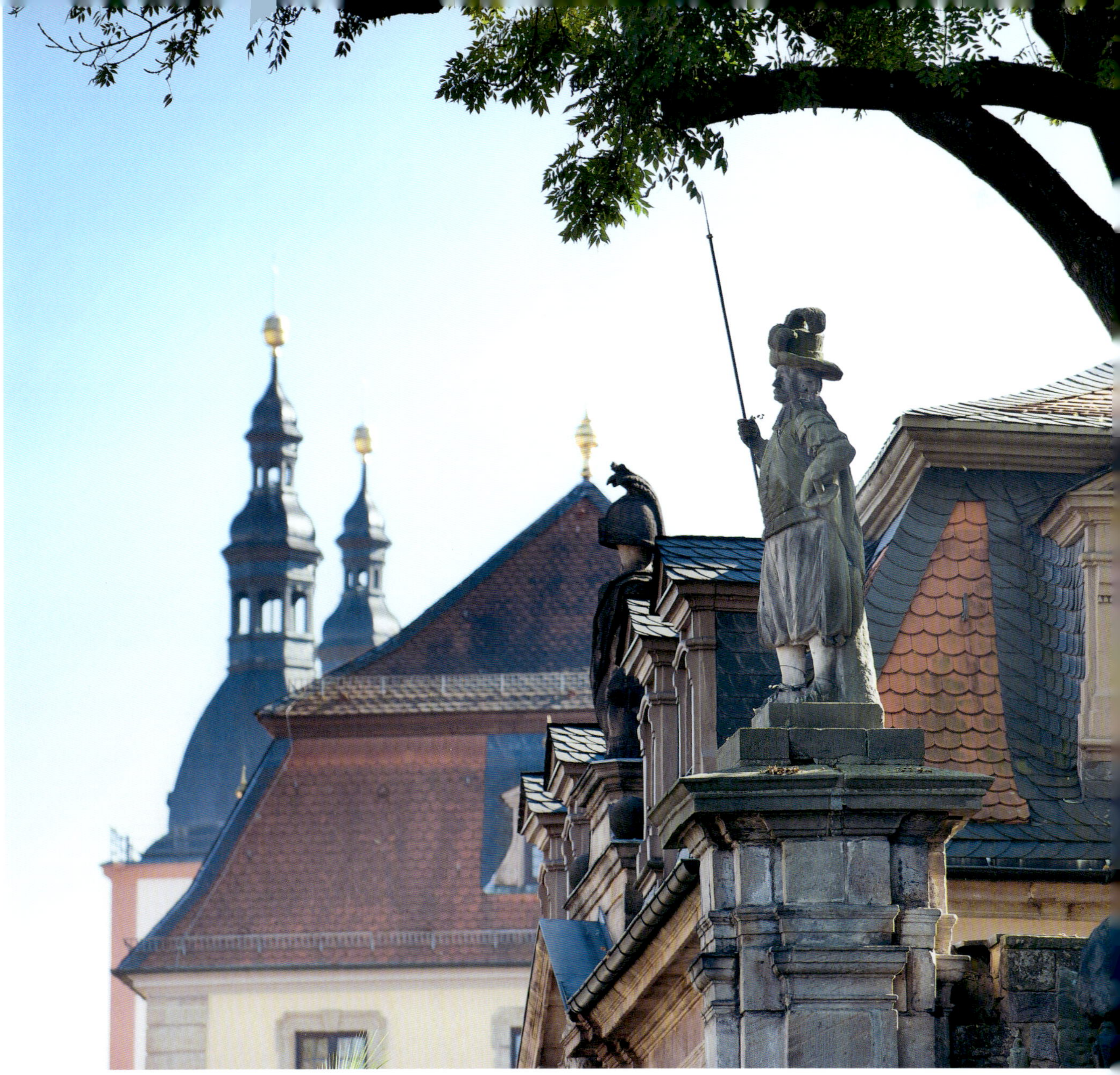

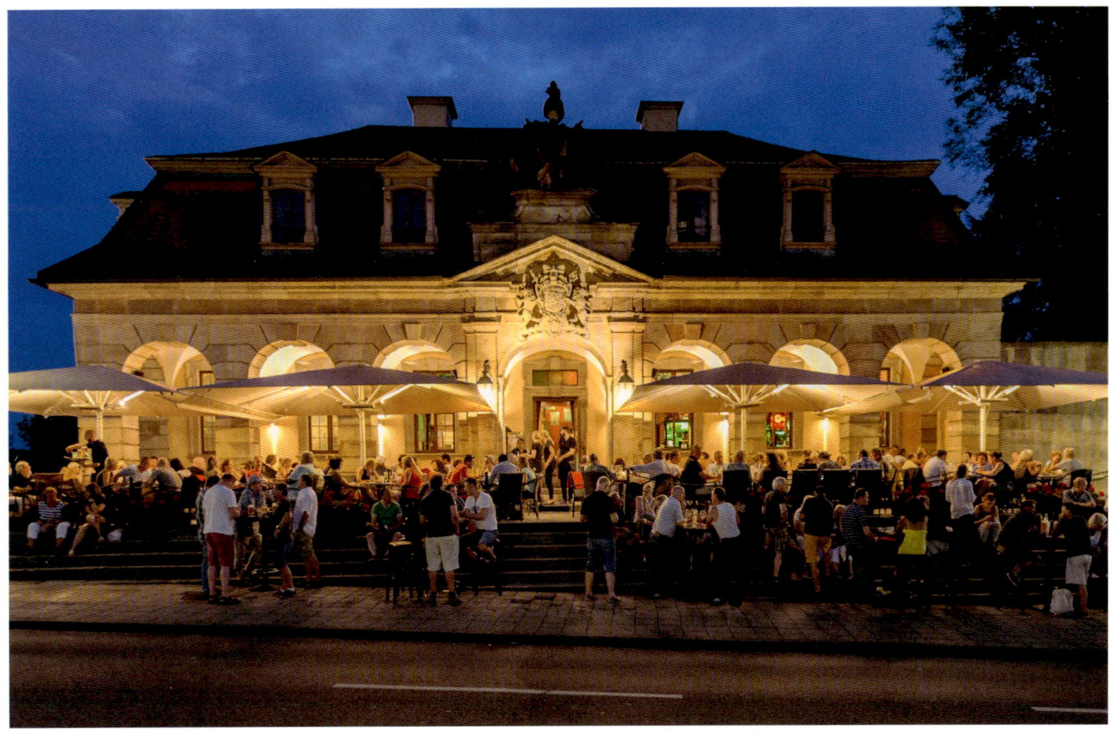

Die Hauptwache entstand – nach Frankfurter Vorbild – in den Jahren 1757 bis 1759 und verfügte im Keller über echte Gefängniszellen. Doch bereits seit dem späten 19. Jahrhundert befindet sich dort Gastronomie.

Modelled on the Frankfurt guardhouse, the Fulda Hauptwache was constructed between 1757 and 1759 and actually had real prison cells in the cellar, but since the late 19th century it has housed a restaurant.

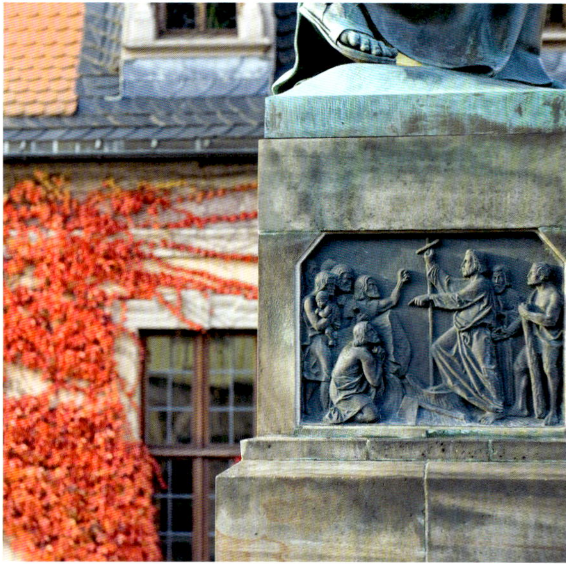

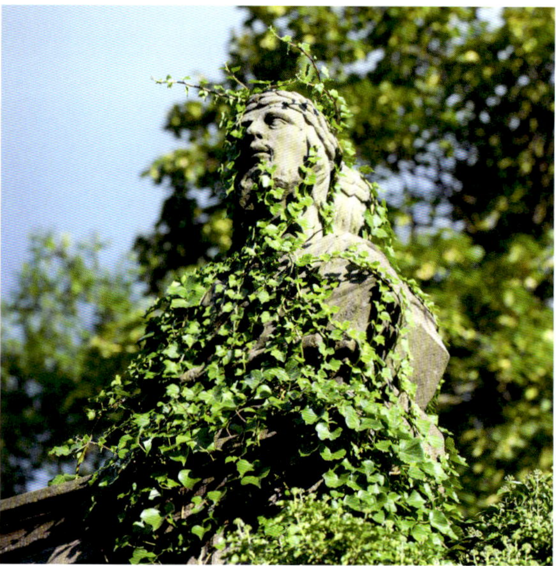

Der Bonifatiusplatz markiert den Eingang zur Bürgerstadt – mit der Achse der breiten Friedrichstraße (früher Schmiedsgasse).

The Bonifatiusplatz marks the entrance into the city area along the Friedrichstrasse (formerly Schmiedsgasse – the blacksmiths' alley)

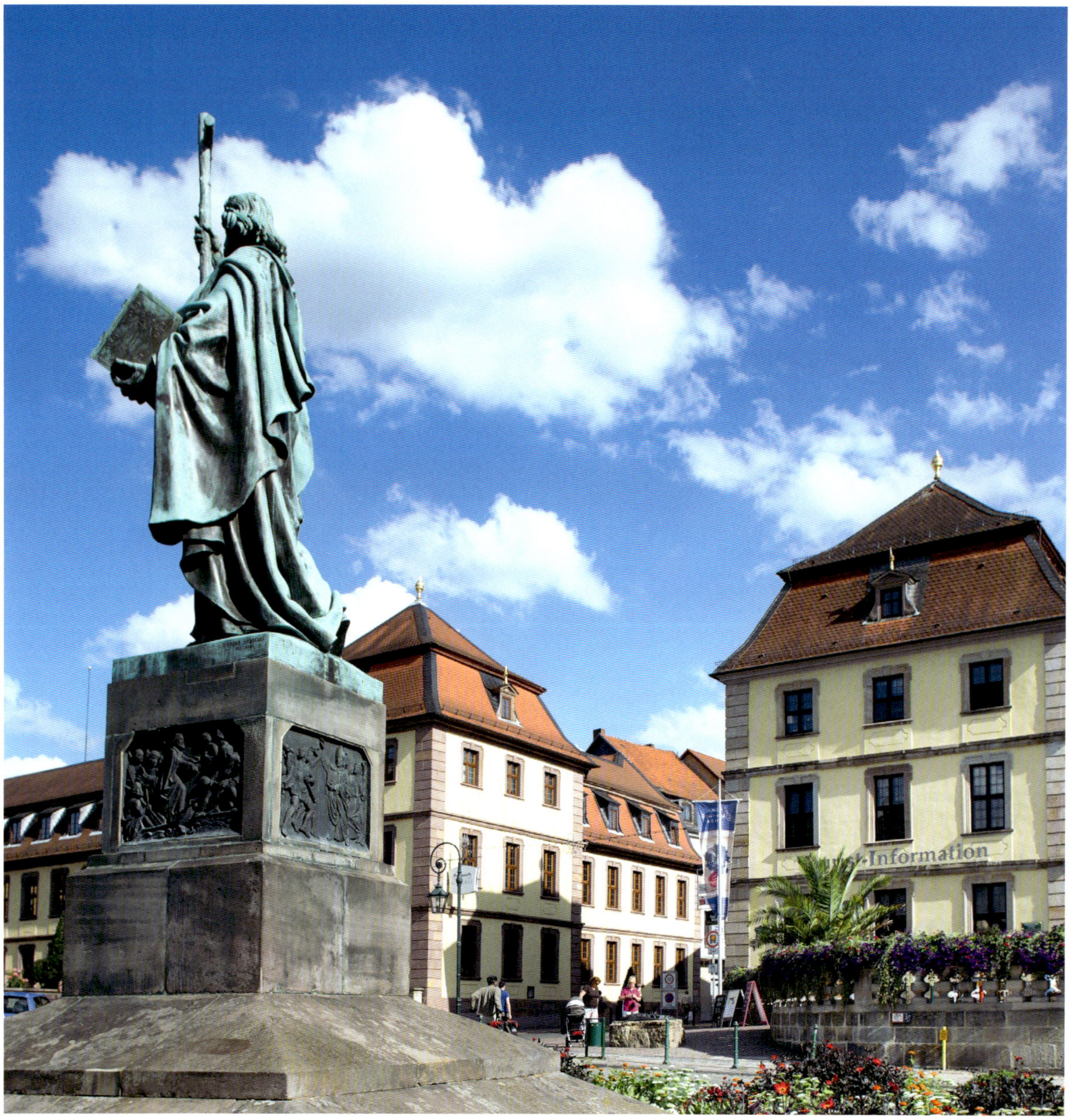

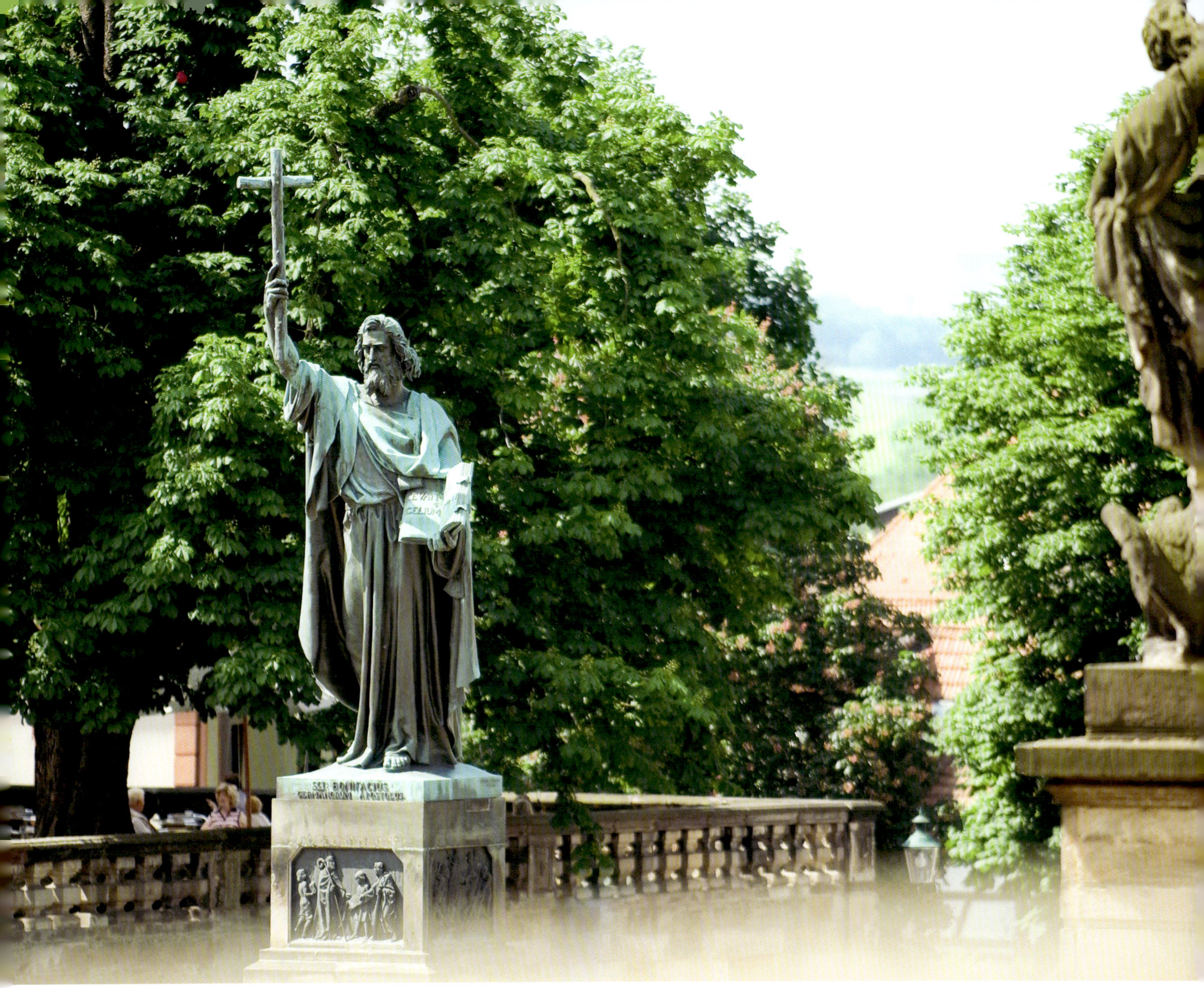

Seit 1842 wacht die bronzene Statue des Bonifatius auf dem ehemaligen Dienstagsmarkt. Das Denkmal – ganz im Stile anderer patriotischer Denkmäler des 19. Jahrhunderts – steht auch für die Vereinnahmung des Heiligen als nationaler Identifikationsfigur.

Since 1842 this bronze statue of St. Boniface has watched over the former "Tuesday Market." The monument – in the characteristic style of other patriotic monuments of the 19th century – also represents the appropriation of the saint as a figure of national identification.

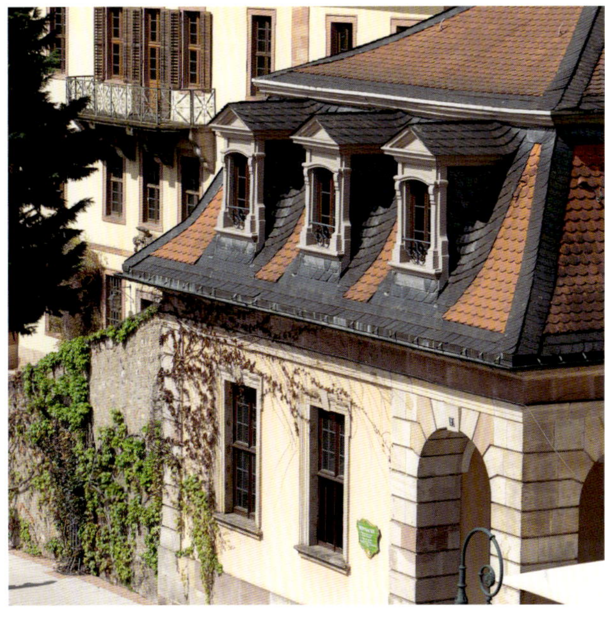

Die einzelnen Palais (hier das Palais von der Tann – bekannt als Haus „Kurfürst") haben ihre eigene bewegte Geschichte und im Laufe der Jahrhunderte eine ganz unterschiedliche Nutzung erfahren.

The nobles' palaces (here the Palais von Tann – known as the "Kurfürst") have their own individual, eventful histories and in the course of the centuries they have been used in very different ways.

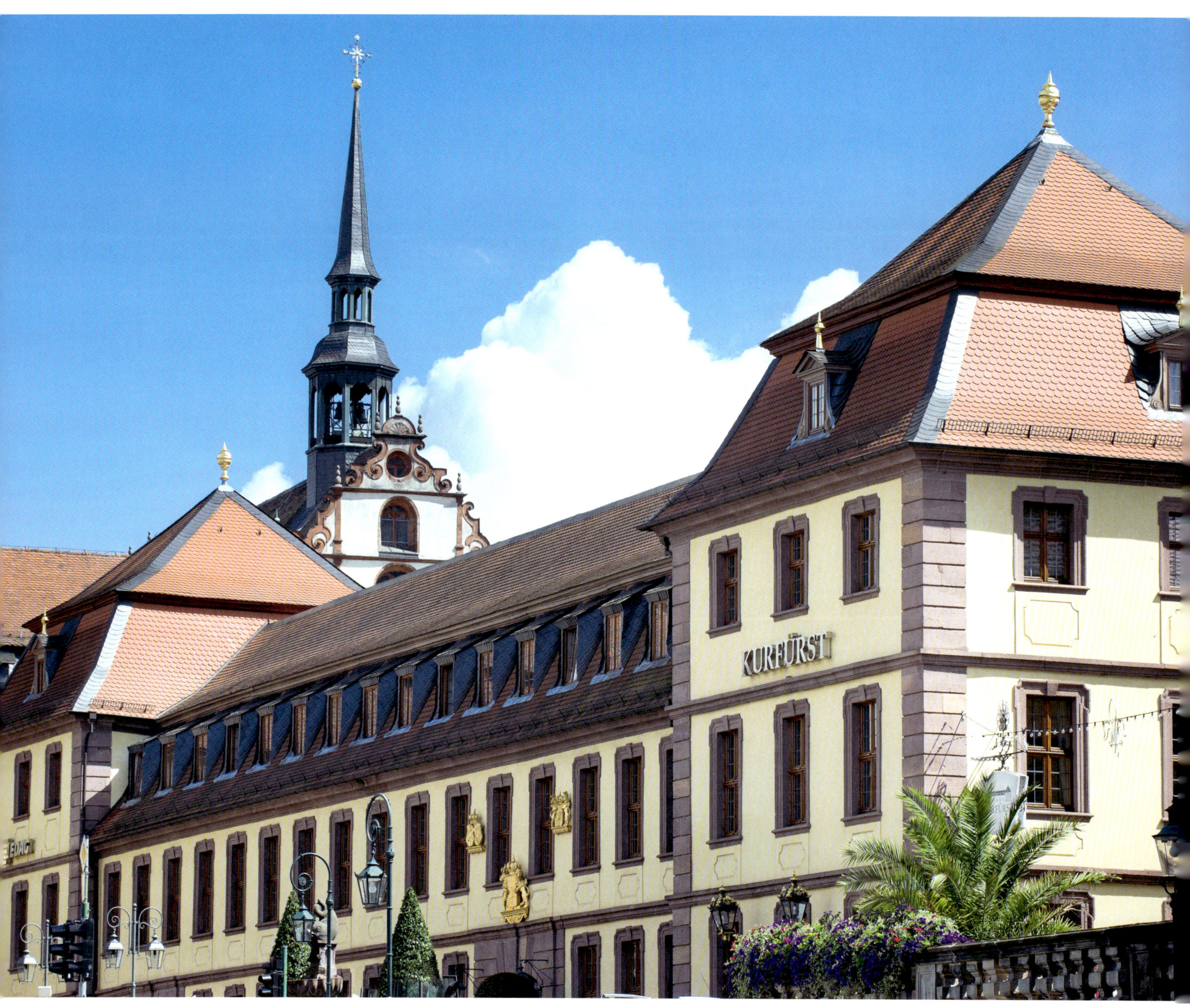

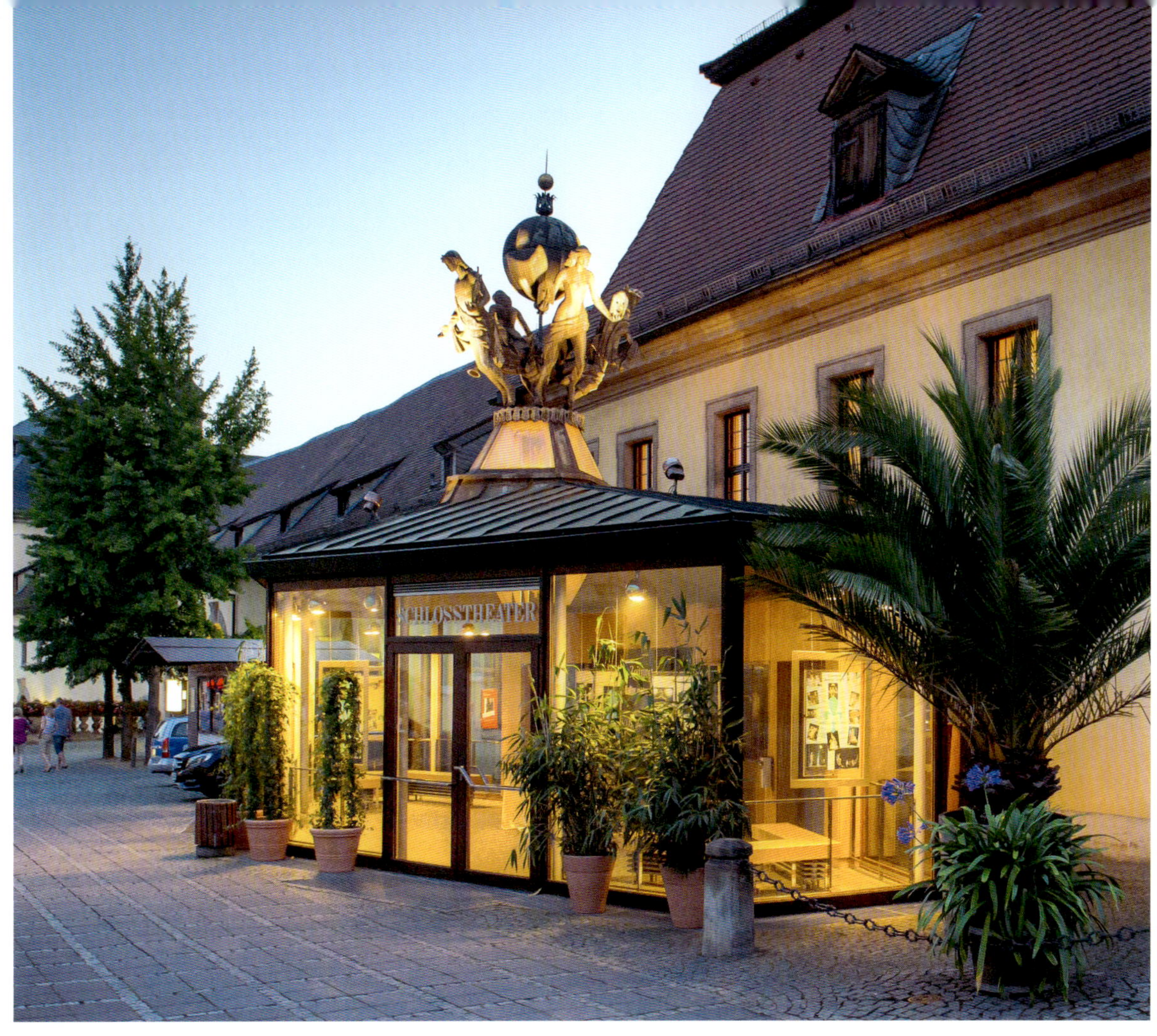

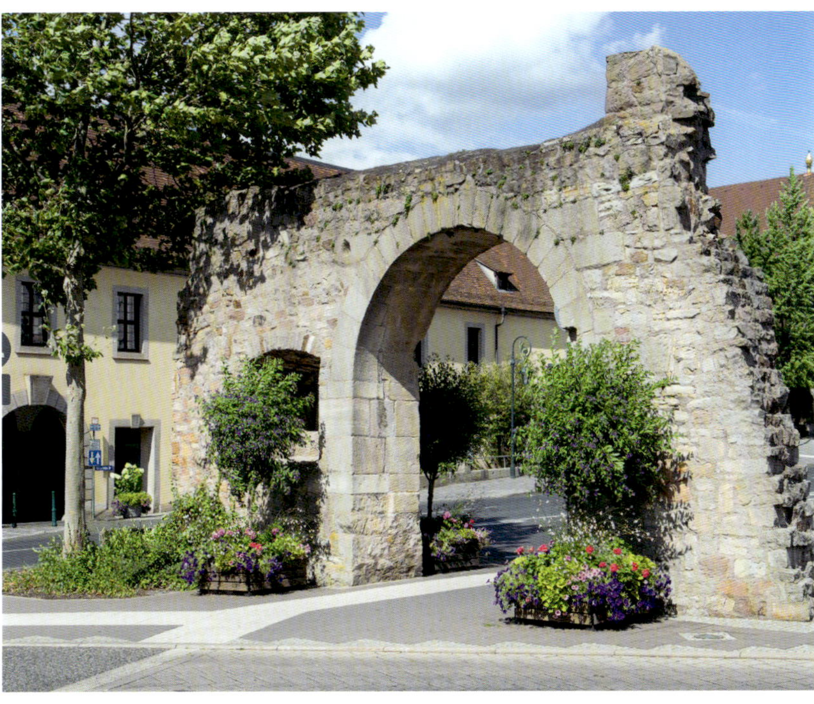

Den östlichen Eingang zum Barockviertel bildet heute das Schlosstheater. Das Heertor (Mitte), das womöglich noch aus dem 12. Jahrhundert stammt, war Teil der Stadtbefestigung und markiert das Ende der Bebauung im Mittelalter.

The eastern entrance to the Baroque quarter is marked by the Schlosstheater. The Heertor (in the middle), which is probably from the 12th century, was part of the wall which completely enclosed the city in the Middle Ages.

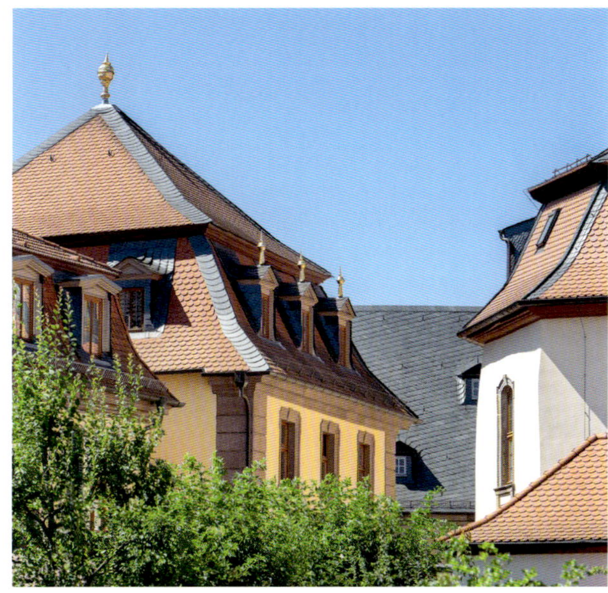

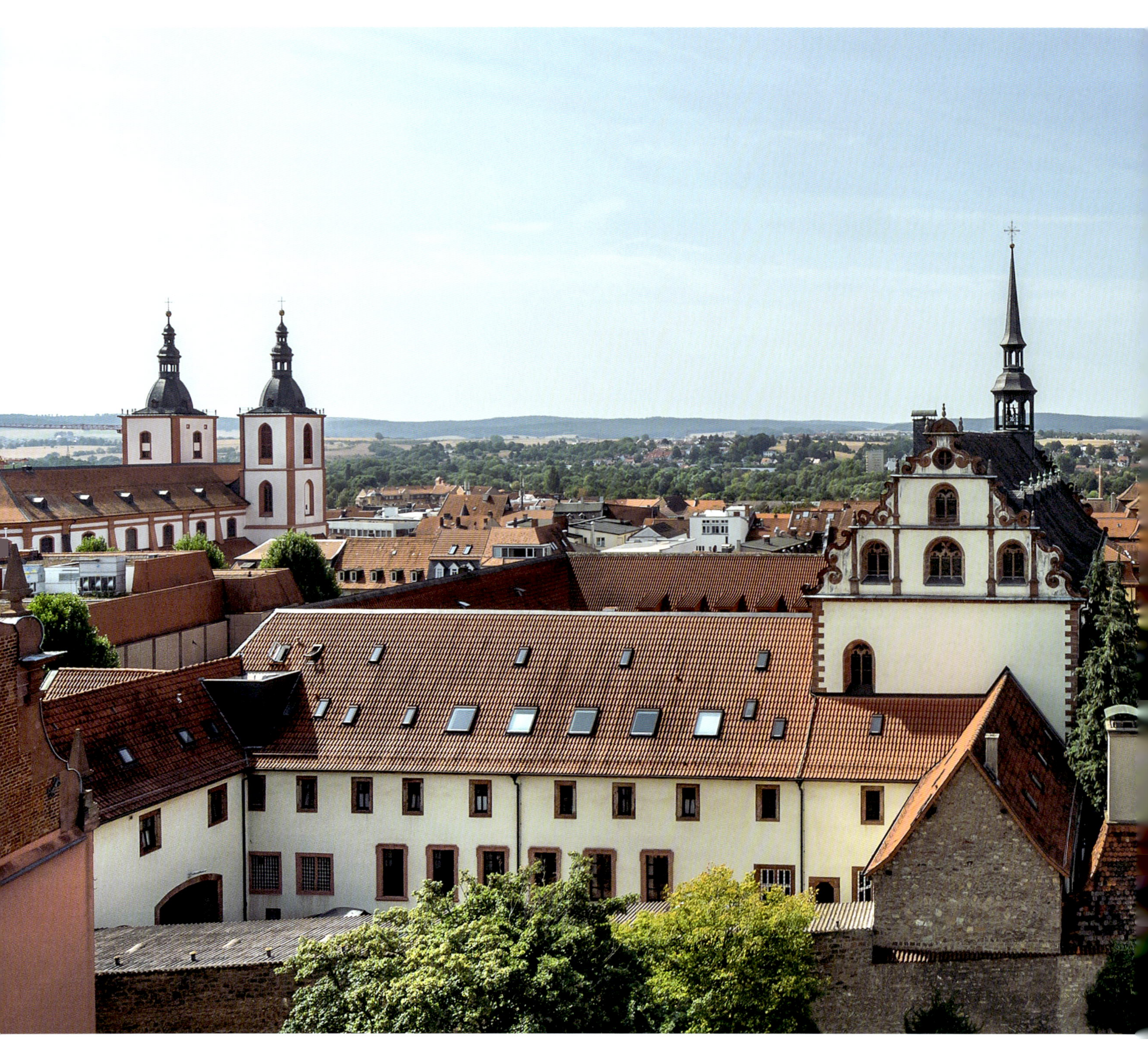

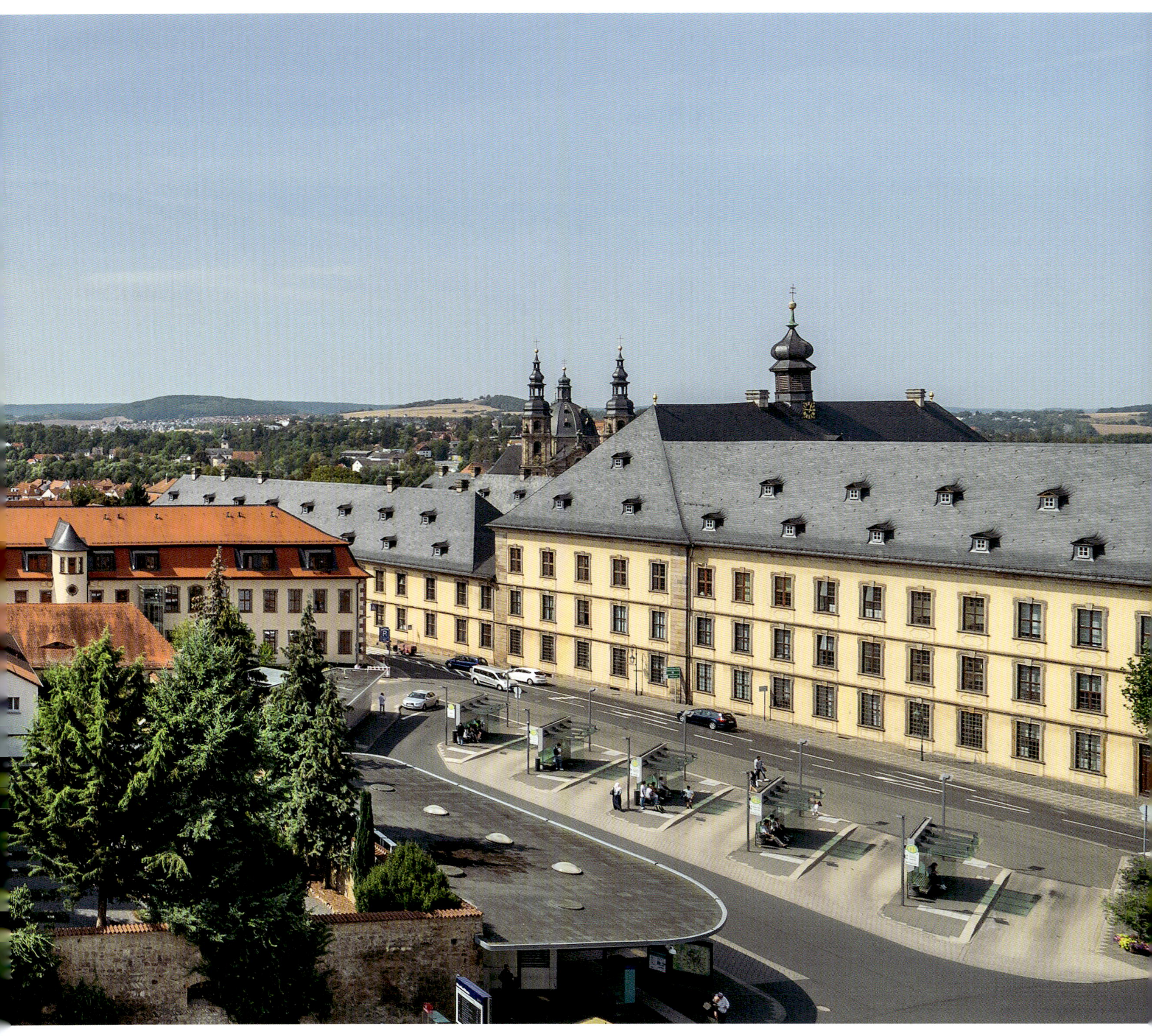

Dom, Schloss und Palais Altenstein stehen für das Barockviertel. Auf der Achse Richtung Stadtpfarrkirche erstreckt sich entlang der alten Stadtmauer das Areal der Benediktinerinnen.

The cathedral, the Residence and Palais Altenstein form part of the Baroque quarter. The old city wall runs past the area of the Benedictine abbey towards the Stadtpfarrkirche.

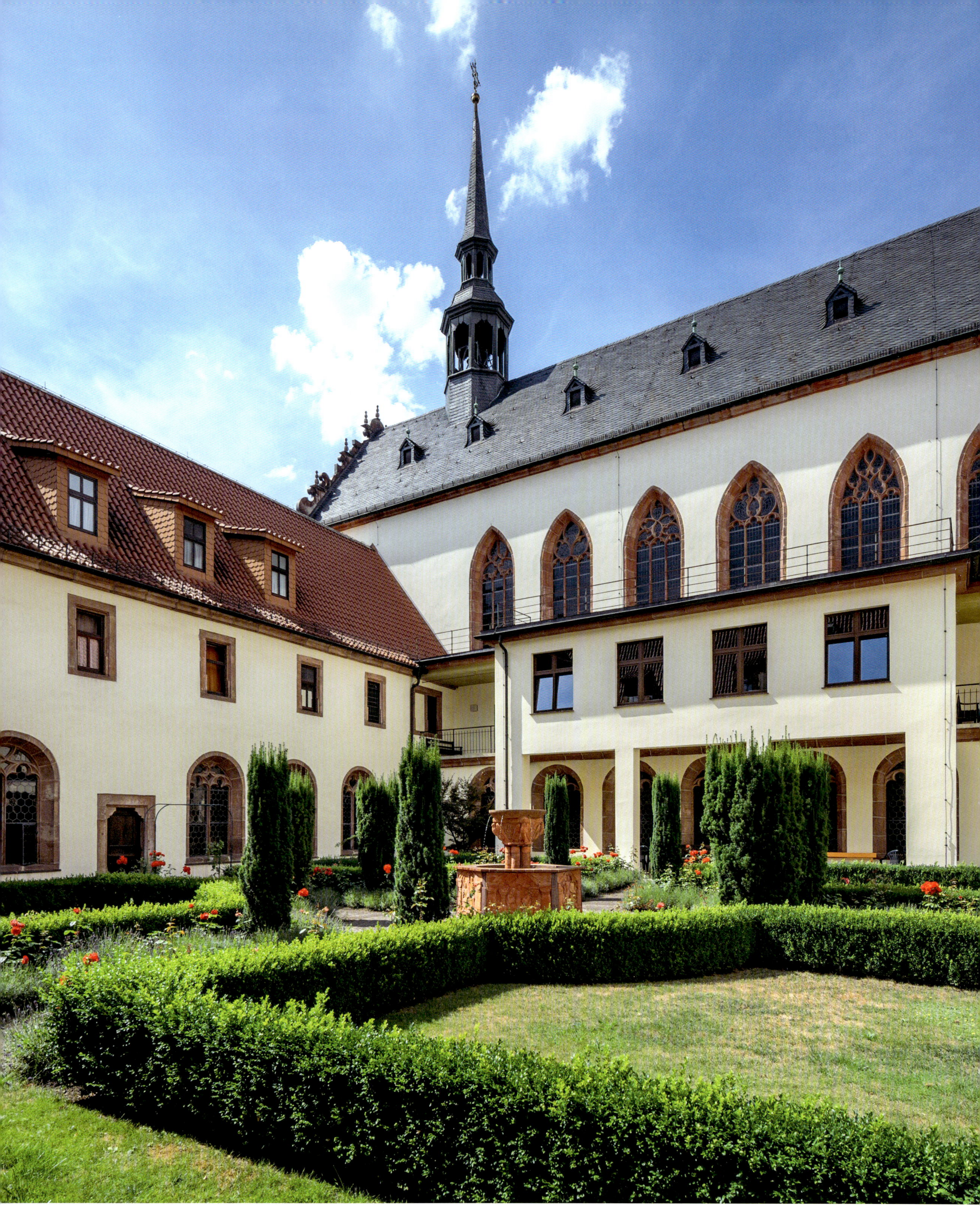

ZWISCHEN HABIT UND HUMOFIX

Die Benediktinerinnen-Abtei St. Maria ist eine Insel der Kontemplation und ein Vorbild des biologischen Gartenbaus

Wenn es in Fulda eine Institution gibt, die man wirklich traditionsreich nennen kann, dann ist es die Benediktinerinnen-Abtei St. Maria. Schließlich stehen die Ordensfrauen, die in ihrem Refugium hinter hohen Mauern zwischen Nonnengasse, Schulstraße und Heertorplatz eine zurückgezogene, aber gleichwohl bemerkenswerte Existenz führen, für den benediktinischen Geist, der Fulda seit der Klostergründung ununterbrochen prägt. Bonifatius und Sturmius waren Benediktinermönche, das von ihnen ins Leben gerufene Männerkloster bildete bis zu seiner Auflösung in der Säkularisation 1802 ein Kontinuum in der Stadtgeschichte, und das benediktinische Frauenkloster, das 1626 gegründet wurde, führt diese Tradition bis in die Gegenwart fort.

Eine Besonderheit ist der idyllische Klostergarten, der von den Schwestern schon lange streng biologisch bewirtschaftet wurde, als das Wort „Nachhaltigkeit" noch kein Modewort war. Und auf die berühmten Tütchen mit „Humofix" als Zusatz für den Kompost oder das Gießwasser, die im Kloster produziert werden, schwören schon Generationen von Fuldaer Hobbygärtnerinnen und -gärtnern.

The Benedictine Sisters and Their "Secret": Humofix

The Benedictine convent of St. Maria provides a place of contemplation and a model for organic gardening

If there is one institution in Fulda that you can truly call traditional, it is the Benedictine convent of St. Maria. Situated behind the high walls between the Nonnengasse, Schulstrasse and Heertorplatz, since its foundation in 1626 this convent has been the home to nuns who have lived secluded, but nevertheless notable lives dedicated to the Benedictine tradition. St. Boniface and St. Sturmius were Benedictine monks who were responsible for the foundation of the brothers' monastery which formed the backbone of Fulda's history until the Secularisation of 1802, and the sisters' Benedictine convent has carried on this tradition into the present.

The idyllic convent garden is particularly noteworthy as the nuns have been gardening strictly organically for decades; long before the word "sustainability" became a catchword. Indeed, generations of Fulda gardeners have sworn by the nuns' sachets of "Humofix", an organic compost accelerator.

Der vom Trubel der Innenstadt abgeschirmte Innenhof der Abtei Hl. Maria gehört zum Klausurbereich des Klosters und ist für Besucher normalerweise nicht zugänglich.

Shut off from the hustle and bustle of the city, the enclosed area within the convent of St. Maria is normally closed to the public.

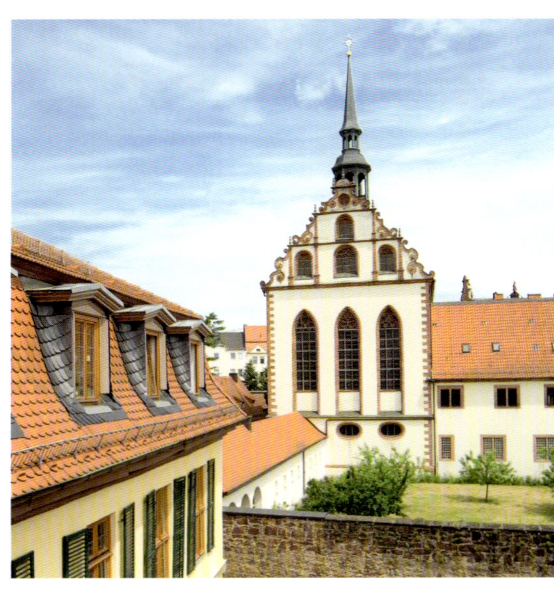

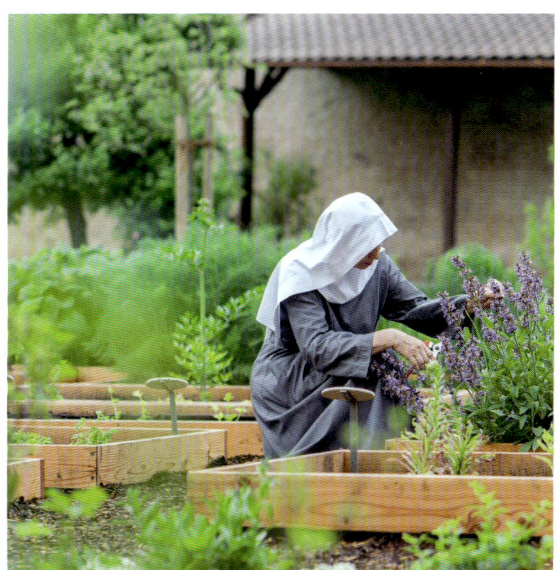

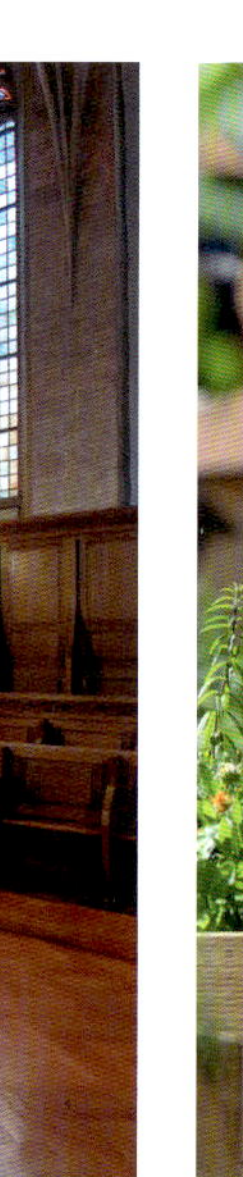

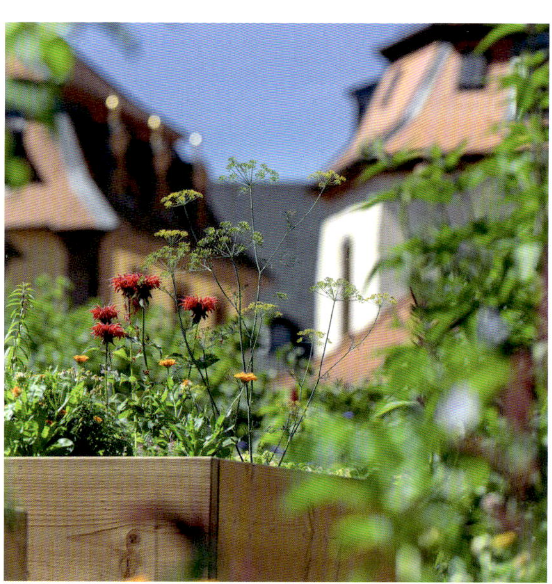

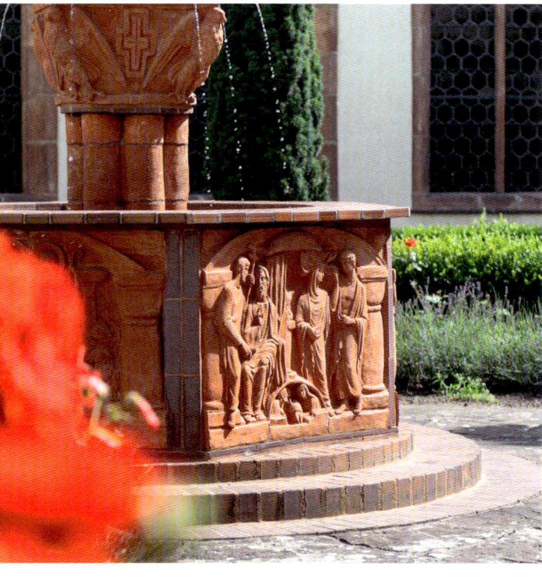

Im Klostergarten wird schon immer nach den Prinzipien des ökologischen Landbaus gewirtschaftet.

The convent garden has always been run according to the principles of organic gardening.

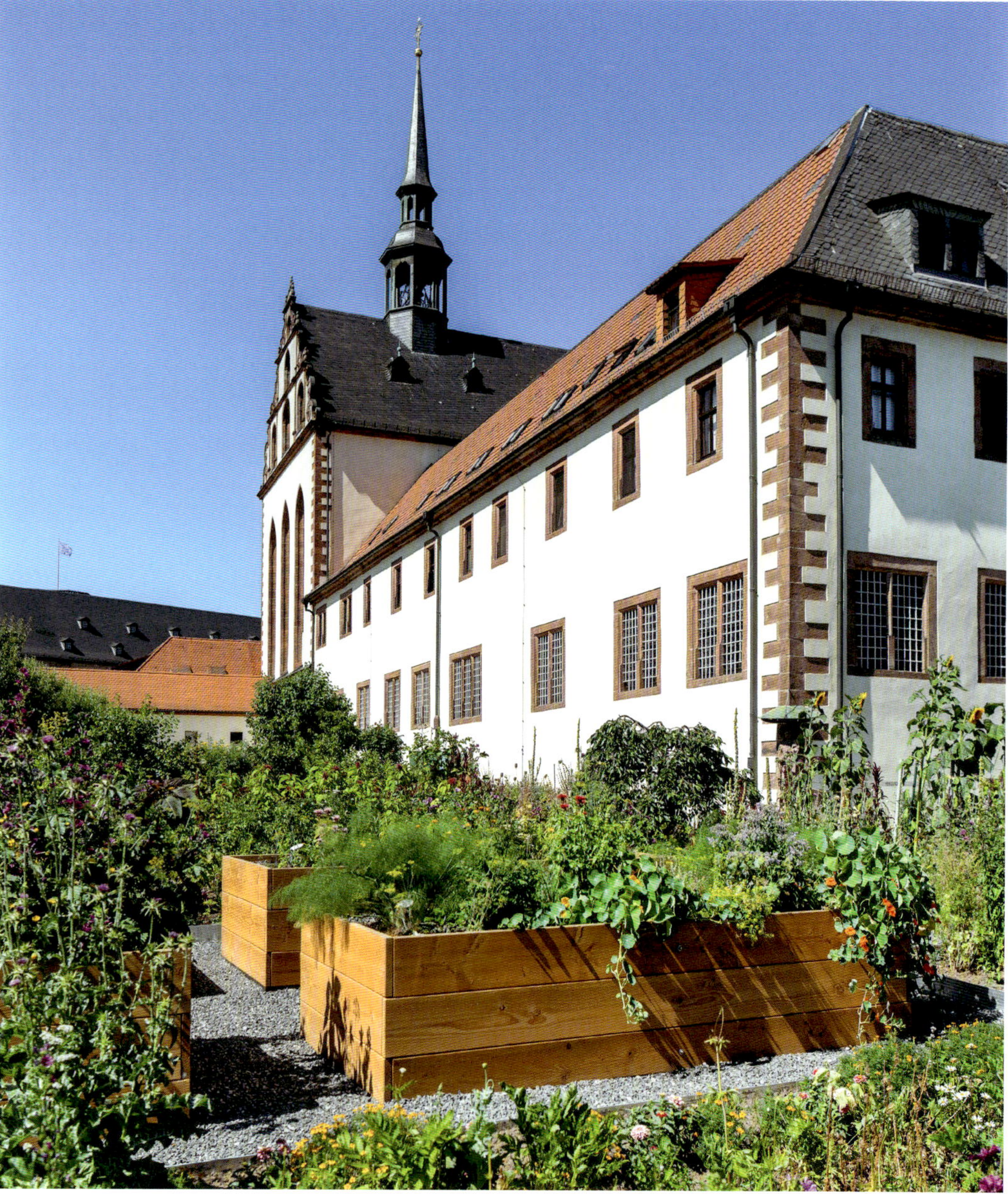

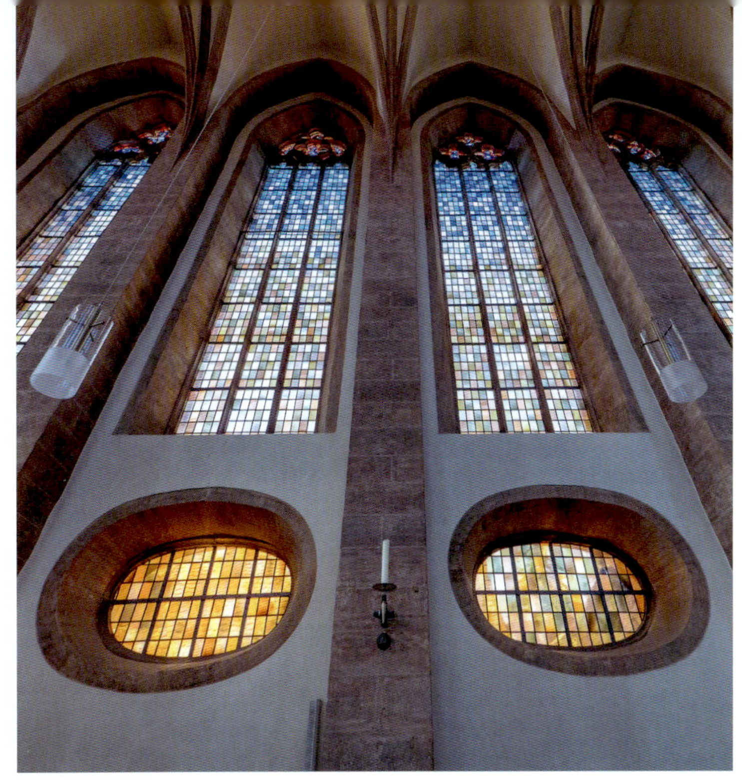

Die Klosterkirche (gebaut 1626–1631) ist eines der wichtigsten baulichen Zeugnisse aus der Zeit der Spätgotik und Renaissance in Fulda. Viele der sakralen Kunstwerke in der Kirche stammen aus der Werkstatt der Fuldaer Benediktinerin Lioba Munz (1913–1997), die jahrzehntelang in der Abtei lebte und arbeitete und als Künstlerin auch international große Wertschätzung erfuhr.

The convent church (built 1626–1631) is one of the most important examples of late Gothic and Renaissance architecture in Fulda. Much of the religious artwork in the church was created by the Fulda Benedictine nun Lioba Munz (1913–1997), an artist of international renown who lived and worked in the convent for many decades.

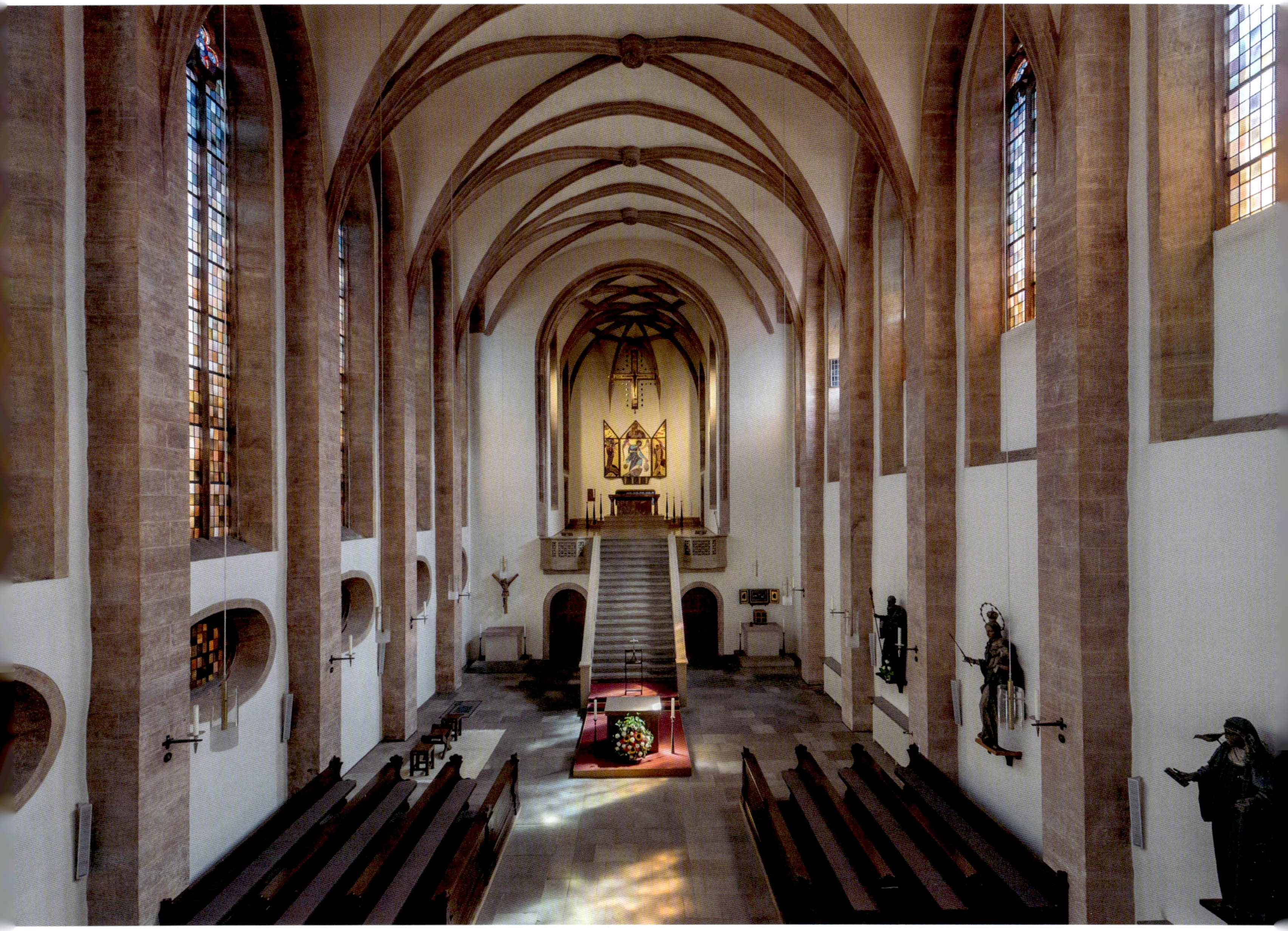

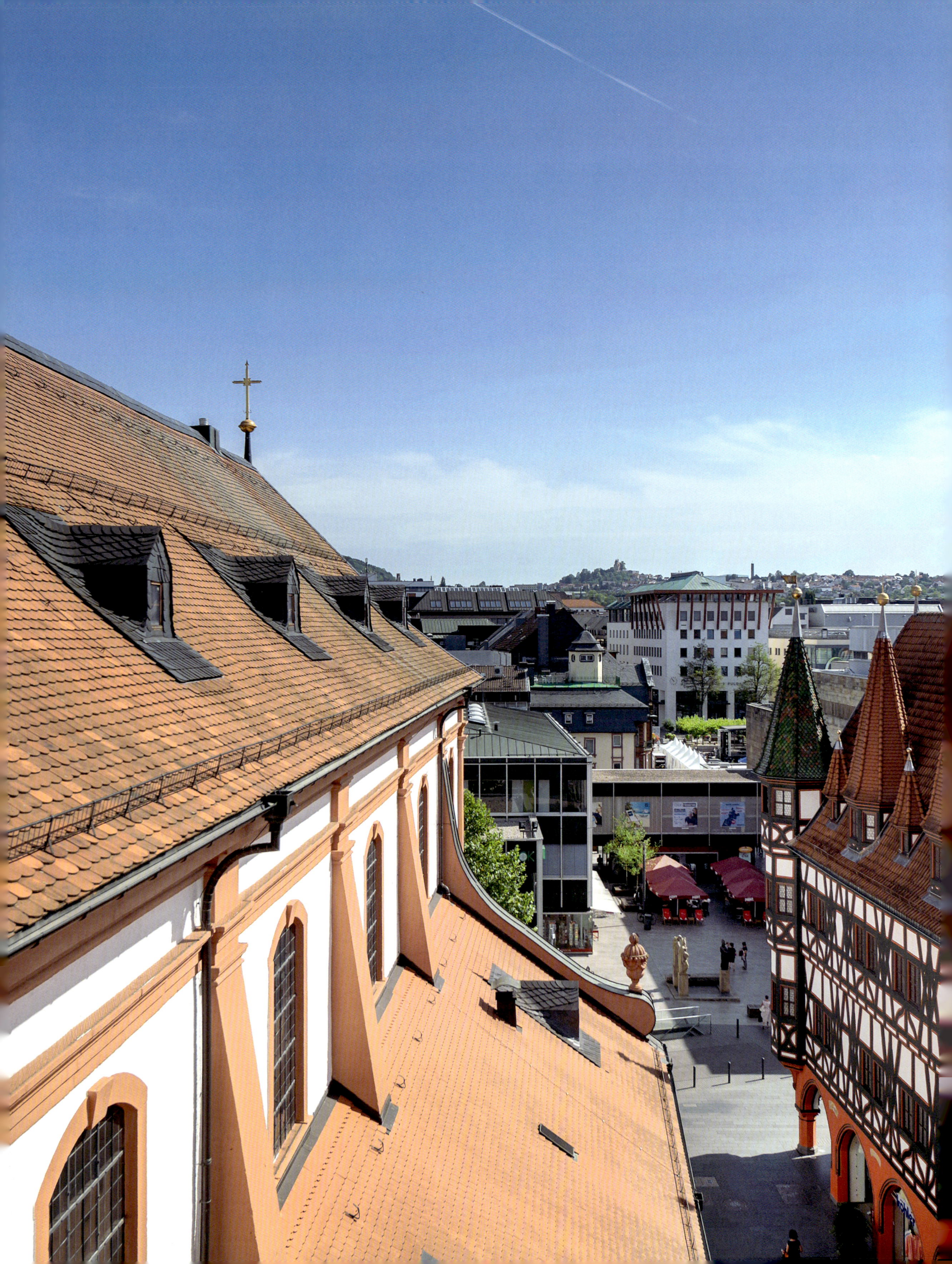

EIN ROT-WEISSER FIXPUNKT IM STADTBILD

Die Stadtpfarrkirche steht schon immer im Schatten des Domes, versprüht aber ihren eigenen Charme

August Heider wusste Bescheid: Der Maler, geboren 1775 in Fulda, wählte als Ausgangspunkt für die bekannten Panorama-Stadtansichten seiner Heimatstadt einen Ort, der kaum besser ausgesucht sein konnte: den südlichen Turm der Stadtpfarrkirche. Rund um diese Kirche schlägt seit Jahrhunderten das Herz der Bürgerstadt, der Standort am Ende der Friedrichstraße ist so prominent, dass so mancher Tourist die Stadtpfarrkirche zunächst für den Dom hält. Dabei stand und steht die Pfarrkirche – wie auch ihre Vorgängerbauten – immer im Schatten des Domes beziehungsweise der Stiftskirche. Während sich im alten Klosterbezirk so mancher Abt, Fürstabt oder Fürstbischof baulich ein Denkmal setzte, war es in der Stadt der Handwerker und Kaufleute, die sich im Mittelalter neben dem Kloster entwickelte, vor allem das Bürgertum, das seine wachsende Bedeutung mit dem Bau einer Kirche im wahrsten Sinne des Wortes untermauern wollte. Gleichwohl blieben die Pfarrkirchen weit bescheidener als die üppigen Sakralbauten der Landesherren oder der Klöster nebenan.

Als die Barockzeit sich schon stark ihrem Ende zuneigte, nahm man schließlich auch die damalige Pfarrkirche aus dem 15. Jahrhundert in den Blick, um sie jenem Stil anzupassen, der bereits seit Jahrzehnten der Stadt seinen Stempel aufdrückte. So entstand ab 1771 das spätbarocke Gotteshaus in seiner heutigen

Vom Südturm der Stadtpfarrkirche aus geht der Blick nach Osten über den Borgias- und den Universitätsplatz zum Petersberg mit der Grabeskirche der hl. Lioba.

View from the south tower of the Stadtpfarrkirche towards the east, stretching from Borgiasplatz and Universitätsplatz (in the foreground) to the burial church of St. Lioba in Petersberg.

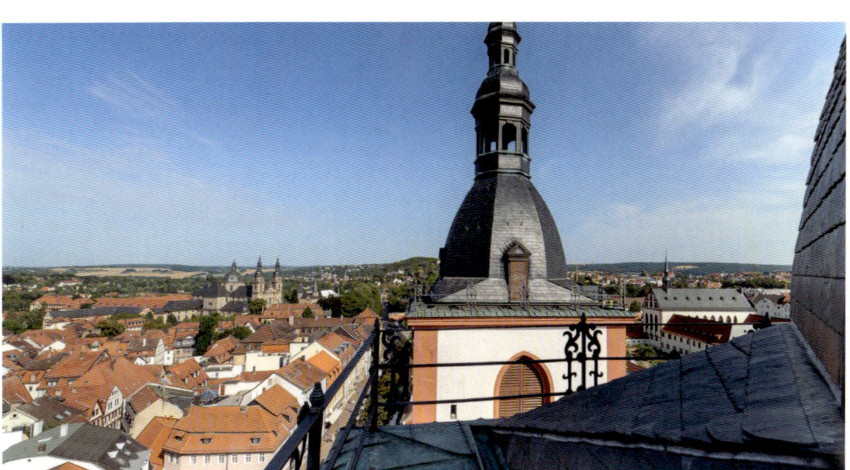

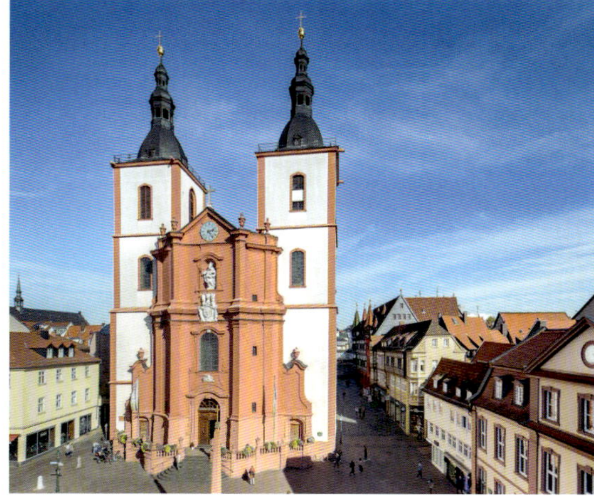

A Red and White Landmark in the City

The Stadtpfarrkirche (the city parish church) has always "stood in the shadow of" the cathedral, but it undoubtedly radiates its own charm.

August Heider knew what was what: the painter, born in Fulda in 1775, chose the best imaginable viewpoint for his well-known city panoramas: the south tower of the Stadtpfarrkirche. The heart of Fulda city life has been beating around this church for centuries. The church's location at the end of Friedrichstrasse is so prominent that tourists frequently mistake it for the cathedral. Yet the Stadtpfarrkirche – like all its preceding churches – was always in the shadow of the cathedral (or formerly the monastery church). While many an abbot, prince-abbot or prince-bishop created a monument to himself in the monastery area, it was the craftsmen and traders, the ever-increasing urban middle class, who wanted to express their growing importance by building an impressive church in the city. Nevertheless, the parish churches which were built in the city from the 10th century onwards were much more modest in design than the nearby religious buildings of the rulers and monastic communities. As the Baroque period was fast coming to end, it was finally decided to transform the old 15th century parish church so that it would fit in with style which had already dominated the city for decades. Thus, in 1771, the

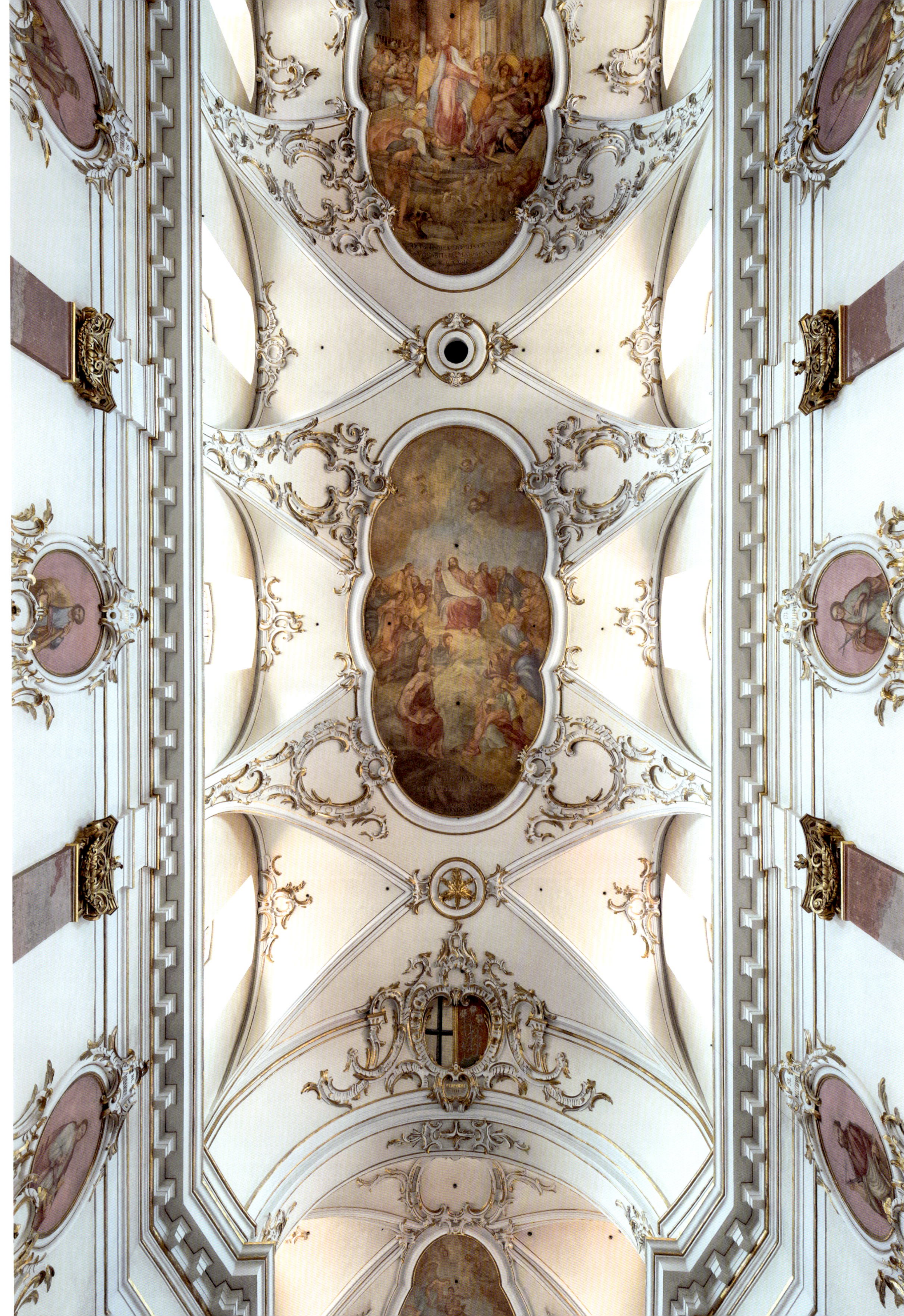

Form. Die charakteristische rot-weiße Farbgebung dürfte den Originalzustand aus der Bauzeit wiedergeben und bildet einen Fixpunkt im Stadtbild. Allerdings war das nicht immer so: Bis zu einer Außenrenovierung in den 1980er Jahren herrschte auch hier jener gelb-graue Putz vor, der auch am Schloss und an vielen Adelspalais zu finden war und der dem natürlichen Ton des Sandsteins nahekam. Als dann hinter den Planen der Verputzer das historisch belegte, kräftige Rot zum Vorschein kam, war die Aufregung in der Stadt groß. Doch die hat sich längst gelegt, und bei einer Umfrage würden heutzutage wahrscheinlich die meisten Fuldaer schwören, dass die Stadtpfarrkirche schon immer rot gewesen ist …

Viel fester im Gedächtnis der Stadt verankert ist indes jene Anekdote, dass einst eine kinderreiche Türmerfamilie im Südturm wohnte. Um sich die vielen Stufen nach unten zu sparen, hatte der Türmer eine Art Flaschenzugmechanik installiert, um Einkäufe nach oben zu transportieren – oder auch Schuhe, die der Turmwächter im Nebenberuf als Schuster reparierte.

late-Gothic church took on its current appearance. The characteristic red and white paintwork, considered to be original design, lends the church a strong presence in the city. This was not always the case: the church was formerly plastered yellow/grey until its exterior was renovated in the 1980s. When, during the renovation, the plasterers discovered the historically recorded, striking red colour while working behind their plastic sheets, it caused quite a stir in the city. The excitement has long since died down and if a survey was carried out today, it is likely that most Fulda people would swear that the church had always been red …

One anecdote which has remained much more firmly anchored in the public memory concerns the tower-keeper and his large family who lived in a flat high in the south tower. In order to avoid having to go up and down the many steps to his abode, the tower-keeper installed a block and tackle so that he could lift heavy purchases up the tower – in fact, shoes were often transported in this way as he also worked as a cobbler.

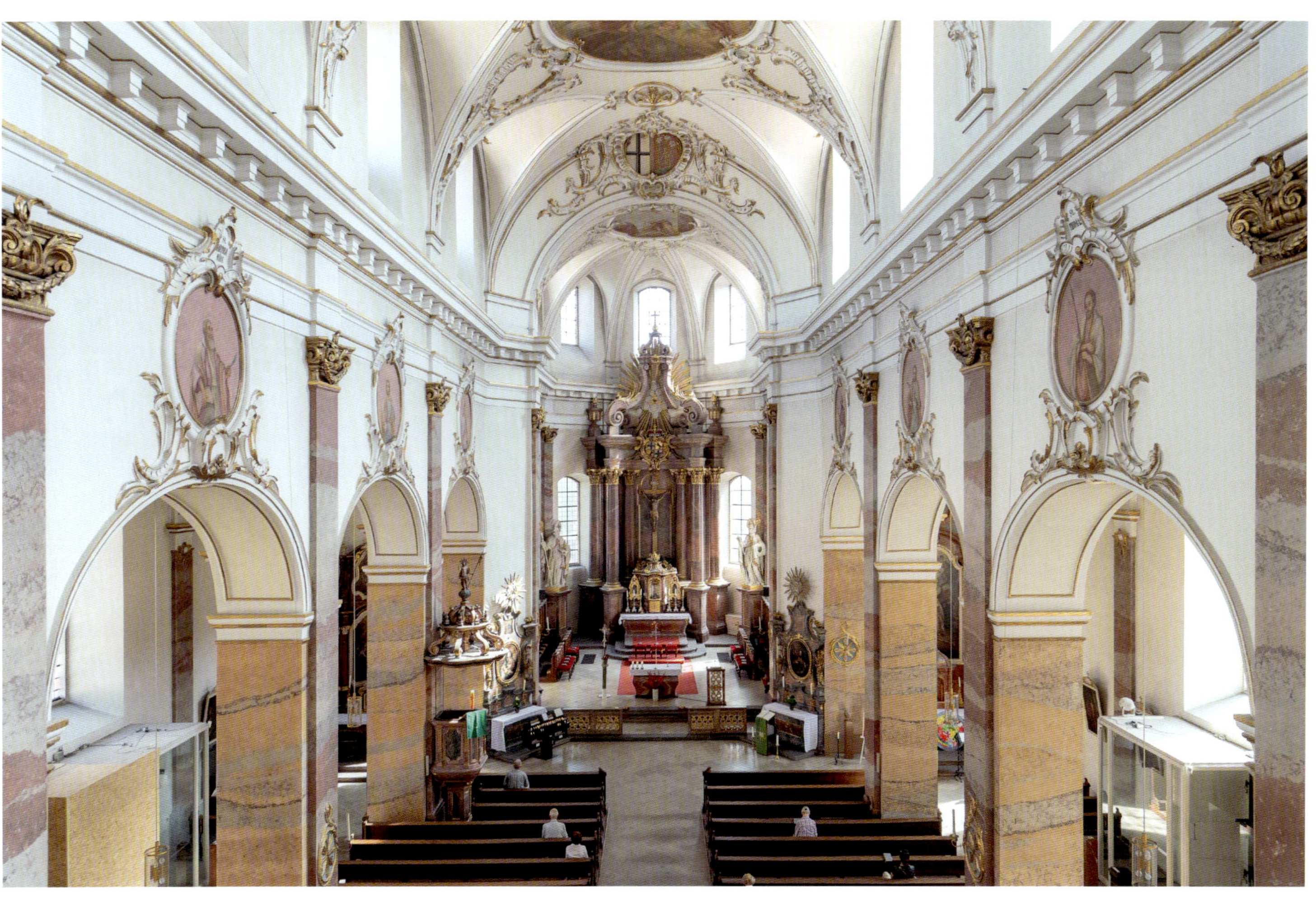

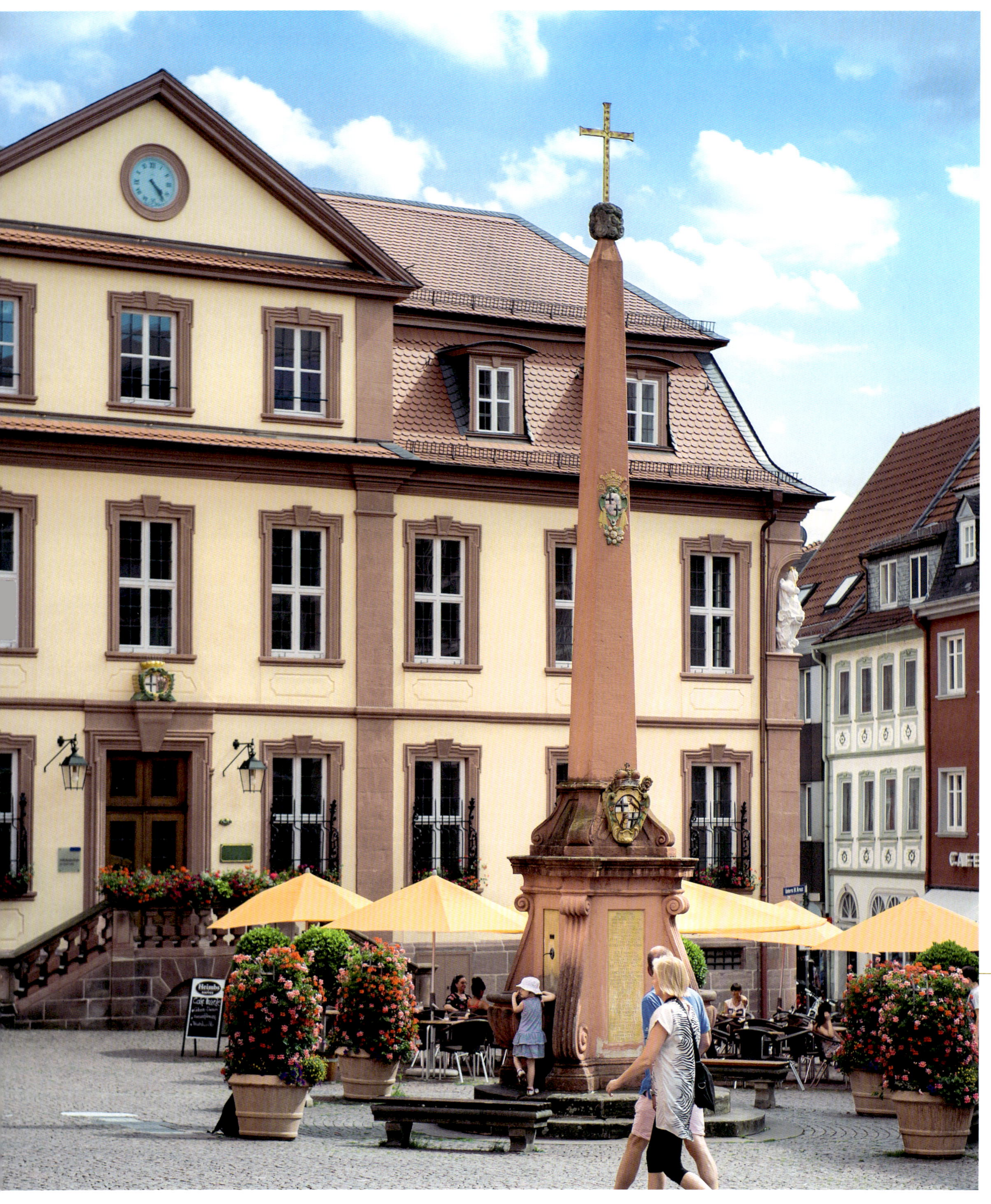

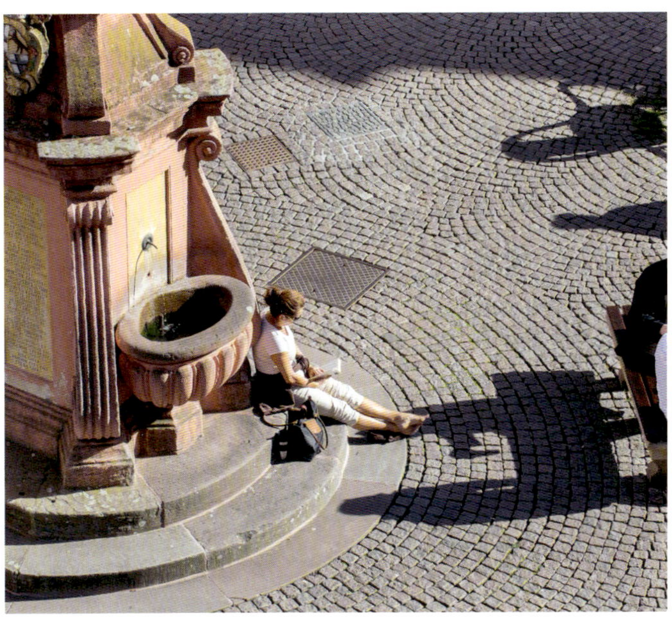

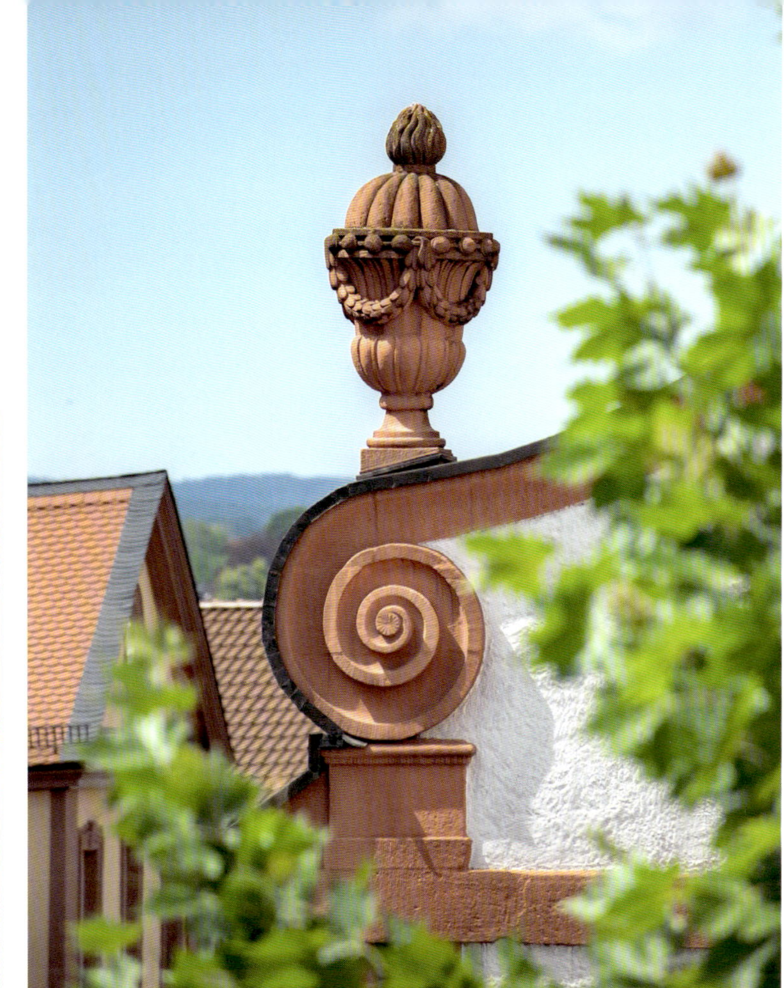

Der Platz „Unterm Heilig Kreuz" wird geprägt von der Stadtpfarrkirche und dem sogenannten Kanzlerpalais. In dem Gebäude von 1735 wohnten einst hohe Beamte des Fuldaer Hofs, später war dort – bis zum Umzug in das Stadtschloss – die Stadtverwaltung untergebracht. Heute ist das Palais unter anderem Sitz der Volkshochschule.

This square "Unterm Heilig Kreuz" is dominated by the Stadtpfarrkirche and the Kanzlerpalais, a building from 1735, in which high-ranking court official once lived. Later the Kanzlerpalais was used as the town hall and now it is the Volkshochschule (the adult education centre).

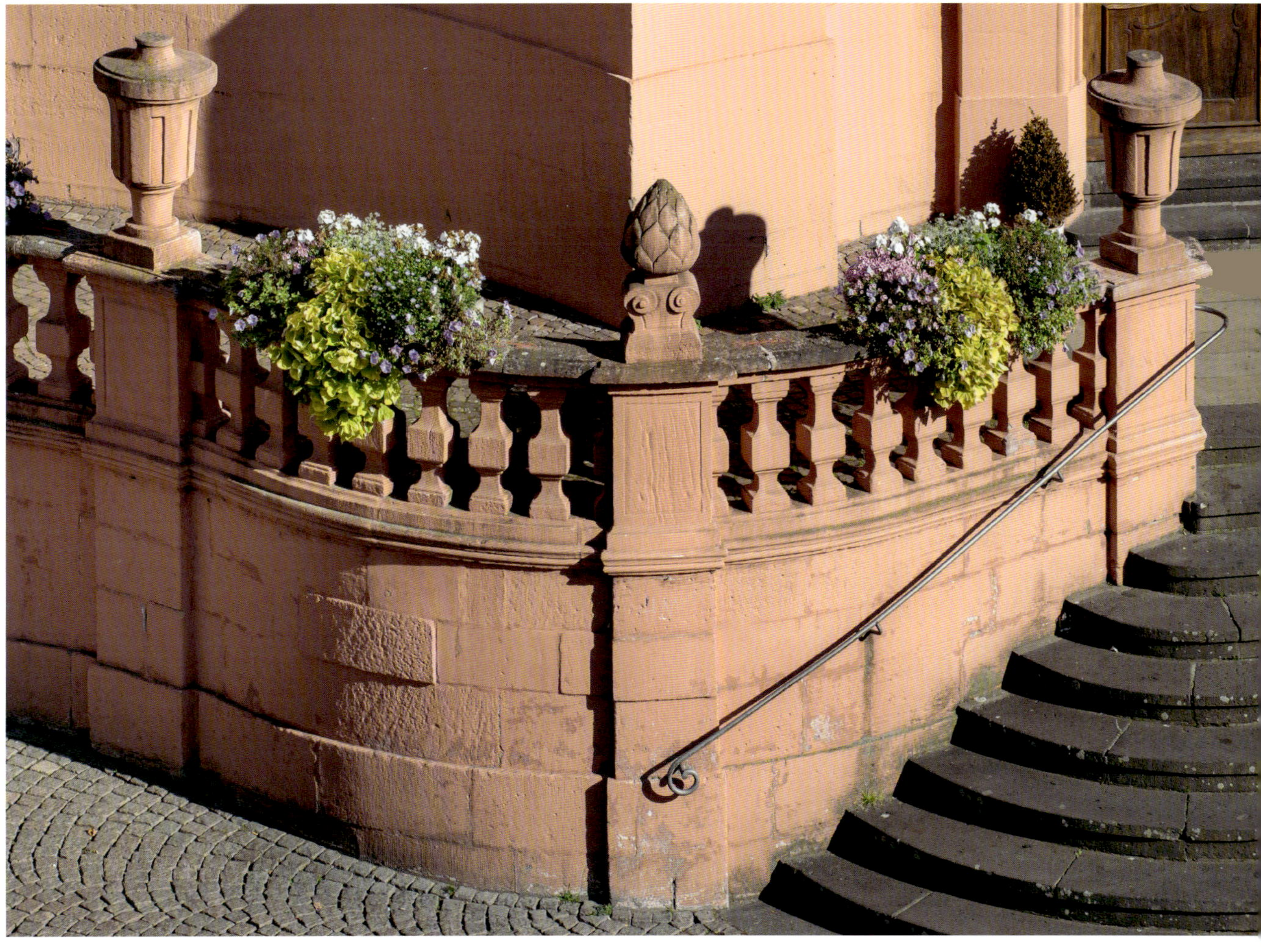

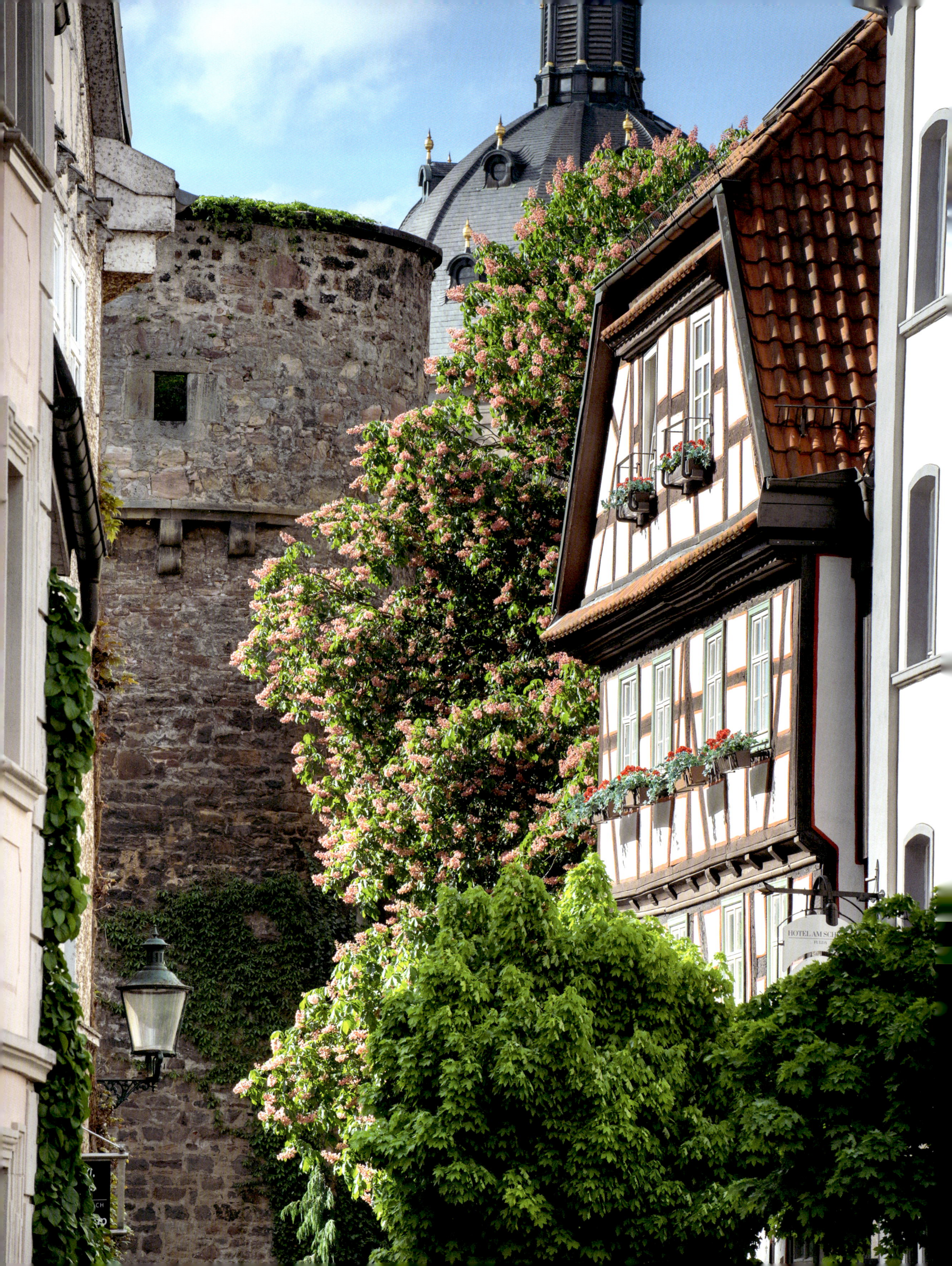
HOTEL AM
FULDA

FACHWERKIDYLLE, IN DER DAS LEBEN PULSIERT

In der Altstadt dominierte einst das Handwerk, heute sind Handel und Gastronomie bestimmend

Bilderbuchansicht aus der Kanalstraße über den Hexenturm auf die Domkuppel. Bei dem Fachwerkhaus rechts handelt es sich um das Geburtshaus des Fuldaer Physikers, Fernsehtechnik-Pioniers und Nobelpreisträgers des Jahres 1909, Ferdinand Braun (1850–1918).

A picture book view from the Kanalstraße over the Witches' Tower to the cathedral dome. The half-timbered house on the right is the birth house of the Fulda physicist, Ferdinand Braun (1850-1918), a pioneer of television technology and Nobel Prize winner in1909.

Ein gewöhnlicher Samstagvormittag am Severiberg: Eine Besuchergruppe hat vor dem gotischen Kirchlein gestoppt, die Stadtführerin erläutert die Besonderheiten; weiter oben am „Roten Löwen" scharen sich weitere Touristen um ihren Gästeführer, fotografieren die pittoresken Gassen; und schon biegt am Mutterhaus der Vinzentinerinnen die nächste Gruppe aus der Kanalstraße um die Ecke. Dazwischen tragen Anwohner ihre Einkäufe vom Gemüsemarkt nach Hause, starten Einkäufer aus dem Umland ihre Shoppingtour. Fuldas Altstadt lebt, die liebevoll renovierten Fachwerkbauten sind kein Museum, hinter den Fassaden wohnen Menschen, in den Erdgeschossen gibt es noch kleine Handwerksbetriebe, einen Bäcker, einen Schuhmacher, einen Restaurator. Kleine Geschäfte und Cafés runden das Bild ab.

Hier war schon im Mittelalter das Zentrum der Stadt der „kleinen Leute". Etliche Gebäude sind aus dieser Zeit erhalten geblieben oder wurden rekonstruiert, die schmalen Kopfsteinpflaster-Gassen tun ein Übriges, um die historische Illusion ein wenig zu schüren. Doch hat Fulda kein geschlossenes Fachwerkviertel wie viele Städte in Nord- und Oberhessen, vielmehr prägt ein Mix aus mittelalterlichen und barocken Steinbauten, Fachwerkhäusern und modernen Gebäuden das Bild in der Altstadt. Die Mischung macht's, in der Idylle pulsiert das Leben. Das gilt insbesondere für die Abendstunden im sogenannten Bermuda-Dreieck im Bereich Kanalstraße/Karlstraße, wo eine junge Szene die gastronomischen Angebote bestimmt. In puncto Kneipendichte kann Fulda ohnehin mit den großen Studentenstädten konkurrieren, und in der Altstadt mit ihren vielen Restaurants und Bars dürfte lukullisch wirklich jeder auf seine Kosten kommen. Häufig befinden sich die Lokale in historischen Gebäuden, was dazu beiträgt, dass viele Straßenzüge zwischen Hexenturm, Buttermarkt und Löherstraße nicht museal, sondern erfrischend lebendig wirken. Die Grenzen der Altstadt, die älteren Fuldaer benutzen übrigens eher den Begriff „Unterstadt", lassen sich bis heute

An Idyllic Cluster of Medieval Houses that Bustles with Life

Once a centre for the crafts, today the old town is more associated with shops and restaurants

A typical Saturday morning on Severiberg: a group of tourists stops in front of the small Gothic church and the guide explains the features of the building. Further up the hill another group gathers around a guide by the house "Zum Roten Löwen" and takes photos of the pretty alleyways. A little later the next group turns the corner of the Kanalstrasse opposite the convent of the Daughters of Charity. Meanwhile, local residents return home from the vegetable market laden with bags, and shoppers from the surrounding area start on their ways. Fulda's old town is full of life – the lovingly restored half-timbered houses are by no means a museum; people live here behind the beautiful façades. On the ground floor of these buildings you can still find small craft businesses – a baker, a shoemaker and a restorer. To complete the picture there are also small shops and cafés.

In the Middle Ages this was the centre of the city for the commoners. The combination of the many surviving, or reconstructed, buildings from this period and the narrow, cobbled alleys very much creates the illusion of a medieval town. However, Fulda does not have a complete quarter with half-timbered houses like in many cities in north and west Hesse. Instead, the old town consists of a mosaic of medieval, Baroque and modern buildings. The combination does it - within the romantic idyll, bustling life! This is particularly the case in the "Bermuda Triangle", in the area between Kanalstraße and Karlstraße, where restaurants and bars cater to the tastes of the younger generation. When it comes to ratio of pubs per person, Fulda need not shy comparison with larger university cities. In the old town all tastes are catered for in the numerous bars and restaurants which are often located in historical buildings, a fact which contributes to making the area between the Hexenturm, Buttermarkt and

gut im Stadtplan ablesen: Der Verlauf der ab 1160 errichteten Stadtmauer, die über Jahrhunderte der Expansion der Stadt enge Schranken setzte, paust sich noch immer durch; Straßenzüge wie die Rangstraße, die Rabanusstraße oder die Königstraße verlaufen in etwa im Bereich der früheren Stadtgräben, an einigen Stellen sind noch Reste der Mauer und Türme erhalten. 1600 Meter lang war die historische Befestigung, und es lohnt ein kleiner Rundgang auf der Suche nach den sichtbaren und den versteckten Relikten, die zum Teil in privaten Häusern verborgen sind.

Löherstraße refreshingly lively – less like a museum. The borders of the old town, known to older Fulda residents as “Unterstadt” (“the lower town”), can be clearly identified on the city map: the course of the city wall, which was first erected in 1160 and which formed the limits of the city for centuries, can still be traced today. The streets Rangstrasse, Rabanusstrasse and Königstrasse all ran alongside the old city moat. In some places you can still see the remaining parts of the wall and towers. The city wall was 1600 metres long and it is well worth the short walk to discover the visible and hidden remnants of the wall, which sometimes now form parts of private houses.

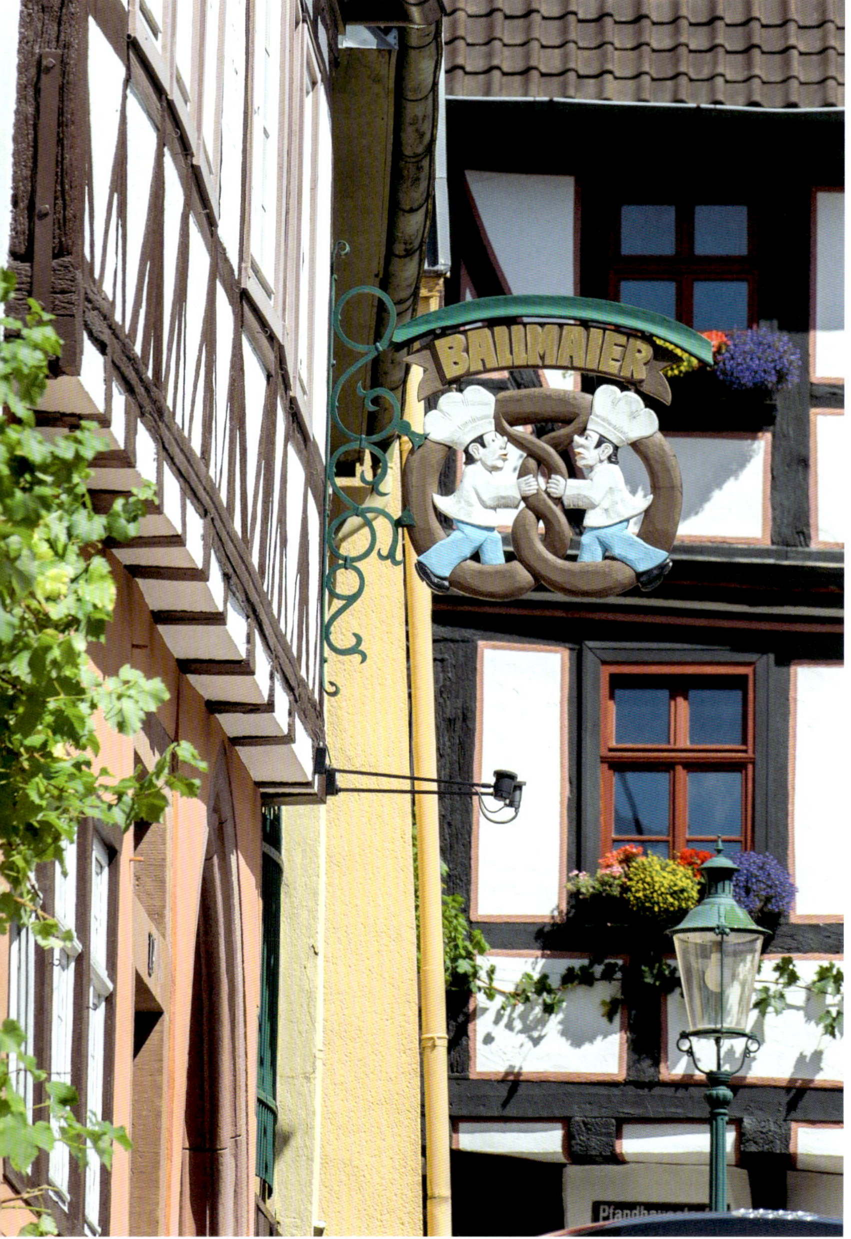

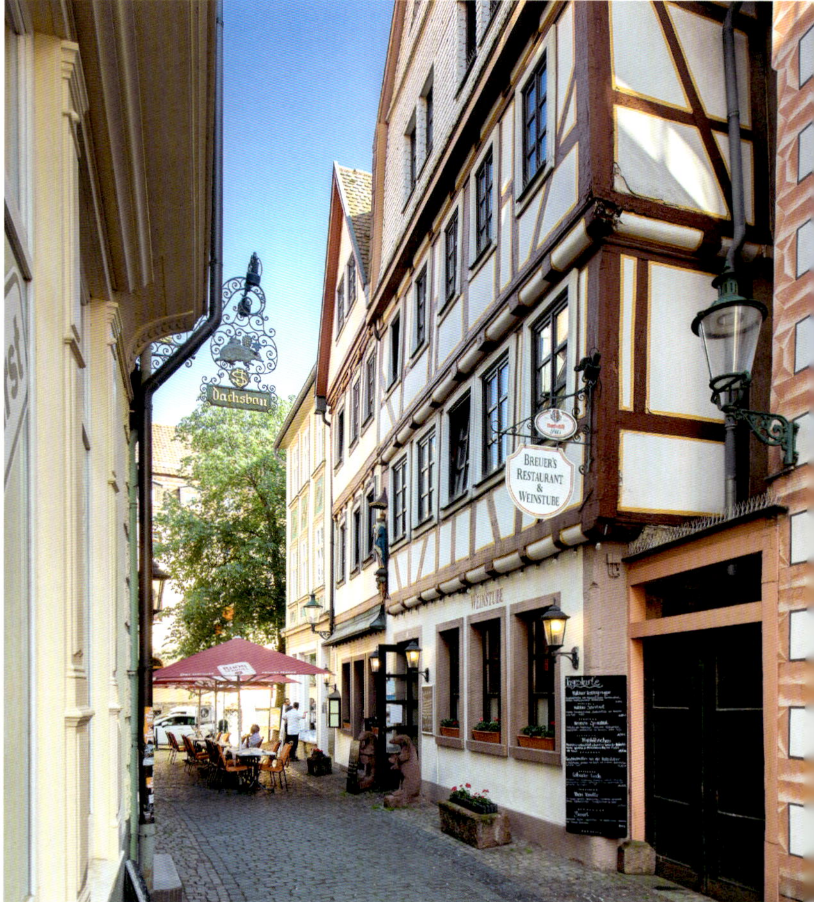

In den Fachwerkgassen rund um den Severiberg und den Luckenberg ist das bürgerliche Fulda am ursprünglichsten erhalten

Fulda old town is best preserved in the medieval alleys in and around Severiberg and Luckenberg.

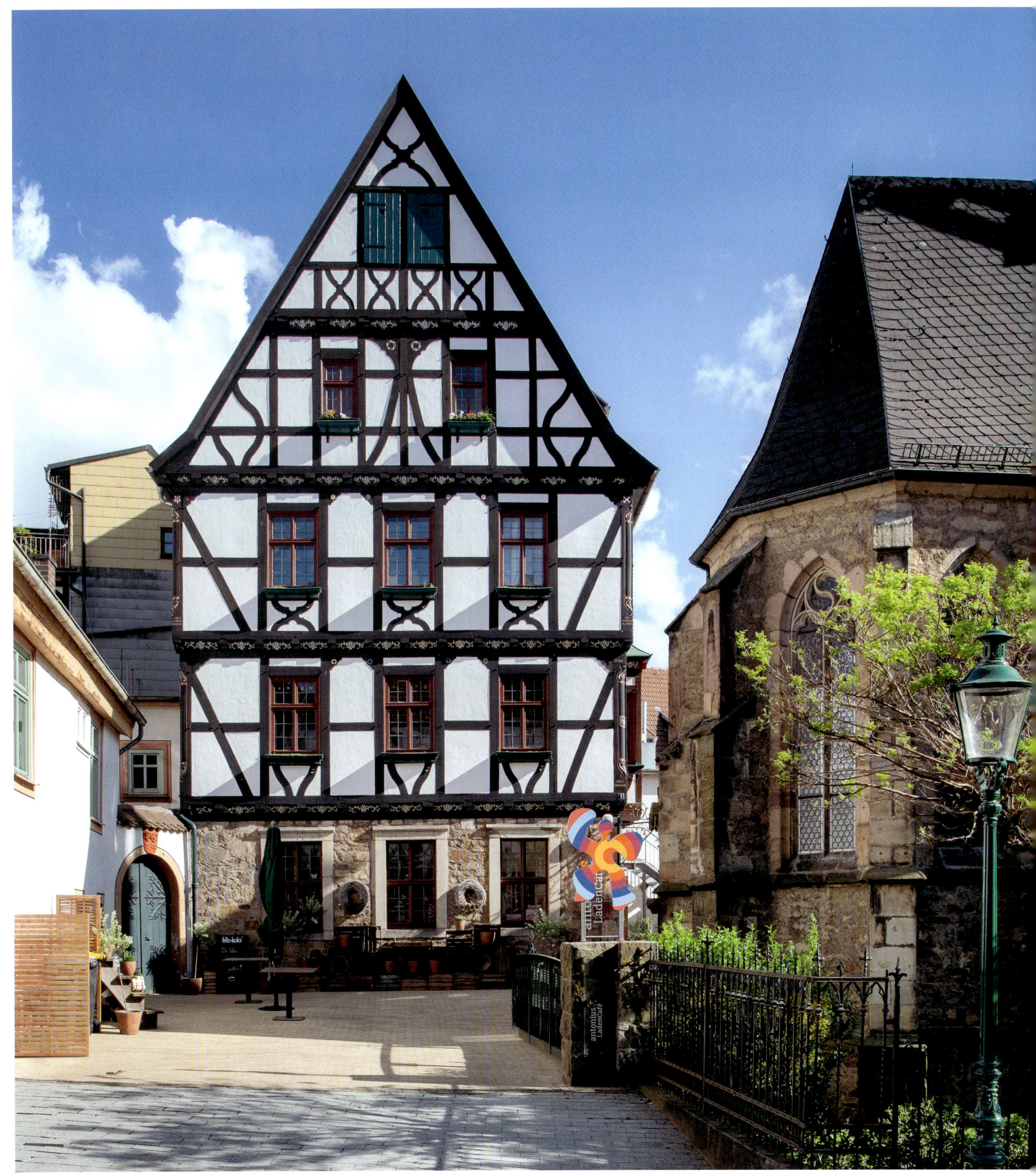
antonius
Ladencafé

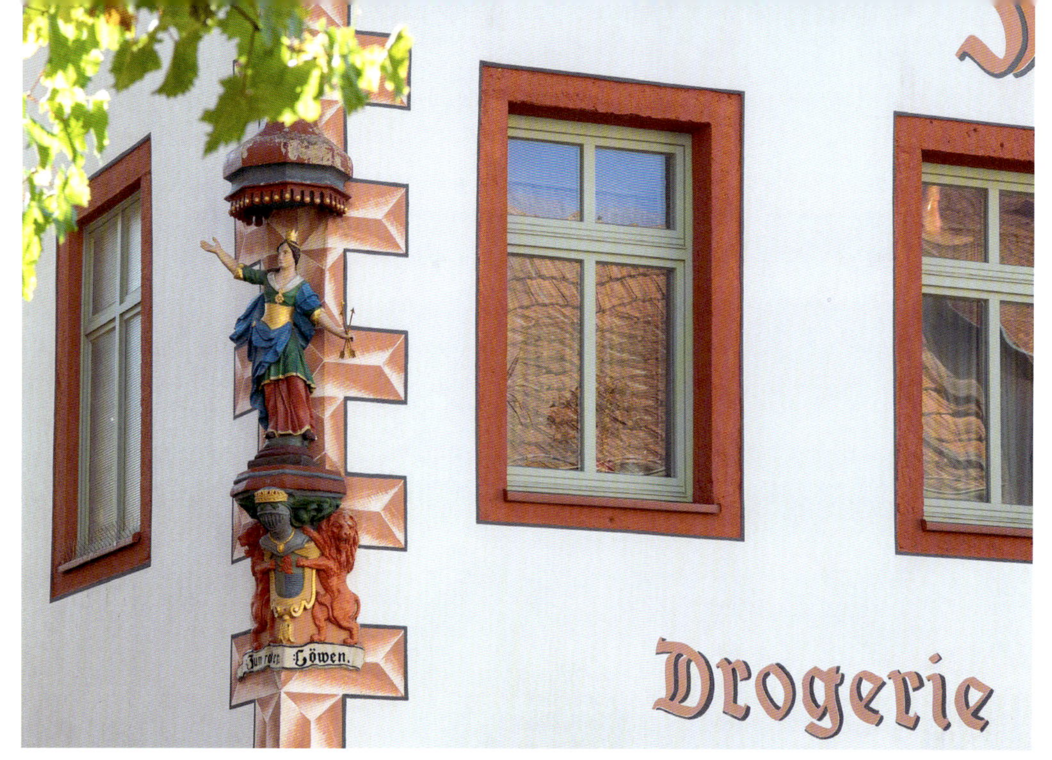

Die Severikirche steht als Paradebeispiel für die in Fulda ansonsten rar vertretene Bauepoche der Gotik. Die Kirche, 1438 bis 1445 erbaut, war die Zunftkirche der Wollweber, deren Schutzpatron wiederum der hl. Severus war, daher leitet sich bis heute der Name ab.

The Severikirche is the finest example of Gothic architecture in Fulda, a style which is rare here. The church, built between 1438 and 1445, was the guild church of the wool weavers, whose patron saint was St. Severus – hence the name of the church.

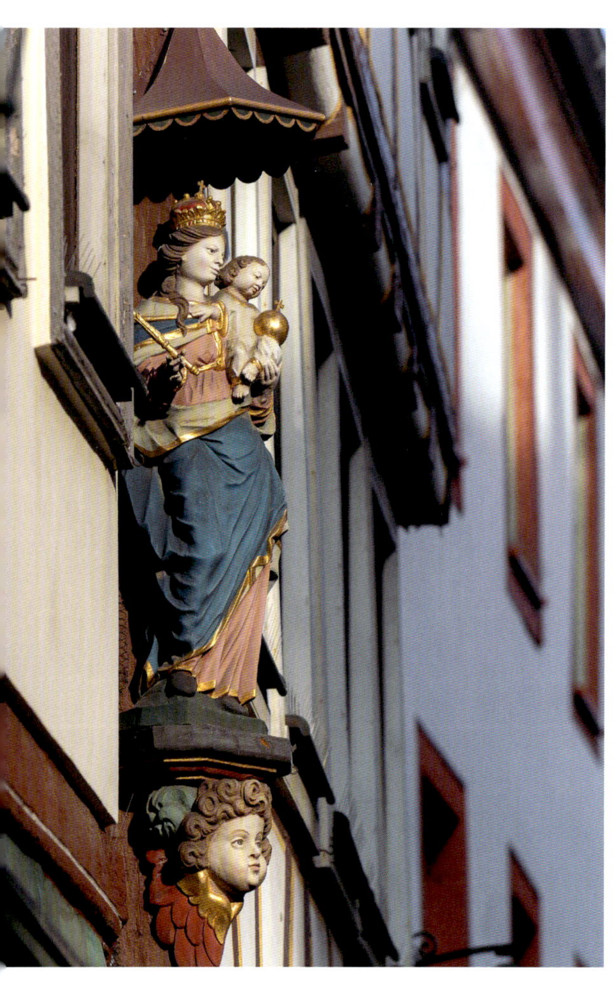

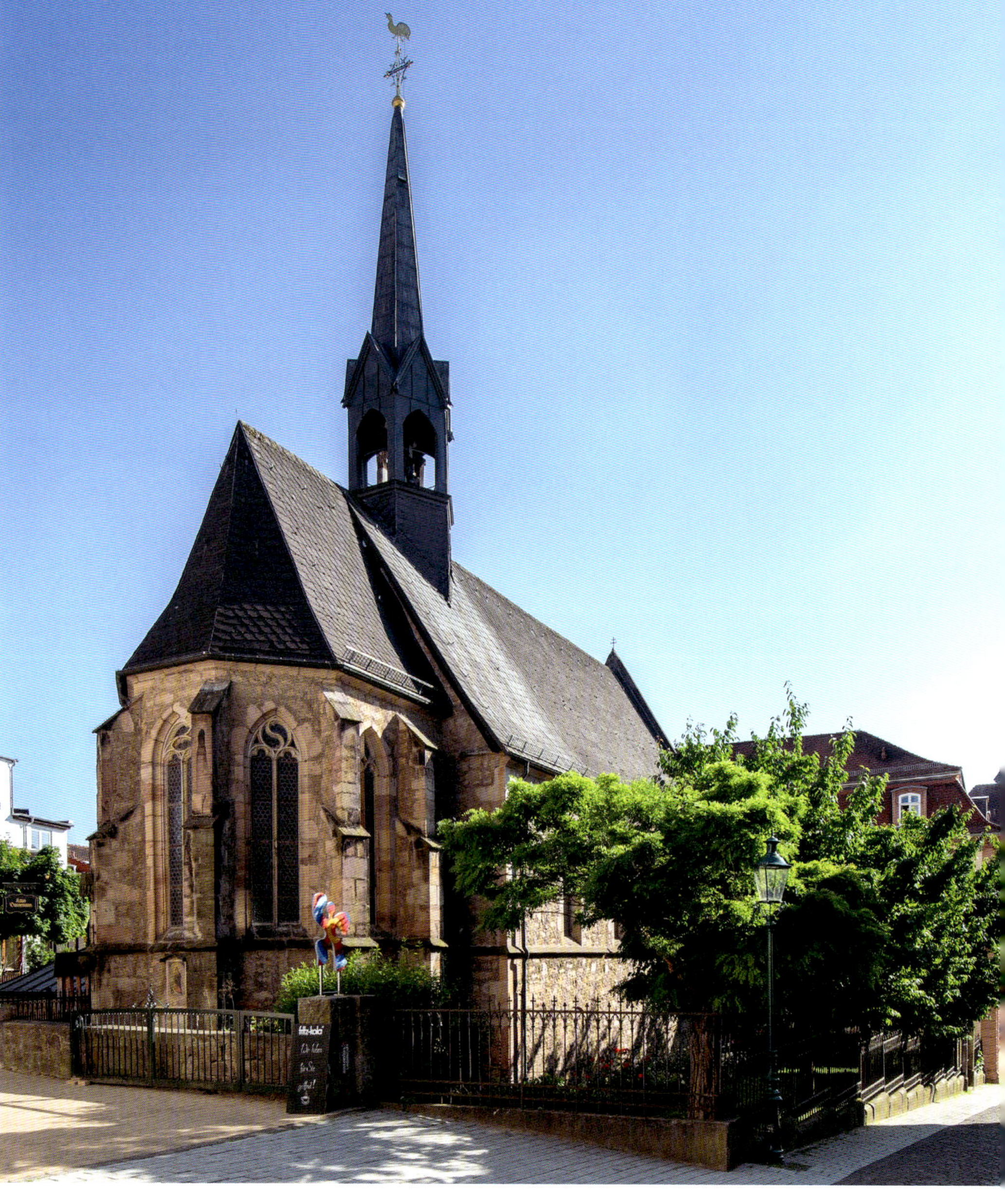

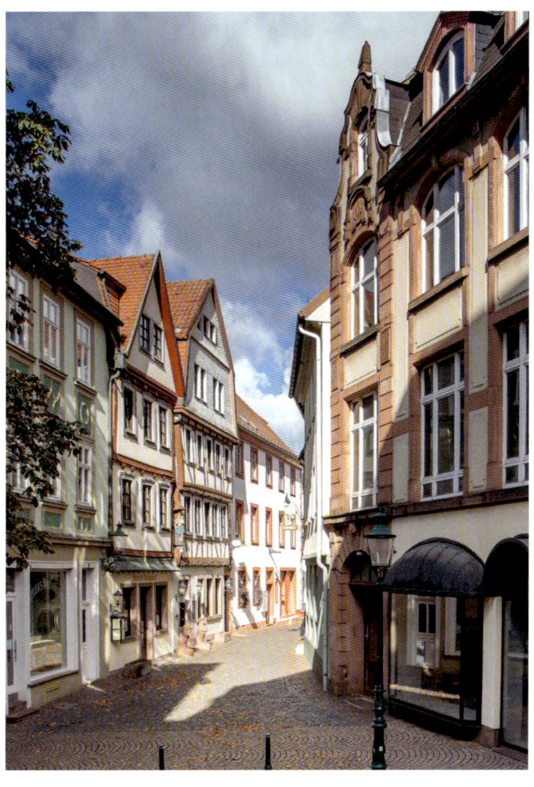

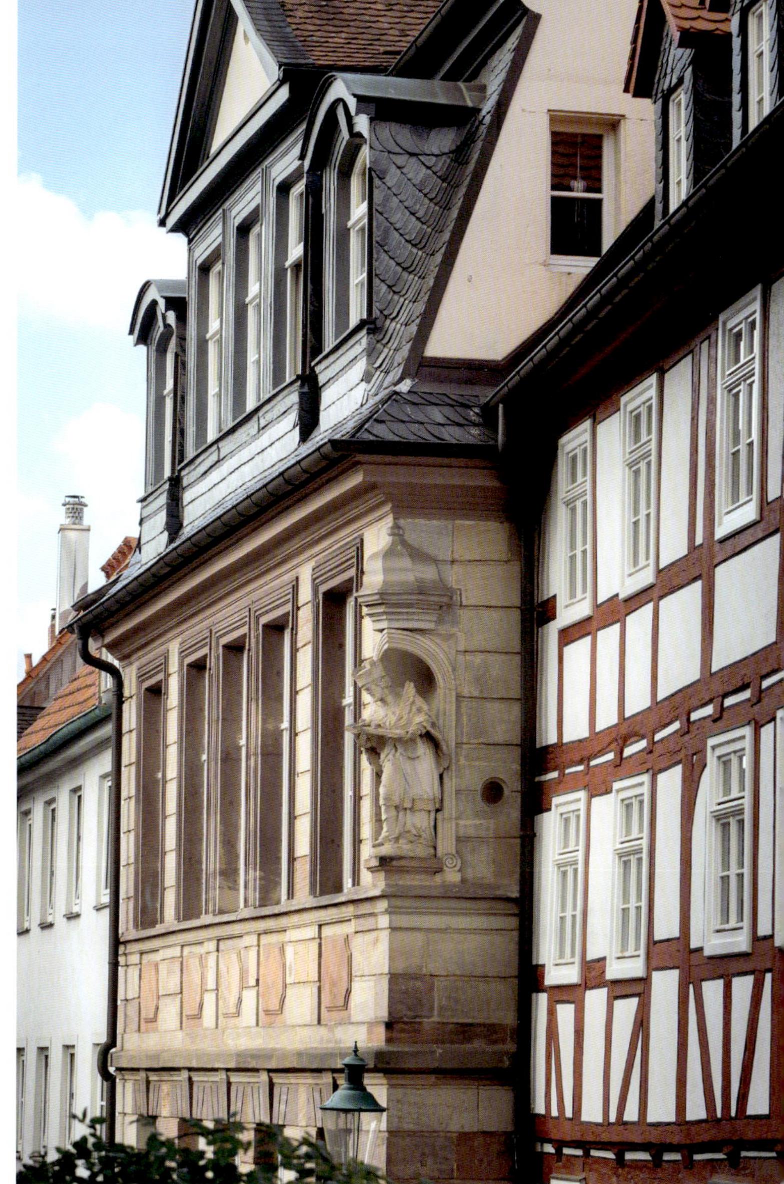

Im sogenannten Dientzenhofer-Haus (oben, rechts) wohnte der berühmte Baumeister – und konnte durch ein kleines Guckloch, das bis heute erhalten ist, die Baufortschritte am Stadtschloss begutachten.

The famous architect Johann Dientzenhofer lived in this house (top right). He could check the progress in the construction of the Residence through a small window which you can still see on the side of the house.

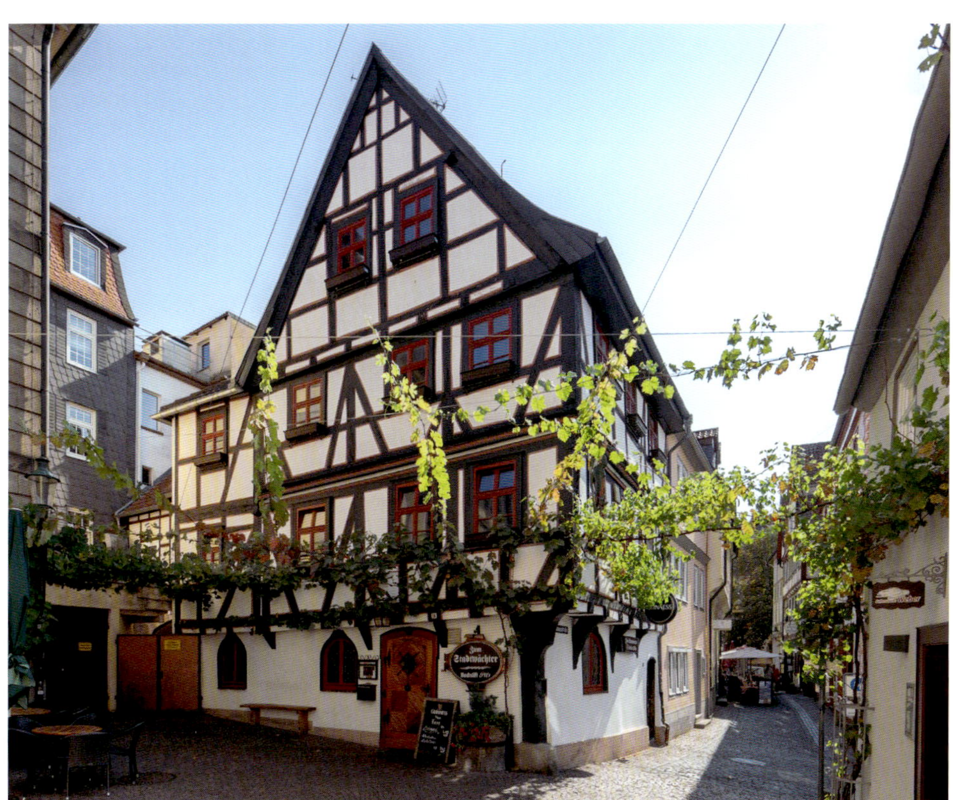

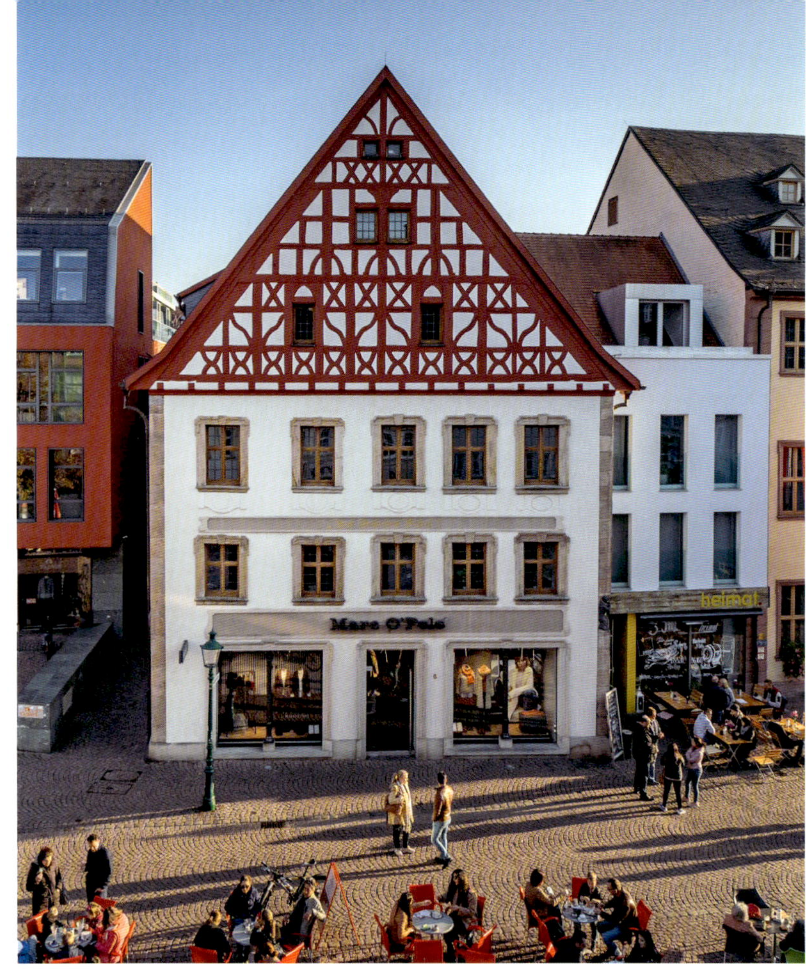

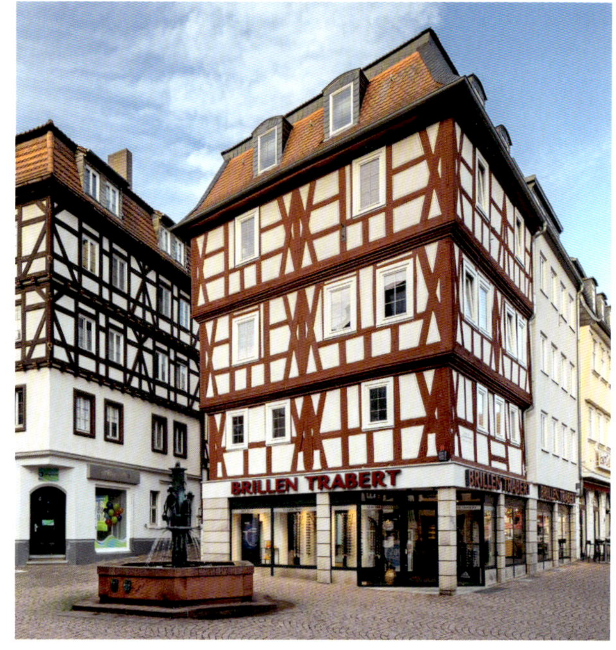

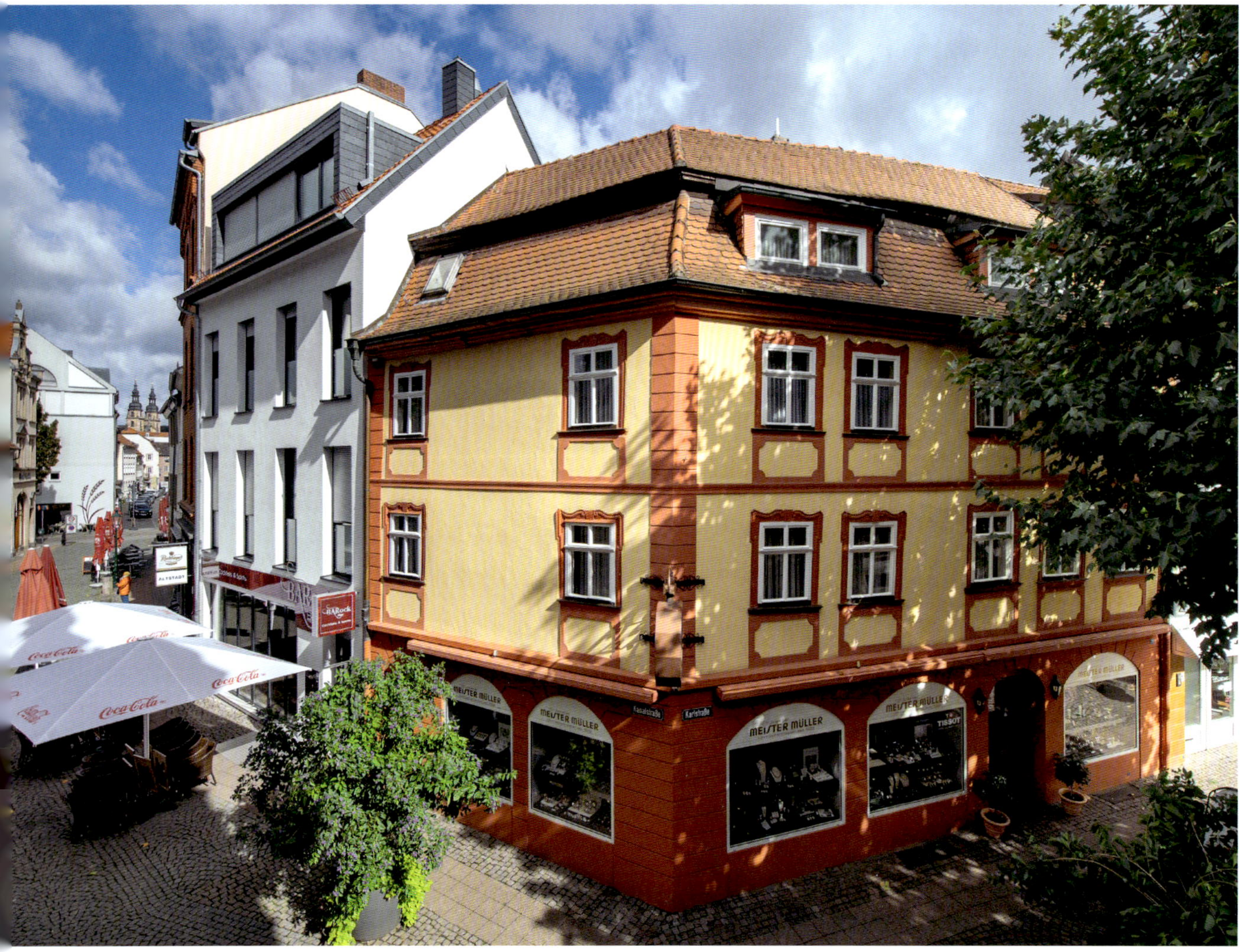

Der Buttermarkt (oben) und das sogenannte Bermudadreieck sind beliebte Treffpunkte in der Stadt.

The Buttermarkt (top photo) and the "Bermuda Triangle" are popular meeting points.

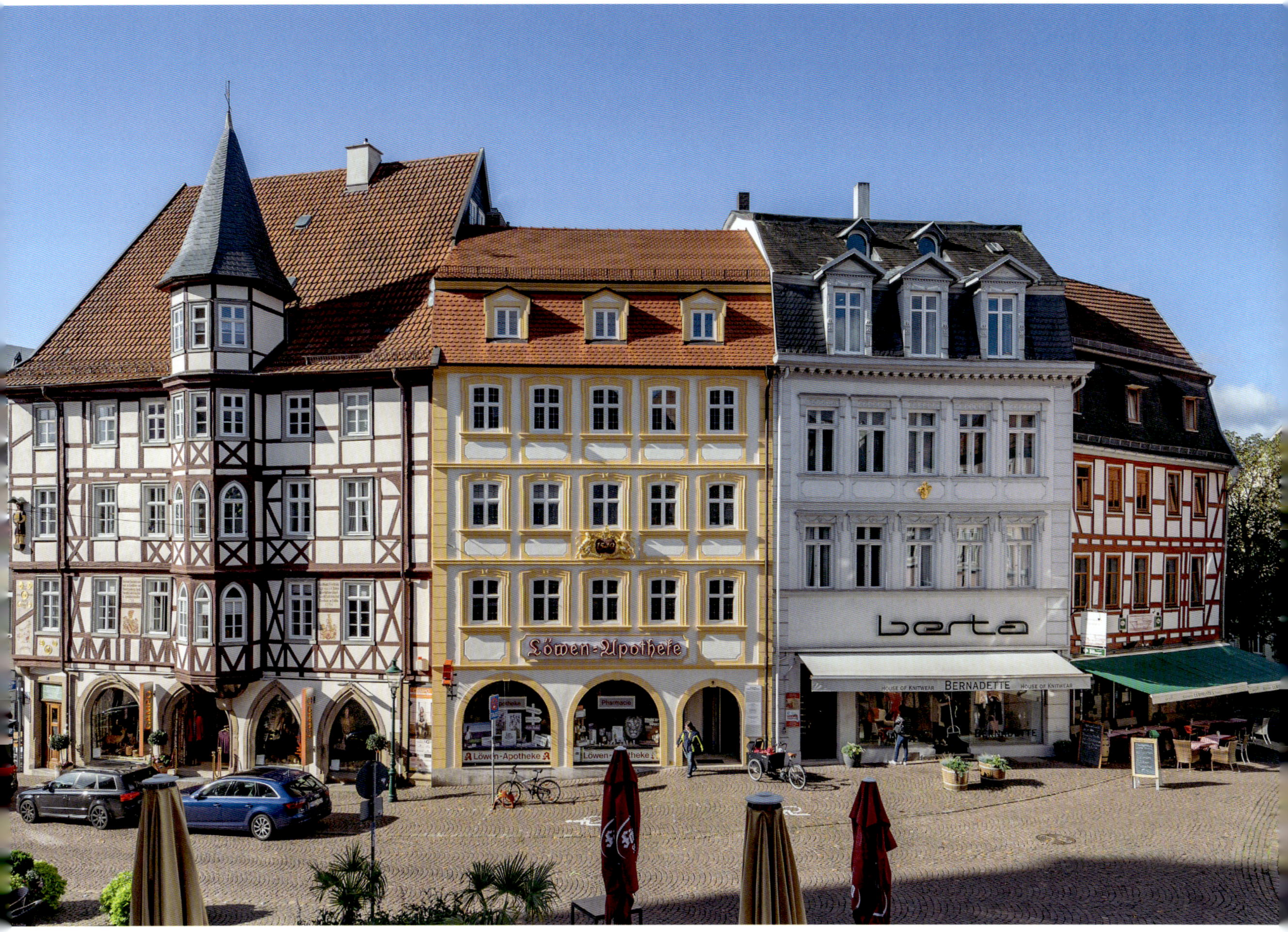

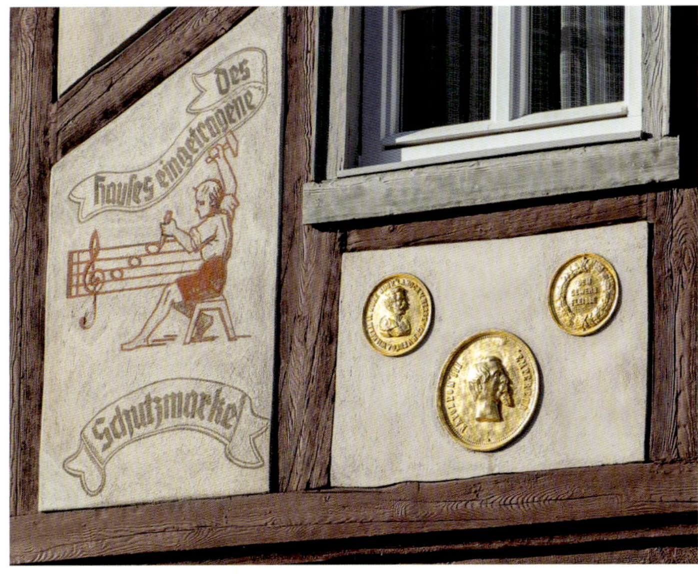

Das stattliche Fachwerkhaus (links im Bild) wurde 1540 im Auftrag von Fürstabt Johann von Henneberg als Salzlagerstätte errichtet. Vielen Einheimischen ist es als „Mollenhauer-Haus" vertraut, da hier jahrzehntelang die berühmte Fuldaer Instrumentenbauerfamilie ihre Werkstatt und ihren Stammsitz hatte. Blockflöten aus Fulda sind auch heute noch international ein Begriff. Das „Berta-Haus" steht wiederum für die einst florierende Fuldaer Kerzenindustrie, die Produkte der Firmen Berta, Eika, Gies und Rübsam gingen in die ganze Welt.

The impressive half-timbered house (on the left of the photo) was constructed as a salt warehouse in 1540. In Fulda it is known as the Mollenhauer House because, for many decades, it was the company office and workshop of the famous family of instrument-makers. Still today, recorders produced by Mollenhauer in Fulda enjoy an international reputation. The nearby Berta House is a reminder of the once flourishing candle industry in Fulda. The products of the companies Berta, Eika, Gies and Rübsam were exported throughout the world.

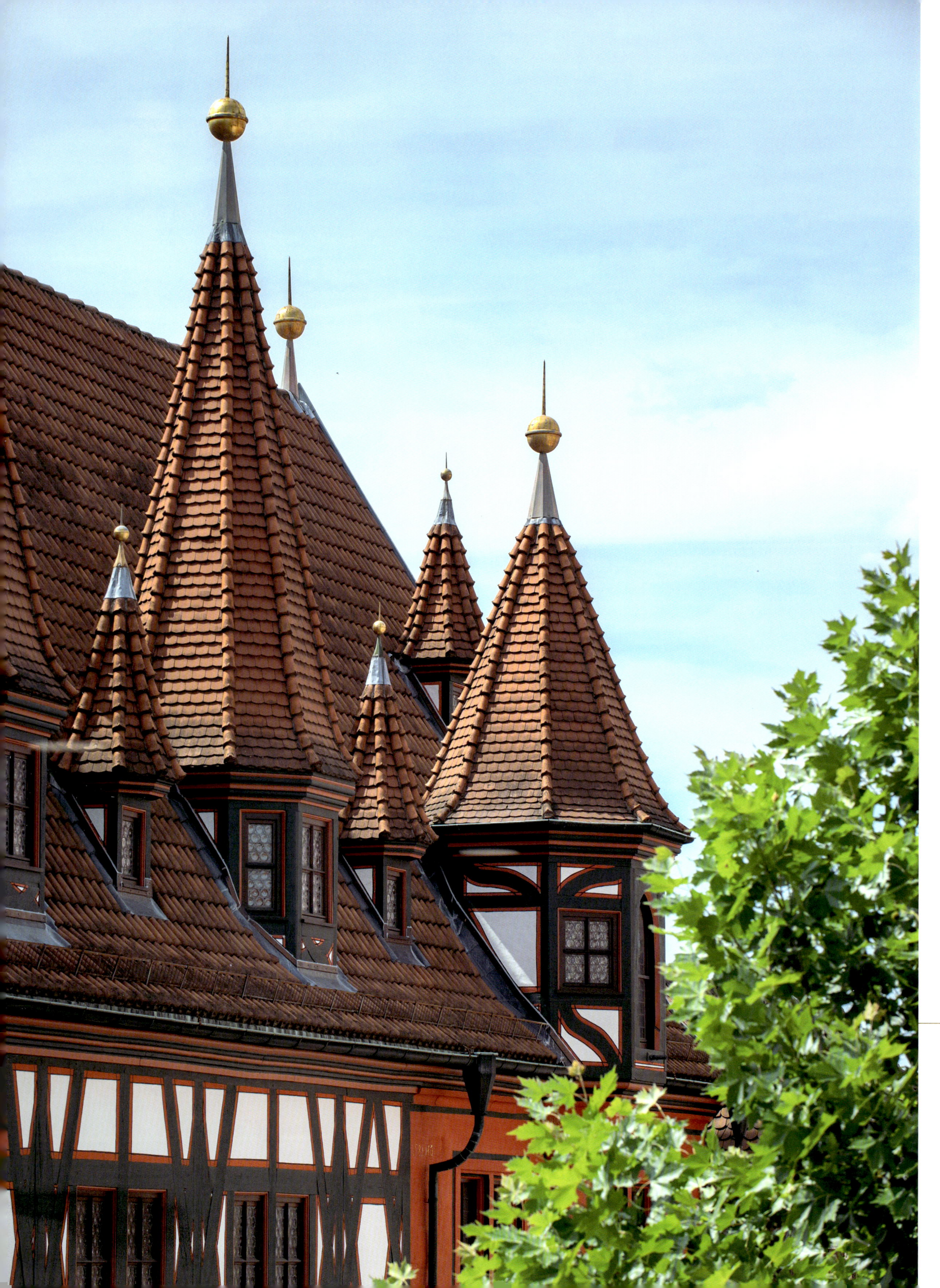

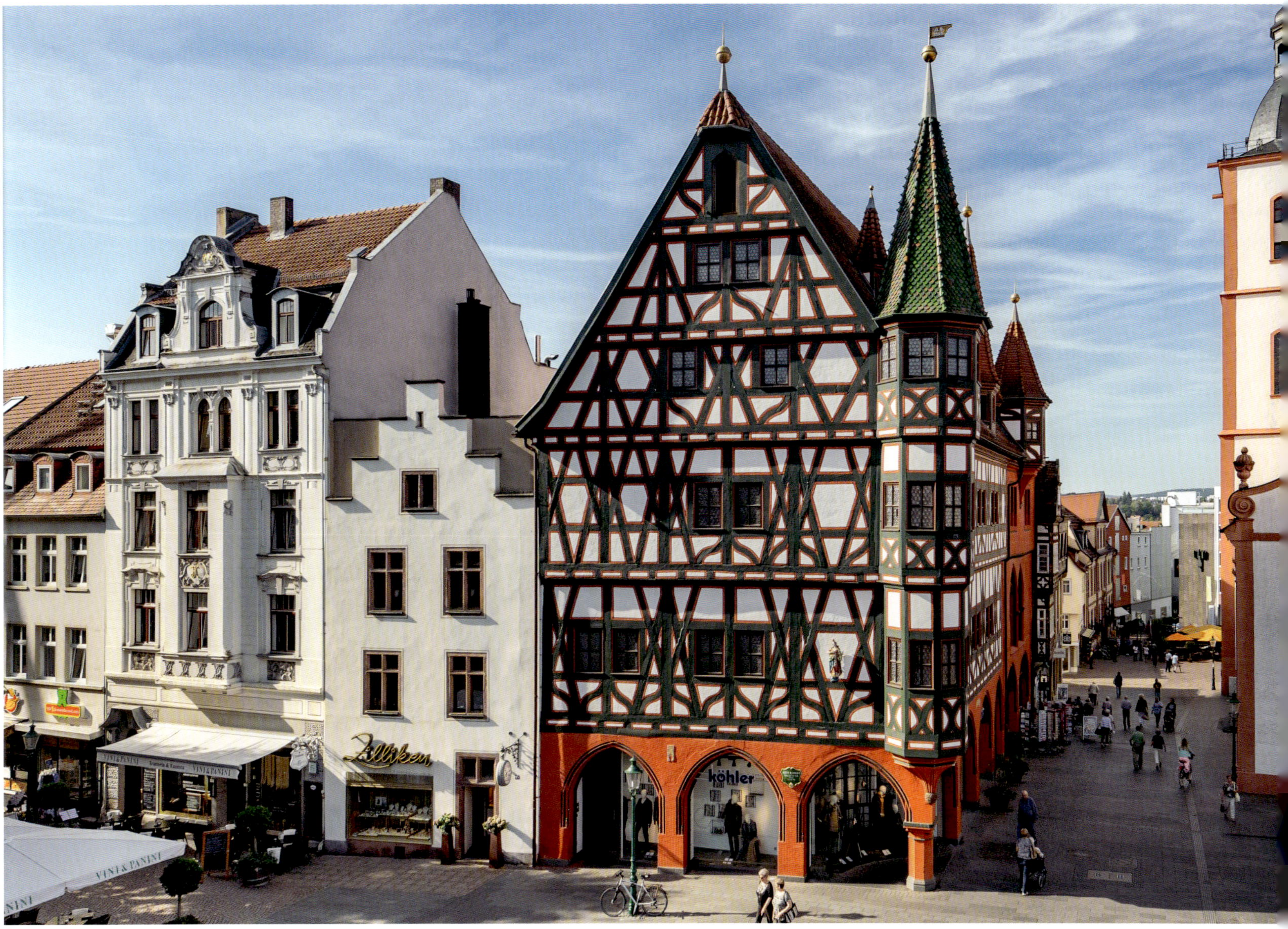

Zu den beliebtesten Fotomotiven der Stadt gehört das Alte Rathaus am Borgiasplatz/ Ecke Steinweg. Allerdings besitzt das Gebäude nur wenig Originalsubstanz, sondern es handelt sich in weiten Teilen um eine Rekonstruktion aus der Nachkriegszeit, die den Zustand im Jahr 1531 simuliert.

One of the most popular photo motifs in the city is the old town hall on the corner Borgiasplatz/ Steinweg. However, little of the building is original and large parts of it were reconstructed in the post-war period as it was in 1531.

Die Brunnenfiguren am Borgiasplatz, der nach dem Jesuiten Franz von Borgia benannt ist, stellen den Missionar Bonifatius („Missio"), den Ordensgründer Benedikt („Regula") und den Fuldaer Klostergründer Sturmius („Fundatio") dar.

These fountain figures on Borgiasplatz, named after the Jesuit Franz von Borgia, represent the missionary St. Boniface ("Missio"), the founder of the order Benedict ("Regula") and the founder of Fulda monastery St. Stumius ("Fundatio").

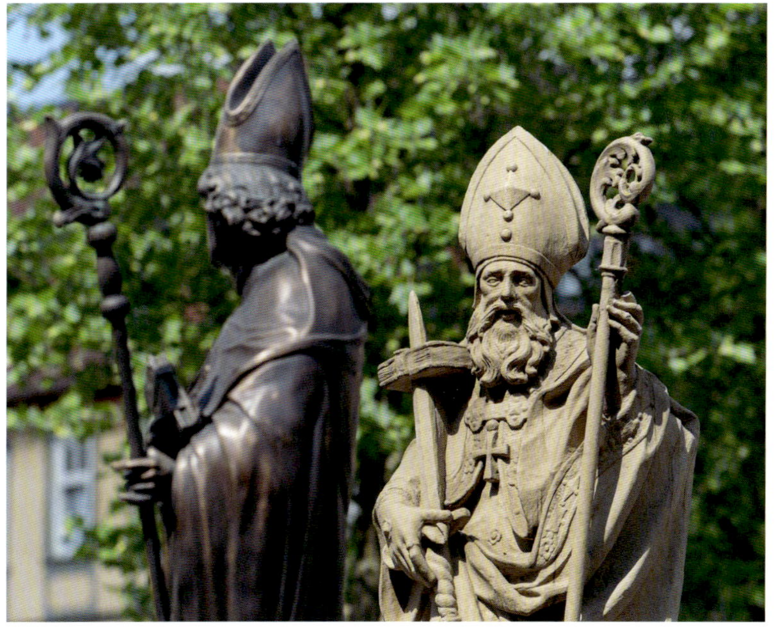

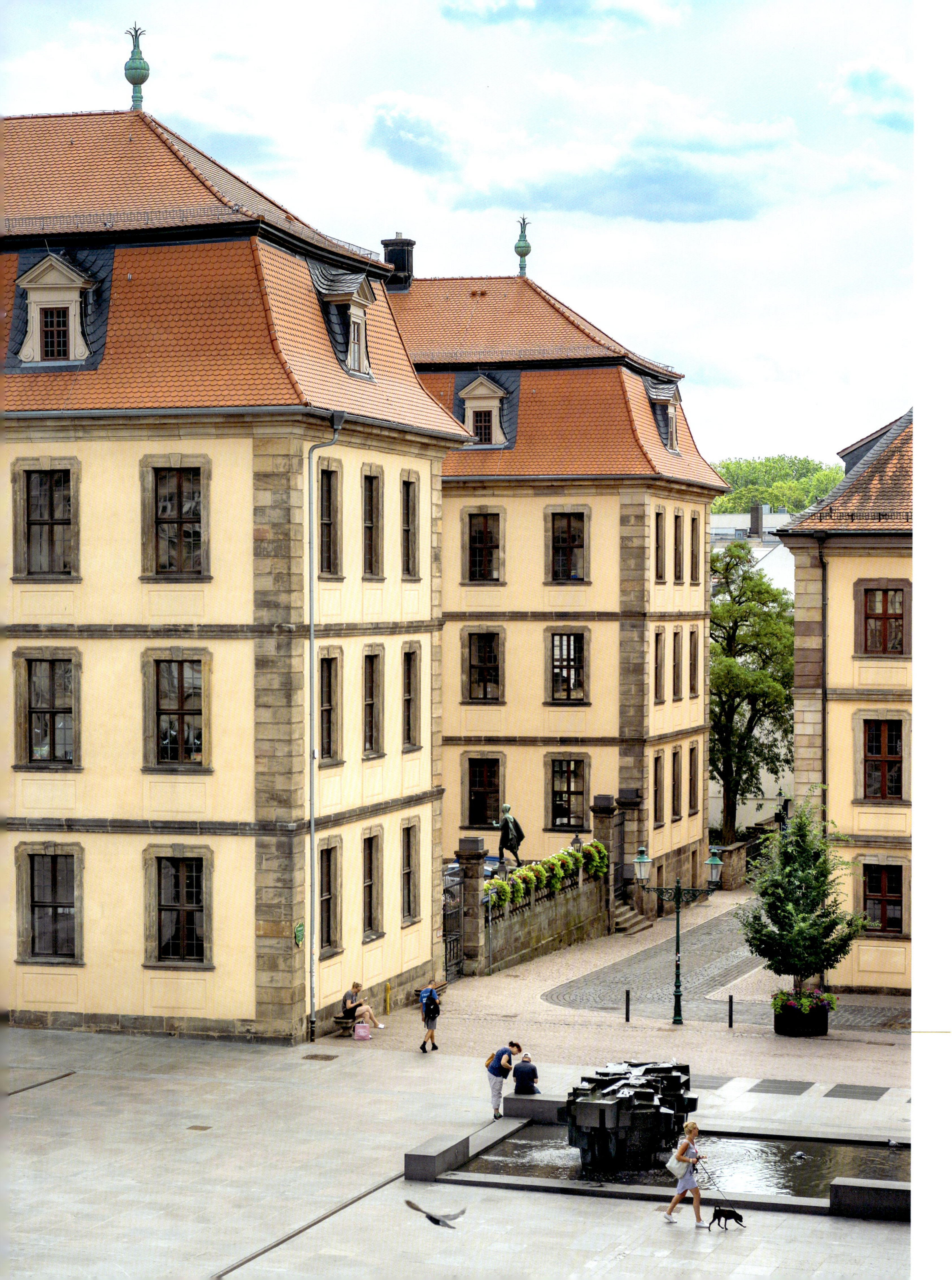

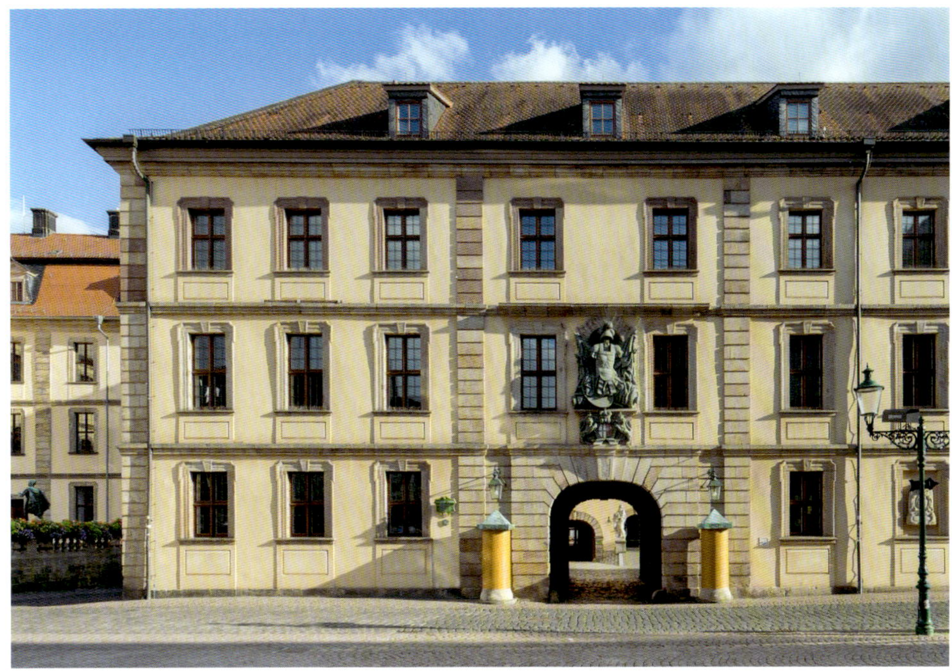

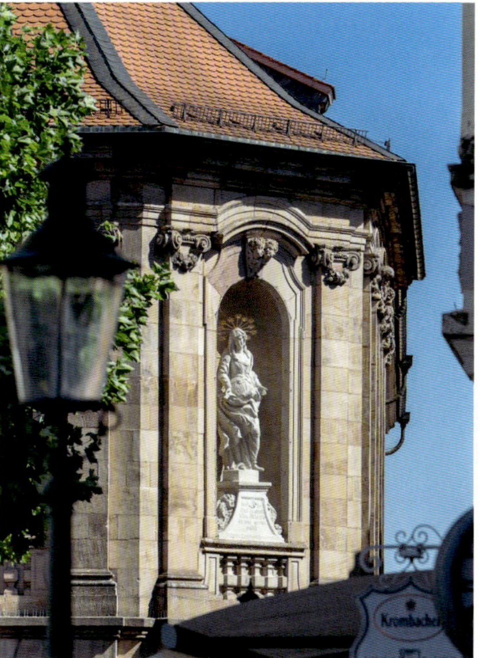

Der wuchtige Komplex des heutigen Vonderau Museums geht ursprünglich auf das Gebäude des Päpstlichen Seminars der Jesuiten zurück, das im 16. Jahrhundert errichtet wurde. Im Laufe der Jahrhunderte gab es einen häufigen Wechsel an Nutzungen sowie diverse Umbauten, so zum Beispiel die Gestaltung der Seminarkapelle im Südwesttrakt durch Gallasini im 18. Jahrhundert. Das Gebäude diente unter anderem als Kaserne sowie als Stadtschule, bevor 1994 das Vonderau Museum in den komplett sanierten Bau einzog.

This massive complex, which is now the Vonderau Museum, was once the building of the Papal Seminary of the Jesuits which was built in the 16th century. In the course of the centuries the building has been used in many different ways and it has often been changed: one example is the new design of the seminary chapel in the south-west wing by Gallasini in the 18th century. The building served as army barracks, and then as a school before it finally became the Vonderau Museum after a complete renovation in 1994.

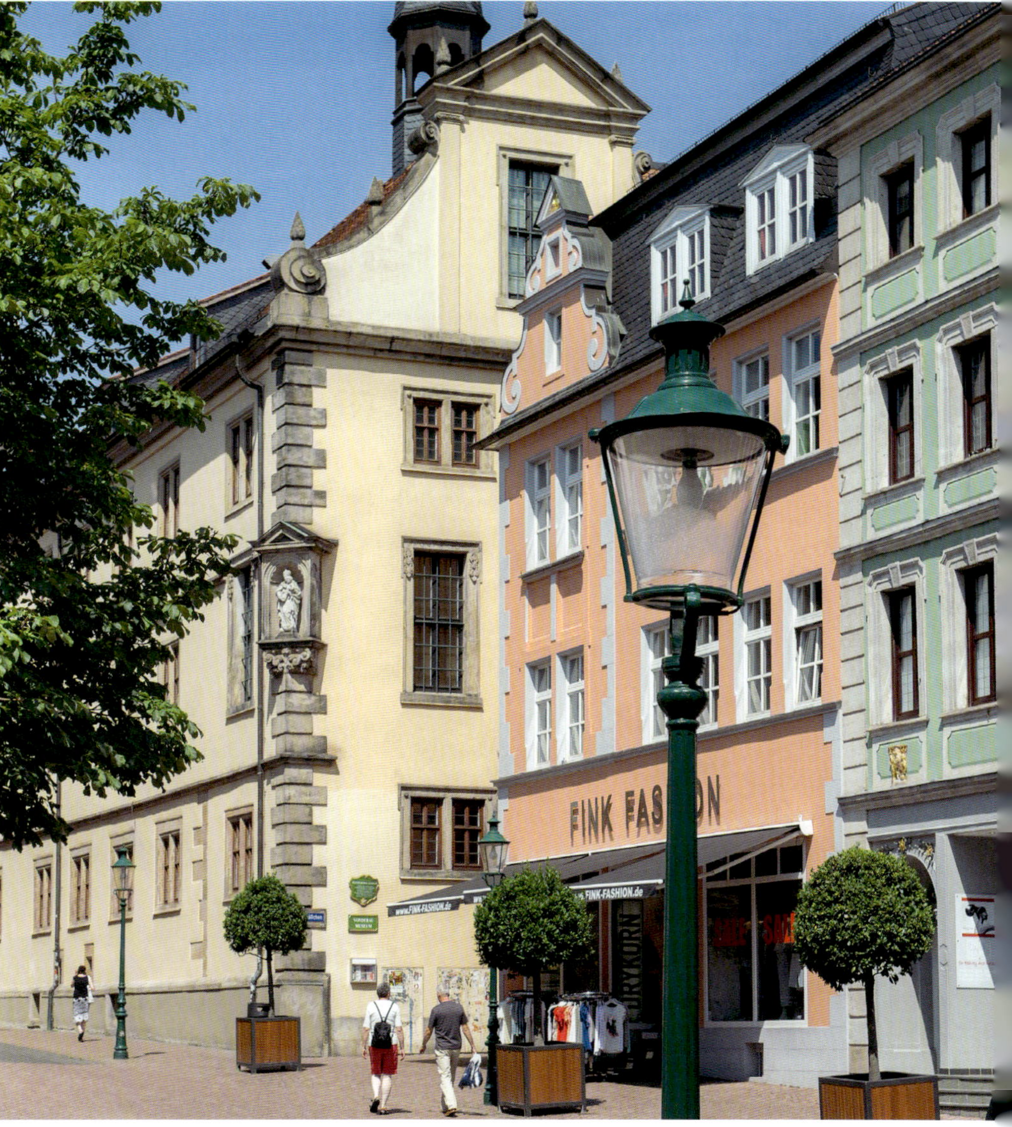

Das alte Universitätsgebäude, 1731 bis 1734 nach Plänen von Andreas Gallasini errichtet, beherbergte einst die nach dem Stifter Adolph von Dalberg benannte Fuldaer Universität („Adolphiana"), die bis 1805 bestand.

The Old University, built by the architect Andreas Gallasin between 1731 and 1734, housed Fulda University, named "Adolphiana" after its founder Adolph von Dalberg. It existed until 1805.

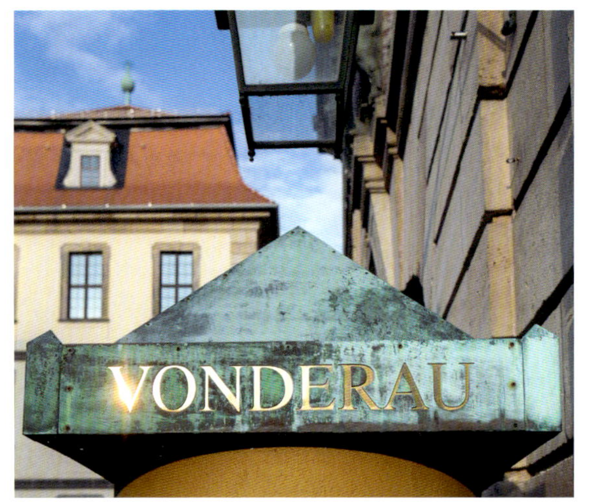

VONDERAU MUSEUM: ARCHÄOLOGIE & MEHR

Regionalgeschichte, Naturkunde sowie Malerei und Skulptur – das sind die Schwerpunkte der Dauerausstellung im Vonderau Museum, dem mit rund 4000 Quadratmetern Ausstellungsfläche größten Museum zwischen Kassel und Frankfurt. Einen Schwerpunkt bildet dabei die Archäologie – kein Wunder, denn der Namensgeber Joseph Vonderau (1863–1951) gilt als wichtiger Vertreter der deutschen Altertumsforschung. Auf den Grabungen, die der Fuldaer Lehrer und Heimatforscher um die Jahrhundertwende unter anderem im Bereich des Domes und der Langebrückenstraße sowie an den prähistorischen Fundstellen am Schulzenberg und Haimberg unternommen hat, beruhen wesentliche Erkenntnisse über die früheste Besiedlung Osthessens.
Mit seinen Sonderschauen und Wechselausstellungen bietet das Museum zugleich immer neue Anregungen für das interessierte Publikum sowie eine Plattform für die zeitgenössische Kunstszene. Museumspädagogische Angebote, die speziell auf Kinder und Schulklassen zugeschnitten sind, sowie ein Planetarium bieten weitere Anreize für einen Besuch des Museums.

The permanent exhibition of the Vonderau Museum focuses on the fields of regional history, natural history, painting and sculpture. The museum has an exhibition area of 4,000 m², making it the largest museum between Kassel and Frankfurt. Archaeology is one of the main areas covered, which is no surprise as the museum is named after Joseph Vonderau (1863–1951), a Fulda teacher who carried out important research into German history. Joseph Vonderau's archaeological excavations at the turn of the century included those near the cathedral, the Langebrückenstraße and at prehistoric sites on Schulzenberg and Haimberg. Our knowledge about the earliest settlements in East Hesse are largely based on Vonderau's findings.
The museum has a full programme of temporary exhibitions which cover a large variety of subjects and regularly exhibits works by local artists.
There are also special events which are specially conceived for children and school classes and a planetarium – plenty of excellent reasons for visiting the museum!

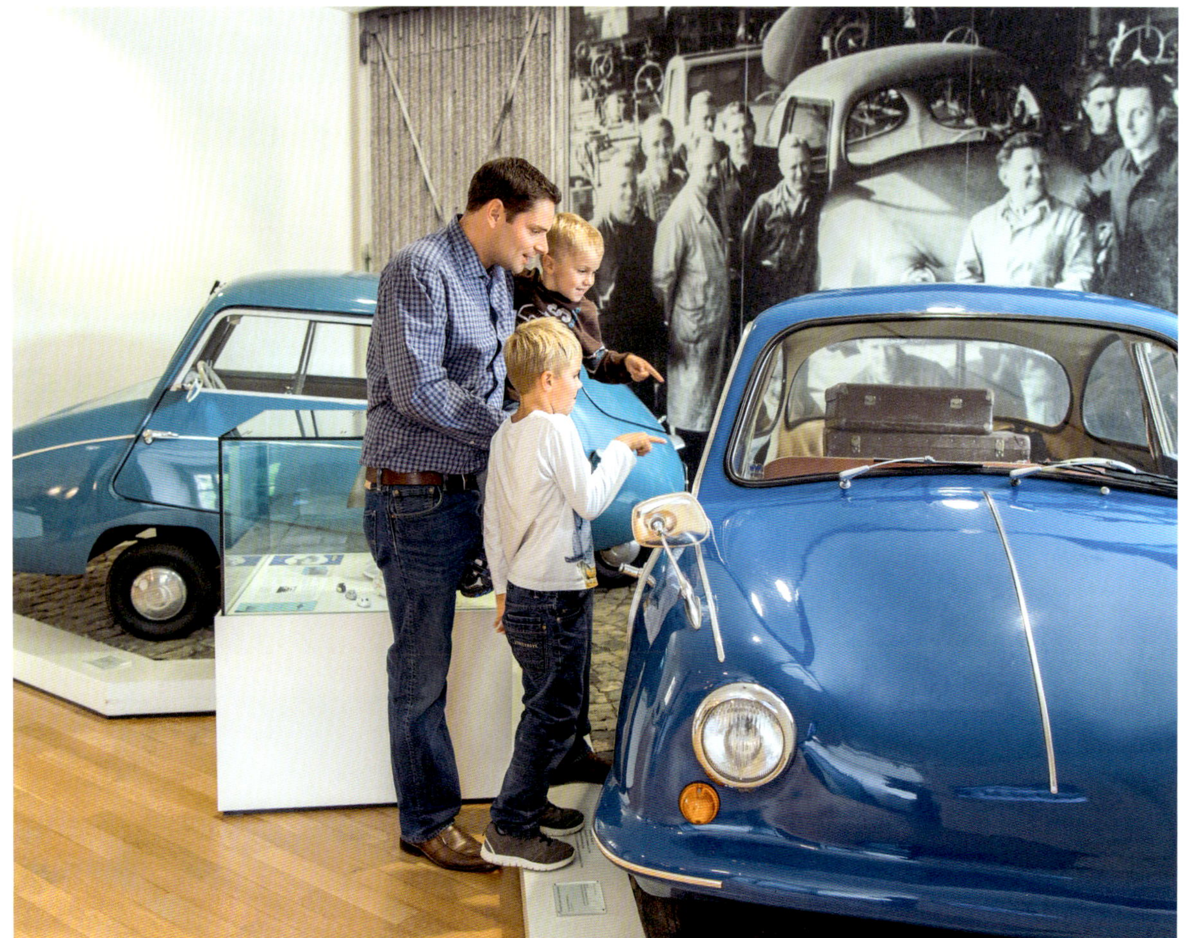

Das Fuldamobil wurde von 1951 bis 1969 gebaut, im Museum sind Originale aus dieser Epoche der Fuldaer Automobilgeschichte zu sehen.

The Fuldamobil was produced from 1951 to 1969. In the museum you can see original cars from this period of Fulda's automotive history.

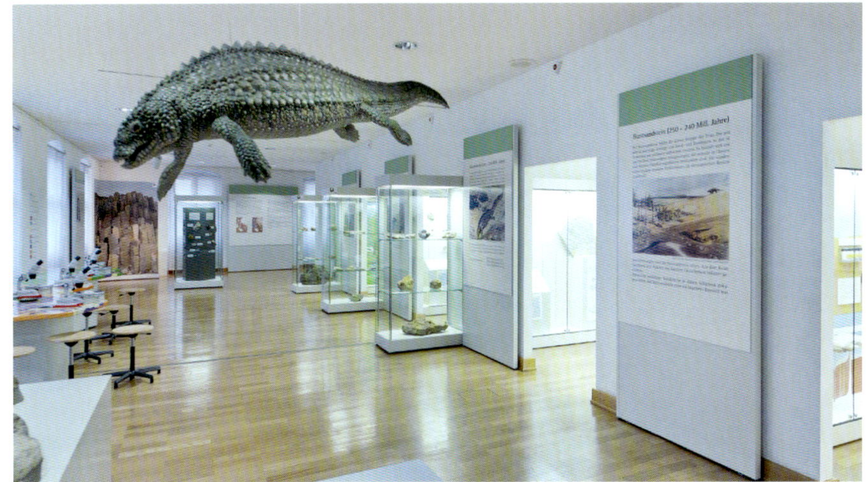

Das Vonderau Museum hat seine Schwerpunkte im Bereich Regionalgeschichte, Archäologie und Naturkunde. Ein Prunkstück ist die sogenannte Austerlitz-Tapete.

The Vonderau Museum focuses on regional history, archaeology and natural history. One special feauture is the Austerlitz Paper Hanging.

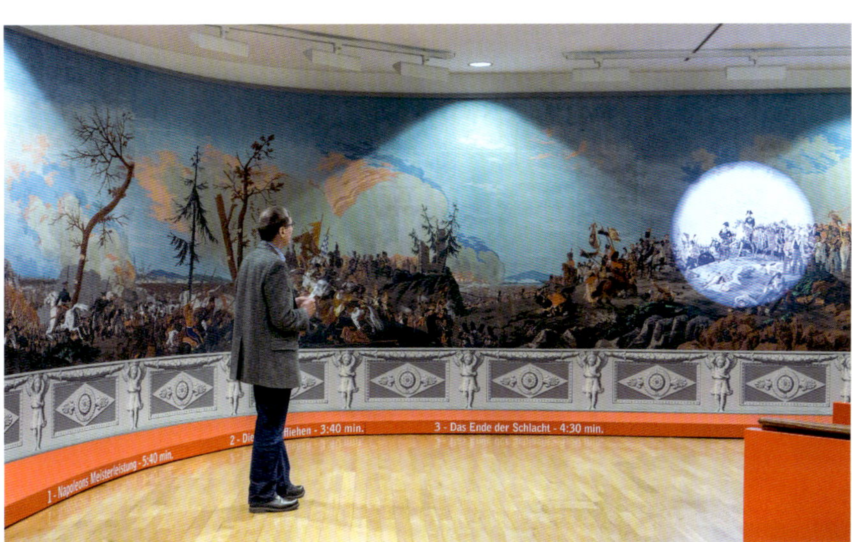

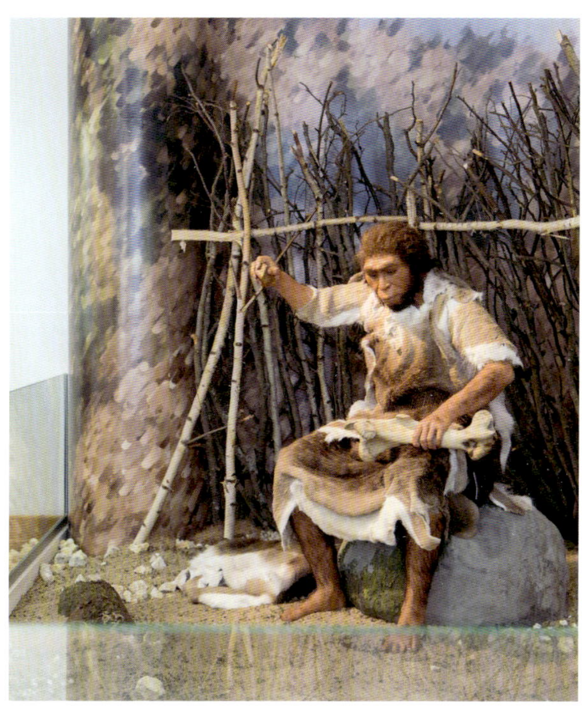

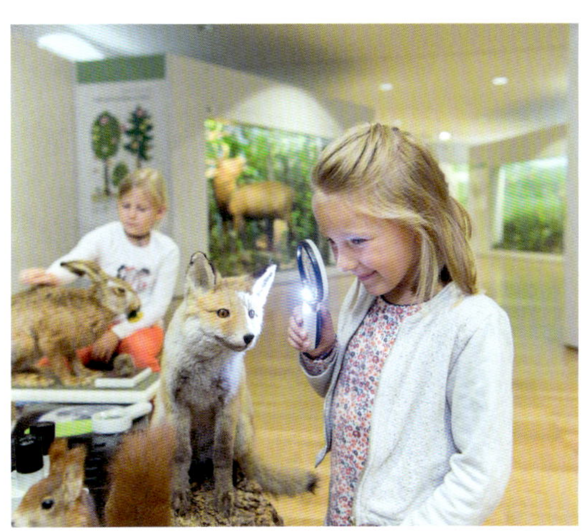

Durch einen Glücksfall konnte die historische Einrichtung der Apotheke und Drogerie „Zum Krokodil" (Karlstraße) erhalten werden und bildet nun einen eigenen Raum im Museum.

By a stroke of luck, the entire historical interior of the chemist's shop "Zum Krokodil" (Karlstrasse) could be conserved and now has its own room in the museum.

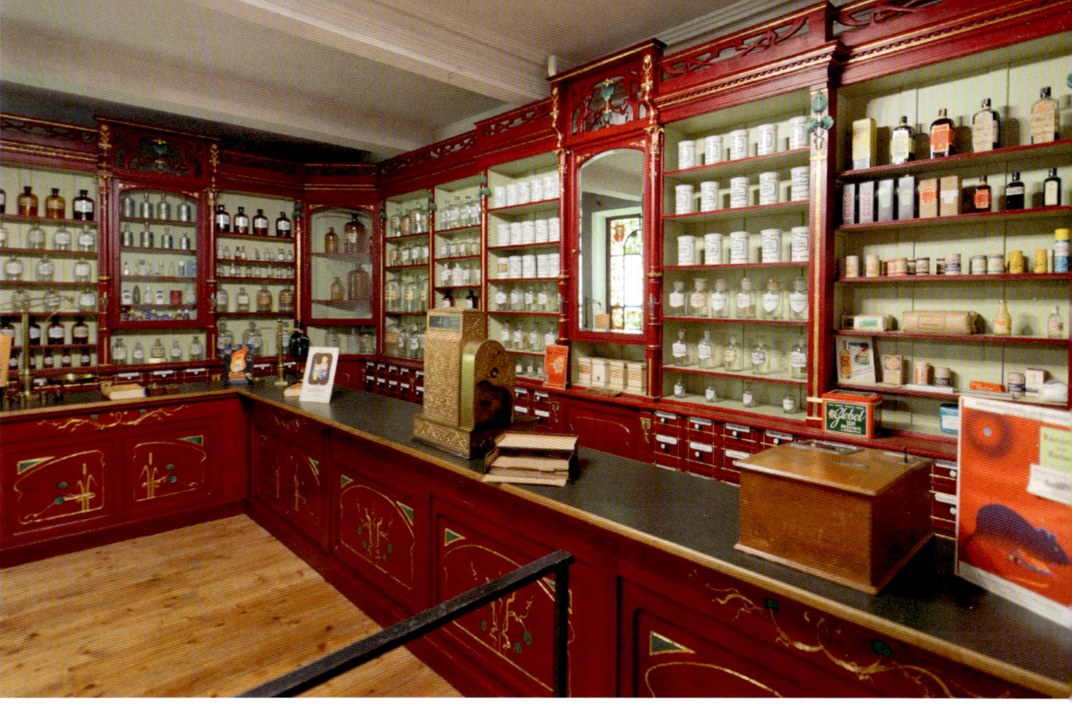

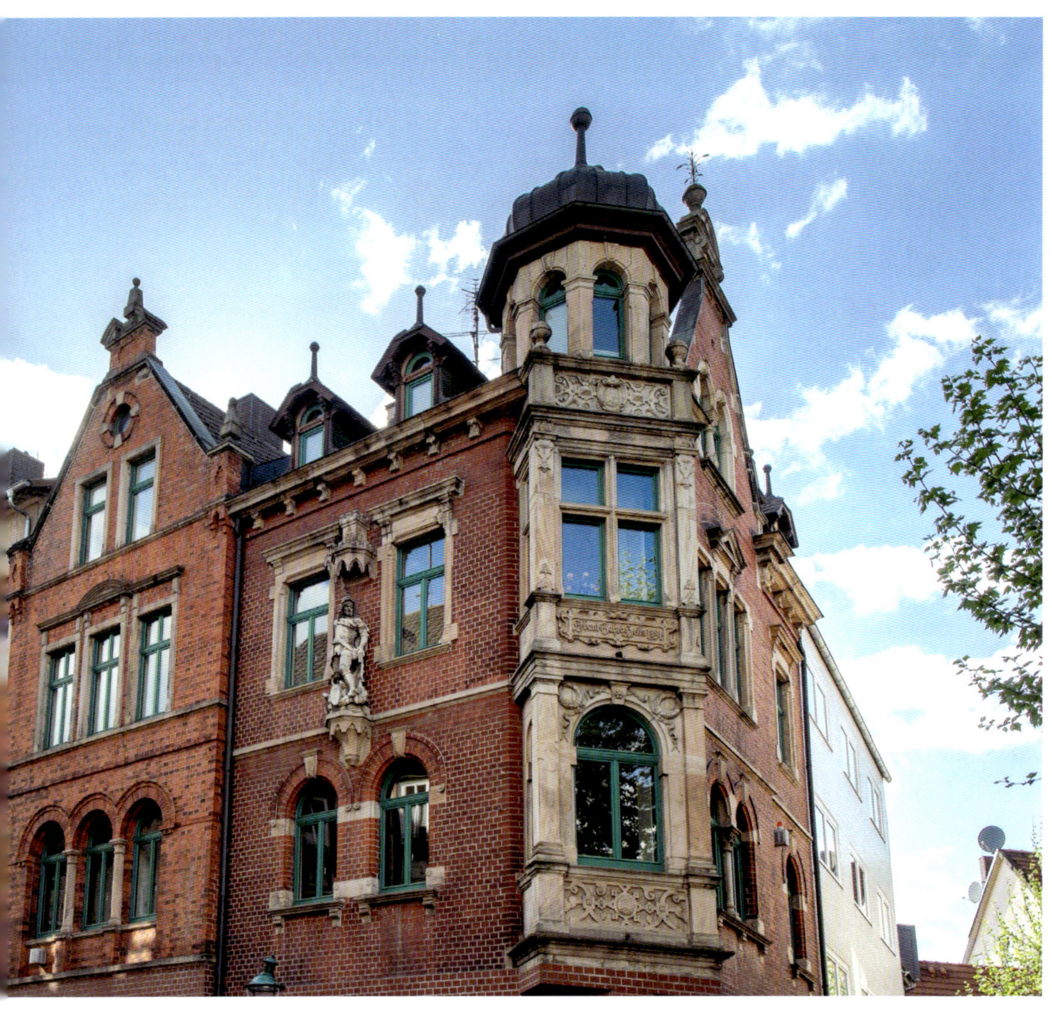

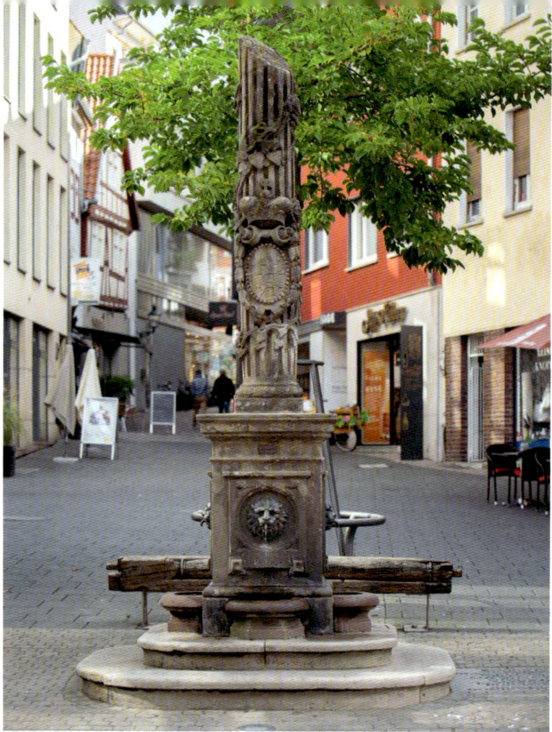

Die Gegend um den Gemüsemarkt (oben) wurde während der Bombenangriffe des Zweiten Weltkriegs schwer zerstört. Der sogenannte Harstall-Brunnen blieb dabei verschont und erinnert heute auch an die vielen Toten des Krieges.

The area around the Gemüsemarkt (top) was badly damaged by bombing in World War II. The so-called Harstall fountain was not hit and now serves as a monument to all victims of the war.

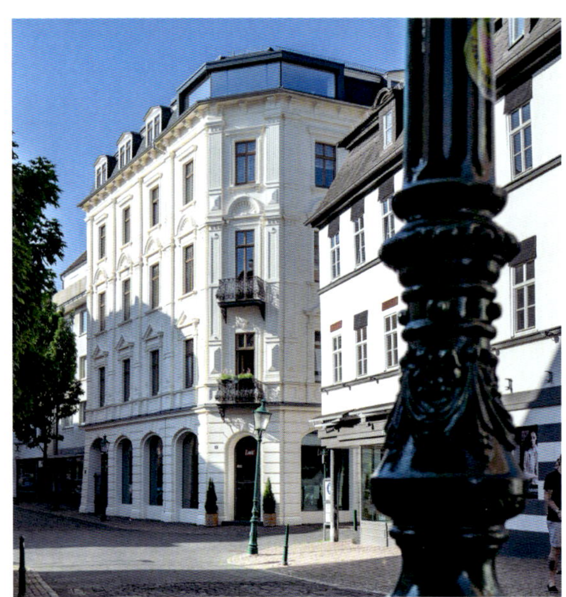

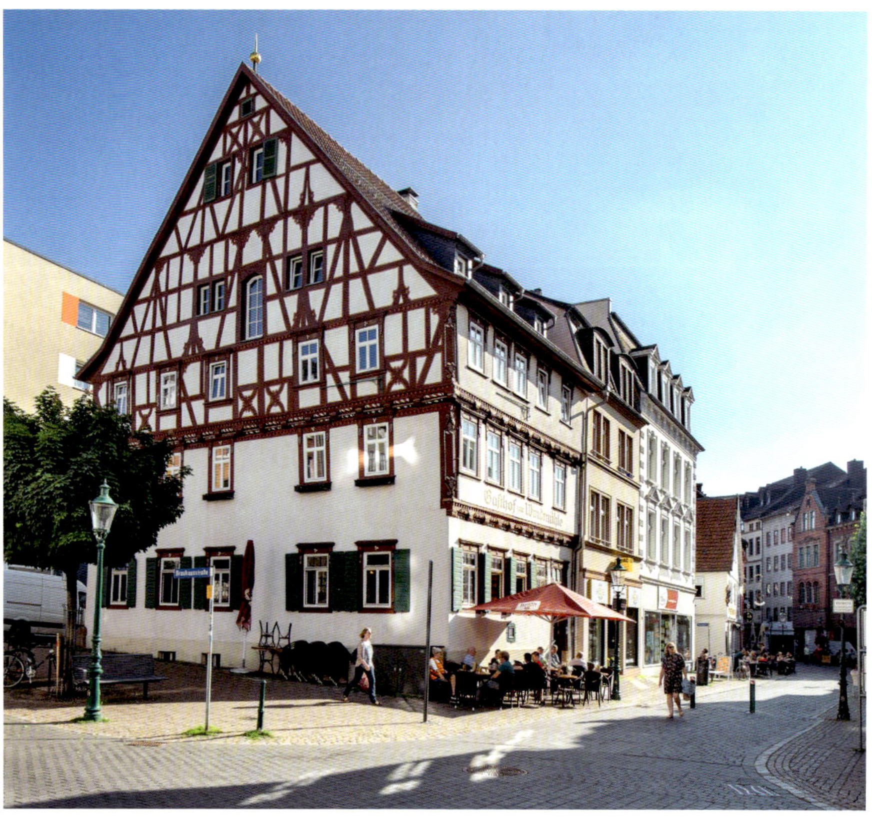

Das historische Gasthaus zur Windmühle markiert den Eingang ins sogenannte Bermudadreieck, wo schon der eine oder andere Nachtschwärmer verloren gegangen sein soll.

The historical pub "Gasthaus zur Windmühle" marks the entrance to the "Bermuda Triangle" where it is said that the odd night owl has not made it back to his nest!

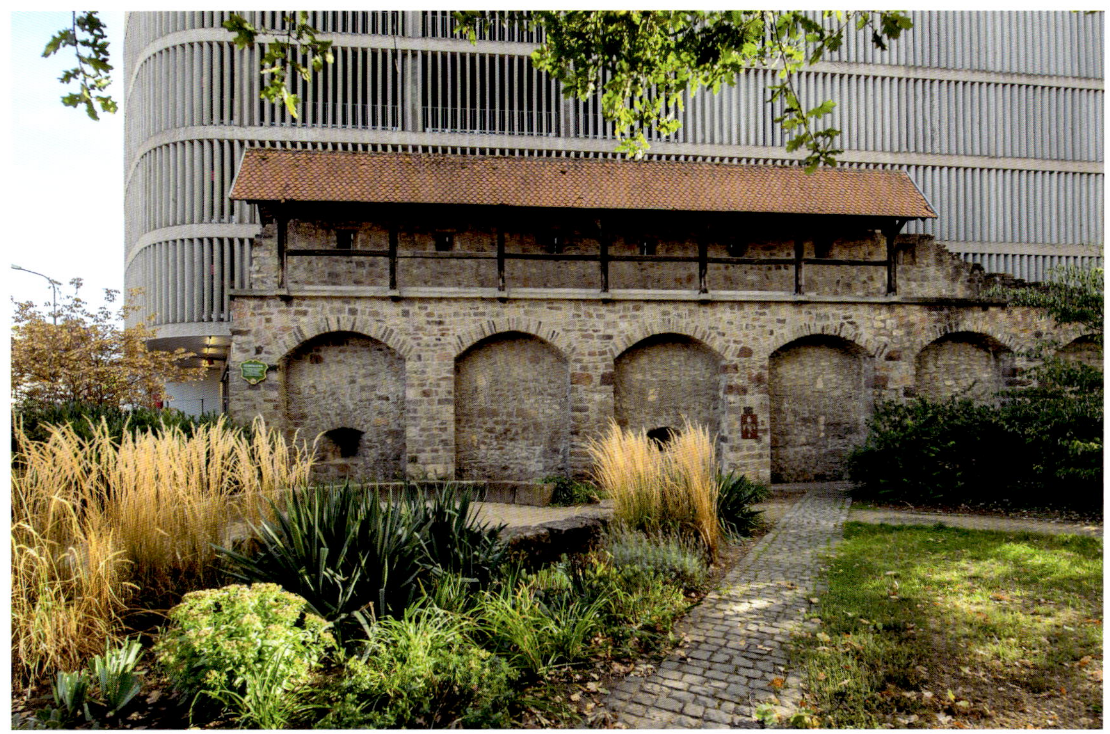

Einen reizvollen Kontrast vor dem modernen Altstadt-Parkhaus bietet die teilweise rekonstruierte Stadtmauer in der Brauhausstraße.

There is a lovely contrast between the modern Altstadt car park and the partly reconstructed city wall in the Brauhausstrasse.

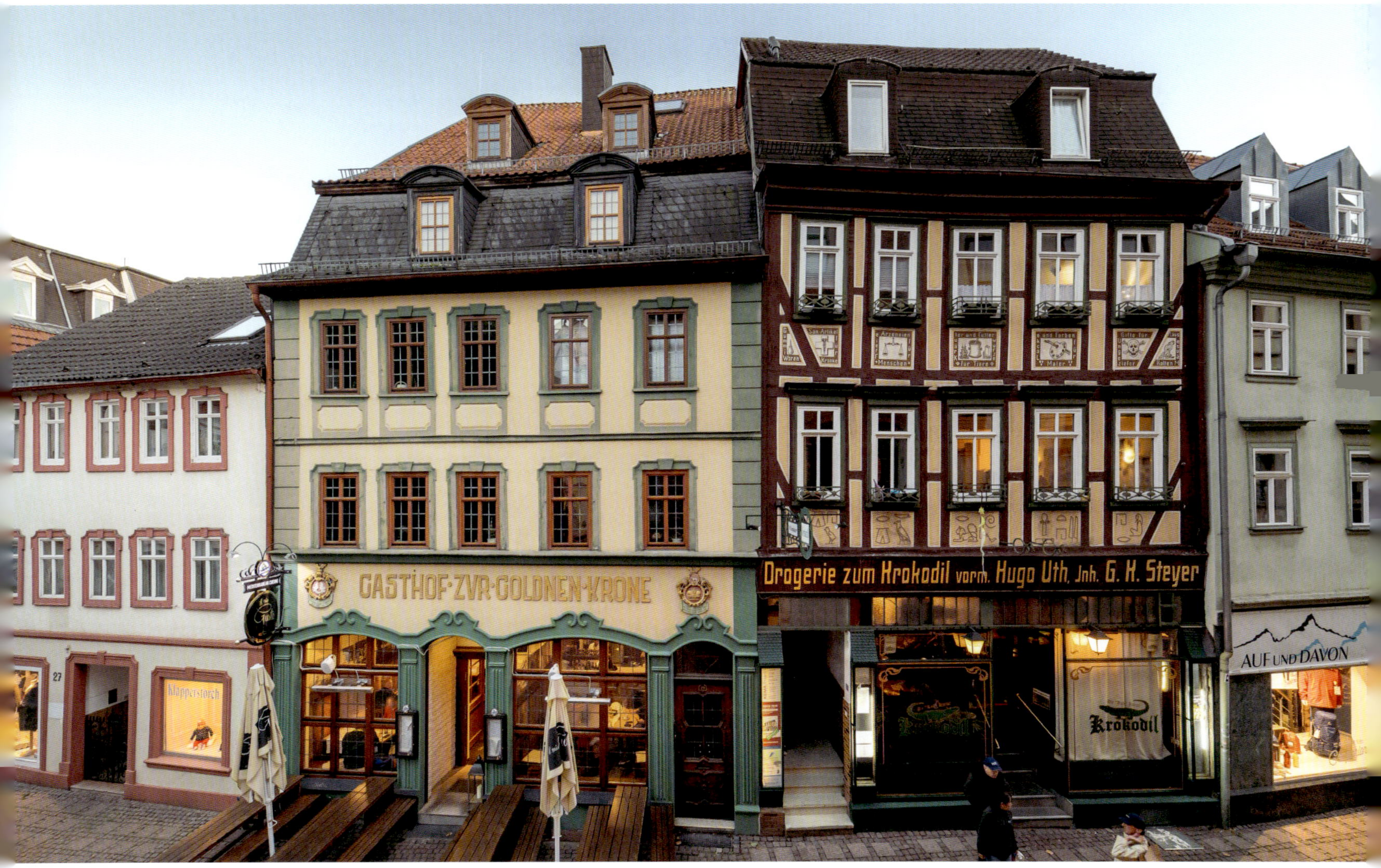

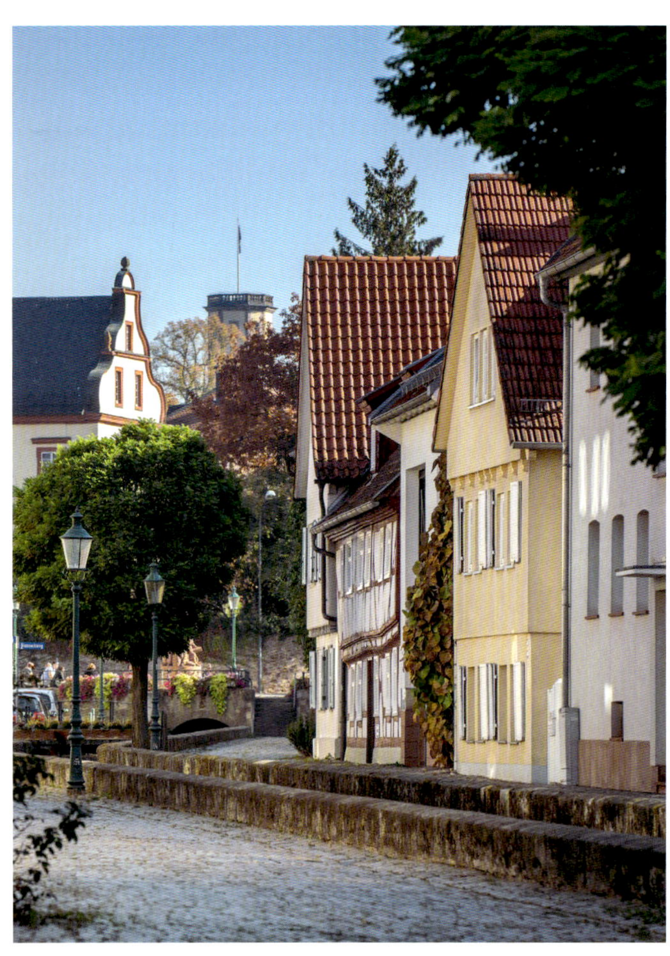

Schon im Mittelalter entstanden vor den eigentlichen Stadtmauern einige kleine Vorstädte. Eine davon befand sich am Areal der Tränke, dem gefassten Bachlauf der Waides, und hat bis heute ihren bezaubernden, kleinteiligen Charme bewahrt. Der Fastnachtsbrunnen erinnert an die karnevalistische Tradition, denn in diesem Quartier ist der älteste Fastnachtsverein der Stadt, der „Vorstädtische Bürgerverein – Türkenbund" von 1888, ansässig.

Already in the Middle Ages small settlements grew up around the city walls. The „Tränke" area, which borders a canalised stream, the Waides, has retained its enchanting, quaint charm. The carnival fountain is a tribute to the Fulda carnival tradition, as the oldest carnival club, the "Türkenbund", has been based here since 1888.

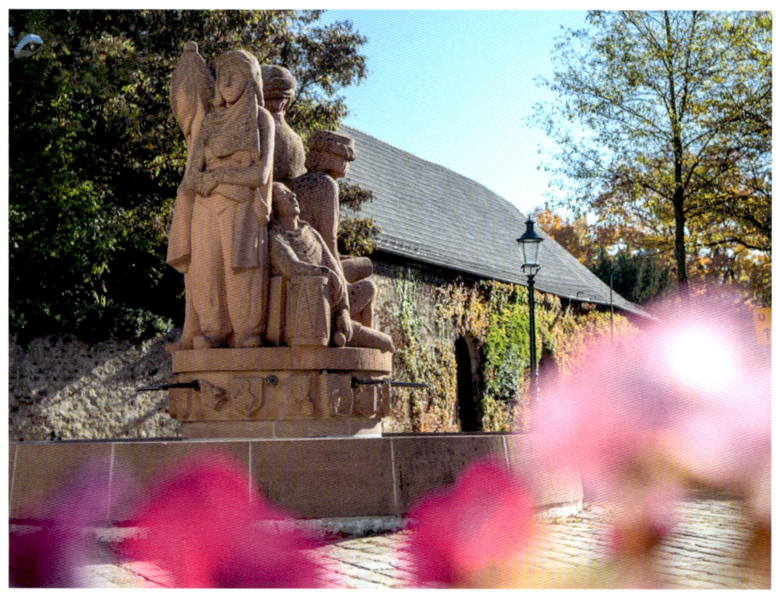

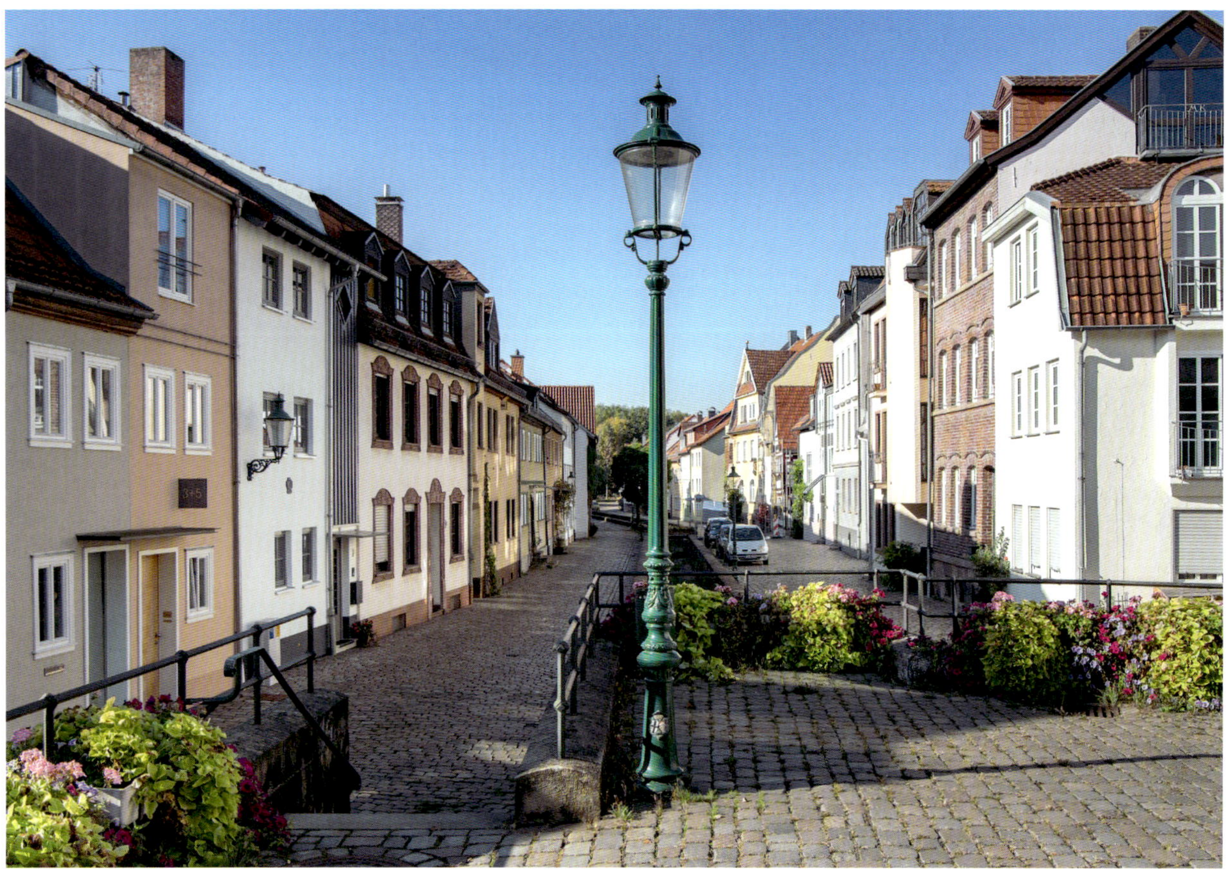

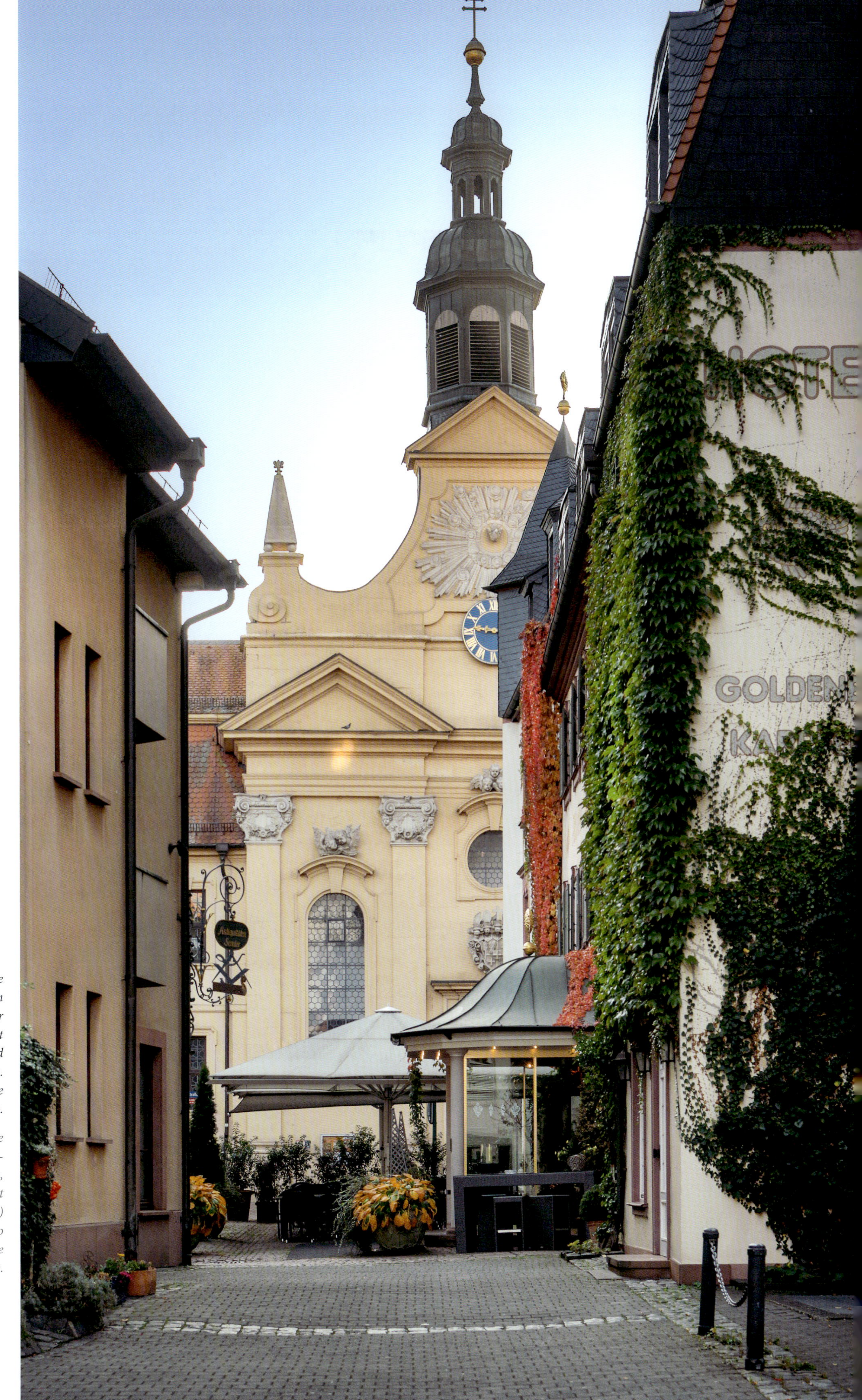

Die südliche Vorstadt bildete sich entlang der wichtigsten Straßenverbindung, der Via Regia, die von Frankfurt über Fulda nach Leipzig und weiter nach Osten führte. Den Eingang zur Löherstraße markiert die Heilig-Geist-Kirche.

The southern outskirts of the city ran along the most important street, the Via Regia, which went from Frankfurt to Leipzig (and further) via Fulda. The entrance to Löherstrasse is marked by the Heilig-Geist-Kirche.

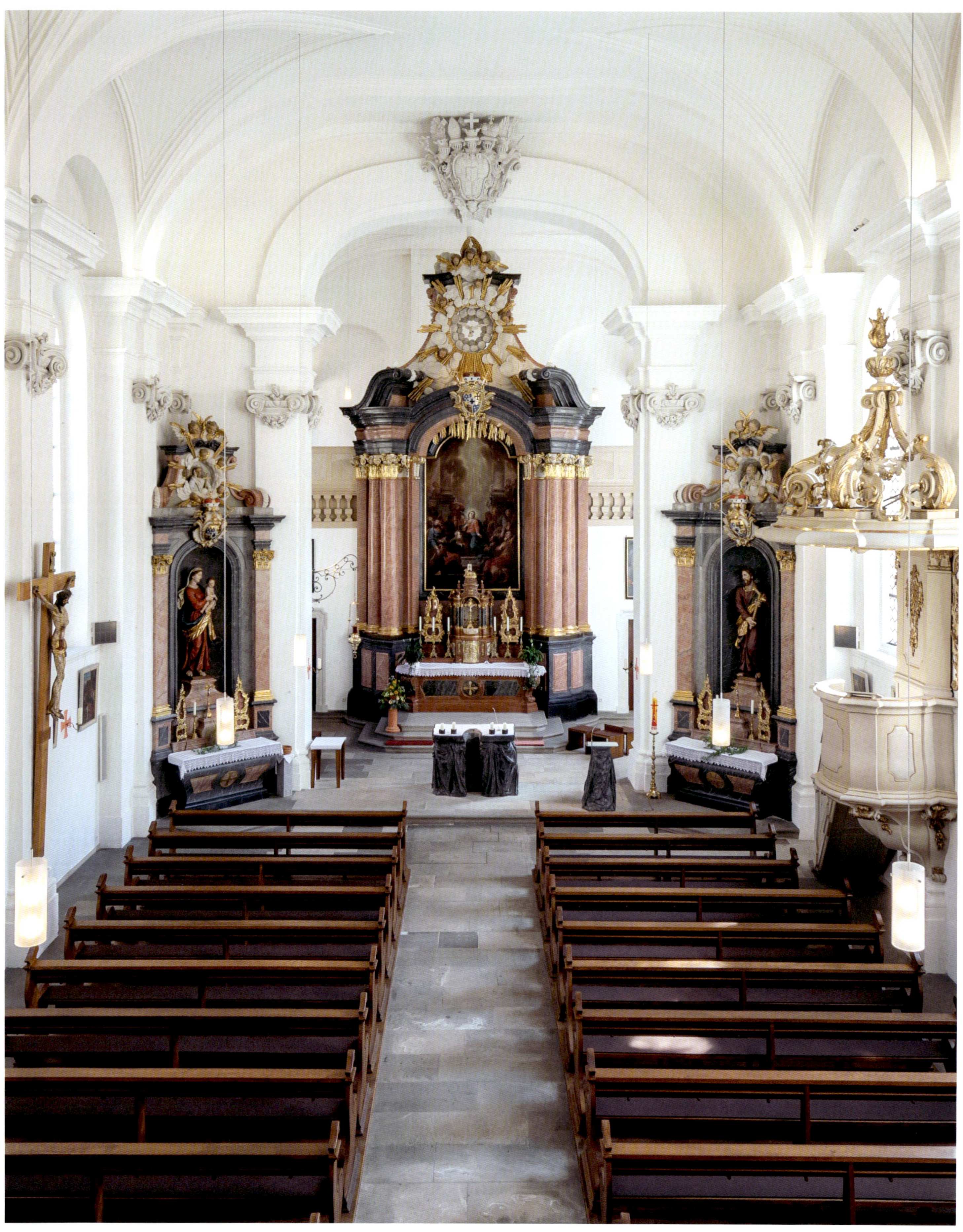

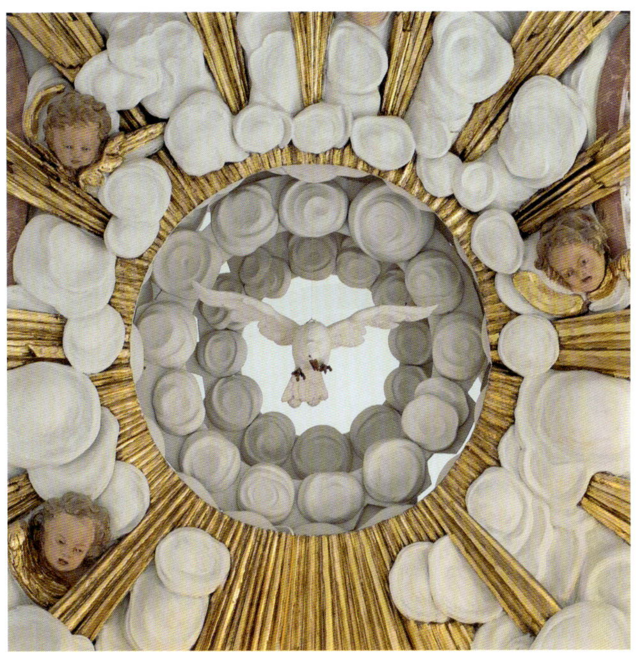

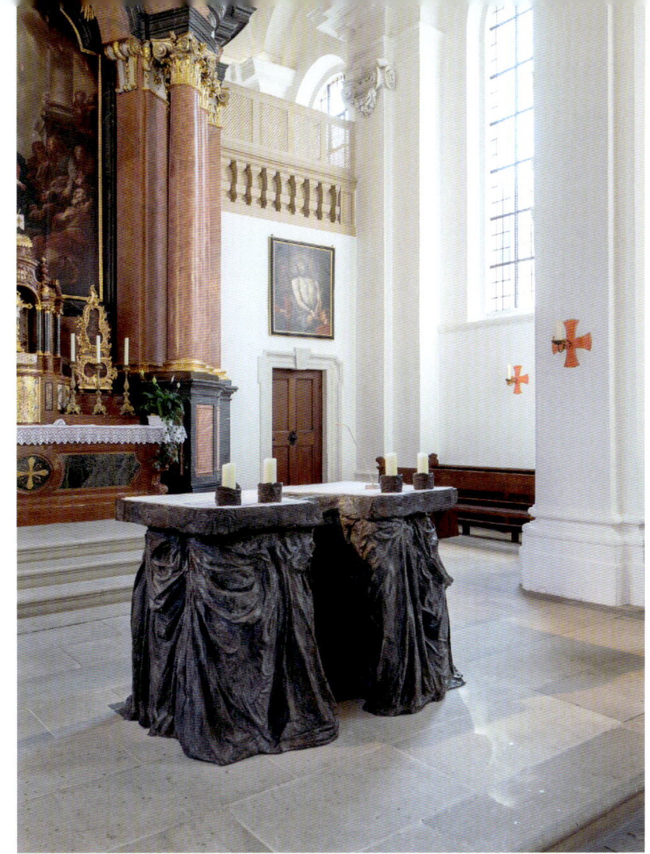

Die Heilig-Geist-Kirche wurde 1729–33 an der Stelle ihres gotischen Vorgängers als Hospitalkirche des Heilig-Geist-Spitals gebaut. Dieses lag – wie im Mittelalter üblich – aus hygienischen Gründen vor den Toren der Stadt. Baumeister Andreas Gallasini schuf dann mit der Kirche ein barockes Kleinod. Das Altarbild im Innern von Emanuel Wohlhaupter zeigt das Pfingstwunder, und die Taube, das Symbol des Heiligen Geistes, ist an mehreren Stellen innen und außen an der Kirche zu entdecken.

The Heilig-Geist-Kirche was built in 1729–33 on the site of its Gothic predecessor as the church of the Heilig-Geist hospital which lay – as was usual in the Middle Ages – outside the city gates for hygienic reasons. The architect Andreas Gallasini then transformed the church into a Baroque gem. The altarpiece by Emanuel Wohlhaupter shows the Pentecost miracle, and the dove, the symbol of the Holy Spirit, is to be found in several places in and outside the church.

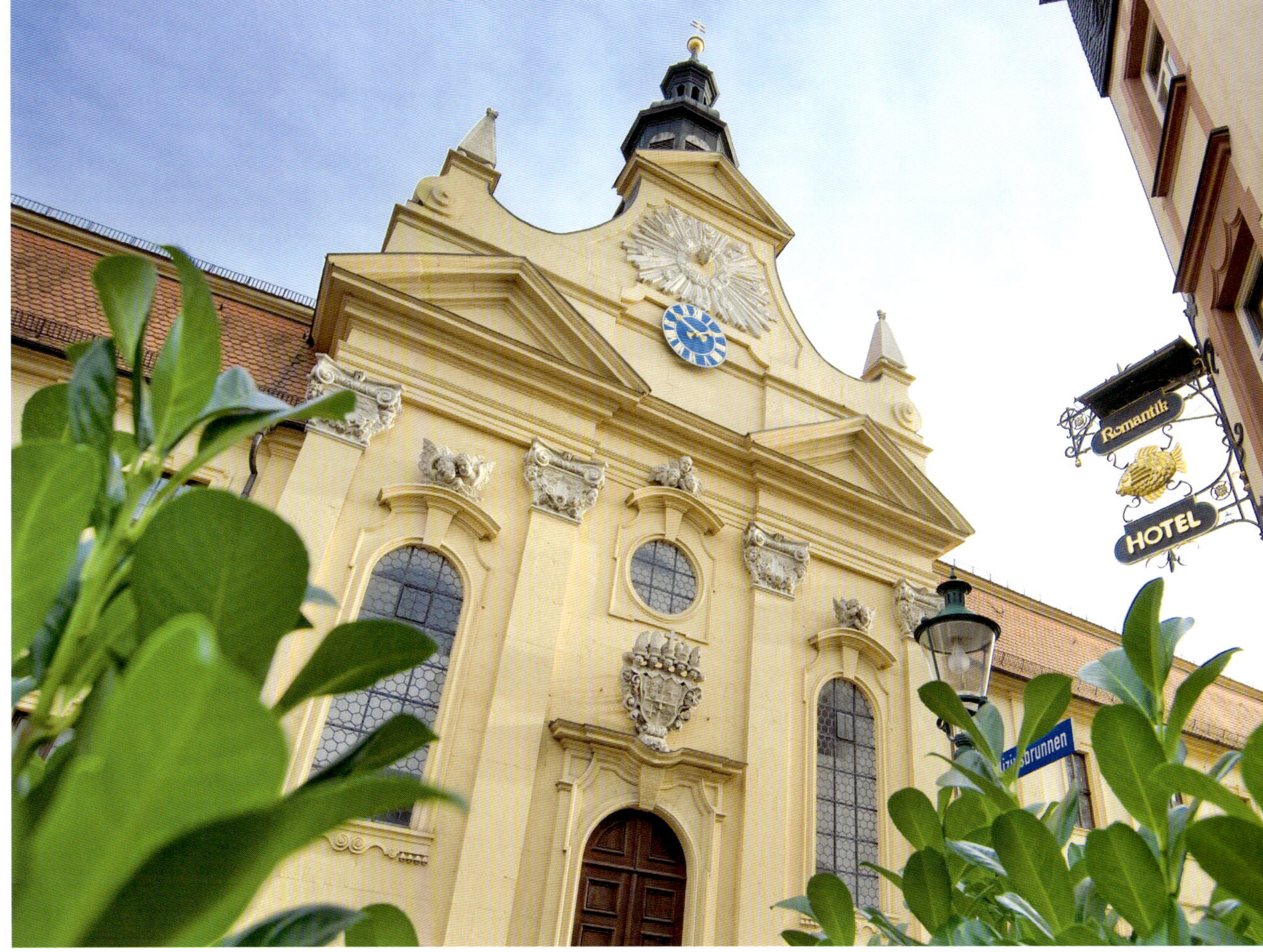

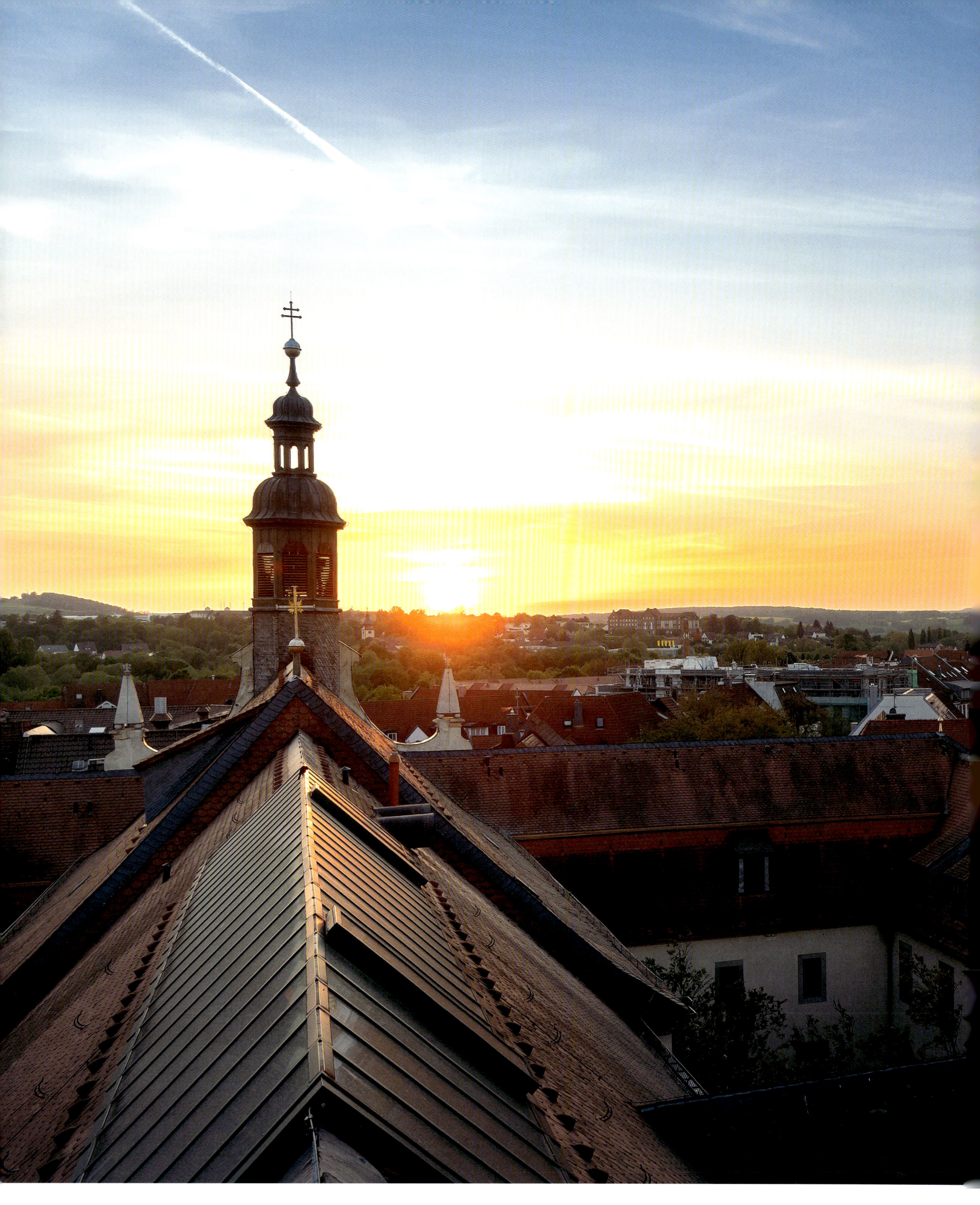

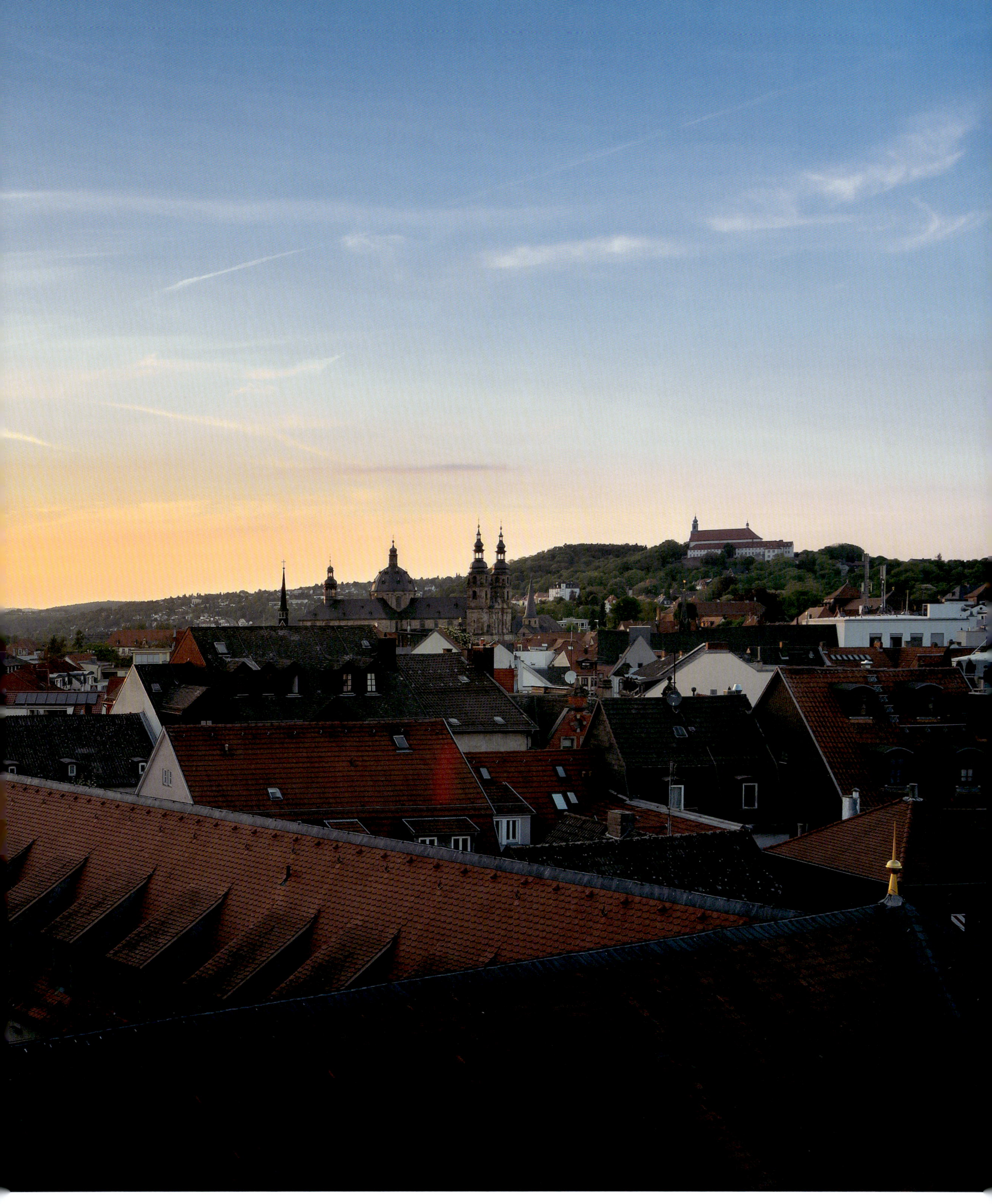

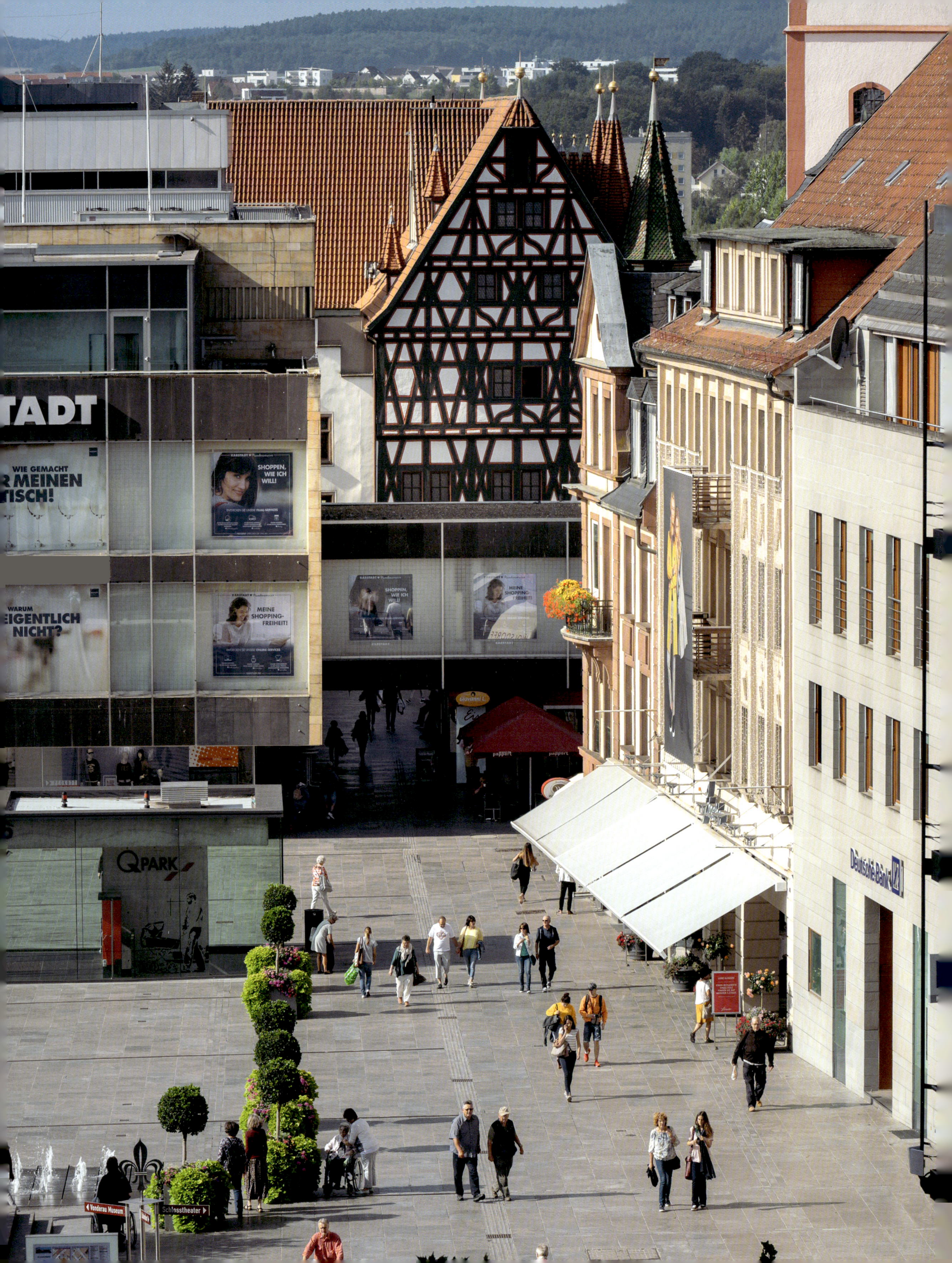
TADT
WIE GEMACHT
R MEINEN
TISCH!
SHOPPEN, WIE ICH WILL!
WARUM
EIGENTLICH
NICHT?
MEINE SHOPPING-FREIHEIT!
QPARK
Deutsche Bank
Vonderau Museum
Schlosstheater

ALS DIE STADT IHRE GRENZEN SPRENGTE

Ab der zweiten Hälfte des 19. Jahrhunderts entstand vor den alten Mauern die heutige City

Als im ebenso ereignis- wie folgenreichen Jahr 1866 die Bebra-Fuldaer Eisenbahnstrecke eröffnet wurde und Fulda damit Anschluss an die modernen Zeiten erhielt, wurde in der Stadt viel gelästert: „Was? Ein Bahnhof so weit draußen? Das kann doch nichts werden …!" Nun, die rasante Entwicklung strafte die Kritiker Lügen: Der Bahnhof, von dem aus man ab 1868 auch Hanau und Frankfurt direkt per Zug erreichen konnte, wurde zum Kristallisationspunkt für die spätere „Oberstadt". Wo jenseits der ehemaligen Stadtmauer zu Beginn des Jahrhunderts in kurhessischer Zeit noch Ziegen und Kühe gegrast hatten, wuchs nun – unter der neuen preußischen Herrschaft – in wenigen Jahrzehnten ein komplettes Stadtviertel in die Höhe. Und wie überall im Reich beherrschen stattliche Mietshäuser, einzelne prächtige Villen und viele schlichtere Blöcke mit dicht bebauten Hinterhöfen diese Gründerzeitviertel. Stolz prangen an vielen Häusern die Jahreszahlen der Fertigstellung – 1897, 1902, 1906 … Der Bauboom dieser Jahre stellte jedenfalls den barocken Modernisierungsschub in Fulda Anfang des 18. Jahrhunderts bei Weitem in den Schatten – zumindest, was die flächenmäßige Ausdehnung angeht. Auch jenseits der Bahnlinie, entlang der traditionsreichen Leipziger Straße wächst die Stadt, erste Industrie- und Gewerbegebiete entstehen. Auf Ansichtskarten dürfen rauchende Schlote nicht fehlen.

Das Scharnier zwischen Alt und Neu, zwischen Ober- und Unterstadt bildet seither der Universitätsplatz. Hier schlägt bis heute das Herz der modernen „City", hier sind die Kaufhäuser und Banken. Auch viele Nachkriegsbauten haben sich ihren Platz erobert. Und doch hat Fulda auch in dieser Phase seiner Expansion nicht die Maßstäblichkeit verloren. Die historischen Gebäude, die natürlichen Erhebungen und die damit verbundenen Blickachsen – sie blieben als Bezugsgrößen erhalten.

When the City Burst its Limits

From the second half of the 19th century on, today's city grew outside the old walls.

The railway line from Bebra to Fulda was opened in the both eventful and portentous year of 1866. The opening of the railway paved the way for Fulda to enter the modern era, but in the city there was some scepticism: "What? A station so far out of the city? Nothing can come out it…!" However, the immensely fast development made nonsense of the criticism: the station, which (from 1868 on) directly linked Fulda to Hanau and Frankfurt, became a crystallisation point for the growth of the later "Upper City". Under the new Prussian rule the area outside the city wall – where at the beginning of the century goats and cows pastured – grew to become a complete city quarter in just a few decades.

As elsewhere in the empire, this area consisted of large apartment buildings, grand villas and very much plainer blocks with densely built courtyards. On many of the houses the date of completion of the building is proudly noted – 1897, 1902, 1906…..the construction boom during these years made the baroque modernisation at the beginning of the 18th century seem minor in comparison – at least in terms of the size of the area covered. On the other side of the railway line, along the old Leipziger Strasse, the first industrial and business areas took form (on postcards of the area you can never fail to notice smoking chimneys!). The Universitätsplatz has always been the "hinge" between old and new, between the "Upper City" and the "Lower City". This is where the heart of the city beats, here are the department stores and the banks. Many postwar buildings have also found their place here, but even in this period of expansion Fulda did not lose its proportions. The historical buildings, the natural rising ground and the resulting lines of view – they all remained as important reference points.

Der Universitätsplatz liegt an der Nahtstelle zwischen Altstadt und gründerzeitlichem Bahnhofsviertel. Handel und Banken prägen hier das Erscheinungsbild.

The Universitätsplatz is situated on the dividing line between the old town and the elegant buildings of the late 19th /early 20th century area towards the station. Banks and shops are the predominant features here.

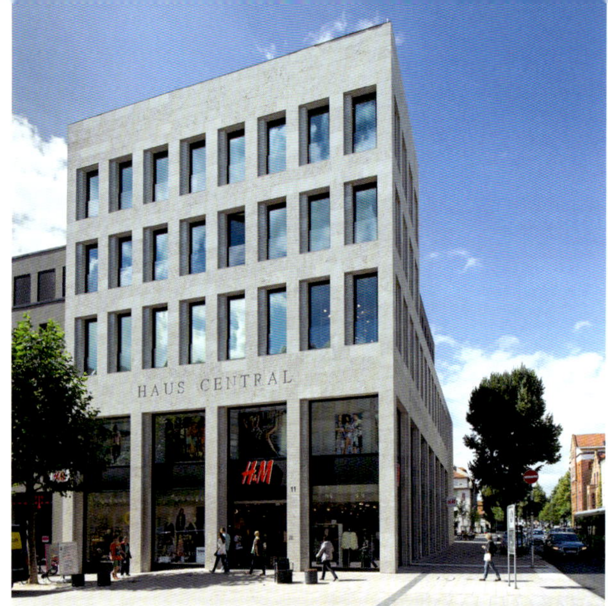

Die Bahnhofstraße als Achse zwischen Universitätsplatz und Bahnhof behauptet ihren Platz als wichtige Einkaufsmeile.

The Bahnhofstrasse, which forms a corridor between the Universitätsplatz and the station, has established itself as an important shopping street.

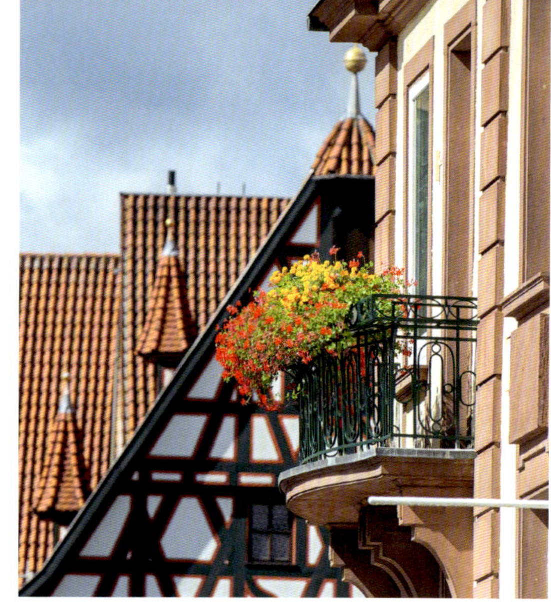

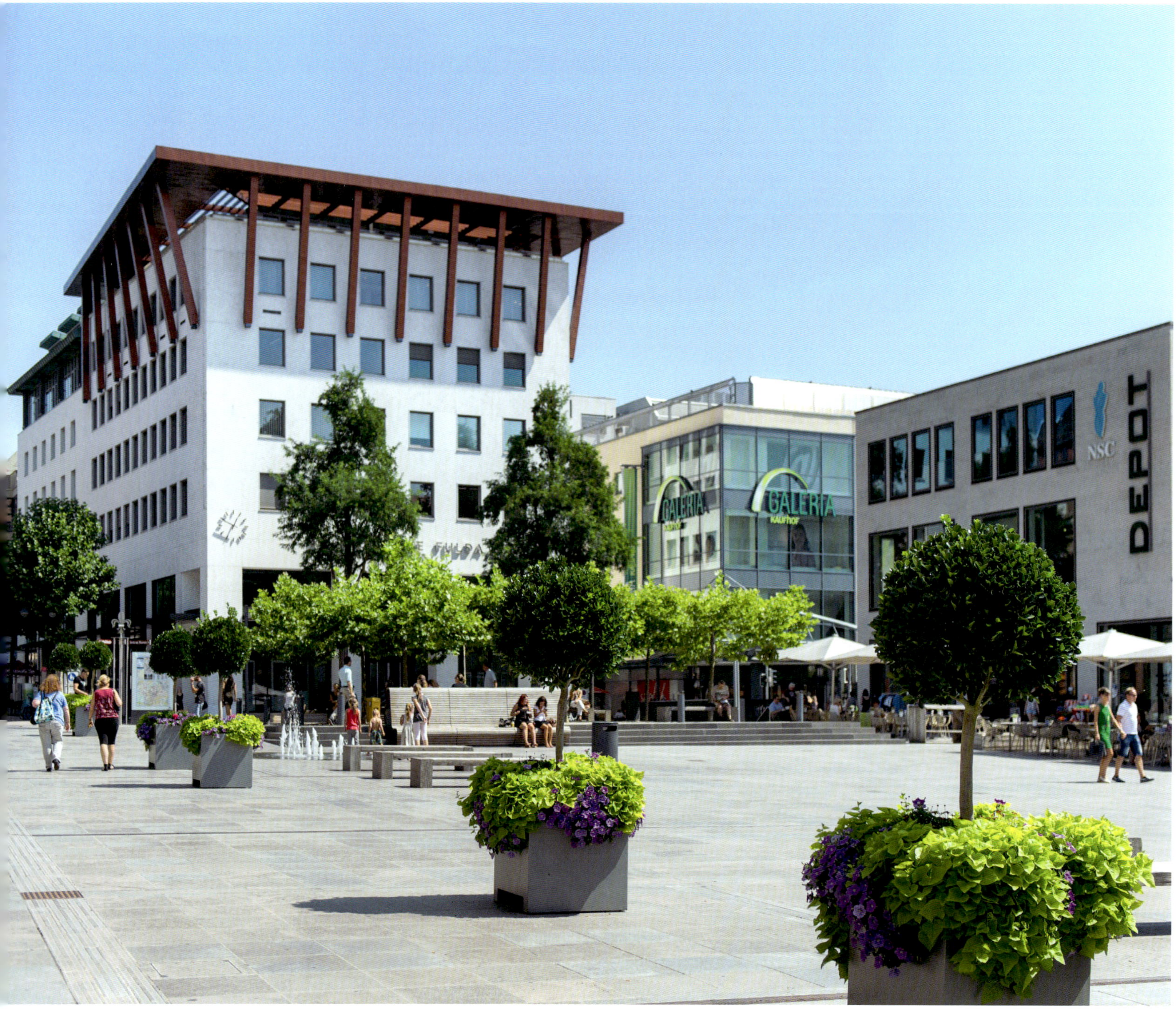

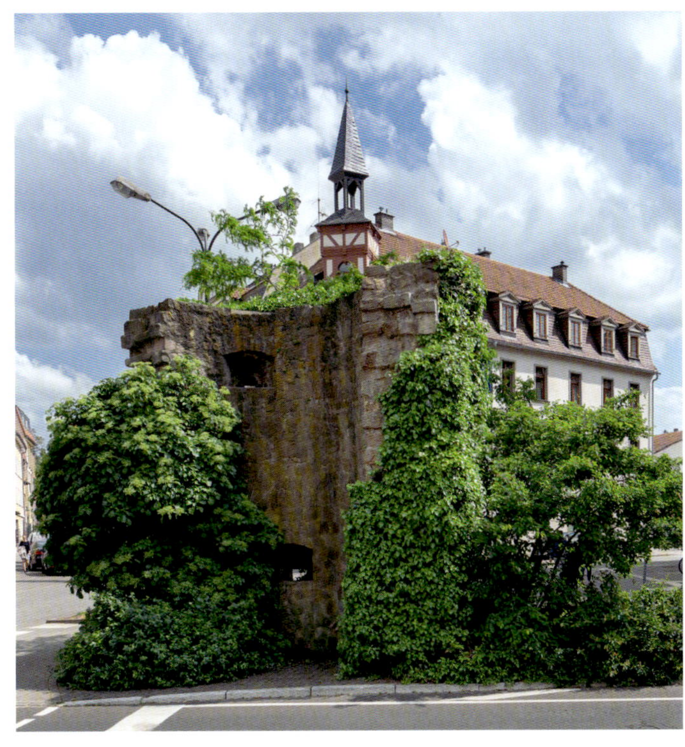

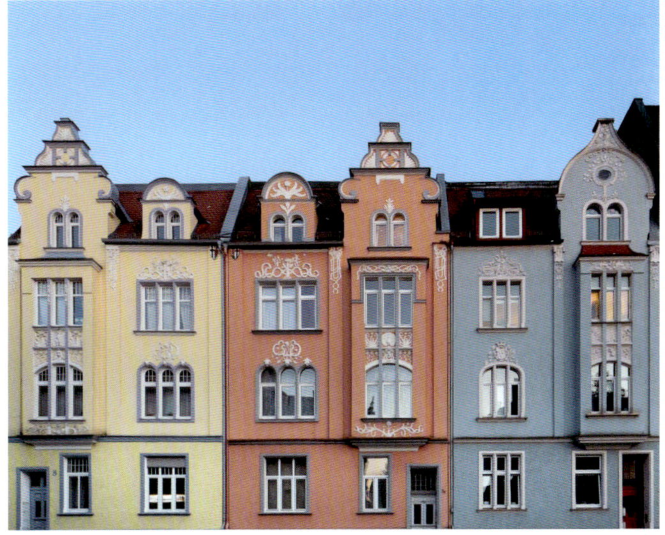

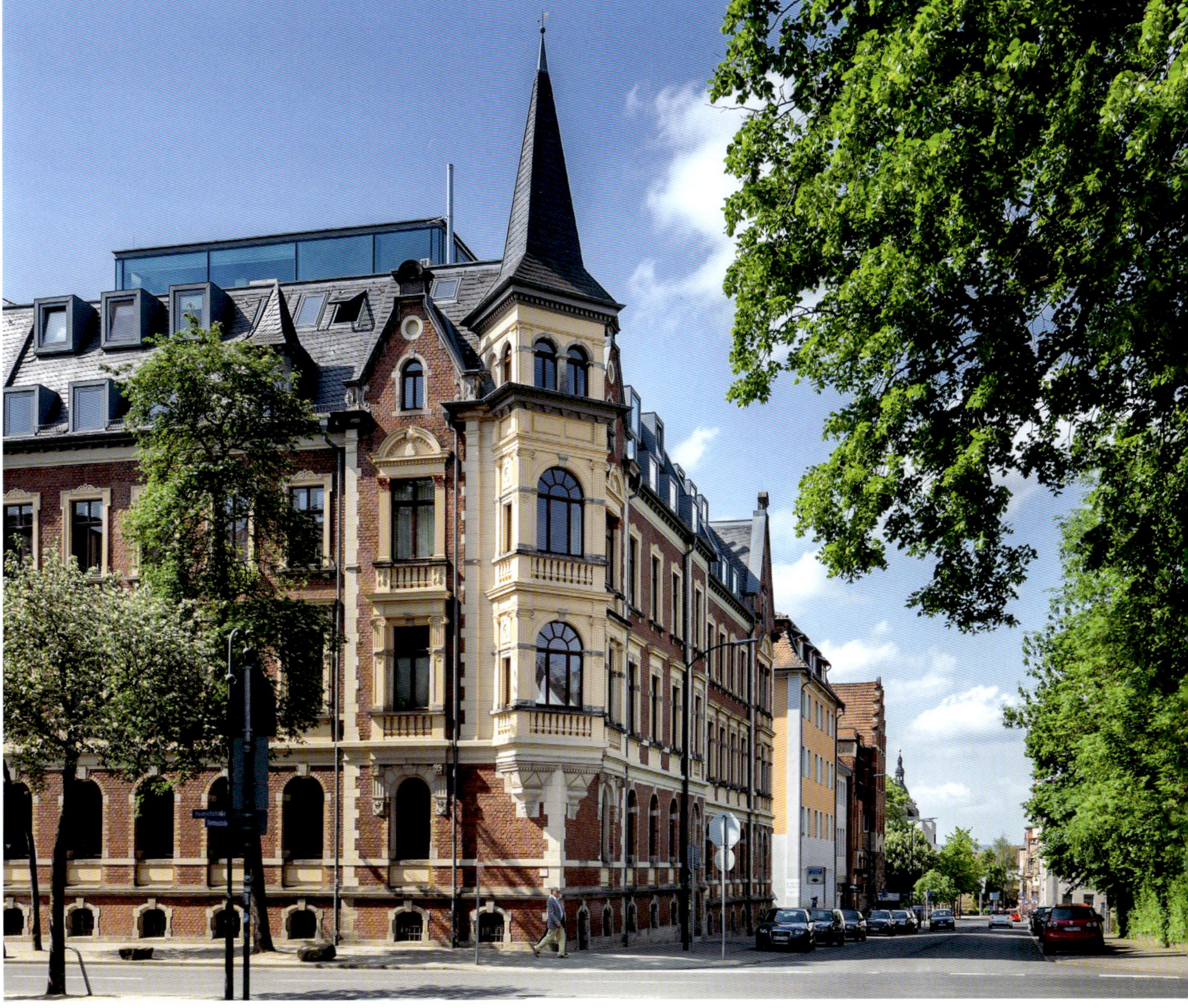

In diesem schmucken Gründerzeitbau in der Sturmiusstraße residierte jahrzehntelang die Polizei, heute ist dort innenstadtnahes Wohnen entstanden – ein Trend, der sich an vielen Stellen beobachten lässt.

This fine, early-20th-century building was once the police station. Today, it has been converted into apartments to provide inner city housing – a trend which you can observe in many places in the city.

Eine verschwenderische Pracht an Türmchen, Erkerchen, Schmuckgiebeln und Stuckornamenten – auch das findet sich zu Hauf im Viertel in Bahnhofsnähe. Punktuell setzt auch die Nachkriegsmoderne architektonische Akzente.

Near the station many buildings boast towerlets, bay windows, fine gables and stucco work. Here and there modern, post-war architecture creates a stark contrast.

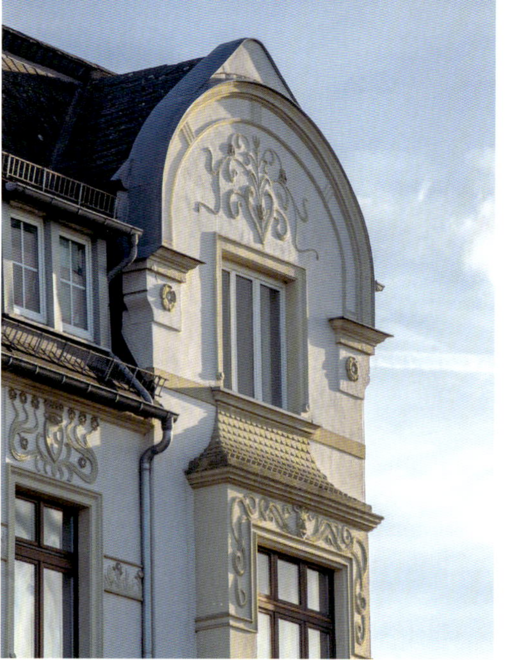

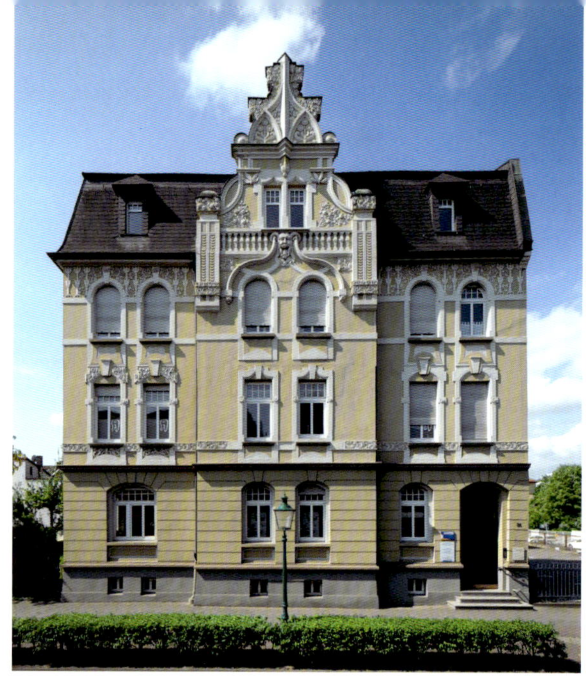

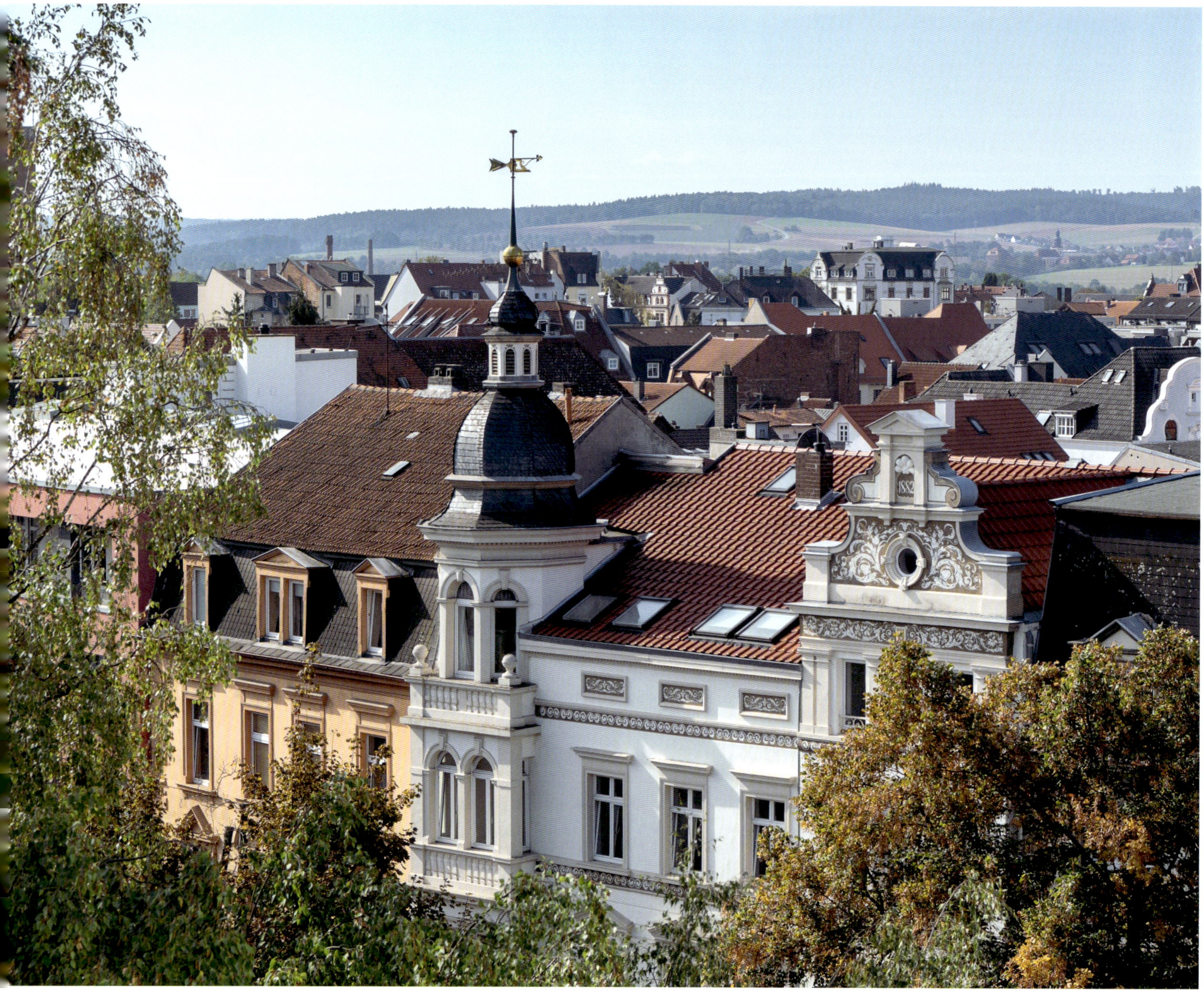

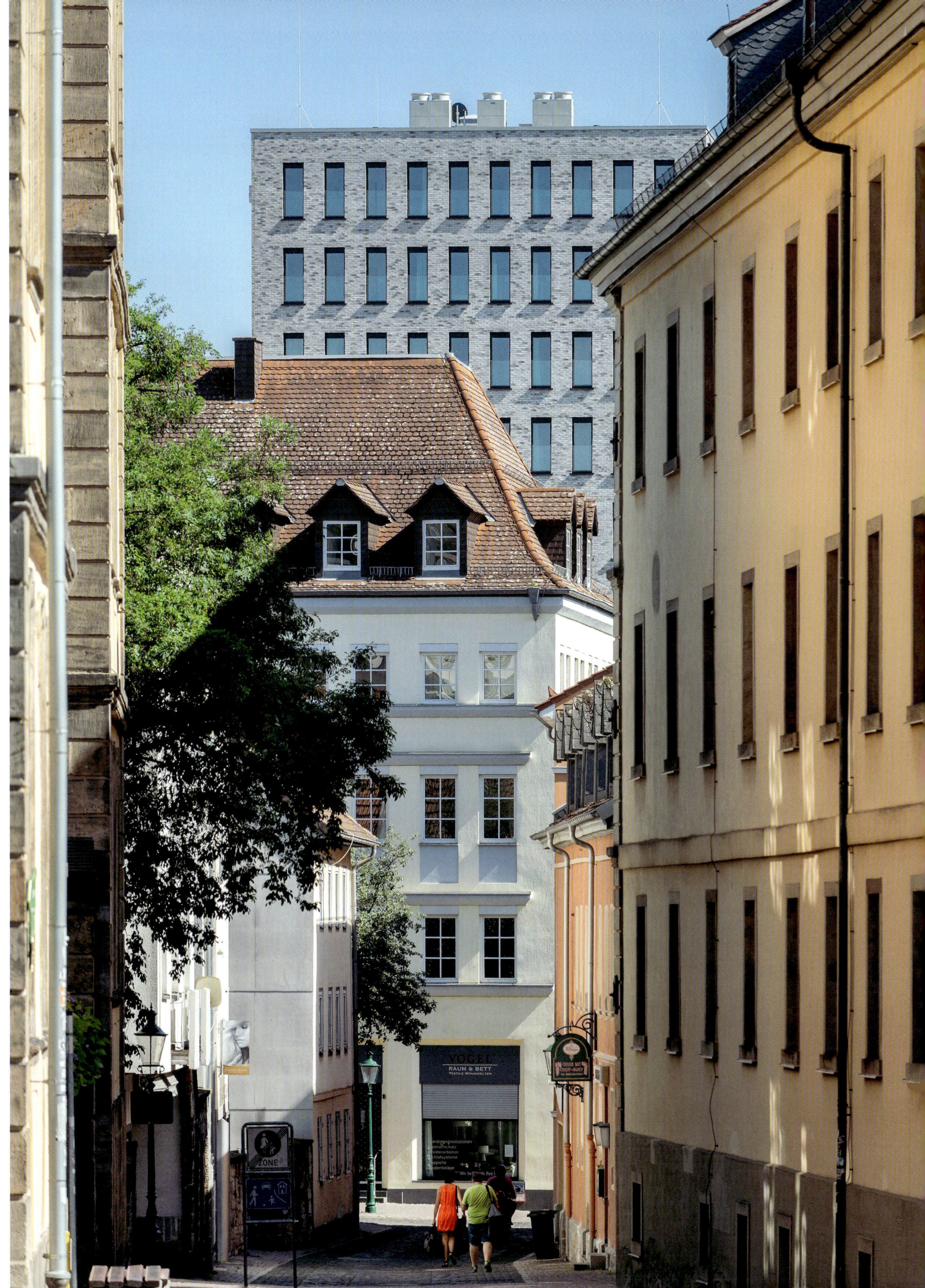
VOGEL
RAUM & BETT
TEXTILE WOHNWELTEN
ZONE

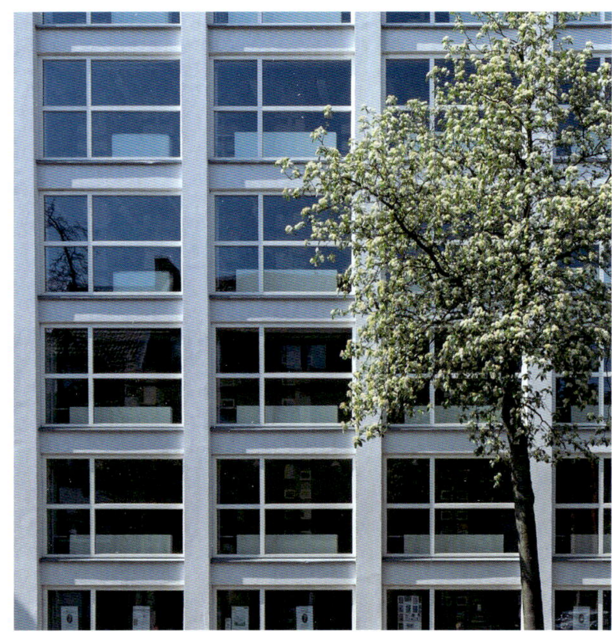

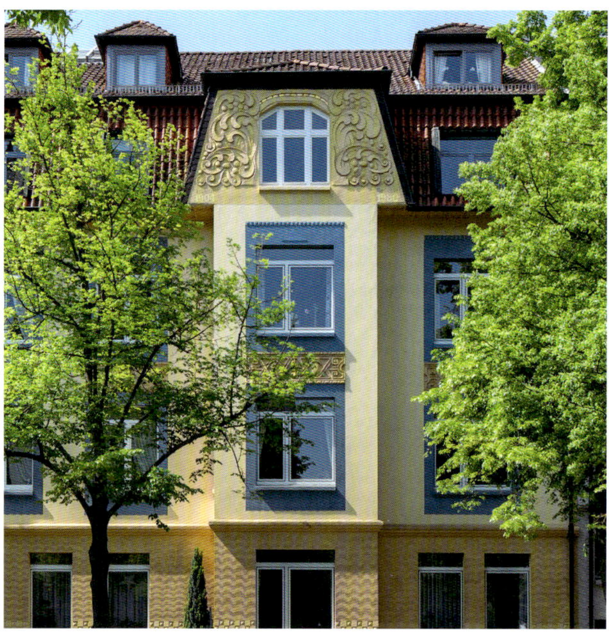

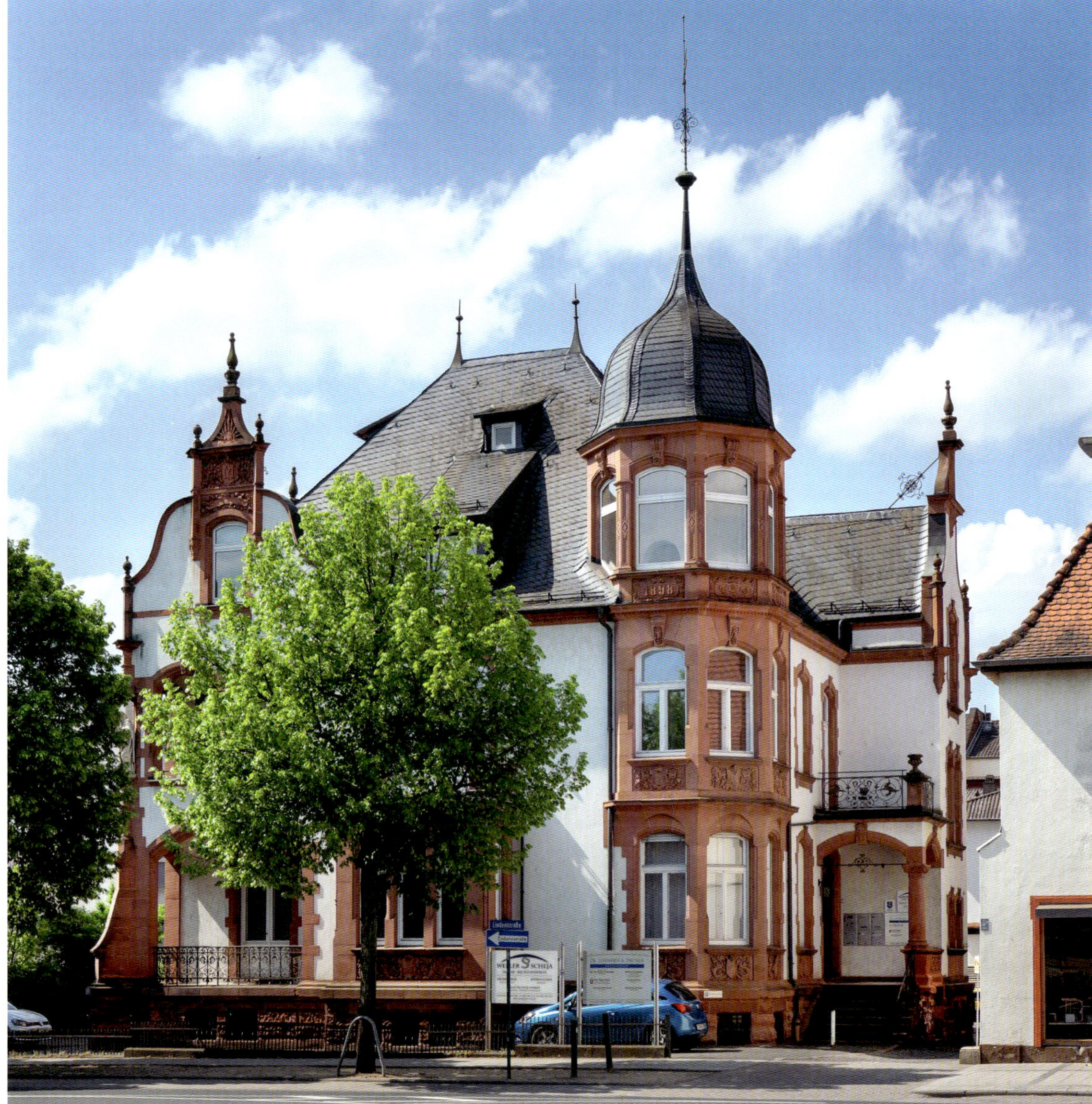

Herrschaftliche Villen wie die des Weinhändlers Müller in der Lindenstraße (gebaut 1898/99) sind im Viertel am Bahnhof an verschiedenen Stellen anzutreffen. Leider wurden in der Nachkriegszeit einige der schönsten Villen abgerissen, um Platz für eine moderne Bebauung – insbesondere für den Einzelhandel – zu schaffen.

Stately villas, like that of the wine merchant Müller in Lindenstrasse (built 1898/99), can be seen in various places in the railway station quarter. Unfortunately, some of the most beautiful of these villas were demolished after the war in order to make space for modern buildings, particularly shops.

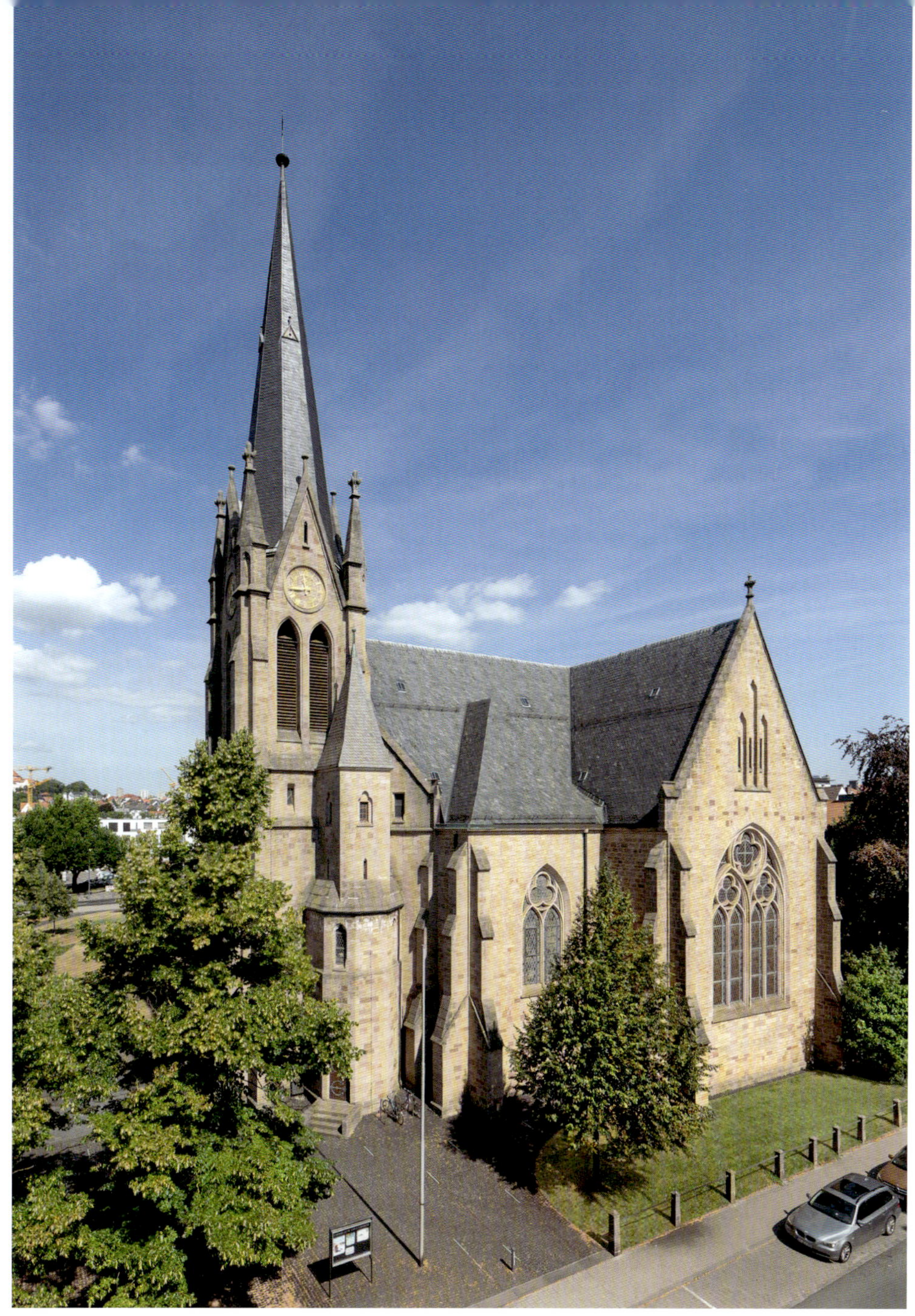

Die Christuskirche, 1894–96 im neugotischen Stil erbaut, ist die zentrale Kirche der evangelischen Christen im ursprünglich rein katholischen Fulda. In oranischer, kurhessischer und preußischer Zeit hatte sich im 19. Jahrhundert der Anteil der Protestanten in der Stadt erhöht, für die dann ein angemessenes Gotteshaus geschaffen wurde.

The Christuskirche, built from 1894 to 1896 in the Neo-gothic style, is the main protestant church in a city which was originally wholly catholic. In the 19th century the number of protestants in the city increased, so an appropriately large church was constructed.

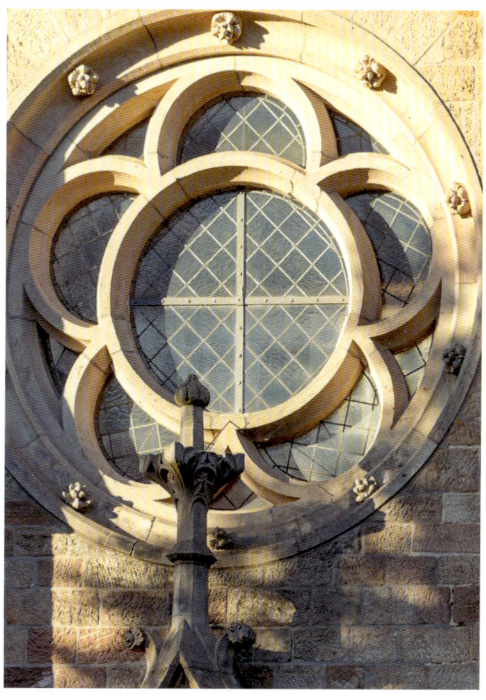

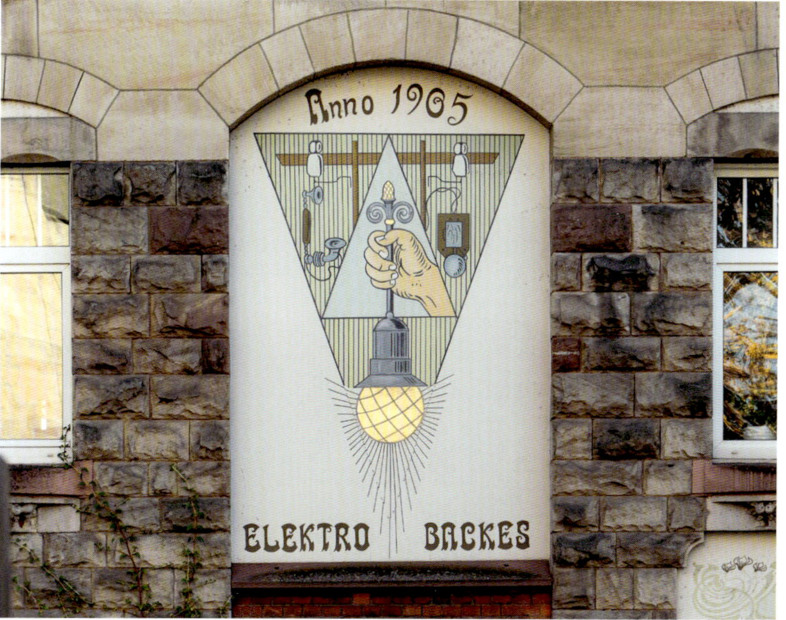

Auch typische Ornamente des Jugendstils gibt es in der Oberstadt – wie hier in der Sturmiusstraße – zu entdecken.

In the "Upper City" (here in the Sturmiusstrasse) you can also discover typical Art Nouveau ornamentation.

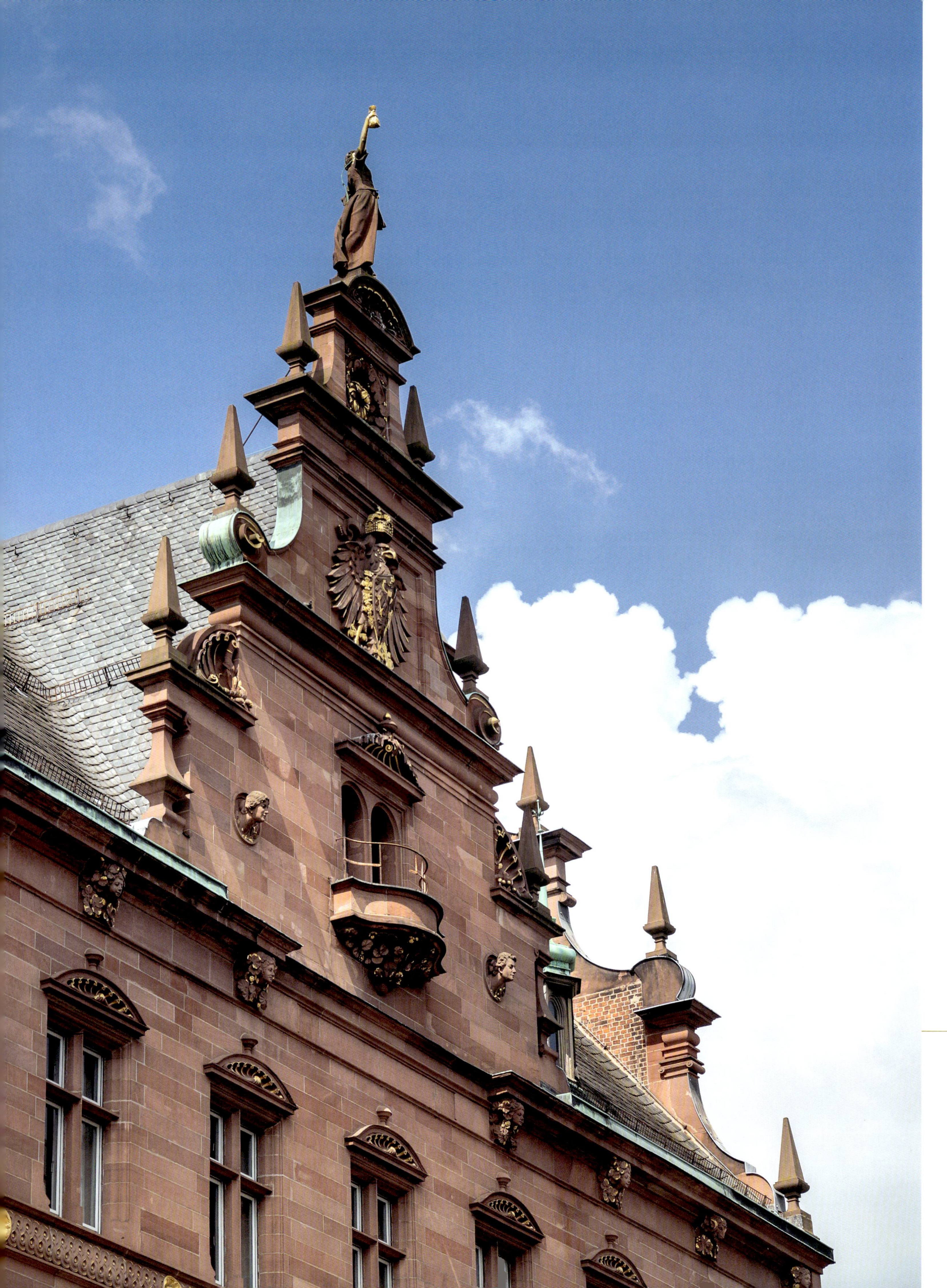

Die traditionsreiche Marienschule prägt einen ganzen Straßenzug zwischen Lindenstraße, Nikolausstraße und Heinrichstraße. Die Maria-Ward-Schule, deren Wurzeln bis in das Jahr 1733 zurückreichen, ist das einzige Mädchengymnasium der Stadt und der weiteren Umgebung.

Rich in tradition, the Marienschule lies between the Lindenstrasse, Niklausstrasse and Heinrichstrasse. The Maria Ward School, whose history dates back to 1773, is the only girls' secondary school (Gymnasium) in the whole area.

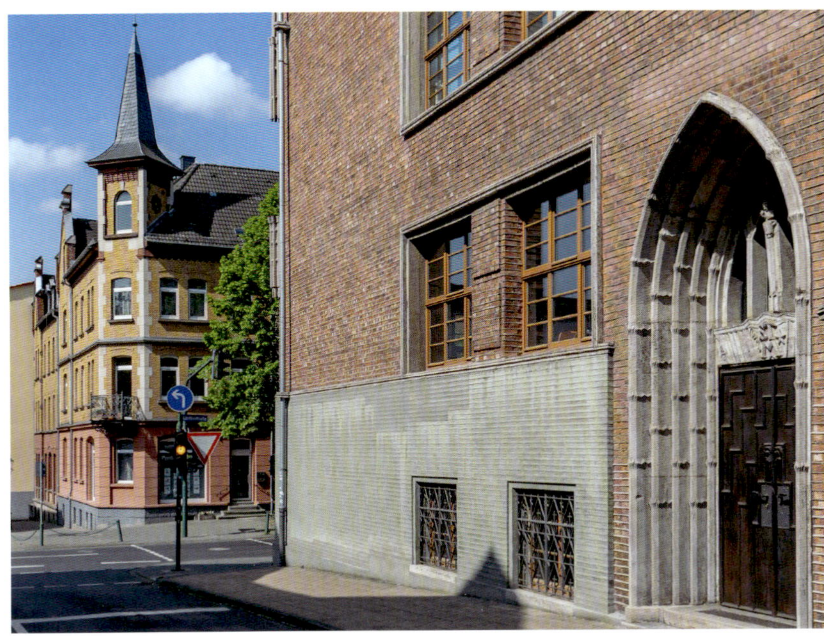

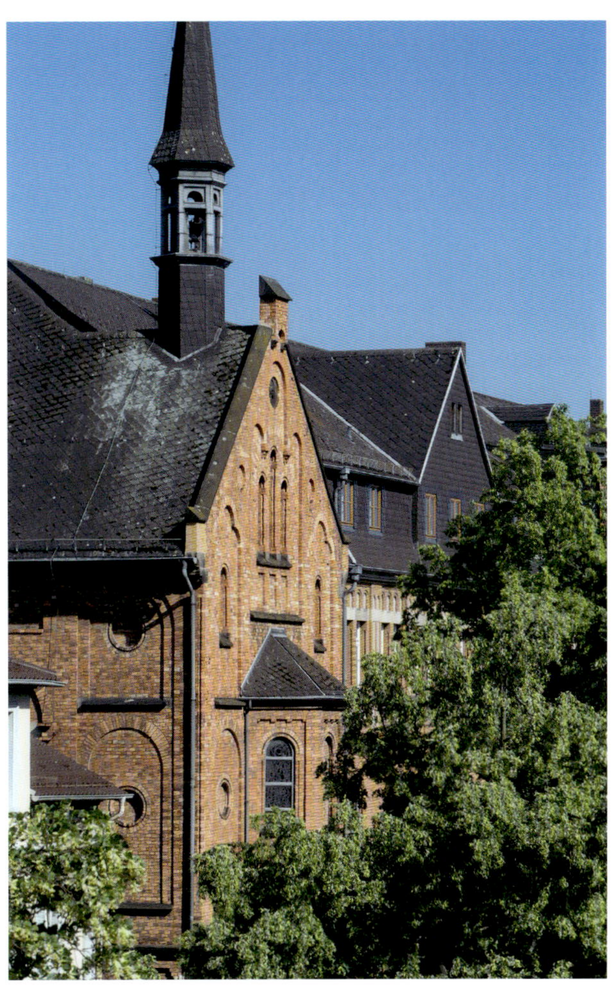

Die ehemalige Landeszentralbank in der Rabanusstraße, 1901/02 im Stil der Neorenaissance gebaut, wird geprägt durch den aufwendig gestalteten Giebel. Inzwischen beherbergt das Gebäude unter anderem ein Café und eine Ballettschule.

The former Hesse state central bank in the Rabanusstrasse features a finely designed gable. Built in 1901/02 in the Neo-renaissance style, the building now houses, among other businesses, a café and a ballet school.

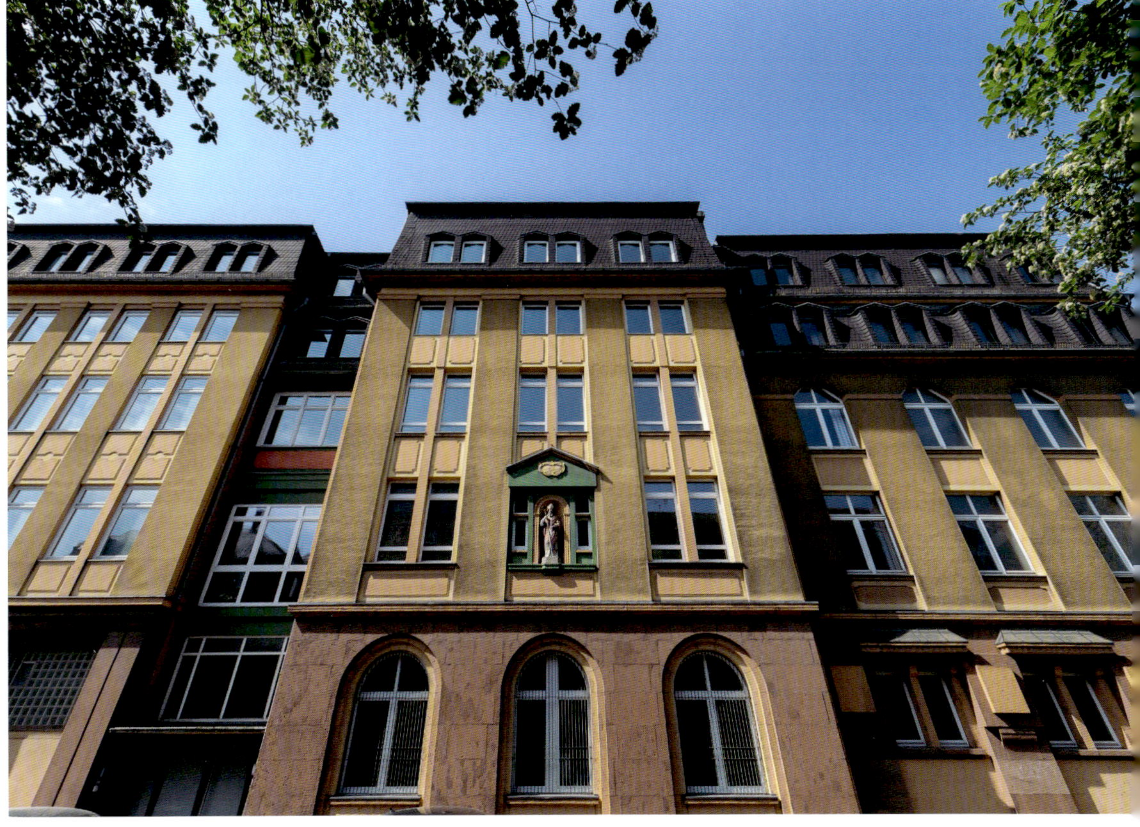

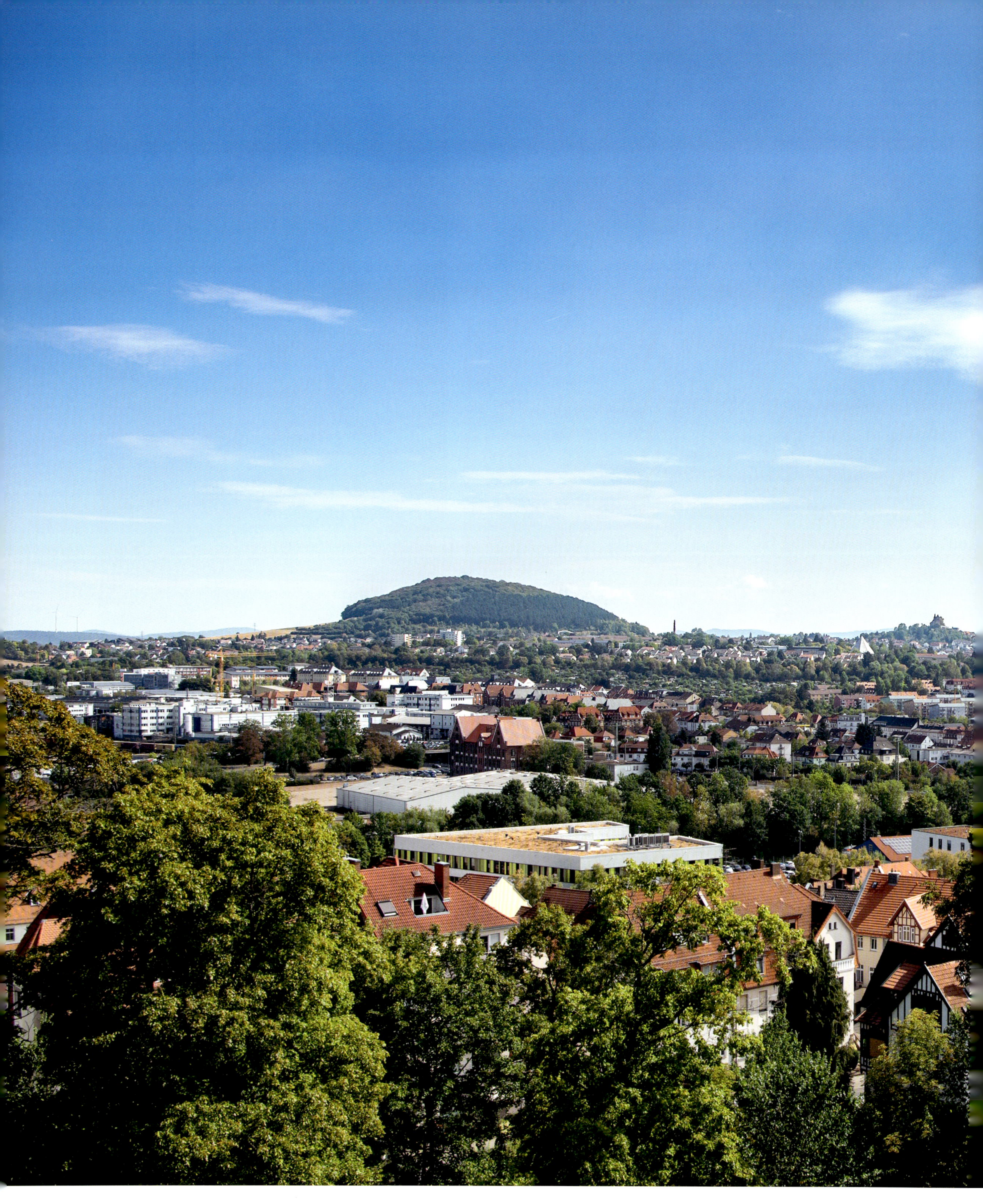

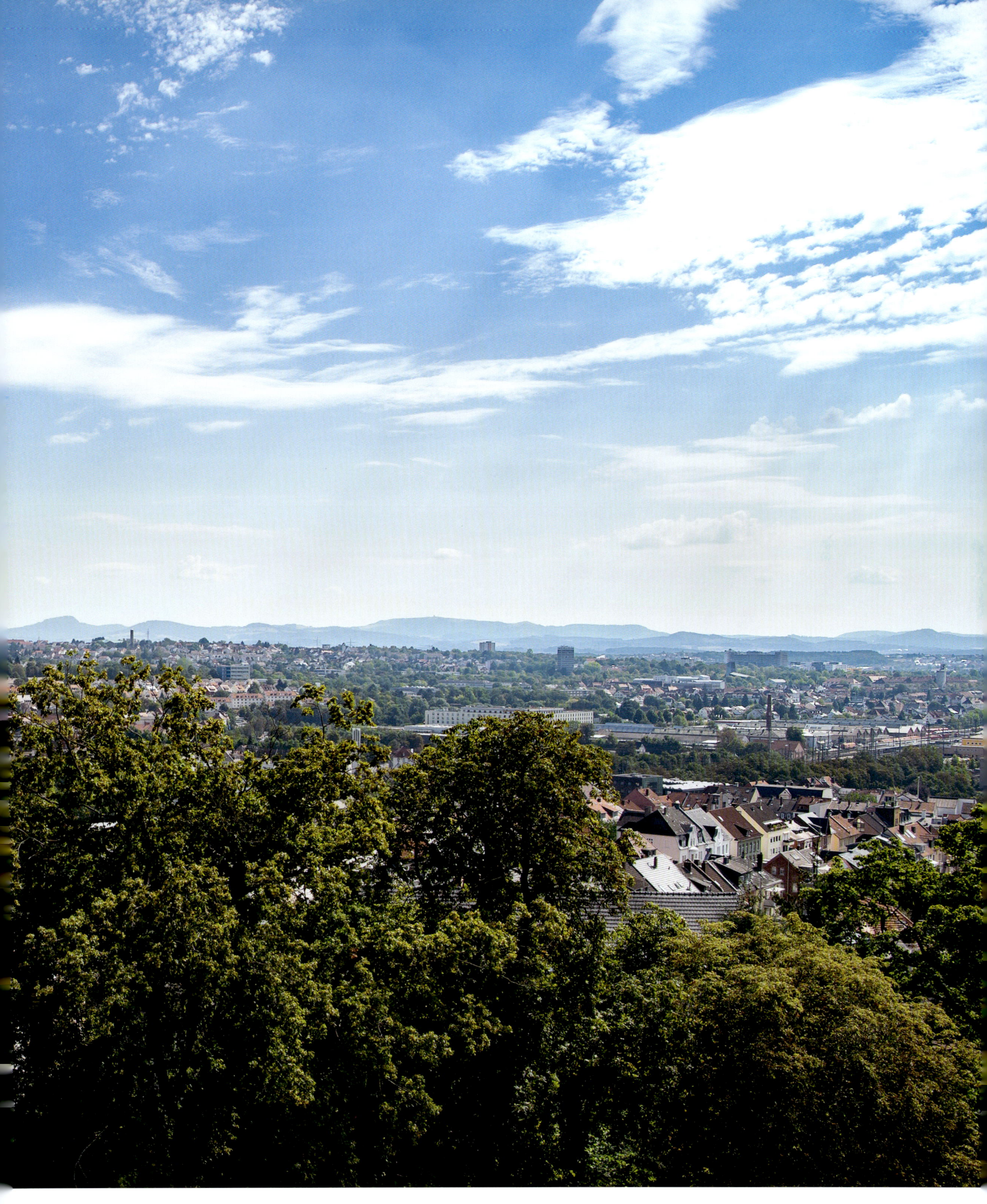

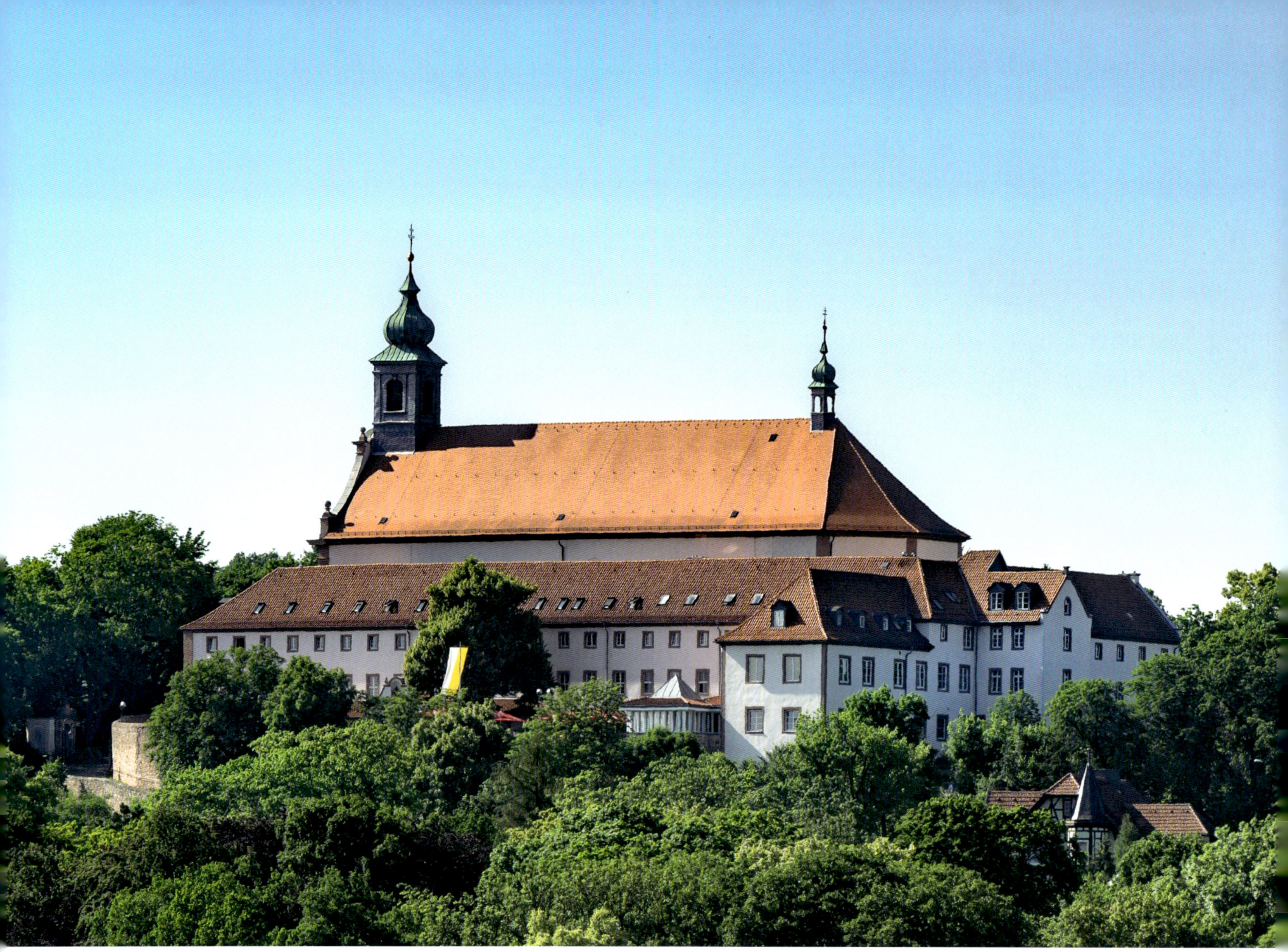

Weithin sichtbar thront das Kloster Frauenberg über Fulda. Der Überlieferung nach beobachtete der heilige Bonifatius von dem Berg aus die Fortschritte des Klosterbaus, für den sein Schüler Sturmius 744 den Anstoß gegeben hatte.

Perching on a hill above Fulda, the Frauenberg monastery can be seen from afar. According to legend, it was from this hill that St. Boniface observed the progress in the construction of the monastery which he had instructed his pupil, St. Sturmius, to build.

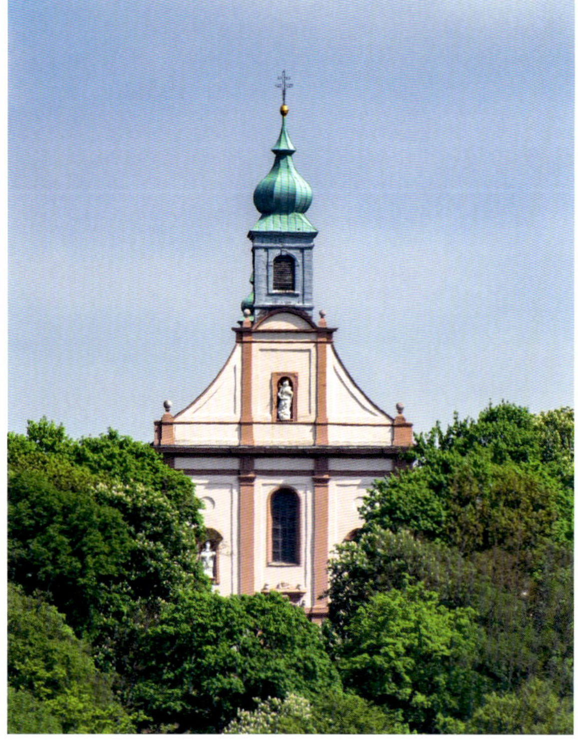

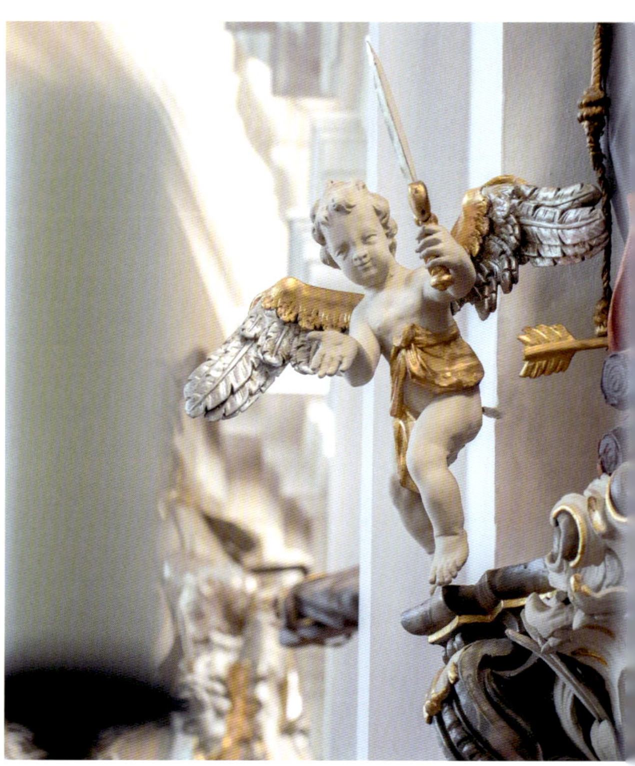

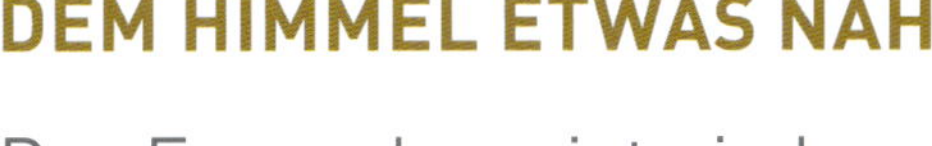

DEM HIMMEL ETWAS NÄHER

Der Frauenberg ist ein besonderer Sehnsuchtsort der Fuldaer – und zugleich ein Spiegel der Stadtgeschichte

Der Anstieg von der Stadt her ist recht beschwerlich, das ausgetretene Pflaster der Treppen könnte sicher unzählige Geschichten erzählen über die vielen frommen und weniger frommen Besucher, die sich im Laufe der Jahrhunderte den Weg zum Frauenberg hinaufbewegt haben. Doch gemeinsam dürfte allen das erhebende Gefühl gewesen sein, am Ende von oben auf die Stadt zu schauen und den Blick weiter schweifen zu lassen zu den anderen Hügeln des Fuldaer Beckens, die – gekrönt mit Klöstern, Kirchen oder Kapellen – einst den etwas vermessenen Vergleich Fuldas als „Rom des Nordens" genährt haben.

Es ist leicht vorstellbar, dass der Ausblick auf diese Landschaft schon dem heiligen Bonifatius ans Herz rührte, als er der Überlieferung nach vom Frauenberg aus die Baufortschritte seines Lieblingsklosters begutachtete – womöglich an einem sonnigen Herbstmorgen, wenn noch Bodennebel in den Talauen wabern, während in den höheren Lagen sich die Konturen schon messerscharf abzeichnen. Nicht nur für Bonifatius, auch für unzählige Fuldaerinnen und Fuldaer ist der Berg ein Sehnsuchtsort, und das sicher nicht nur deshalb, weil in den versteckten Ecken Richtung Kalvarienberg dem Vernehmen nach so manche zarte Bande geknüpft wurde ...

Der Frauenberg lag einst außerhalb der befestigten Stadt – entsprechend häufig ist er in unruhigen Zeiten erobert, sind Kirchen und Gebäude zerstört worden. Seine heutige Gestalt erhielt er erst ab 1758, als die seit 1623 hier ansässigen Franziskanermönche ihr Kloster und die Klosterkirche im spätbarocken Stil erbauten. Die Franziskaner, bei der katholischen Bevölkerung des Fuldaer Landes unter anderem als gute Beichtväter und Prediger beliebt, machten den Frauenberg 1894 für mehr als 100 Jahre zum Mittelpunkt ihrer Thüringischen Ordensprovinz. Heute werden die Gebäude gemeinsam mit „antonius – Netzwerk Mensch" unter anderem für ein inklusives Wohnprojekt genutzt.

Closer to the Heavens

Fulda locals have a special affection for the Frauenberg - a place which also reflects Fulda's history.

The ascent up from the city is fairly hard-going and the worn, cobblestone steps could surely tell a few tales of the many pious, and not so pious, visitors who have made their way up the Frauenberg over the course of history. Yet, they must have all experienced that up-lifting feeling of looking back down over the city on reaching the top. From this vantage point you can let your view drift over the other hills of the Fulda valley which – crowned as they are by monasteries, churches or chapels – once earned Fulda the somewhat exaggerated epithet "the Rome of the North".

It is not hard to imagine that this view also touched St. Boniface's heart as he looked down on the completion of the construction of this favourite monastery – perhaps on a sunny autumn morning, when the mist hangs in the river meadows while in the higher areas the contours are cut sharply. Not just for St. Boniface, but for many, many Fulda people the hill is a place of inner longing – and not only because it is said that in hidden corners up towards Kalvarienberg many tender ties of affection have been formed. The Franciscans – who have always been appreciated as good preachers and confessors by the Catholics in the Fulda area – made the monastery the centre of the Thuringian province of their order in 1894, which it then remained for a hundred years. Today, the buildings are used in cooperation with "antonius - Netzwerk Mensch" for, among other things, an inclusive residential project.

In former times the Frauenberg lay outside the city walls, so in periods of strife the churches and the buildings were often destroyed. The current appearance of the monastery and the church dates back to 1758 when the Franciscan friars, who had been here since 1623, constructed the buildings in the late-Baroque style.

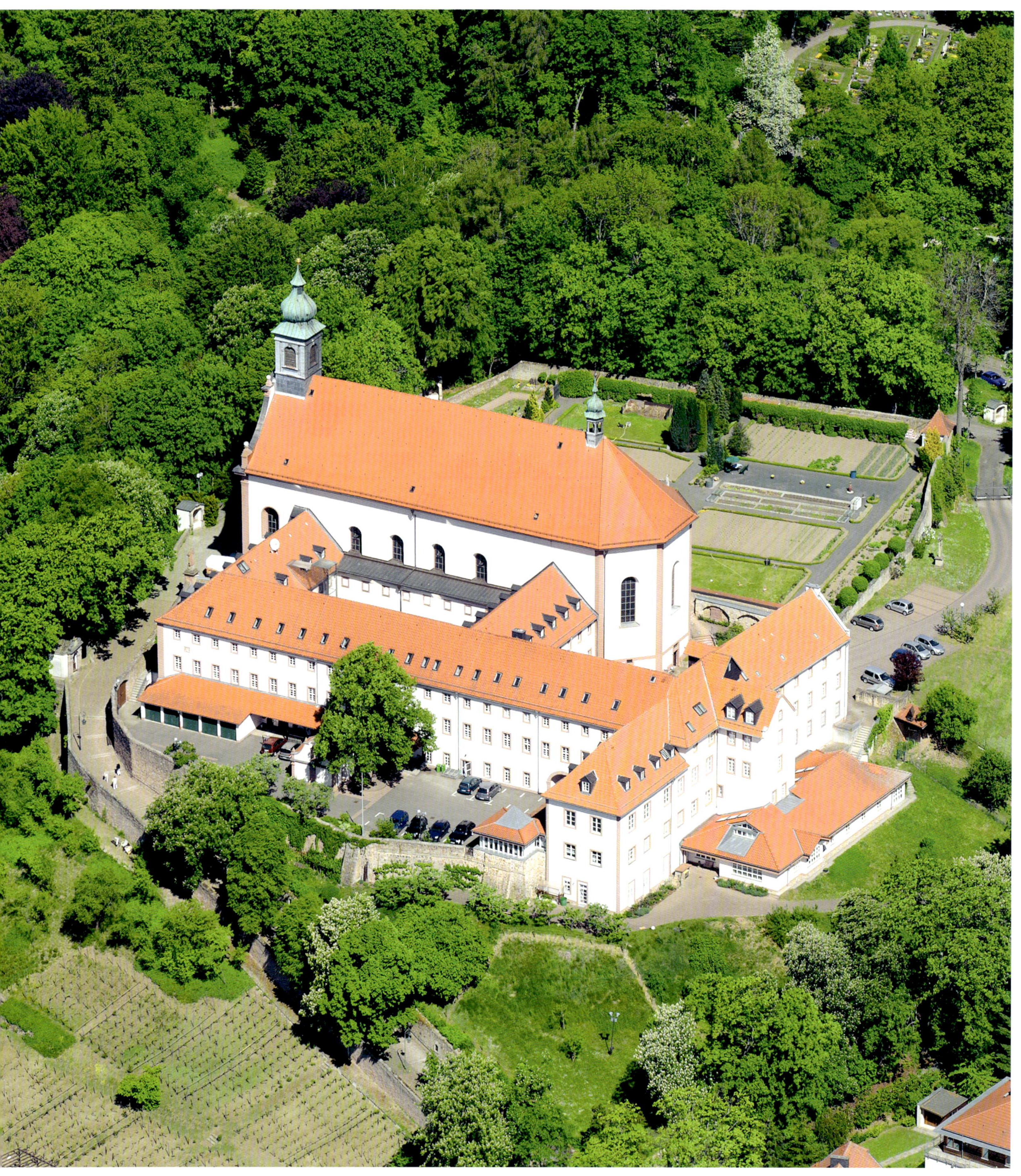

Die spätbarocke Klosterkirche entstand nach einem Großbrand 1757, bei dem das Kloster massiv zerstört wurde. Beim Neubau waren die Franziskaner selbst federführend: In ihren Reihen gab es namhafte Baumeister, Kunsthandwerker und Künstler.

This late-Baroque monastery church was built after a fire destroyed much of the monastery in 1757. The Franciscans themselves were greatly involved in the reconstruction project as there were reputable architects, craftsmen and artists among the friars.

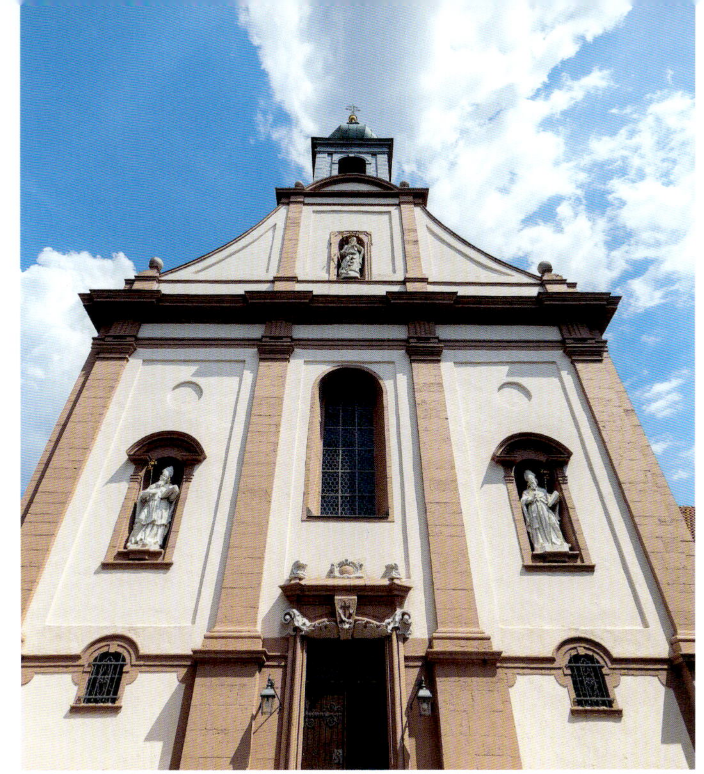

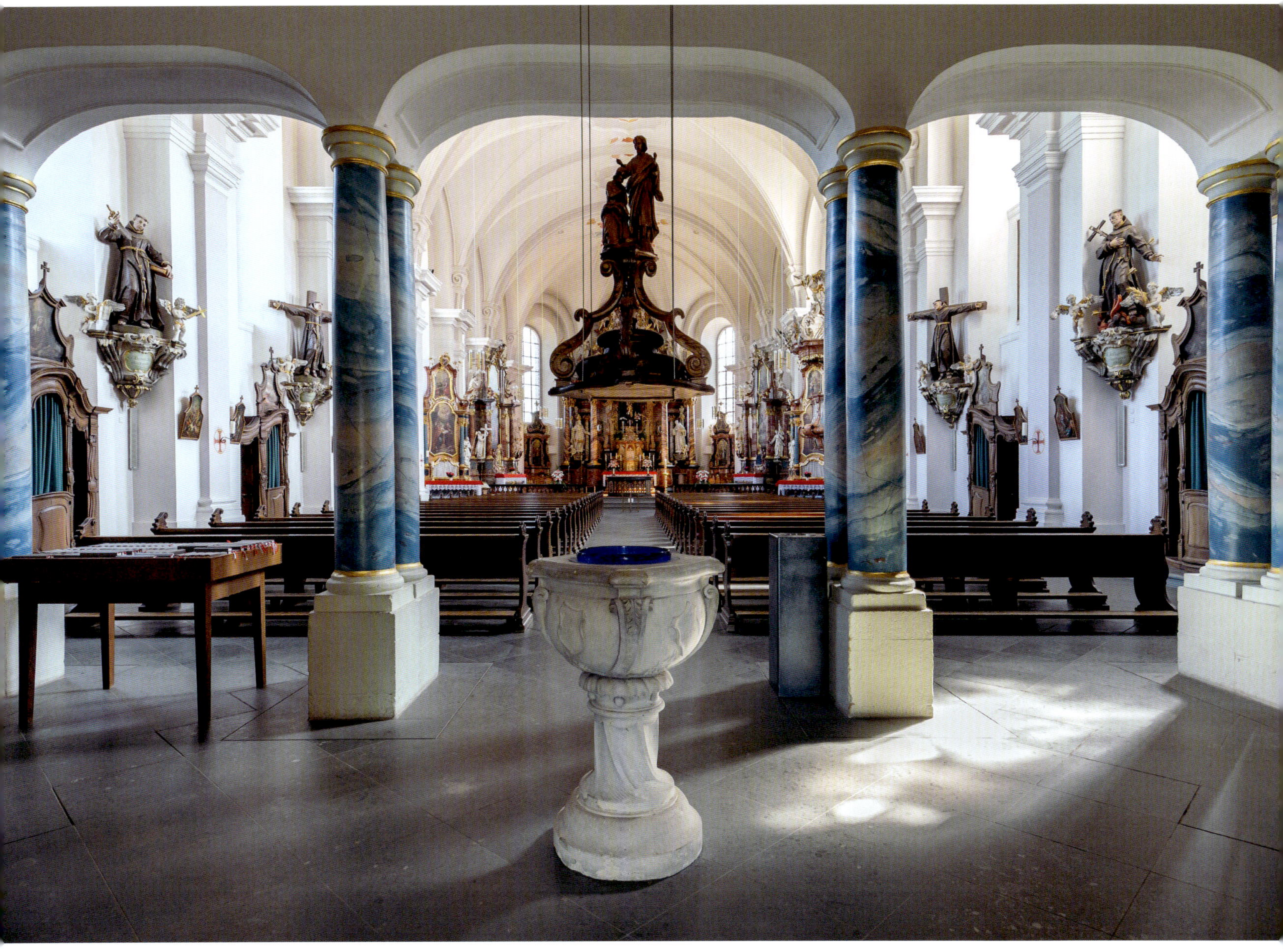

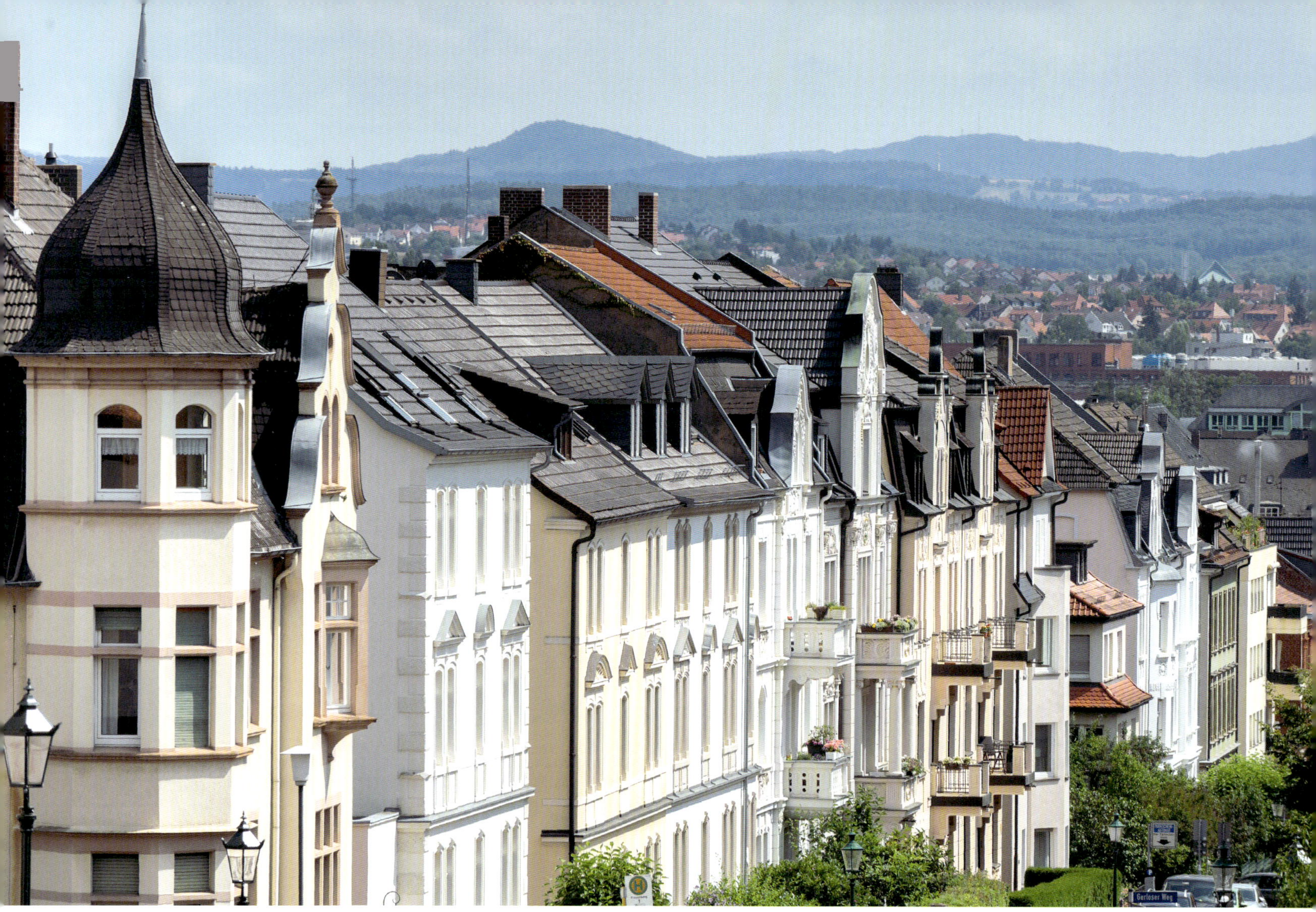

In wilhelminischer Zeit wuchs die Stadt auch über die Leipziger Straße hinaus in Richtung Frauenberg. Es entstand in relativ kurzer Zeit ein bevorzugtes Wohngebiet, das sich nur der wohlhabendere Teil der Bevölkerung leisten konnte.

At the turn of the 20th century the city grew over the Leipziger Strasse towards the Frauenberg. Within a short time this area became a desirable residential area with houses which could only be afforded by the wealthy.

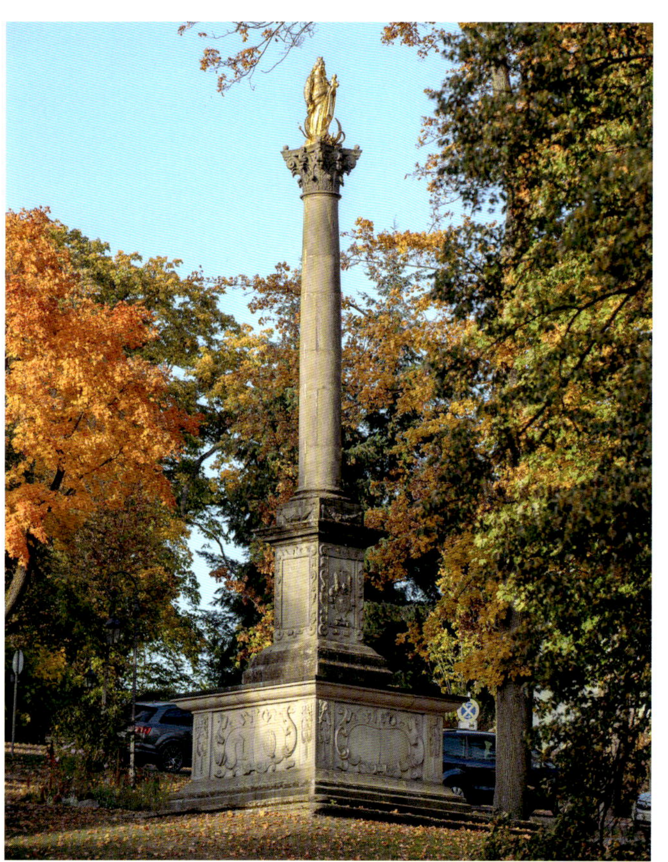

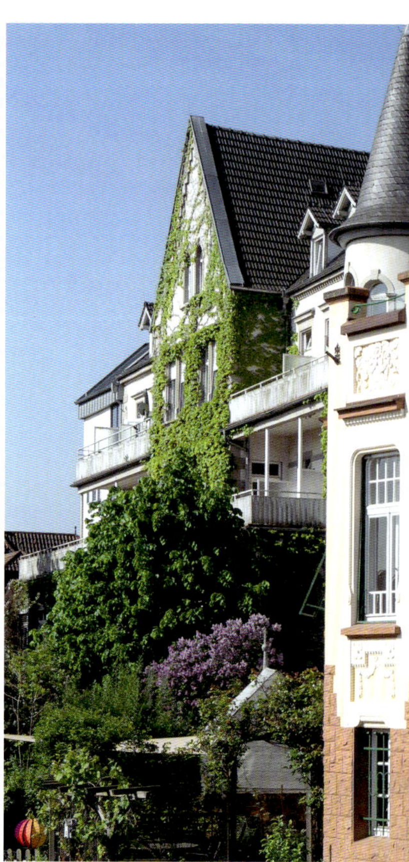

HERRSCHAFTLICHES WOHNEN IM GRÜNEN

Die Villen am Frauenberg zeugen vom Selbstbewusstsein des Fuldaer Bürgertums in der Zeit der Industrialisierung

Marienstraße, Elisabethenstraße, Klosterweg und Gerloser Weg, Adalbertstraße und Parkstraße – diese Adressen haben in Fulda seit mehr als hundert Jahren einen besonderen Klang. Hier – am Süd- und Westhang des Frauenbergs, klimatisch begünstigt und mit frischer Luft aus Richtung Westen versorgt – entwickelte sich um die Wende vom 19. zum 20. Jahrhundert das bevorzugte Wohngebiet der Wohlhabenden. Die herrschaftlichen Villen – die im Volksmund nach der Profession ihrer Besitzer bald Spitznamen wie die „Eier-“ oder „Kartoffelburg“ erhielten – schienen miteinander um Größe und Pracht zu wetteifern und traten optisch sogar in Konkurrenz zum Kloster auf dem Berg. Fabrikanten und erfolgreiche Händler demonstrierten mit den Gebäuden bürgerliches Selbstbewusstsein. Und noch heute ist der durchgrünte Stadtteil die teuerste Wohnlage der Stadt.

Elegant Living in Leafy Surroundings

The villas illustrate the growing confidence of the middle class during the period of the industrialisation. Marienstrasse, Elisabethenstrasse, Klosterweg und Gerloser Weg, Adalbertstrasse and Parkstrasse are street names which have had a special ring to them for more than a hundred years. The south and west slopes of the Frauenberg enjoy a favourable climate and a good supply of fresh air from the west – just two of the reasons why this area became popular with the wealthy at the turn of the 20th century. The elegant villas were soon given names by the local people like the "Egg Castle" or the "Potato Castle" which referred to the profession of the owner. Factory owners and successful businessmen demonstrated their improved social status by means of these buildings. Still today this leafy area contains the most expensive property in the city.

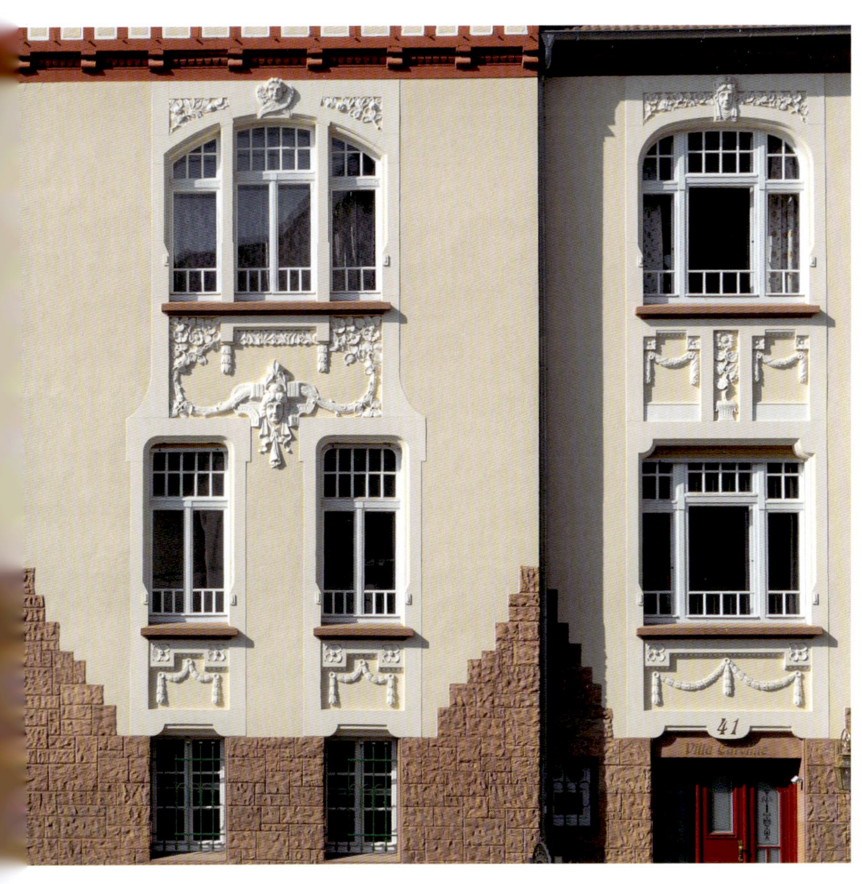

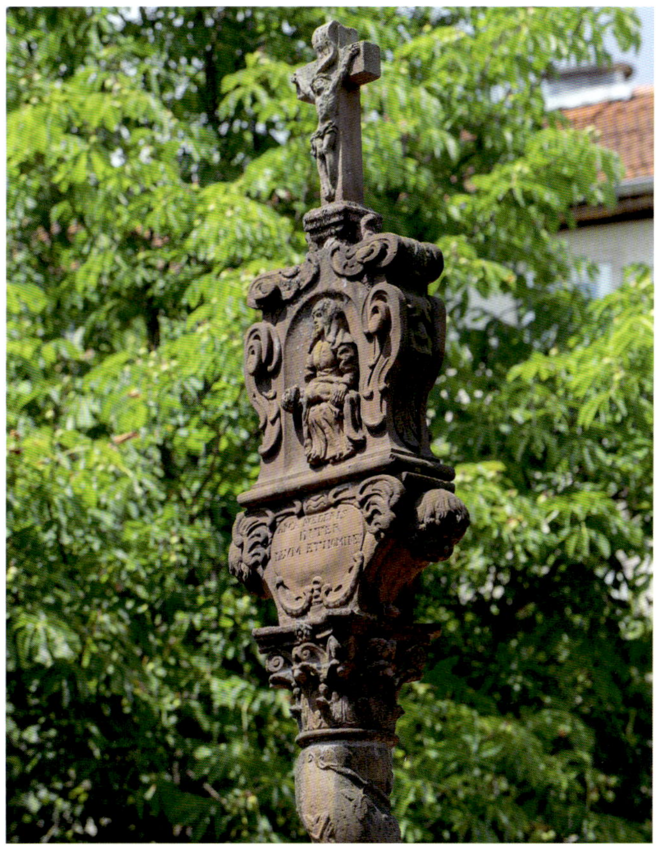

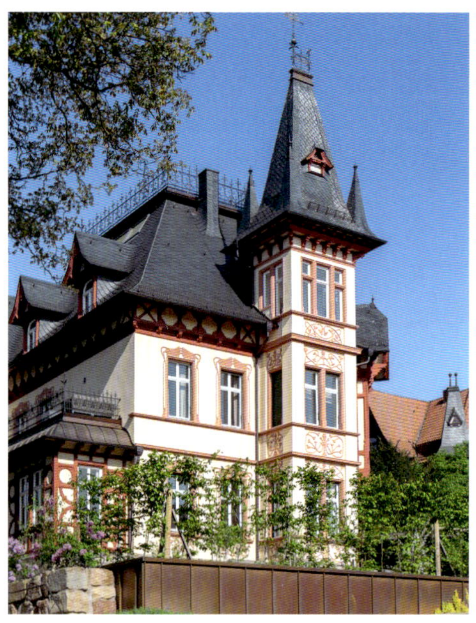

Der Historismus der wilhelminischen Epoche hinterließ auf dem Frauenberg viele bauliche Zeugnisse.

The influence of Historicism at the beginning of the 20th century can be seen in many of the houses on Frauenberg.

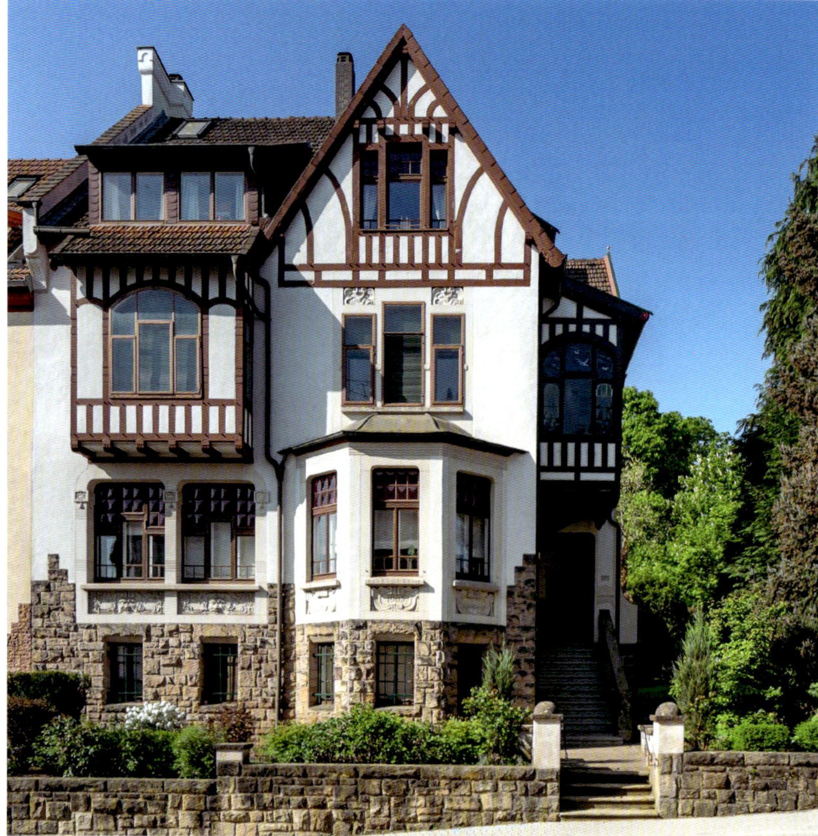

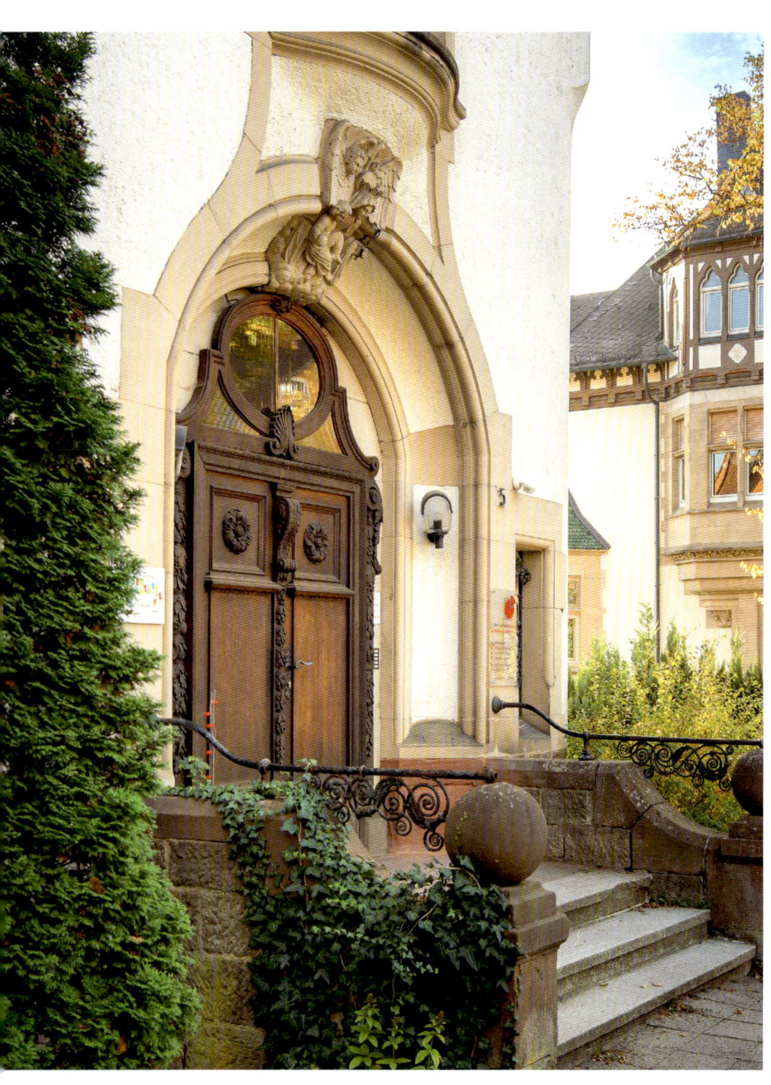

Viel Grün durchzieht das Wohngebiet Frauenberg – und macht es auch heute noch zu einer der teuersten Lagen der Stadt.

The residential area on Frauenberg is very green, making it one of the most expensive property locations in Fulda.

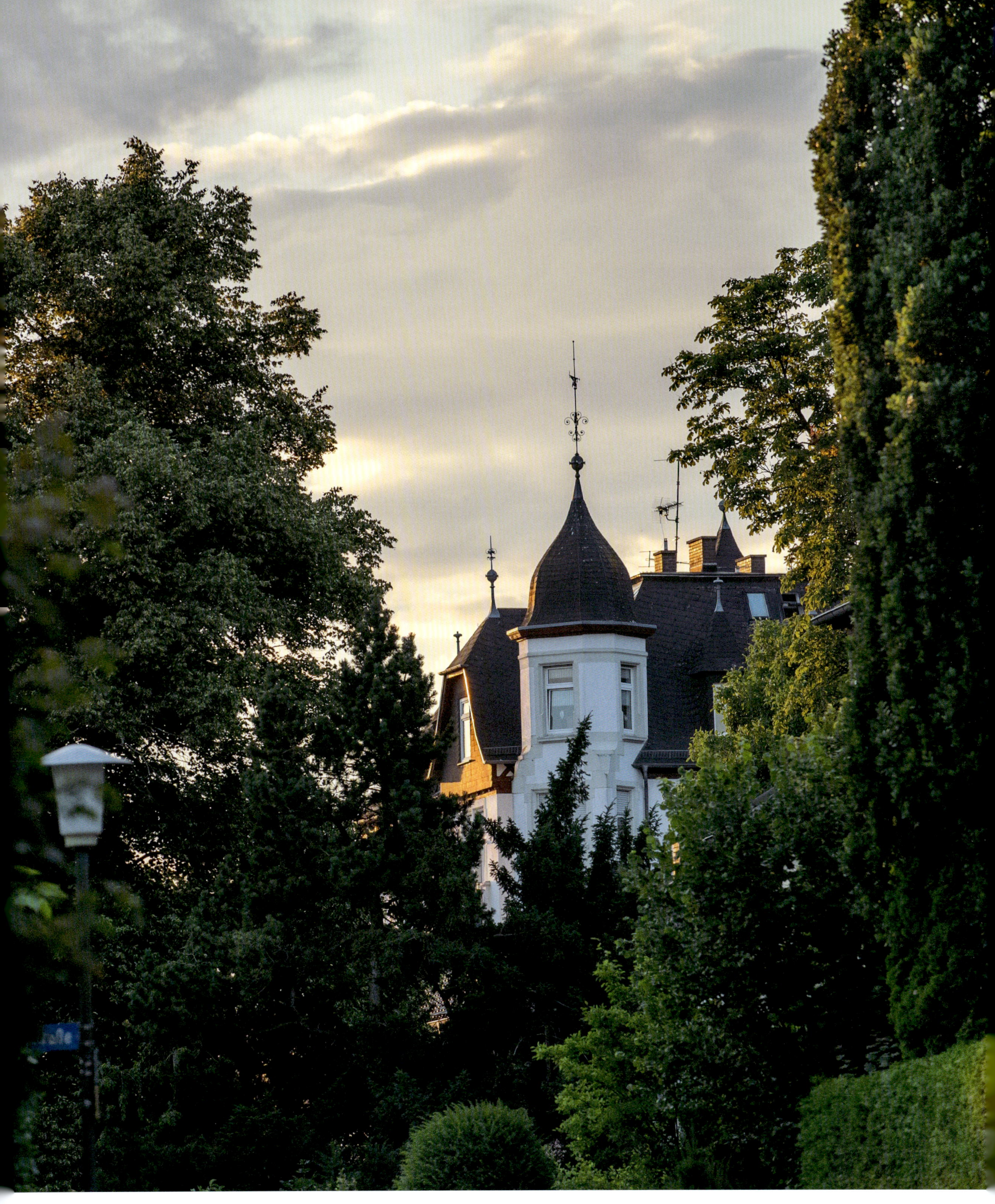

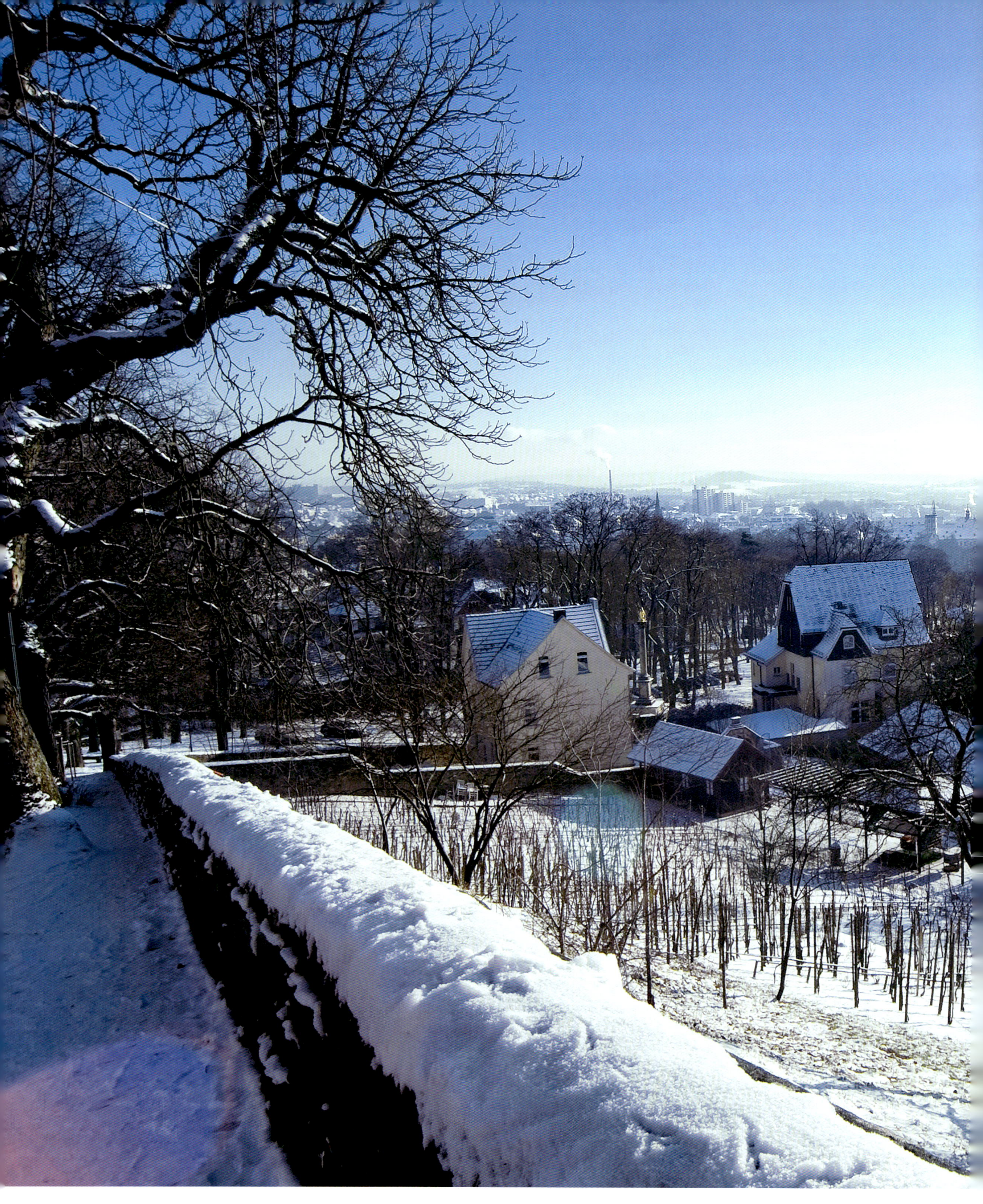

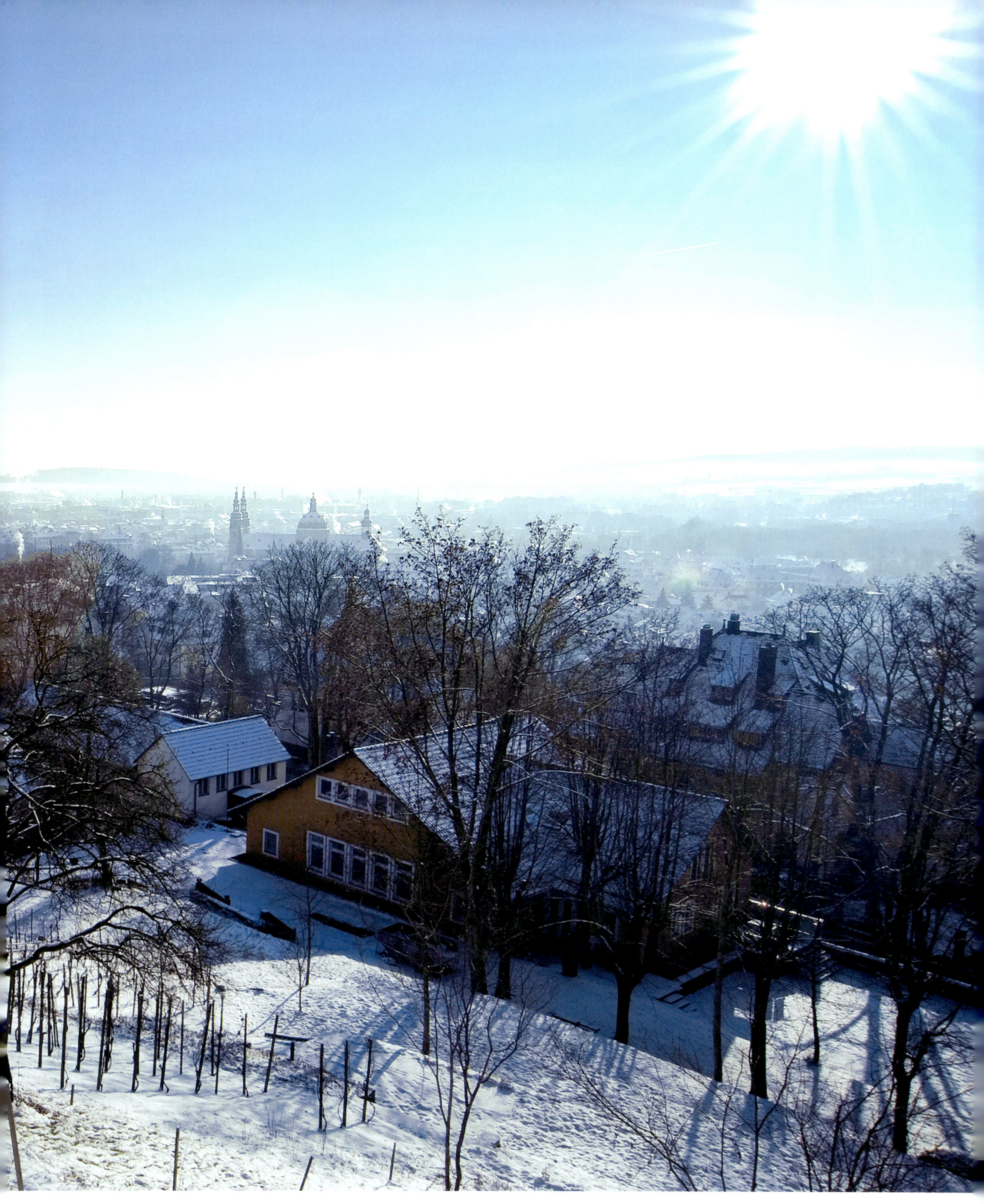

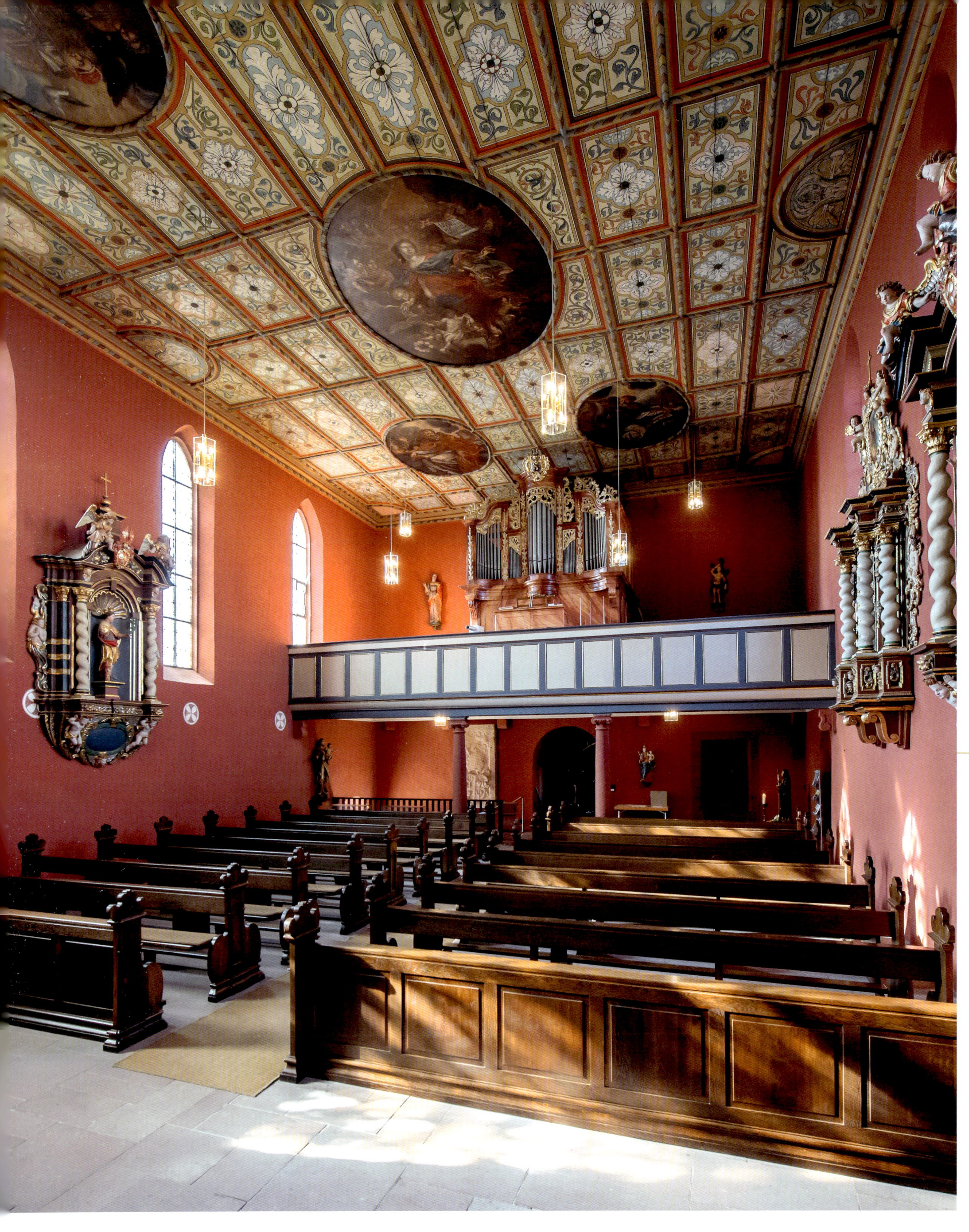

EIN PERLENKRANZ UM DIE STADT

Auf den Hügeln um Fulda bildeten – in Kreuzform verteilt – vier Klöster die Keimzellen für weitere Orte

Zieht man eine Linie vom Kloster Frauenberg (siehe Seite 133) zur Propstei Johannesberg im Süden der Stadt sowie eine imaginäre Verbindung von der Kirche St. Andreas im westlichen Stadtteil Neuenberg zur Bergkirche St. Peter im Osten, so entsteht ein (etwas schiefes) Kreuz, dessen Balken sich nahezu exakt am Fuldaer Dom kreuzen. Diese geometrischen Bezugspunkte sind keineswegs ein Zufall: Denn schon in karolingischer Zeit legte man sehr bewusst auf den Hügeln rings um Fulda Nebenklöster an, und die christliche Symbolik des Kreuzes drängte sich angesichts der topografischen Gegebenheiten geradezu auf. Die ehemaligen Klöster bilden heute einen Perlenkranz um die Stadt, die einen touristischen Abstecher unbedingt lohnen. Da ist zunächst die Propstei

The String of Pearls Around the City

There are four monasteries on the hills around Fulda, around each of which settlements grew, their positions making up the shape of a cross.

If you draw a line from Frauenberg monastery (see p. 133) to the Propstei Johannesberg to the south of the city, then a further line from the church of St. Andreas in the west to the hill church of St. Peter in the east, you form a (somewhat bent) cross. The beams of this cross meet almost exactly over the cathedral. These geometric patterns are by no means coincidental: in the Carolingian period subsidiary monasteries were very intentionally built on the hills around Fulda and the Christian symbolism of the cross obviously became apparent due to the topography of the area. The

Der einschiffige Kirchenraum von St. Peter (Liobakirche) auf dem Petersberg stammt aus dem Jahr 1479, der Chorraum und die Krypta sind jedoch wesentlich älter.

The aisle-less church of St. Peter (Liobakirche) on Petersberg is from the year 1479. The sanctuary and the crypt, however, are much older.

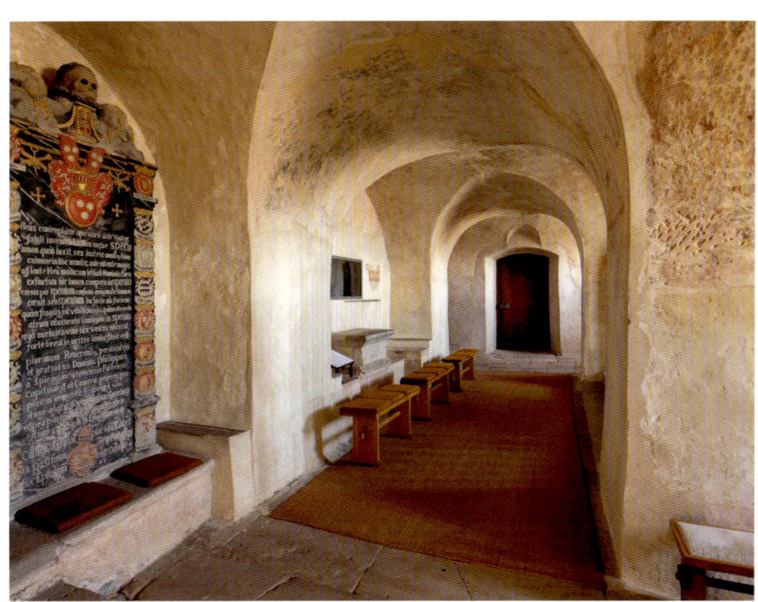

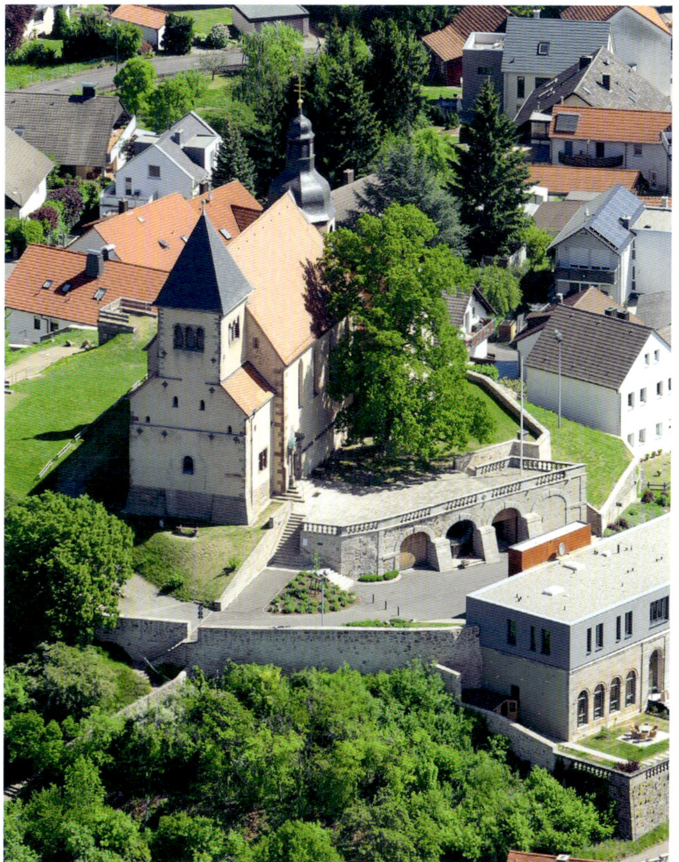

Petersberg mit der Grabeskirche der heiligen Lioba. Die Kirche wurde zwischen 836 und 838 unter Abt Rabanus Maurus, der hier auch einen Teil seines Lebens als Gelehrter verbrachte, geweiht. Die Fresken in der Krypta zählen zu den ältesten erhaltenen Wandmalereien in Deutschland. Der Standort auf dem Hügel war ideal gewählt: Auf der Wasserscheide zwischen Fulda und Haune reicht der Blick von hier sowohl über die gesamte Fuldaer Senke als auch bis zur Kette der Rhönberge. Die Propstei Petersberg bildete zugleich die Keimzelle eines Ortes, der bis heute als selbstständige, aber eng mit der Stadt Fulda verflochtene Gemeinde besteht.

Die Orte Neuenberg und Johannesberg – wie Petersberg aus früheren Propsteien hervorgegangen – sind dagegen heute Stadtteile von Fulda. Doch auch sie bergen mit ihren Sehenswürdigkeiten – den Wandmalereien aus ottonischer Zeit in Neuenberg etwa oder der barocken Gartenanlage in Johannesberg – wahre Schätze der Region.

former monasteries now form a string of pearls around the city which are well worth a short detour as a tourist. Built between 836 and 838 under Abbot Rabanus Maurus (who spent a part of his life as a teacher here), the Propstei Petersberg contains the burial church of St.Lioba. The frescoes in the crypt are among the oldest wall paintings in Germany. The location on the hill was perfectly chosen: lying on the hills between the Fulda and Haune valleys, the view from here stretches out over the Fulda hollow and, on the other side, all the way to the Rhön mountains. The Propstei Petersberg formed the basis for the development of today's independent council area, which has close ties to the City of Fulda.

By contrast, Neuenberg and Johannesberg, which like Petersberg originated from church foundations, are still parts of Fulda. Both places have interesting sights of their own; the 11th-century frescoes in Neuenberg and the Baroque gardens in Johannesberg – real local treasures.

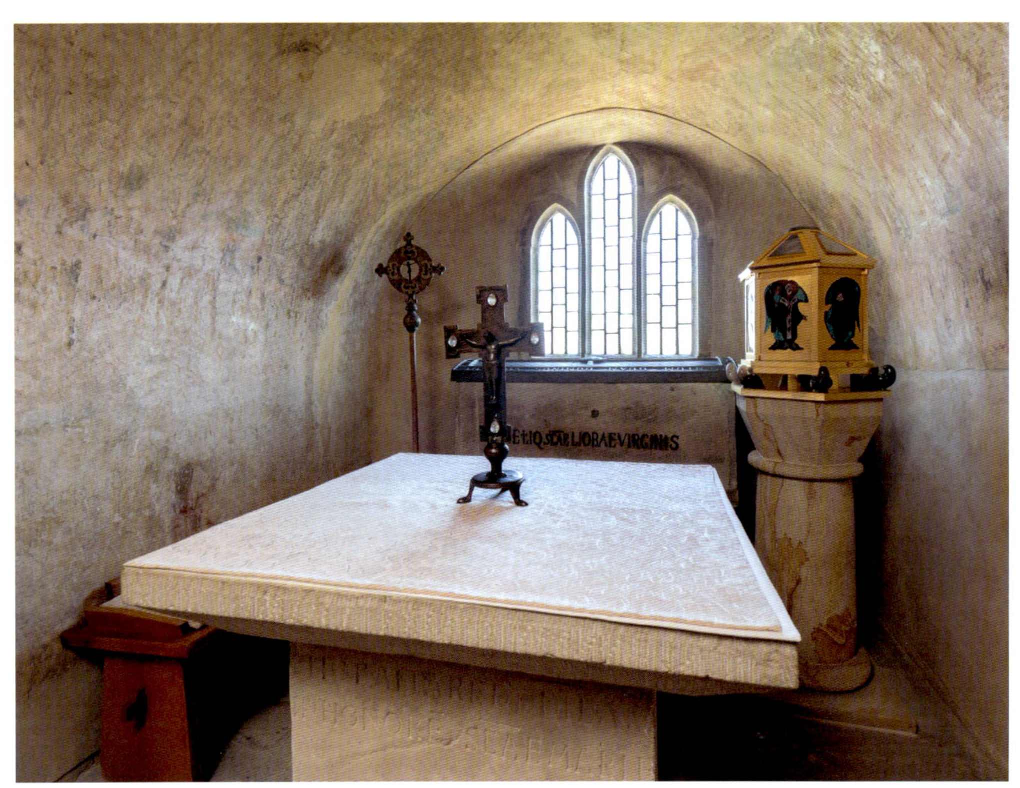

Während der jüngsten Renovierung (2002–2007) erhielt der Kirchenraum einen Anstrich in der mutmaßlichen Originalfarbe. Die beiden Sandsteinreliefs an den Pfeilern stammen vermutlich aus dem 12. Jahrhundert.

During the most recent renovation (2002–2007) the church interior was repainted in its original colour. The sandstone reliefs date from the 12th century.

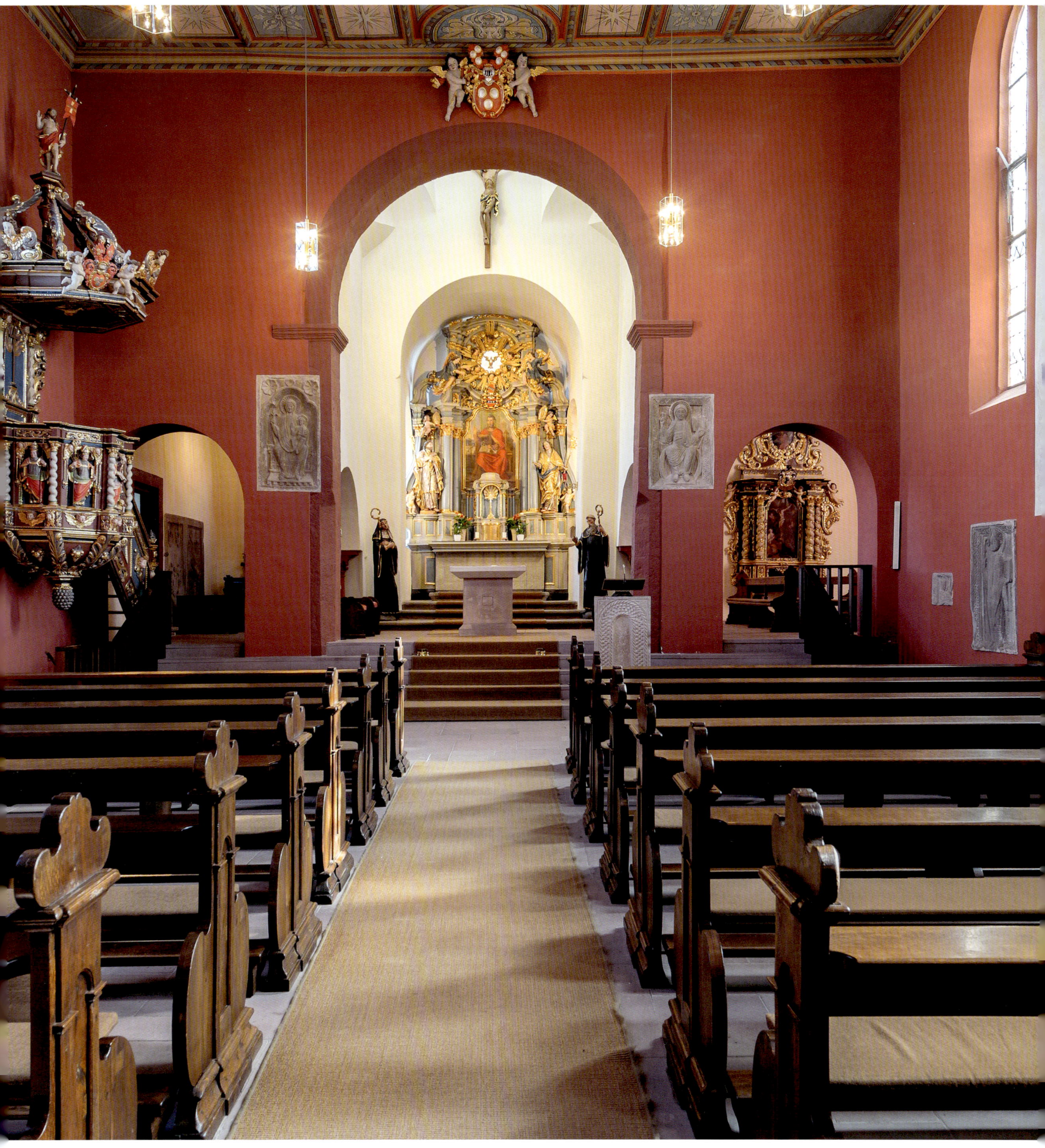

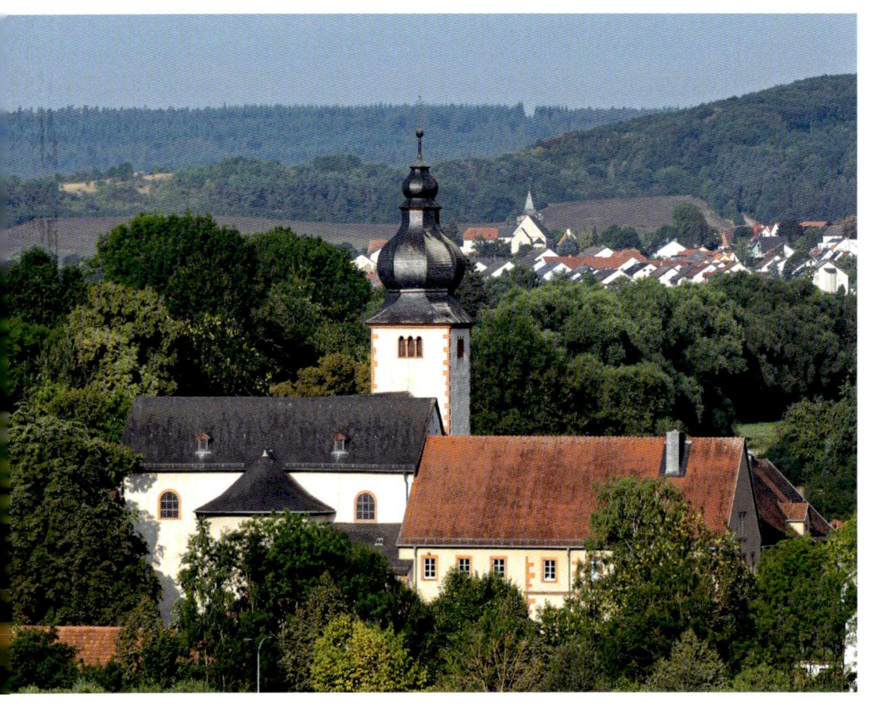

Die St.-Andreas-Kirche in Neuenberg stammt in ihren ältesten Teilen aus dem 11. Jahrhundert. Die Wandmalereien in der Krypta sind herausragende Beispiele der Kunst der ottonischen Epoche.

The oldest parts of St. Andreas in Neuenberg originate from the 11th century. The wall paintings in the crypt are exceptional examples of art from this period.

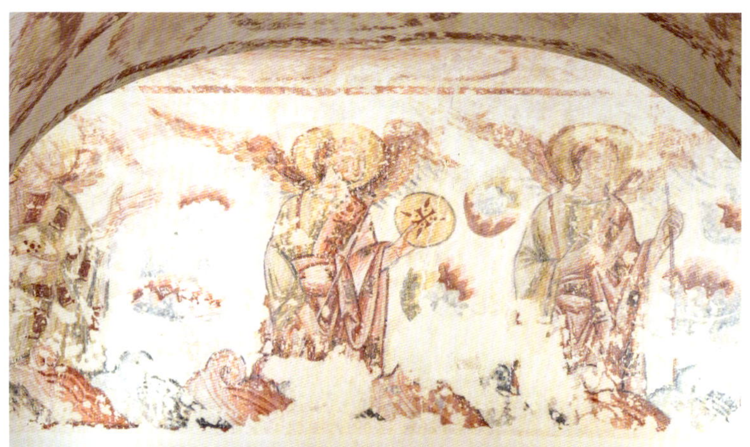

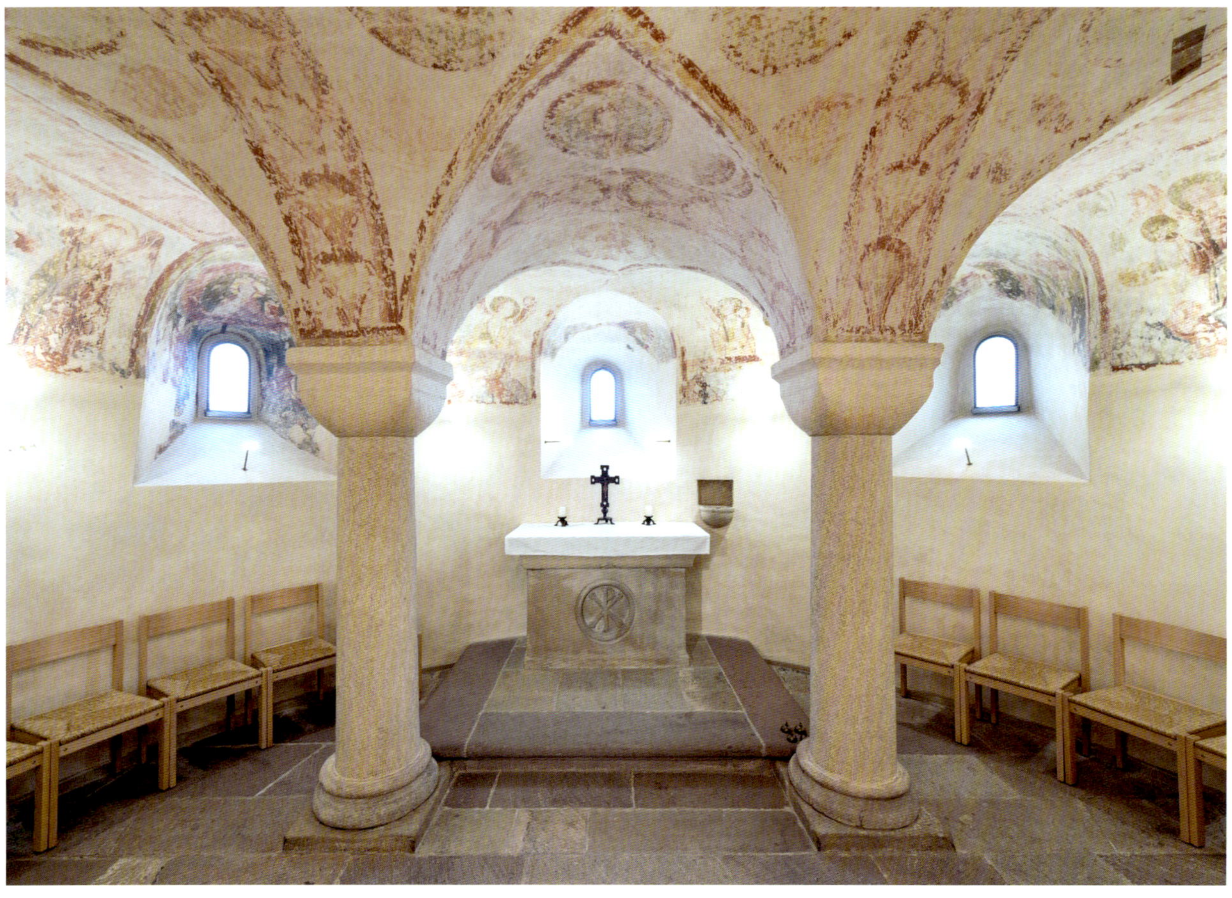

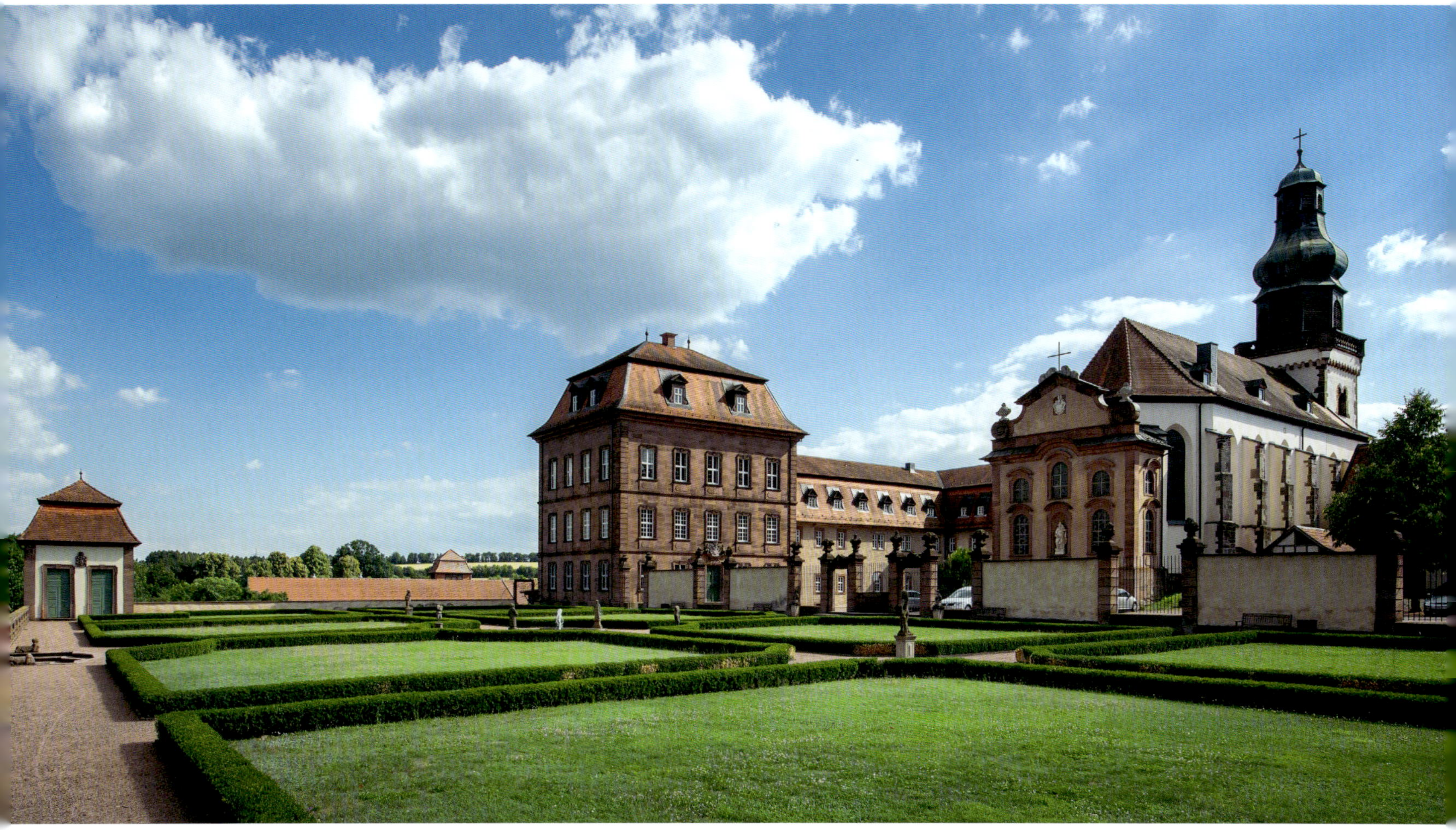

Die Propstei Johannesberg geht ebenfalls auf eine benediktinische Klostergründung im 9. Jahrhundert zurück. In der Barockzeit wurde die Propstei unter Propst Conrad von Mengersen komplett umgestaltet. Andreas Gallasini lieferte auch hier die Entwürfe. Eine Besonderheit für Fulda ist die terrassenförmige Gartenanlage, die herrliche Ausblicke über das Fuldatal hinweg ermöglicht.

The Johannesberg Priory also has its origins in a Benedictine monastery founded in the 9th century. In the Baroque period Prior Conrad von Mengersen had the priory completely redesigned by the architect Andres Gallasini. A particular feature here is the terraced garden which offers magnificent views over the Fulda valley.

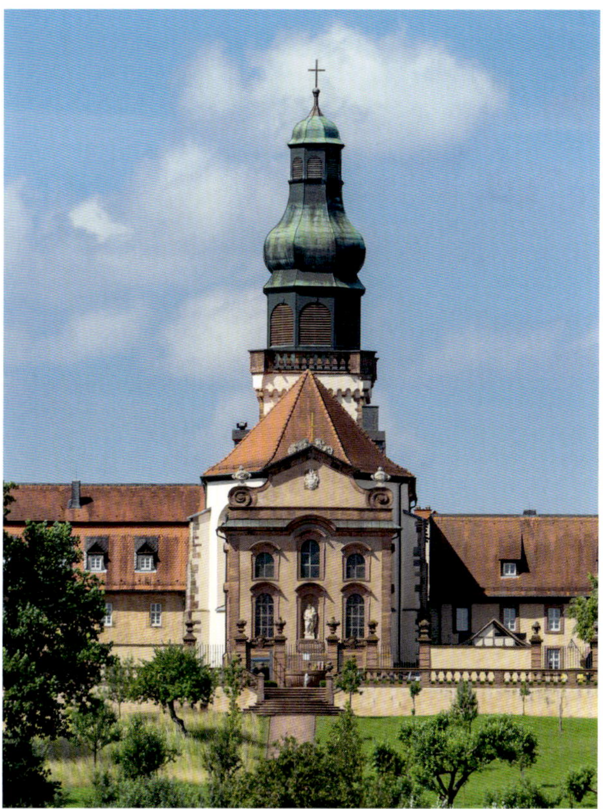

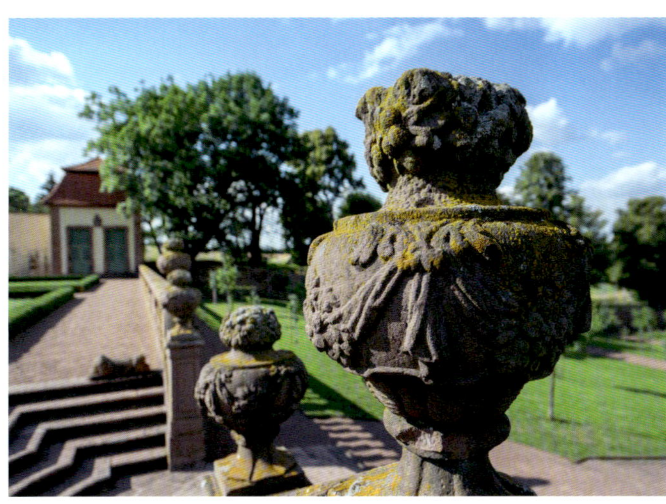

DER PERFEKTE ORT FÜR SOMMERFREUDEN

Schloss Fasanerie gilt als schönstes Barockschloss Hessens – und dafür spricht einiges

Anders als bei den Propsteien gab es für die Sommerresidenz der Fuldaer Regenten keine Keimzelle aus dem frühen Mittelalter. Sie entstand „auf der grünen Wiese" zunächst als kleines Schlösschen mit Jagdpark unter Fürstabt Adalbert von Schleiffras. Unter seinem Nach-Nachfolger Adolph von Dalberg erfolgte ab 1730 der erste Ausbau des Schlosses, das seither den Beinamen „Adolphseck" trägt. Seine endgültige Form erhielt das Schloss dann unter Fürstbischof Amand von Buseck, und auch hier sorgte der in Fulda omnipräsente Baumeister Gallasini für den architektonischen Feinschliff. Genutzt wurde es als Sommerresidenz – im Winter sind die herrlichen Räume schwer zu heizen. Noch heute ist das Schlossmuseum in den Wintermonaten geschlossen. Im Gegensatz zu allen anderen ehemaligen Herrschaftsgebäuden Fuldas befindet sich Schloss Fasanerie noch immer in adeliger Hand: Besitzer ist die Hessische Hausstiftung, die im Museum die schönsten Stücke der Privatsammlung der hessischen Landgrafen versammelt hat. Gleichzeitig ist es auch heute noch der perfekte Ort für Sommerfreuden – etwa das Fürstliche Gartenfest.

The Perfect Place for Enjoying the Summer

Schloss Fasanerie is regarded as the most beautiful Baroque palace in Hesse – not without reason.

In contrast to the priories, the summer residence of the Fulda rulers did not develop from medieval beginnings: it all started with a small hunting lodge and deer park for Prince-abbot Adalbert von Schleiffras. Von Schleiffras' successor, Adolph von Dalberg, then extended the building in 1730 – since this time the palace has also had the name "Adolphseck" ("Adolph's Corner"). Under Prince-bishop Amand von Buseck the palace then took its final form, and the ubiquitous Andreas Gallasini was once more responsible for the architectural finishing touches. The palace was used as a summer residence – in winter the beautiful rooms are difficult to heat. Still today the palace museum is closed in the winter months. Unlike the former nobles' houses in Fulda, Schloss Fasanerie is still in noble hands: the owner is the Hessische Hausstiftung which has brought together the most beautiful pieces from the Hesse Landgraves' private collection for this museum. It is also the perfect location for enjoying the summer events – such as the Princely Garden Festival.

Die sonnige Gartenterrasse lädt zum Verweilen ein – unter einer Inschrift aus kurhessischer Zeit.

The perfect Place for enjoying the summer Schloss Fasanerie is regarded as the most beautiful Baroque palace in Hesse – not without reason.

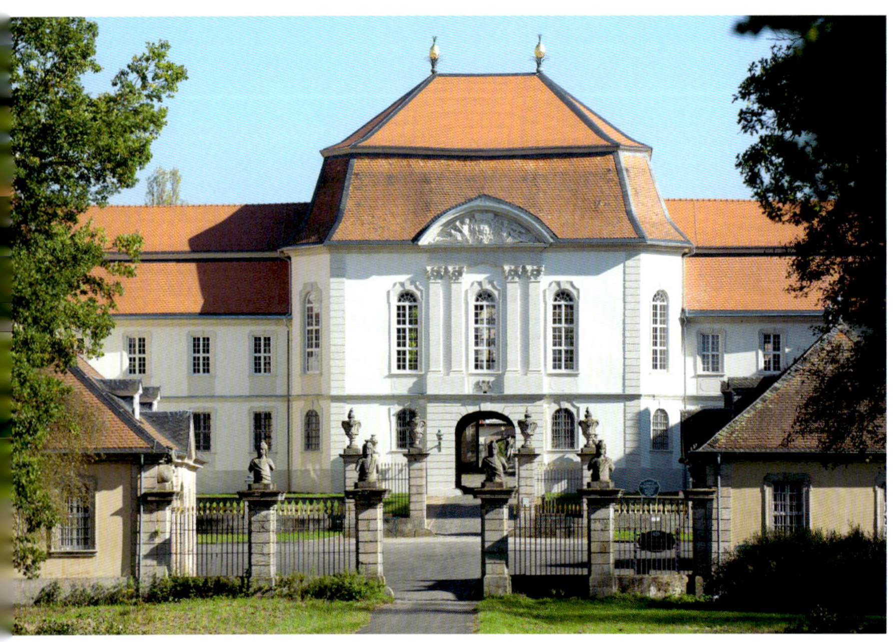

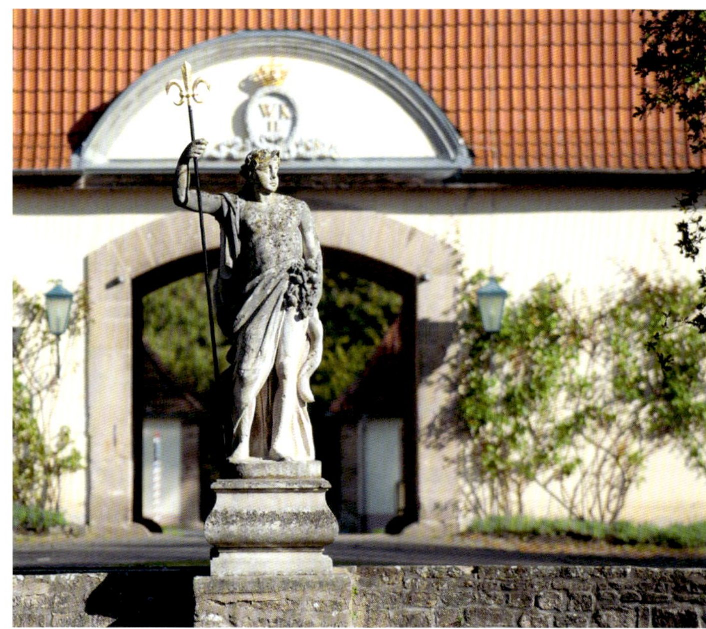

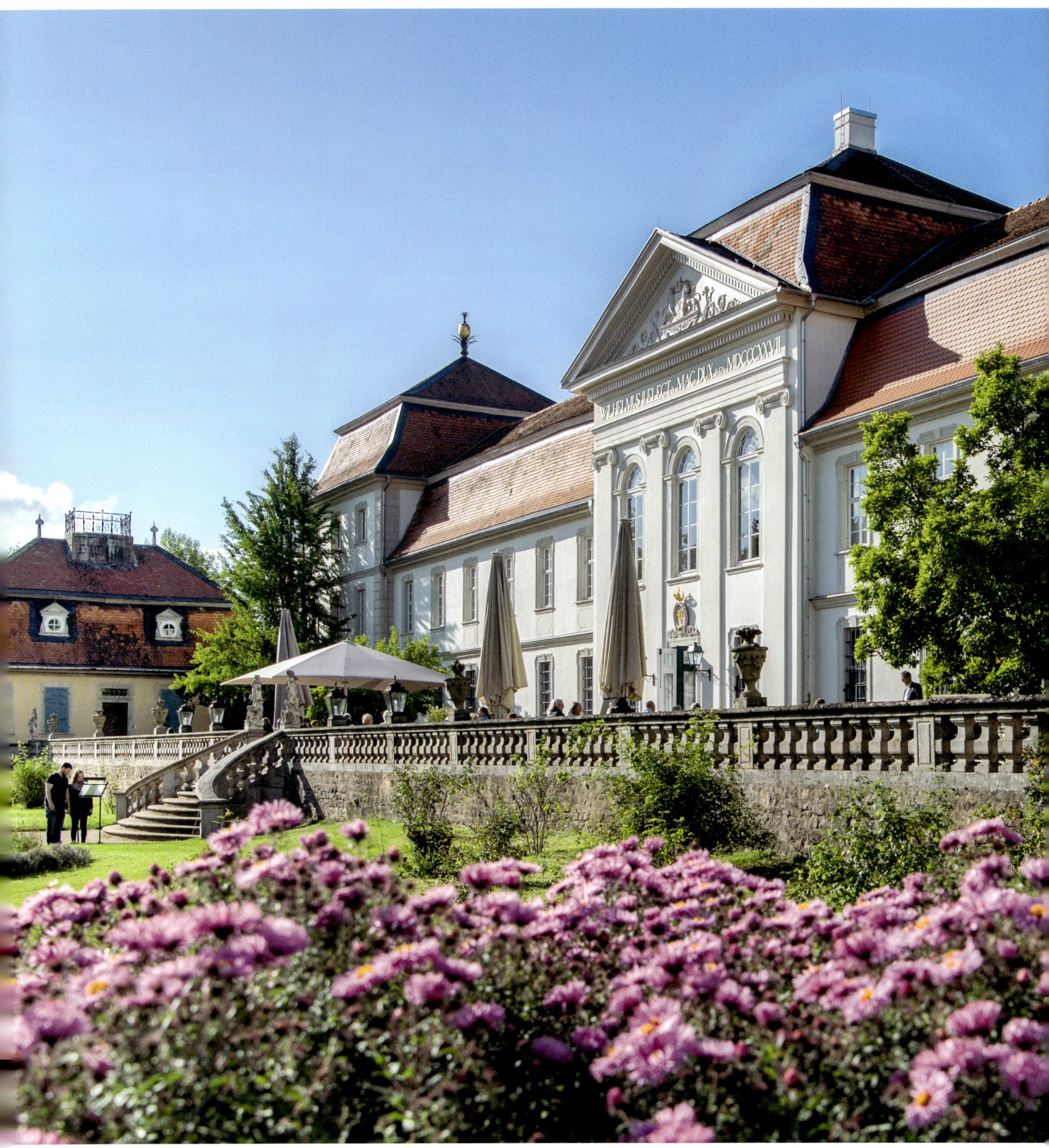
WILHELMUS II ELECT. & MAG. DUX REN: MDCCCXXVII.

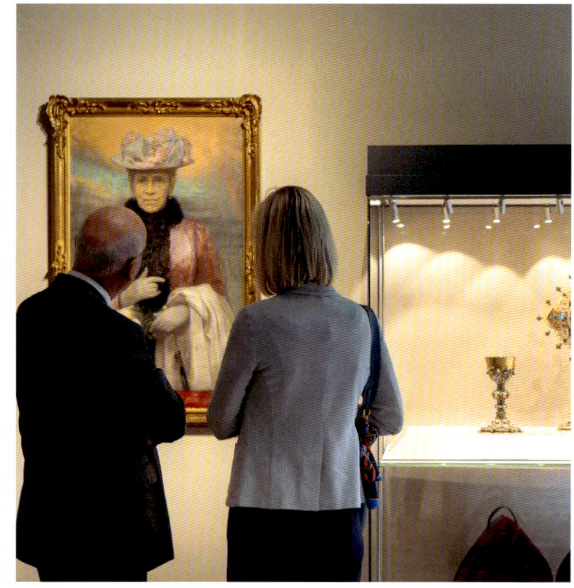

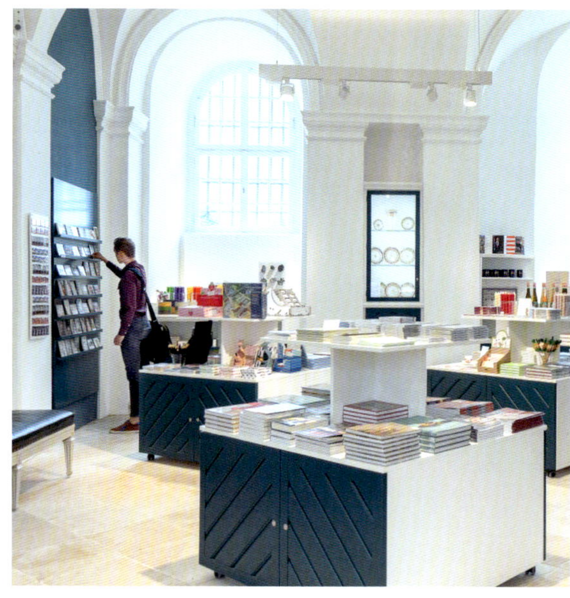

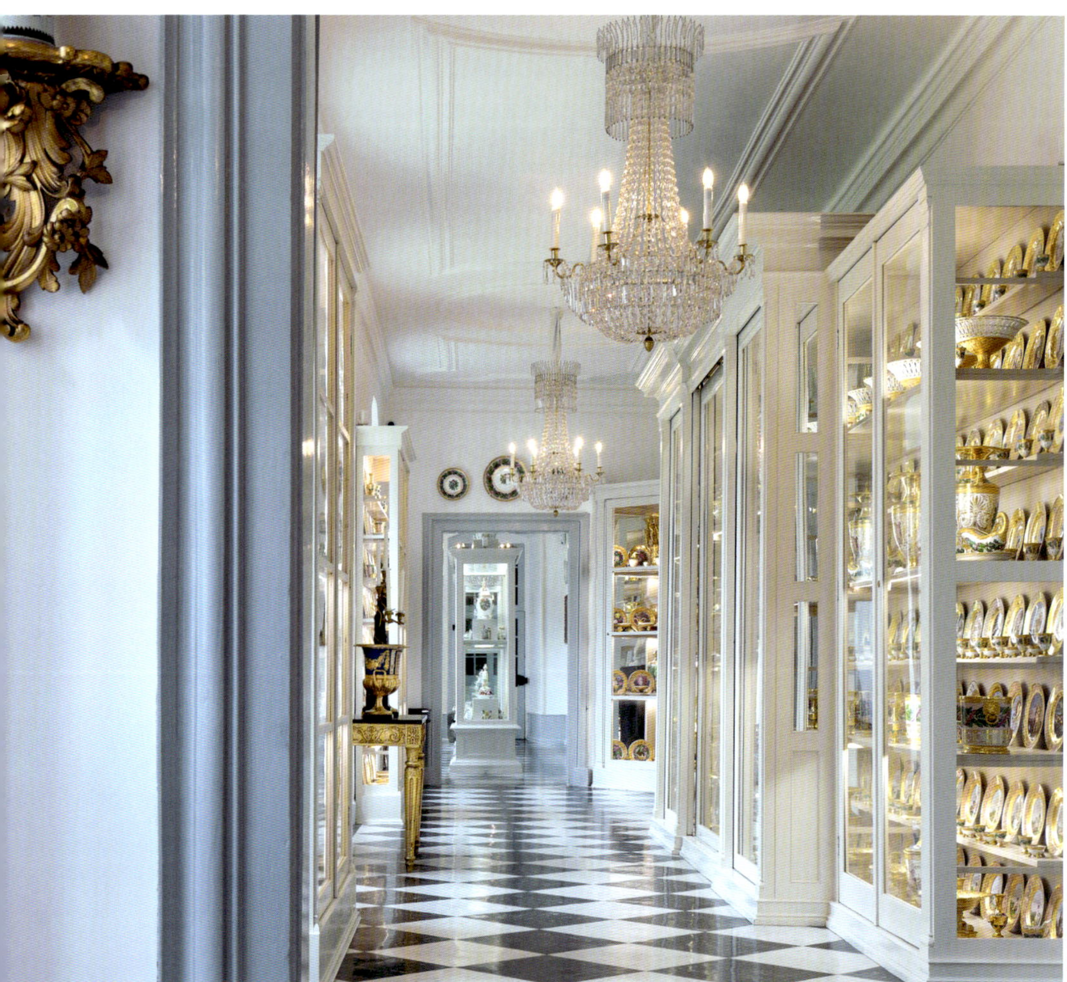

Das Museum zeigt unter anderem eine reichhaltige Porzellansammlung. Auch die Antiken des Hauses Hessen, das auch Beziehungen zum englischen Königshaus pflegt, sind berühmt.

The museum has a very large, valuable collection of porcelain. The House of Hesse's collection of art from the classical period is renowned.

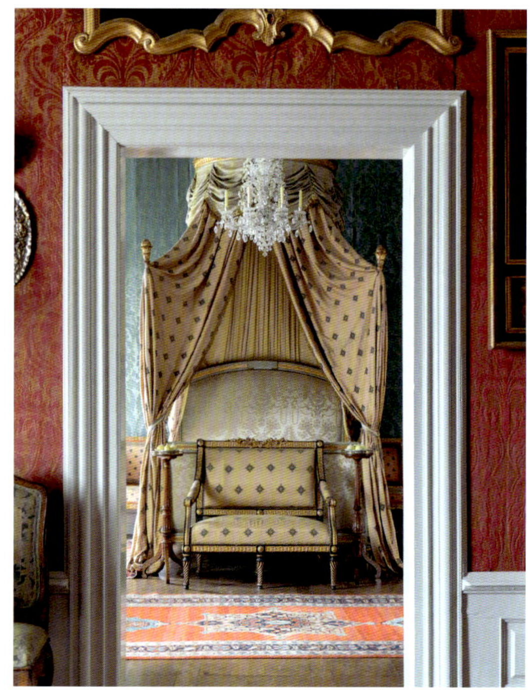

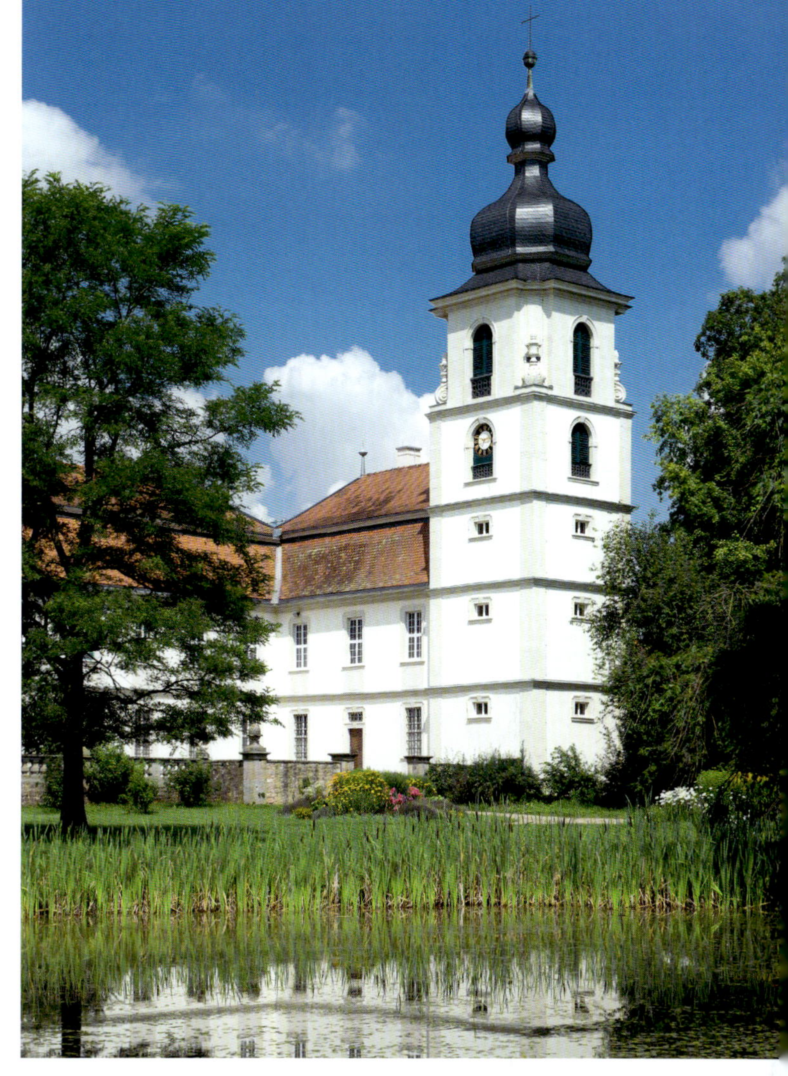

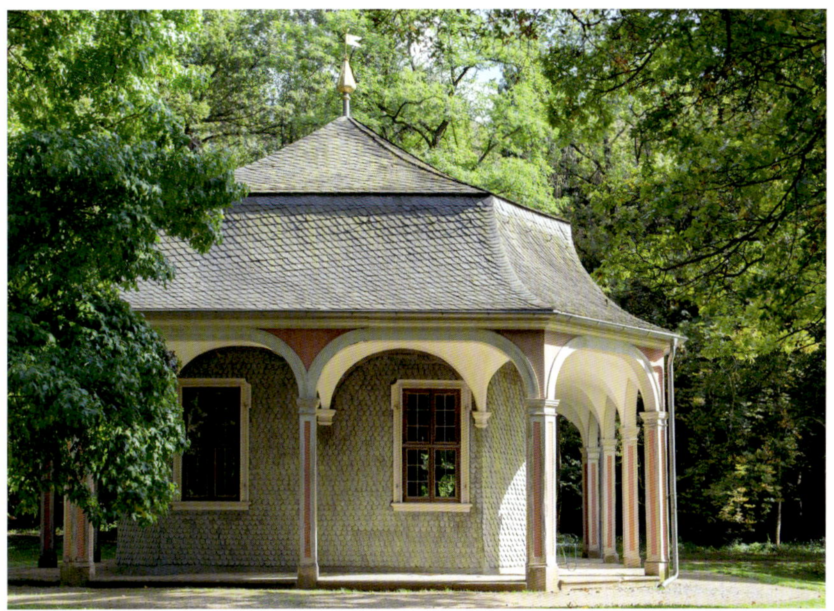

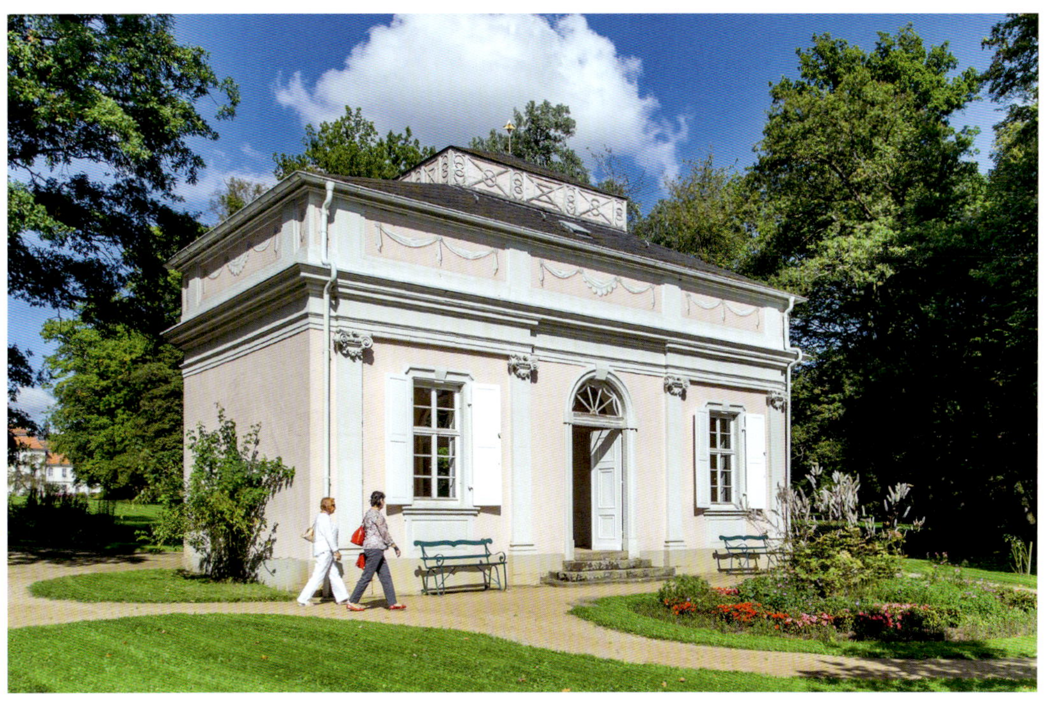

Das Schloss und die weitläufigen Parkanlagen, die heute auf dem Gebiet der Gemeinde Eichenzell liegen, laden zum Spazierengehen und Verweilen ein – etwa an den barocken Pavillons. Der ursprünglich barocke Garten wurde in kurhessischer Zeit zu einem naturnahen Landschaftspark im englischen Stil umgestaltet.

The palace and the large landscaped park are now part of Eichenzell district. Here you can enjoy a pleasant walk, perhaps pausing for a while at the Baroque pavilions. In the 19th century the original Baroque garden was transformed to the more natural style of "English" landscape garden.

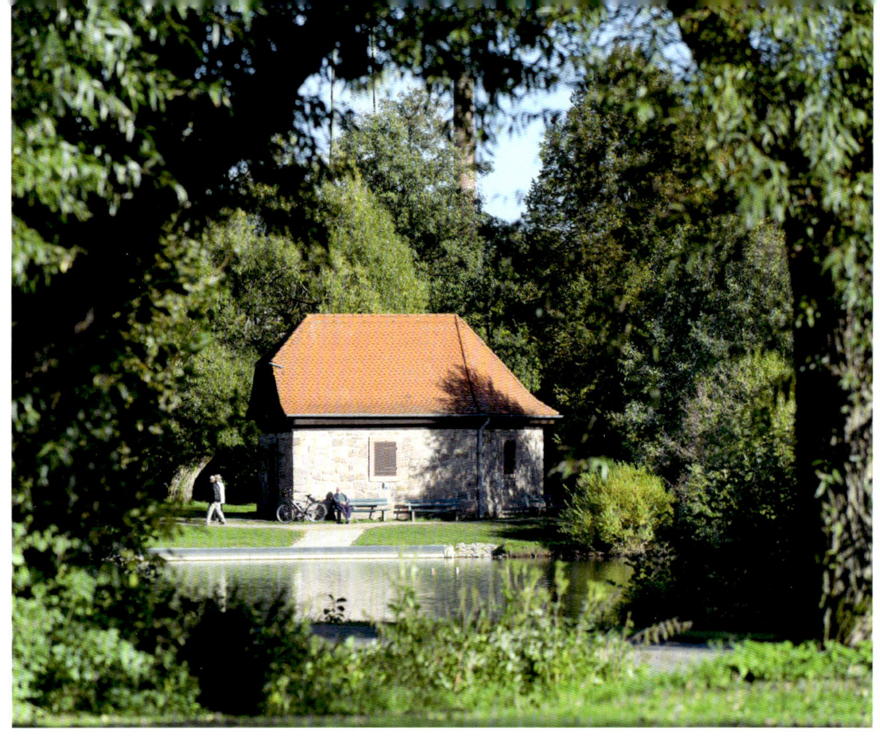

Grüne Idylle: Die Fulda-Aue mit den beiden Aueweihern bildet ein weitläufiges Naherholungsgebiet.

Green idyll: the river meadows with the two small lakes form an extensive park area which is ideal for free time activities.

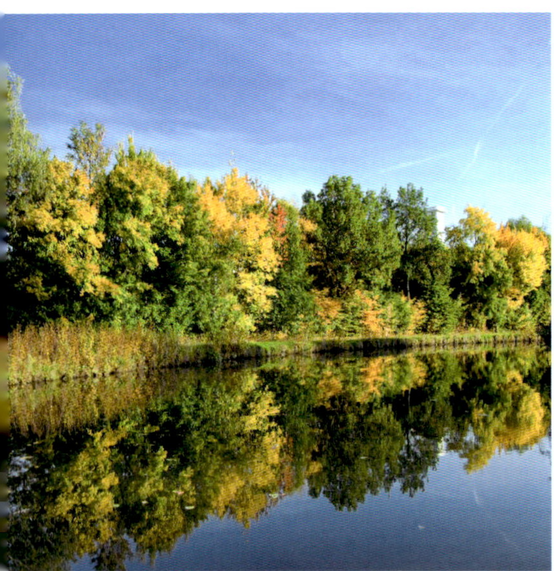

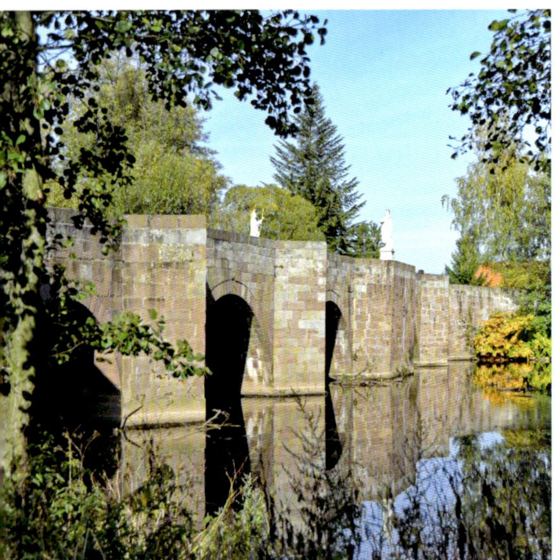

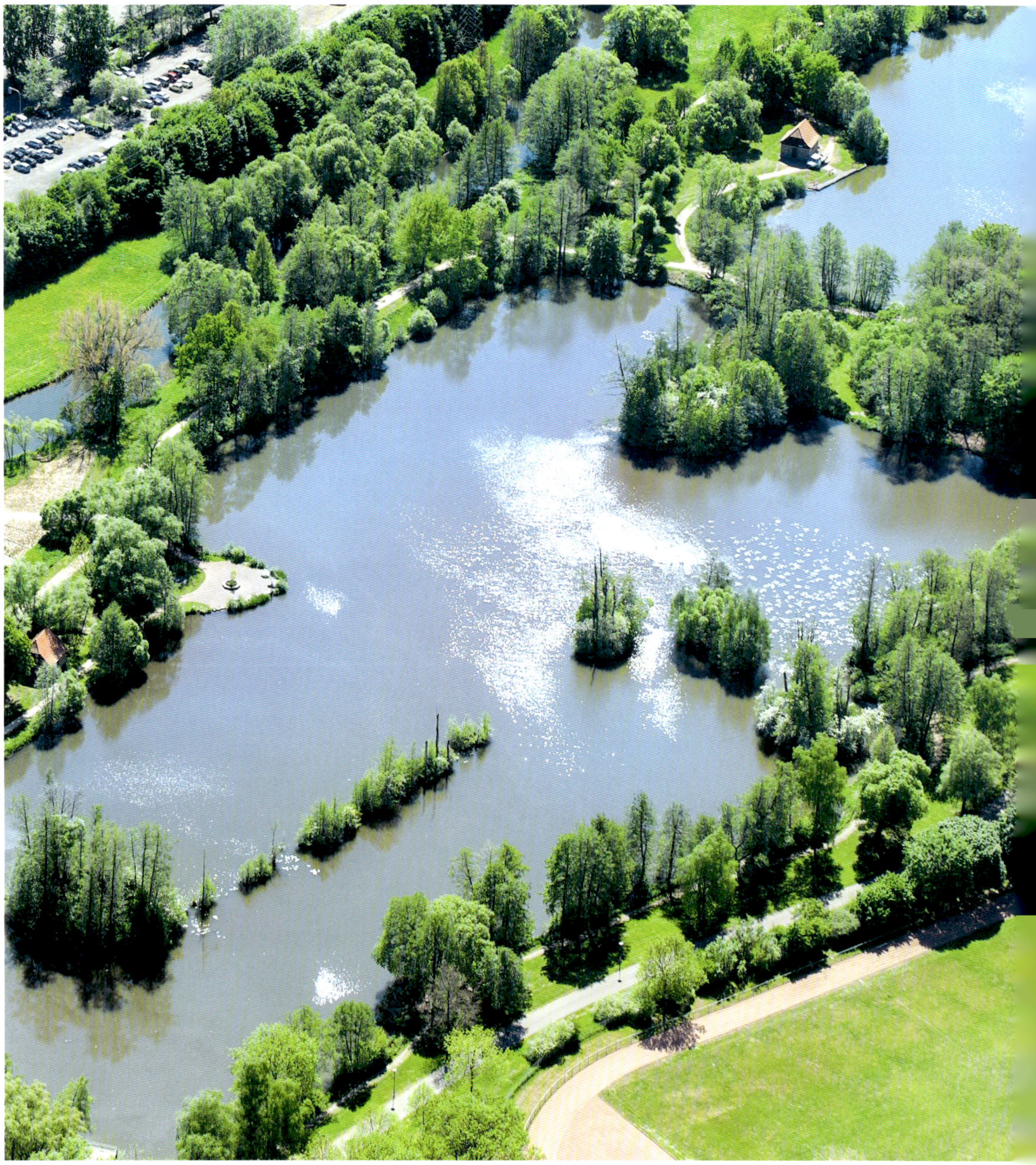

DIE FULDA-AUEN: GRÜNES KLEINOD AM STADTRAND

Ideale Bedingungen für Jogger, Radfahrer und Spaziergänger – und ein besonderes Angebot für Feuerwehrfreunde

Lange Zeit waren die Stadt Fulda und der gleichnamige Fluss keine Freunde: Die Stadtbebauung wendete ihre hässlichen Seiten in Richtung Wasser, frühe Industrien leiteten giftige Abwässer ein. Doch spätestens seit der ersten Hessischen Landesgartenschau 1994 hat sich das Bild gewandelt: Die Fulda-Auen sind zum beliebten Naherholungsgebiet geworden, unter anderem an der Tränke und an der Rosenmauer wendet sich die Wohnbebauung dem Fluss zu, attraktive Quartiere sind so entstanden. Auf den Hauptwegen in der Aue herrscht an schönen Tagen reger Verkehr von Radfahrern, Inline-Skatern, Joggern, Spaziergängern, Gassi-Gehern, … und alle Feuerwehrfans kommen gleich nebenan im Deutschen Feuerwehrmuseum voll auf ihre Kosten.

Die Aueweiher, einst entstanden aus den Hinterlassenschaften des Kiesabbaus, wirken inzwischen so natürlich, dass so manche Einheimische schwören würden, dass sie schon immer dort gewesen sind.

A Recreation Area on Your Doorstep

The Fulda river meadows provide perfect conditions for joggers, cyclists and walkers … and fire brigade fans! For a long time Fulda city and the Fulda River were not friends: the city turned its uglier side to the river and early industries polluted the water, but this changed in 1994, if not before, when the Hesse Garden Show took place in Fulda: the meadows have become a popular place for free time activities. In the "Tränke" and along the lane "an der Rosenmauer" houses were built facing the river, creating attractive residential areas. On nice days there is a lot of toing and froing on the main paths of the meadows – cyclists, inline skaters, joggers, strollers and people walking their dogs. Just nearby, fire brigade fans can feast their eyes on the fascinating exhibits of the German National Fire Service Museum. The river meadows, once the remains of a gravel pit, look so natural these days that many local people would swear that they had always been there.

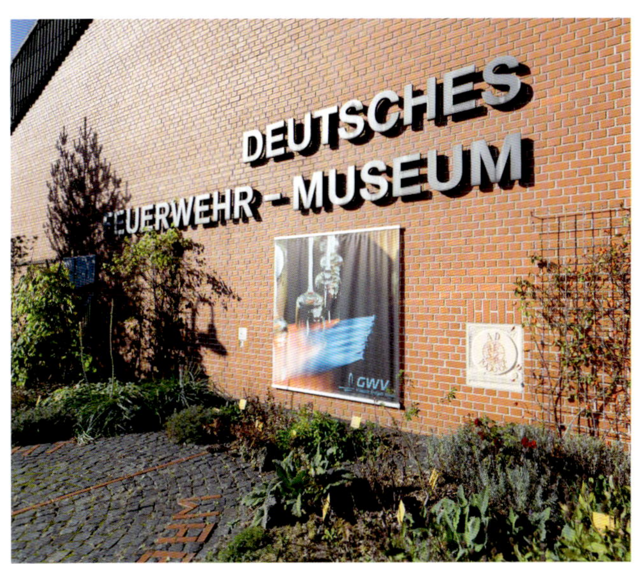

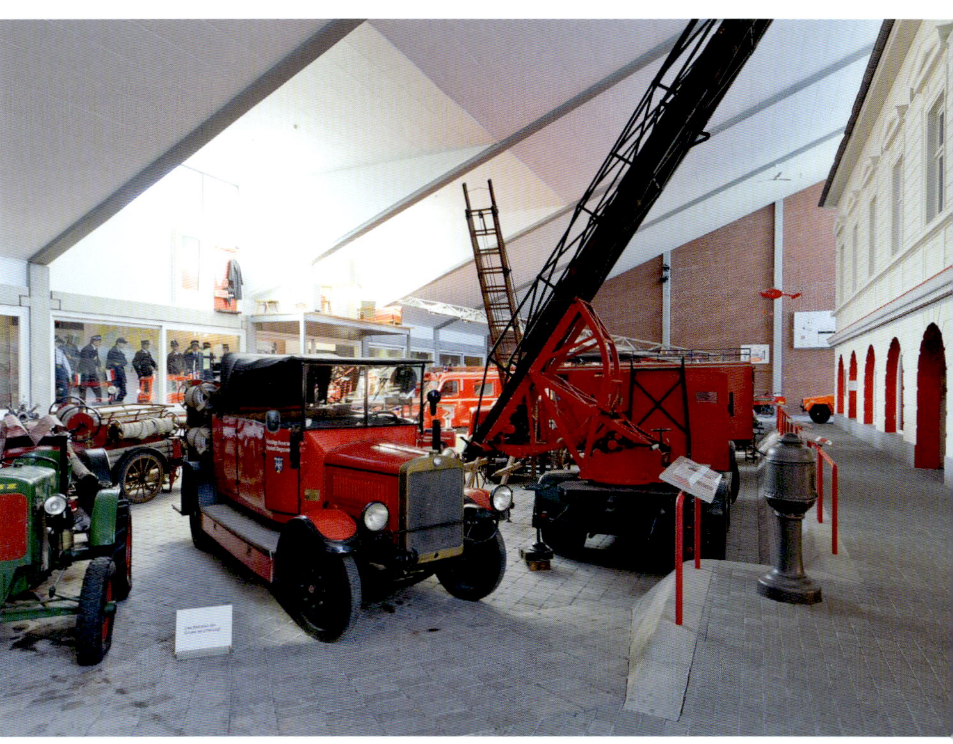

Das Deutsche Feuerwehrmuseum bietet Interessantes rund um den Brandschutz – von einer fahrbaren Handdruckspritze von 1624 bis zu modernsten Löschfahrzeugen.

The German National Fire Service Museum has a collection which ranges from a mobile, manually operated fire pump from 1624 to the most modern fire vehicles of today.

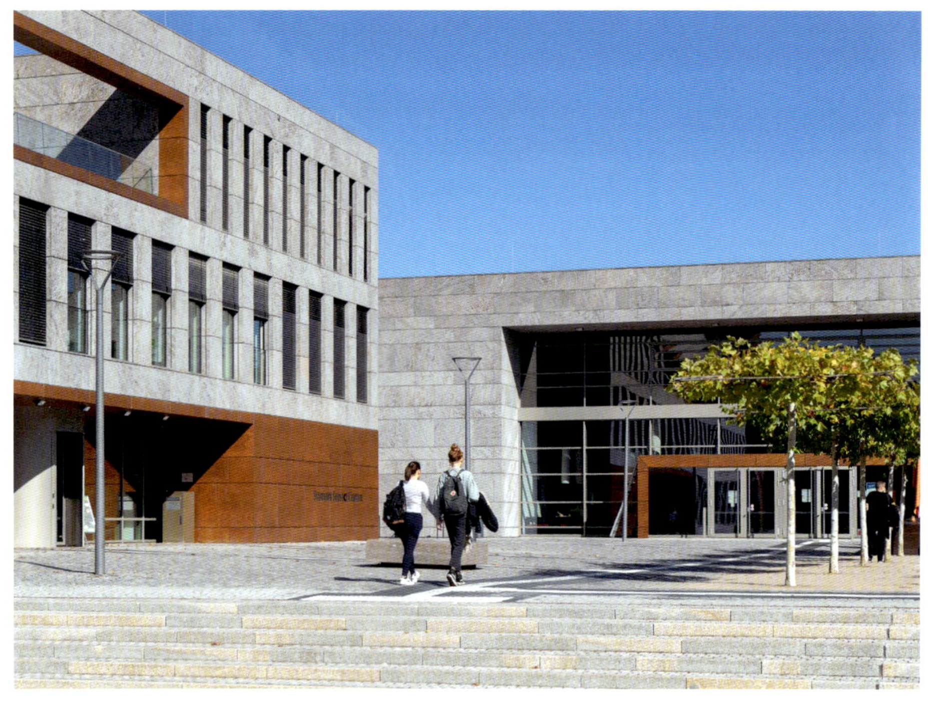

Die gewachsene Bedeutung der Hochschule Fulda fand 2013 auch architektonisch einen angemessenen Rahmen: Der neue Campus mit der Mensa (oben) und der Bibliothek (unten) bietet eine Qualität, wie man sie an vielen Universitäten vergeblich sucht.

The increased importance and size of Fulda University led to the construction of two new principal buildings in 2013: the university refectory (top) and the library (below) are of a quality that you would struggle to find at other universities.

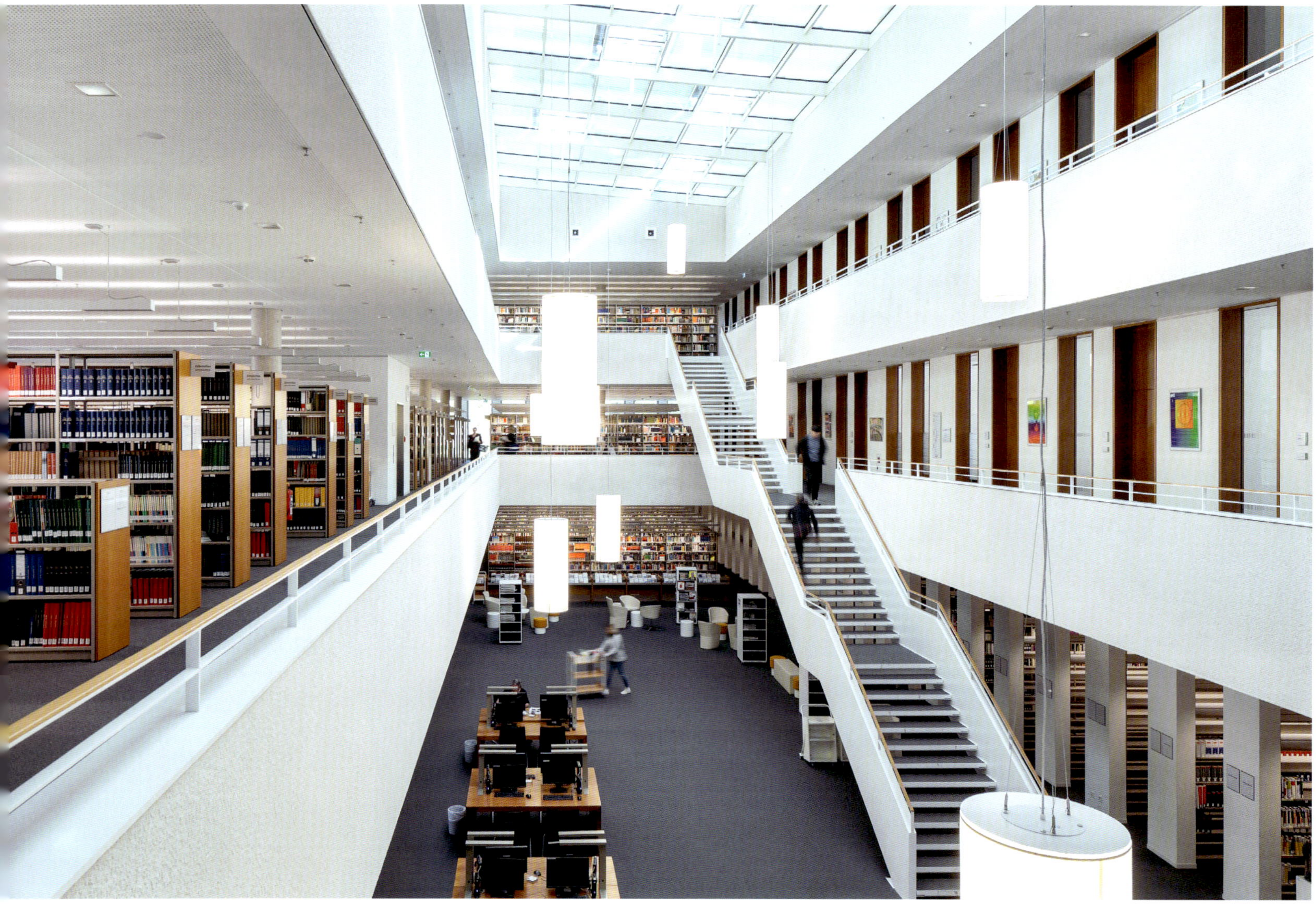

STADT DER BILDUNG

Von der Kinderakademie bis zur Hochschule: Fuldaer Bildungseinrichtungen sind bundesweite Magneten

Sicher: An die herausragende Bedeutung, die das Kloster Fulda im frühen Mittelalter für die Schreibkunst und die Literatur besaß, konnte die Stadt in späteren Jahrhunderten kaum wieder anknüpfen. Die Universität bestand nur von 1737 bis 1805. Doch seit Ende des Zweiten Weltkriegs hat sich Fulda immerhin zu einem überregional relevanten Bildungsstandort gemausert. Da sind zunächst die Schulen: Allein vier reine Gymnasien gibt es im Stadtgebiet mit insgesamt fast 4000 Schülern. Das Einzugsgebiet der beruflichen Schulen reicht bis nach Südthüringen und Unterfranken. Und da wäre natürlich die Hochschule Fulda, die in nicht einmal 50 Jahren eine rasante Entwicklung von einem kleinen pädagogischen Fachinstitut zu einer international renommierten „University of Applied Sciences" mit gut 9 000 Studenten genommen hat und inzwischen in einigen Fächern sogar das Promotionsrecht besitzt. Aber auch für die Bildung der Jüngsten wird viel getan: Exemplarisch steht hier die Kinderakademie Fulda, eines der bundesweit ersten Mitmachmuseen für Kinder, das jährlich Tausende Besucher aus ganz Deutschland anzieht.

An Educational City

From the Children's Academy to the University – Fulda's educational institutions attract people from all over Germany

Of course, it is hardly likely that the city will never again reach the heady heights in education that the Fulda monastery once did: however, since World War II Fulda has gradually become a place of education that has a good reputation throughout Germany. The schools include four Gymnasien (grammar schools) with almost 4,000 pupils, and two large vocational training colleges. Needless to say, there is also the internationally renowned University of Applied Science, which has grown very rapidly in the last fifty years and now has 9,000 students and the right to confer doctorates in some faculties .

In addition, a great deal is done for the young: the popular Children's Academy, one of the first hands-on children's museums in Germany, is a pioneer in its field.

Das „begehbare Herz" sowie fantasieanregende Mitmachangebote sind Markenzeichen der Kinderakademie Fulda.

The "Walk-through Heart" and other hands-on activities intended to stimulate children' s minds are central to the concept of the Fulda Children's Academy.

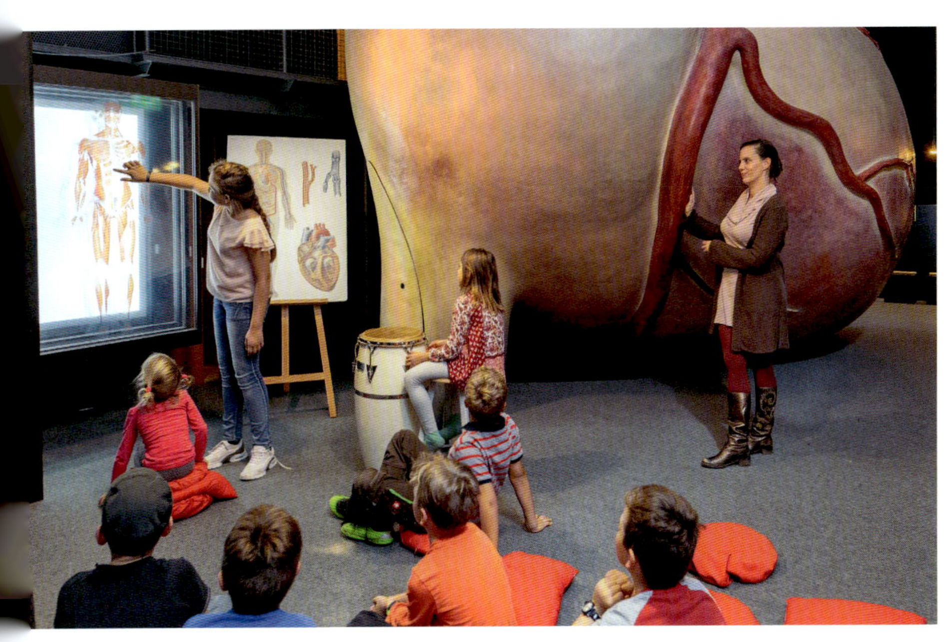

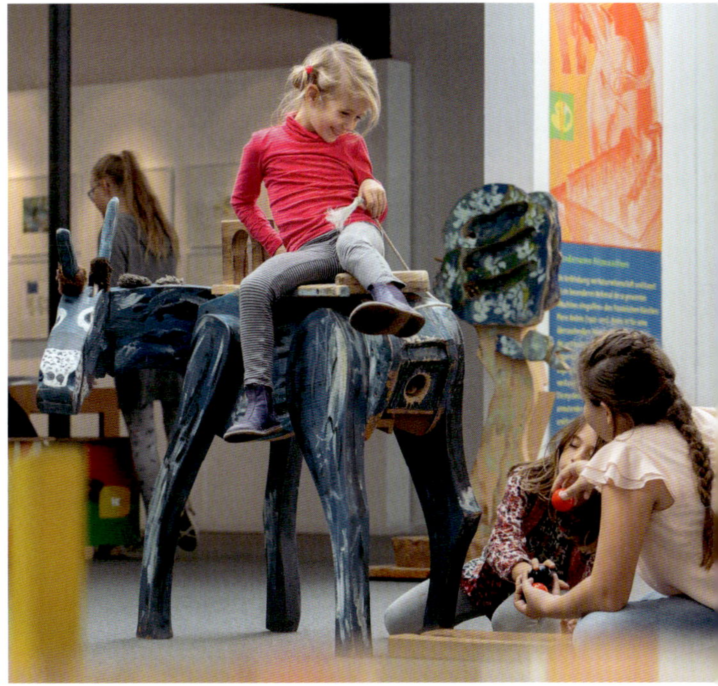

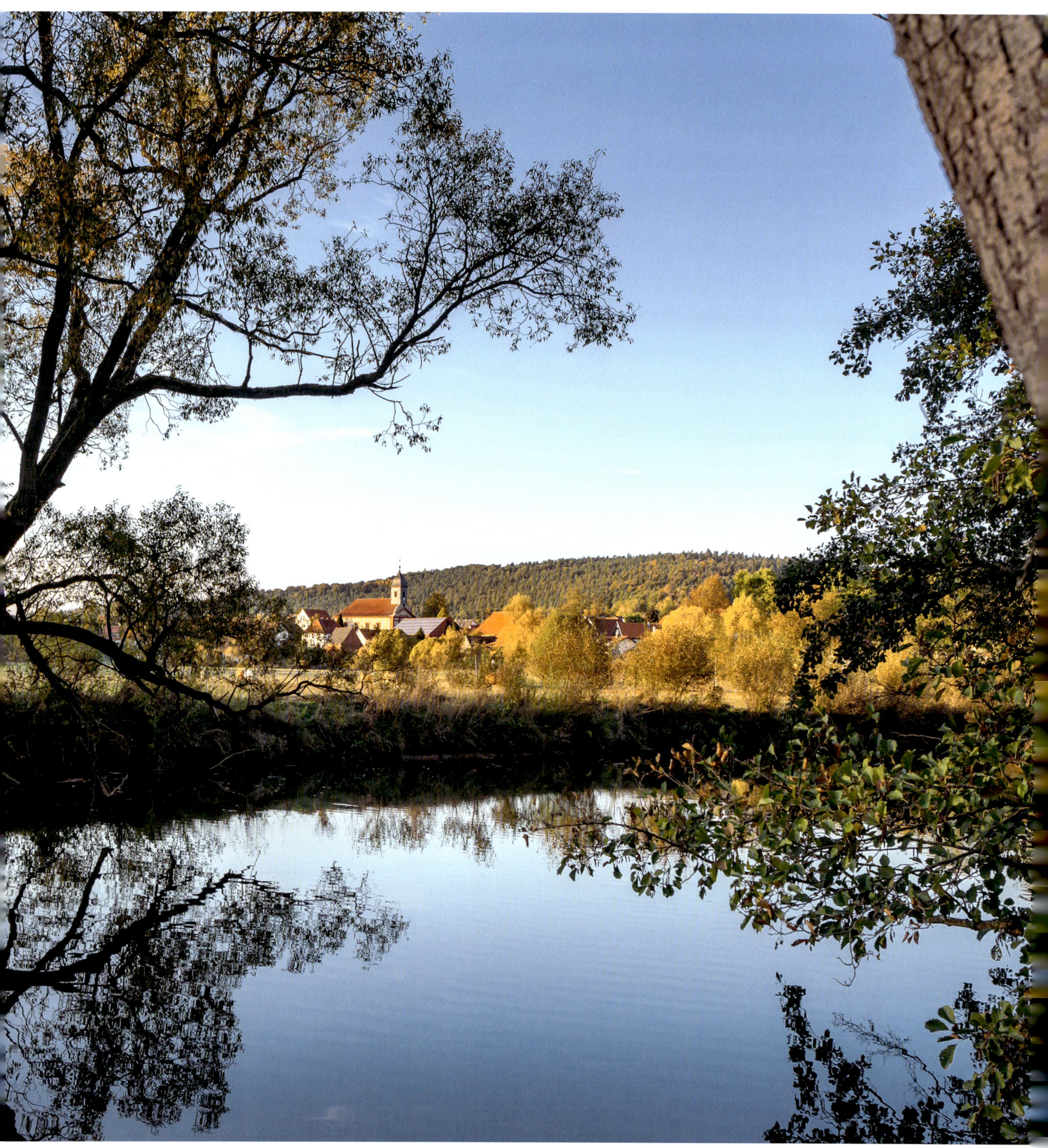

VOM WEILER BIS ZUR VORSTADT

24 Stadtteile gehören zur Stadt Fulda – und bereichern sie mit eigenen Traditionen und Festen

Das Jahr 1972 markiert einen Einschnitt in der Fuldaer Stadtgeschichte: Im Zuge der hessischen Gebietsreform kamen 24 ehemals eigenständige Gemeinden – vor allem im Westen und Süden der Stadt – als Stadtteile zu Fulda, darunter bessere Weiler bis zur urban anmutenden Vorstadt. Der „große Wurf" freilich – ein Zusammenschluss mit Künzell und Petersberg und damit der mögliche Sprung über die 100 000-Einwohner-Grenze – war nicht zustande gekommen. Gleichwohl bedeutete der Zuwachs an Stadtteilen einen Gewinn an Fläche (auf mehr als 10 000 Hektar) und damit Entwicklungsmöglichkeiten sowie eine Bereicherung des städtischen Veranstaltungsreigens durch die vielen Traditionen, Feste und lebendigen Vereinsgemeinschaften, welche die Stadtteile ins Leben der Stadt einbringen.

From Hamlet to Suburb

24 city districts that belong to Fulda city, enriching the city with their own traditions and festivals

The year 1972 marks a decisive point in the history of Fulda city: the State of Hesse carried out district reforms whereby twenty-four, formerly independent parishes – mainly to the west and south of the city – became parts of Fulda; some were no bigger than country hamlets while others were more like city suburbs. However, the "big coup" of Fulda merging with Künzell and Petersberg, and thus reaching a population exceeding 100,000, did not materialise, although the changes did mean that the total area of Fulda increased to more than 10,000 hectares.

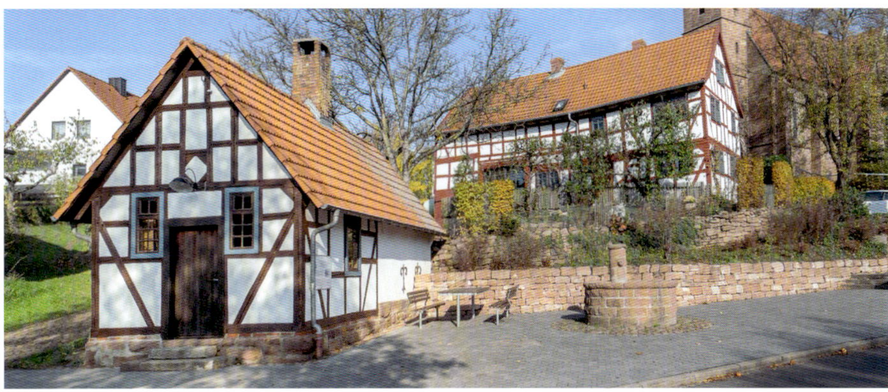

Viele Fuldaer Stadtteile – hier: Kämmerzell – haben sich ihren ländlichen Charme bewahrt und bieten familienfreundliche Wohnmöglichkeiten.

Many villages that belong to the Fulda city area, like Kämmerzell, have retained their rural charm and provide good housing opportunities for families.

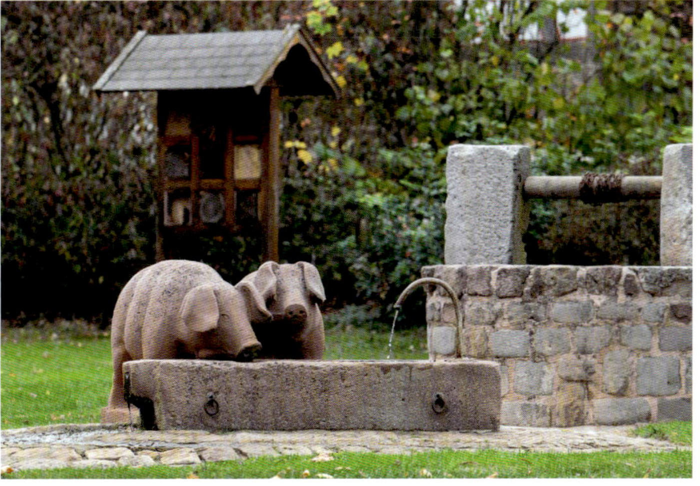

Die Landwirtschaft ist auch in den Stadtteilen vielerorts auf dem Rückzug, doch der dörfliche Charakter bleibt meist erhalten (wie hier in Dietershan und Malkes).

The importance of agriculture in many of the rural parts of the Fulda city area has diminished, but their village-like character has remained (as here in Dietershan and Malkes).

WENN DIE „PÄPSTIN“ AUF „DER PRINZ“ TRIFFT …

Feste und Veranstaltungen sind Anker der Lebensfreude und Selbstvergewisserung im städtischen Jahreslauf

Fulda feiert gerne und ausgelassen. Dafür reicht ein Blick in den Jahreskalender der Stadt. So beginnt die „fünfte Jahreszeit“ alljährlich am 11.11. mit der alles entscheidenden Frage – inklusive original Fuldaer Akkusativ: „Wer macht der Prinz?“ Und bevor dann die Fastnachtssaison ihrem Höhepunkt am Rosenmontag mit dem größten Romo-Umzug Hessens zustrebt, lockt in der Adventszeit der Fuldaer Weihnachtsmarkt Tausende Besucherinnen und Besucher in die festlich geschmückte Innenstadt.

Während die katholischen Feste wie Fronleichnam oder die Bonifatiuswoche Anfang Juni, die Pilgergruppen aus allen Teilen des Bistums anzieht, auf jahrhundertelange Traditionen in der Stadt zurückschauen können, haben sich der Fuldaer Musicalsommer, die Domplatzkonzerte oder das Genussfestival erst jüngst etabliert. Gleichwohl ziehen auch sie Gäste in solchem Maße an, dass sie zum Teil wirklich relevante Größen im jährlichen Tourismusgeschäft sind. Musicalproduktionen wie die „Päpstin“ oder der „Medicus“ stoßen sogar international auf Resonanz.

Und ob Weinfest oder Weihnachtsmarkt: Jeder Fuldaer hat seinen Lieblingsanlass, auf die Straßen und Plätze zu gehen und sich mit Freunden zu treffen. Und immer mehr Gäste finden ebenfalls Geschmack daran …

When “Pope Joan” meets “the Prince”

Festivals and events are a source of joy and provide a sense of continuity over the course of the year

Fulda likes to celebrate festivals – to the full! You just need to take a look in the city event calendar to see this. The carnival season, also known as the “fifth season”, begins on 11 November every year (the big question is always who is to be the new carnival Prince. Yet, before the carnival reaches its climax with the biggest Carnival Monday parade in Hesse, the Fulda Christmas market, attracts thousands of guests to the charmingly decorated city centre during Advent. While some festivities like the Catholics’ Feast of Corpus Christi or the Bonifatius Week at the beginning of June go back hundreds of years in the city’s history, others like the Fulda Summer of Musicals, the concerts on the cathedral square or the Gourmet Festival have only established themselves fairly recently. The “new” events, however, attract guests in such numbers that they have become really important factors in the local tourism business. Musical productions like “Pope Joan” and “The Physician” are also internationally highly acclaimed. Whether the wine festival or the Christmas market, everybody in Fulda has their favourite reason for going out onto streets and squares to meet their friends. An increasing number of guests are also developing a taste for it …

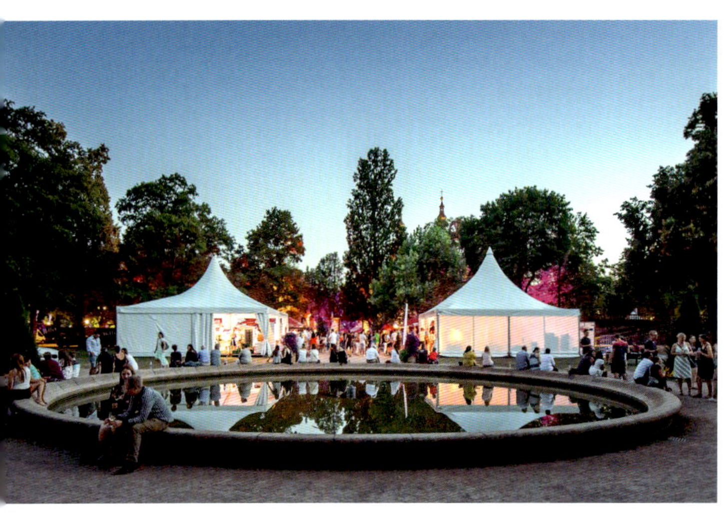

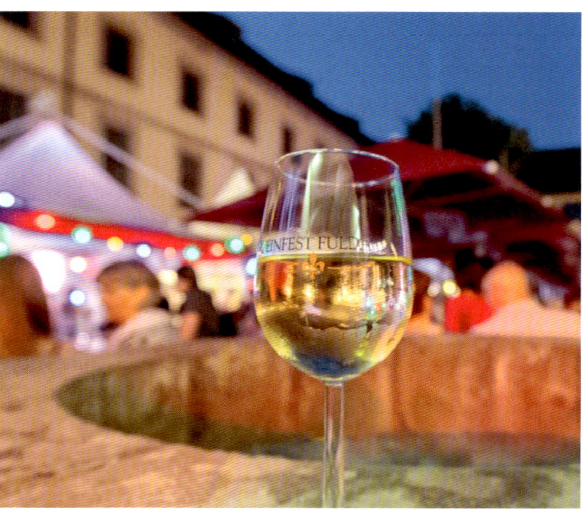

Konzerte mit Weltstars wie Elton John oder Sting vor der nächtlichen Kulisse des Doms: Das sind die Markenzeichen der Domplatzkonzerte.

Concerts with international stars like Elton John or Sting playing in the night shadows of the cathedral: the successful concept behind the cathedral square concerts.

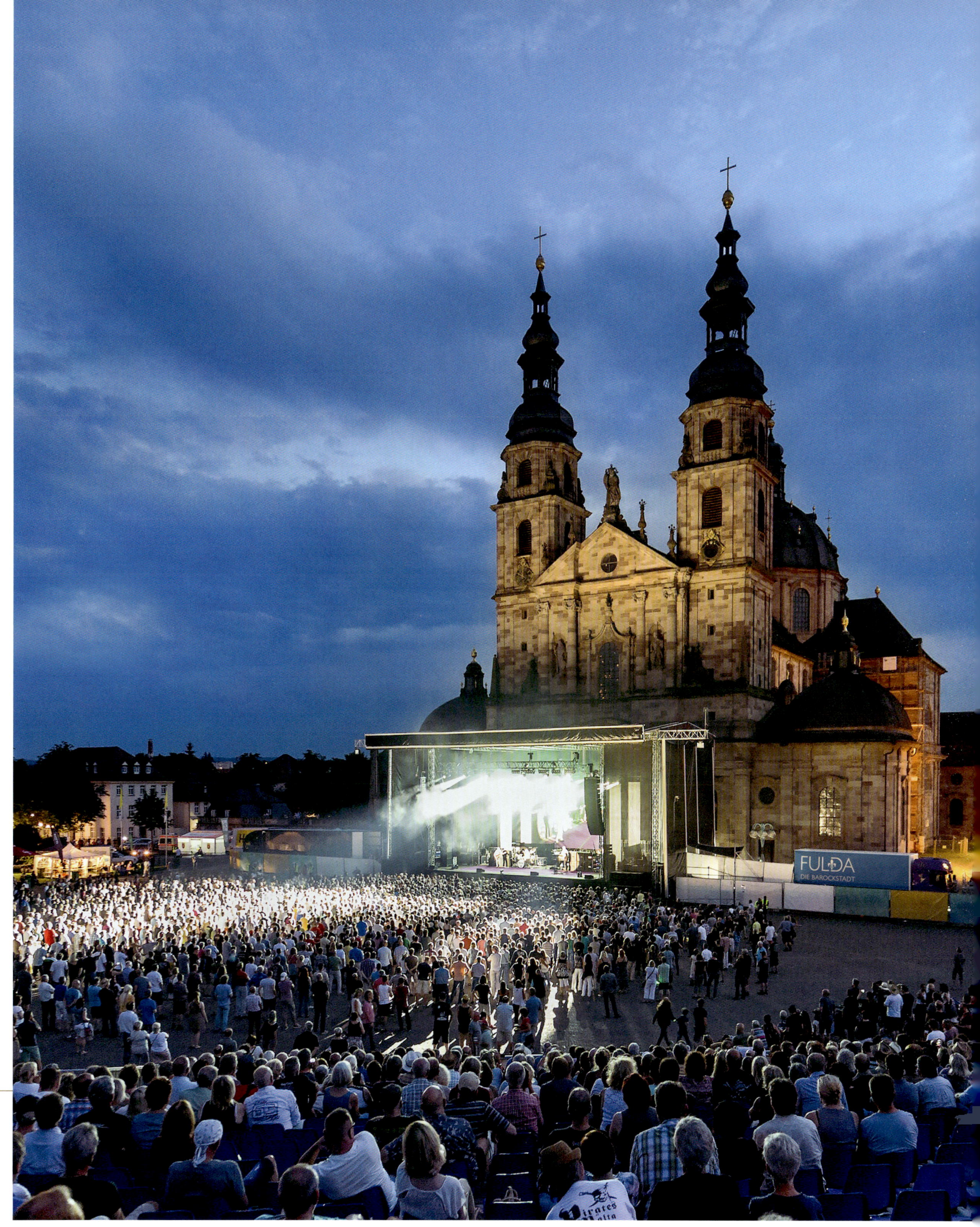
FULDA
DIE BAROCKSTADT

Seit der Premiere des Musicals „Bonifatius“ 2004 hat sich das Fuldaer Schlosstheater zu einem Hotspot der deutschen Musicalszene entwickelt. In Fulda entstandene Produktionen wie „Die Päpstin“, „Die Schatzinsel“ oder „Der Medicus“ haben viele Branchenpreise abgeräumt und sind Publikumsmagneten.

Since the premiere of the musical "Bonifatius" in 2004 the Fulda Schlosstheater has developed into a hotspot of the German musical scene. The productions staged in Fulda like "Pope Joan", "Treasure Island" and "The Physician" have been major hits and have picked up many prizes.

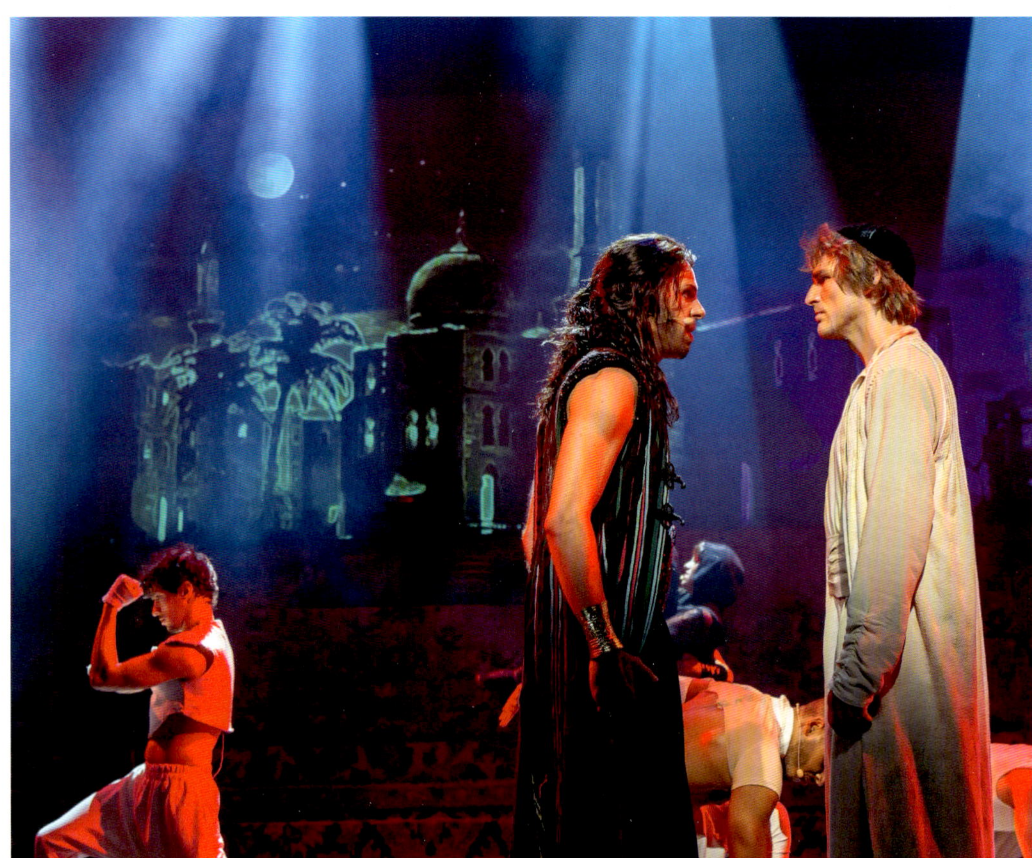

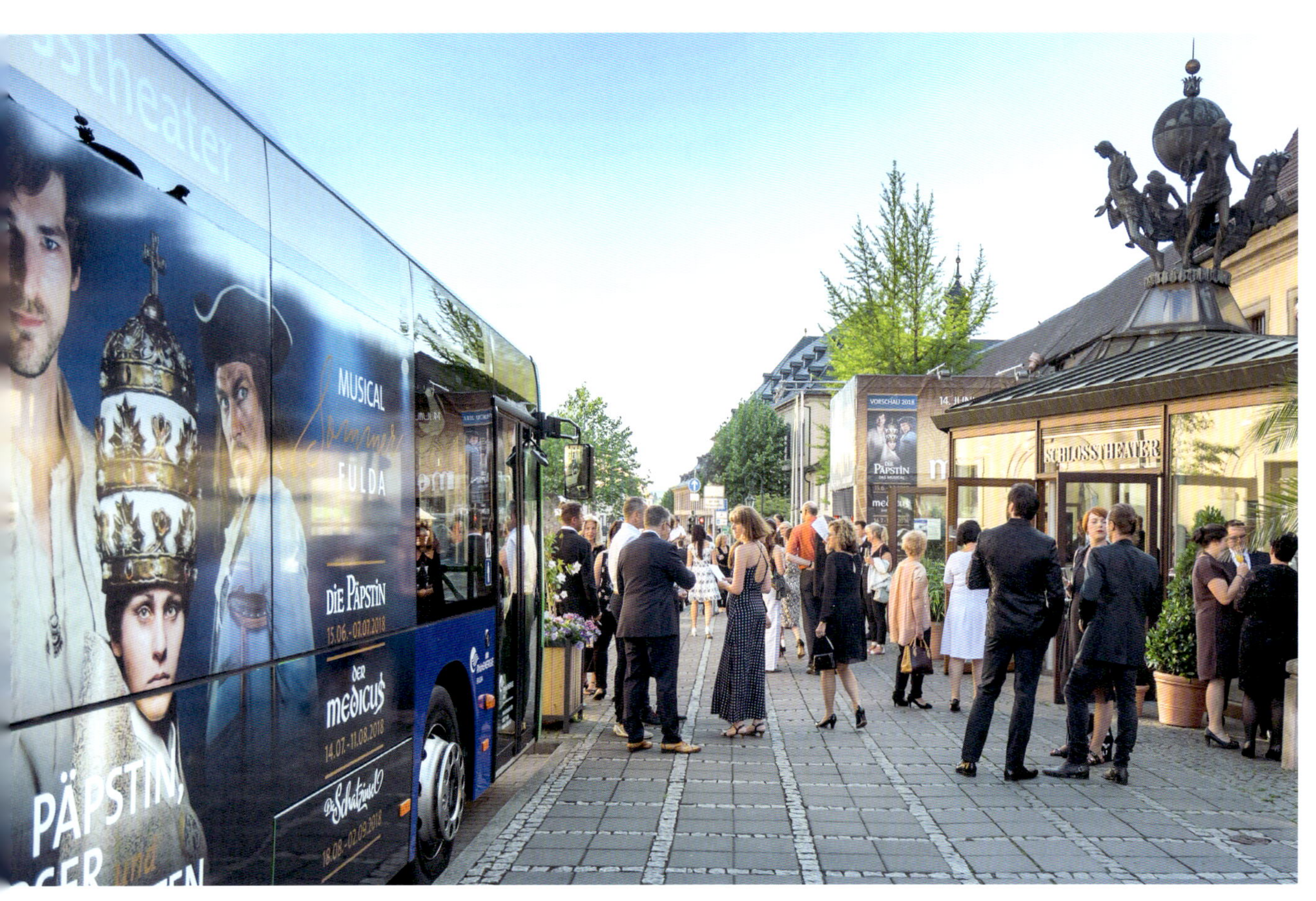

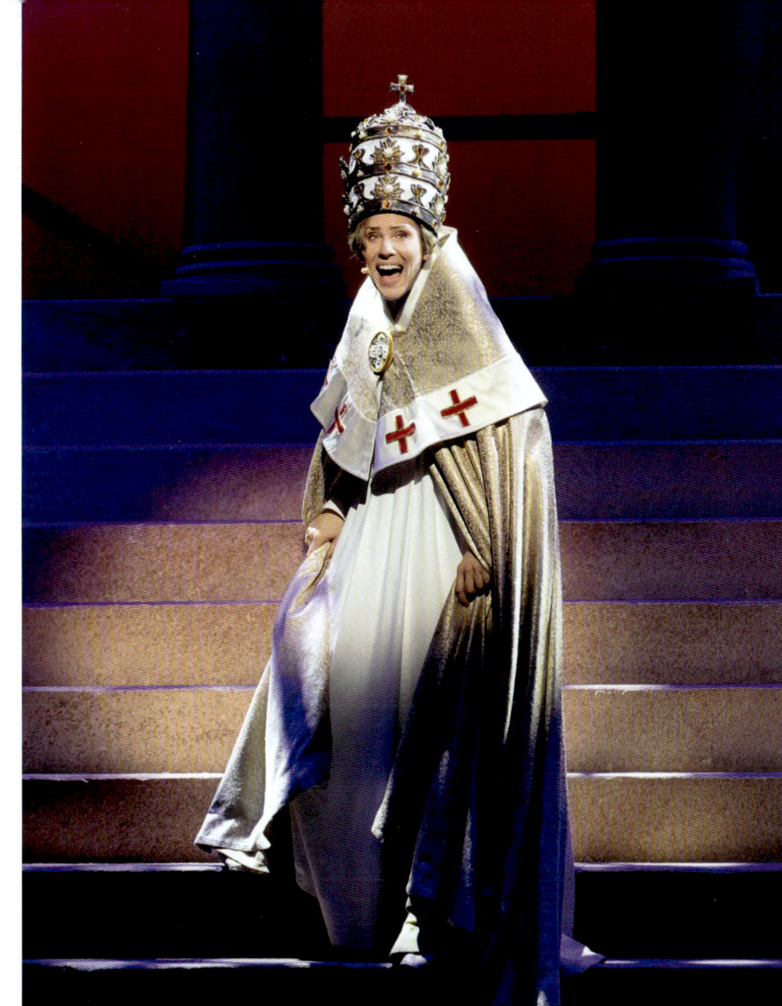

International renommierte Sängerinnen und Sänger, mitreißende Choreografien sowie knallige Bühneneffekte machen den Musicalbesuch zum Erlebnis.

Internationally acclaimed singers, thrilling choreography and spectacular stage effects ensure that the musicals are a really wonderful experience.

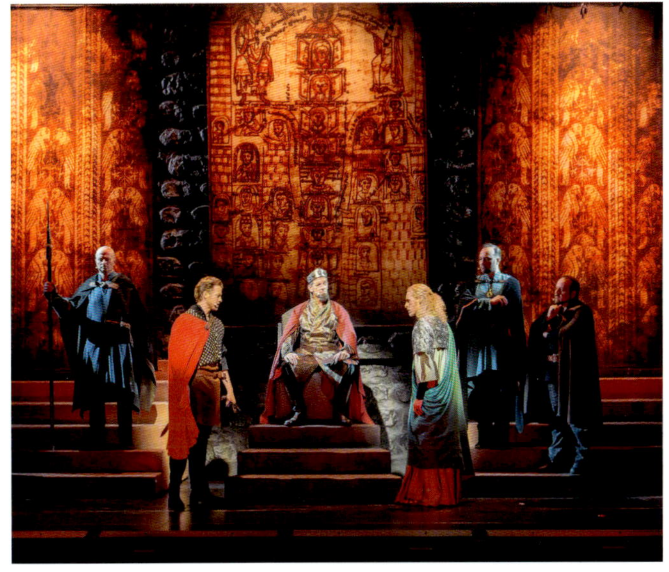

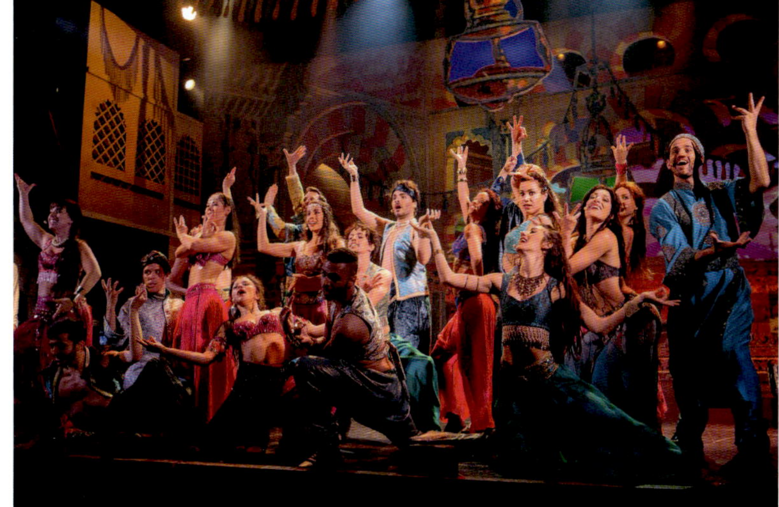

Aber auch außerhalb der Musicalsaison lockt das Fuldaer Schlosstheater mit einem ambitionierten Programm in den Sparten Theater, Ballett, Oper und Konzert.

But also outside the season of musicals the Fulda Schlosstheater has an attractive programme of events which includes drama, ballet, opera and concerts.

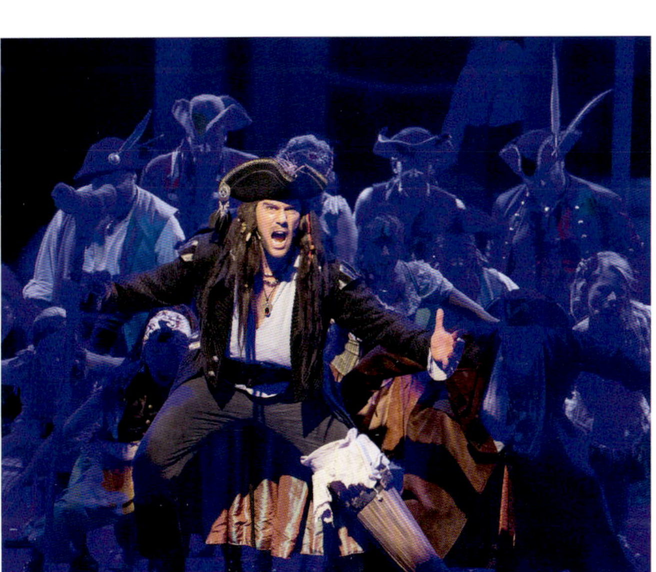

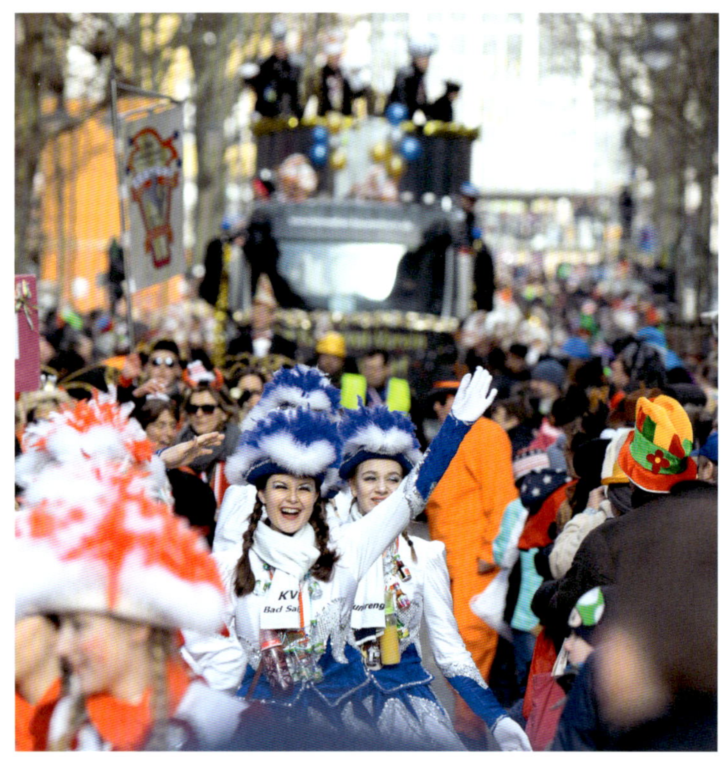

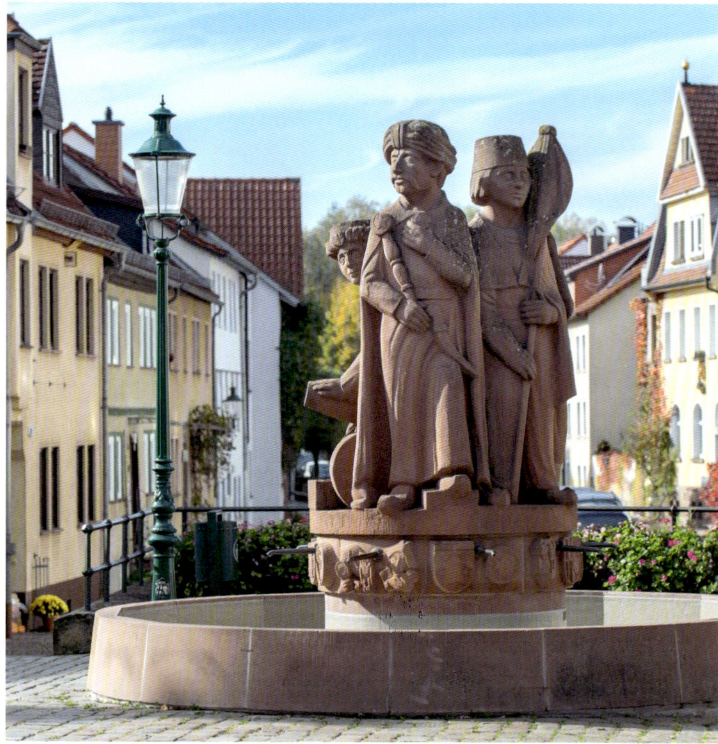

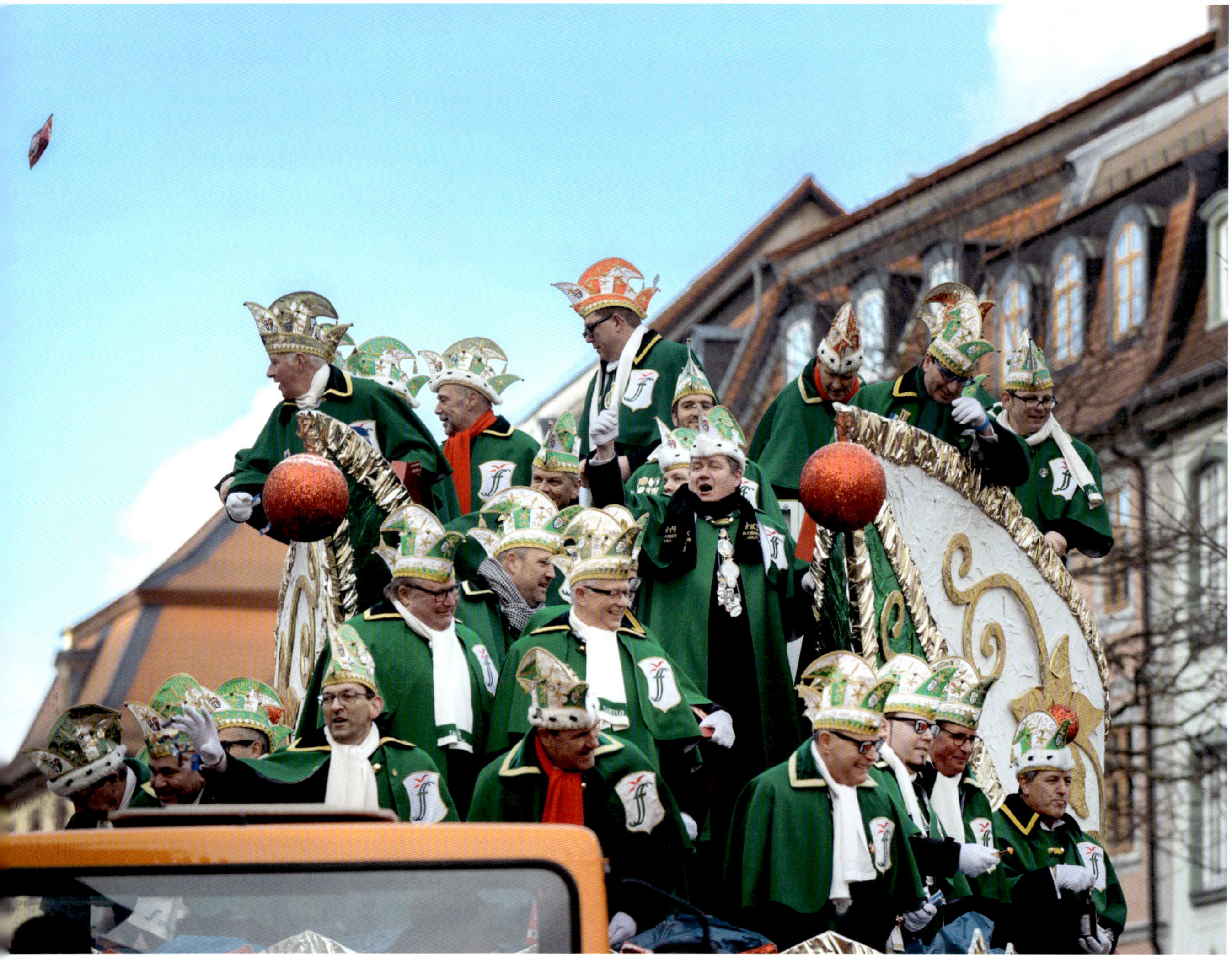

An die Fastnachtstradition und die Vielzahl an aktiven Vereinen erinnert der Fastnachtsbrunnen (oben rechts) ganzjährig, während sich der eigentliche Straßenkarneval in der Innenstadt auf den Fastnachtssonntag und den Rosenmontag konzentriert.

Throughout the year the carnival fountain is a reminder of the city's carnival tradition and its many active clubs (top right), but the actual street carnival in the city centre is concentrated on just two days – Carnival Sunday and Rosenmontag (Carnival Monday).

Große und kleine Gartenfreunde kommen beim Fürstlichen Gartenfest auf Schloss Fasanerie auf ihre Kosten. An den Veranstaltungstagen strömen jedes Jahr aufs Neue Tausende Besucher auf das Schlossgelände.

Young and old garden fans all find something that is just right for them at the Princely Garden Festival at Schloss Fasanerie. Every year thousands of visitors flock to this event in the palace grounds.

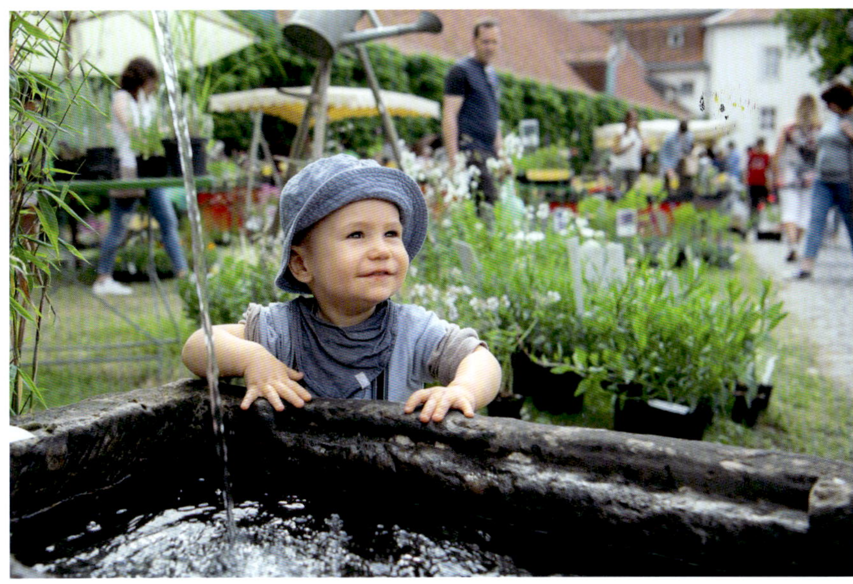

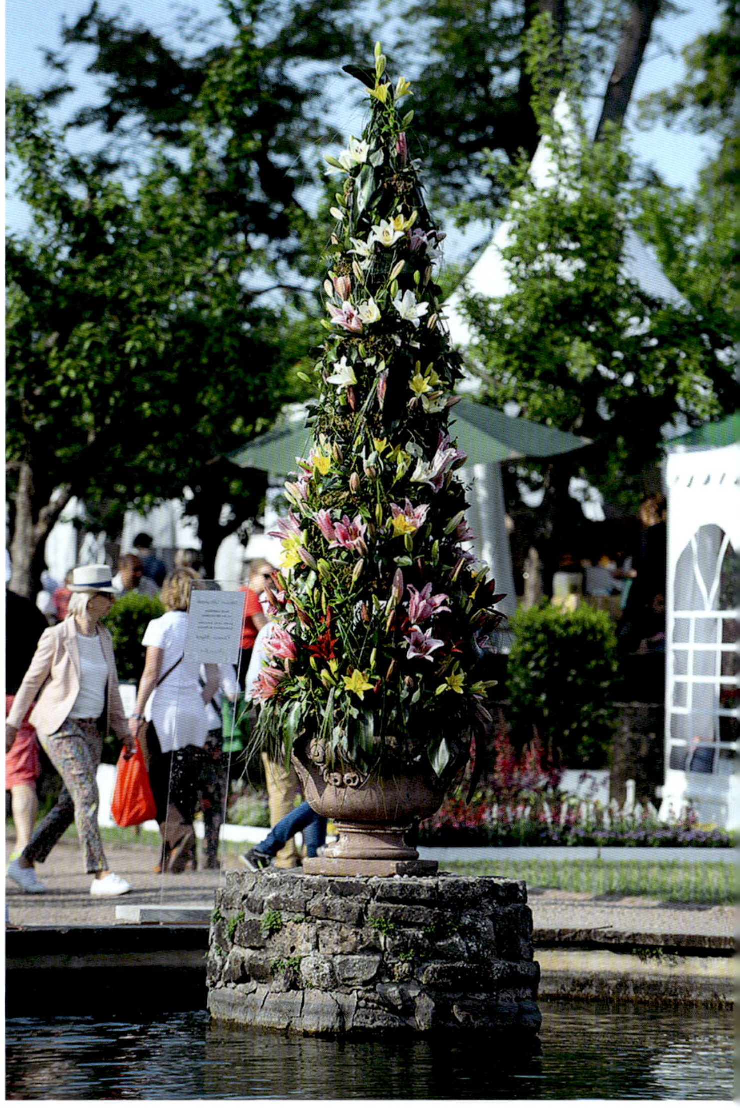

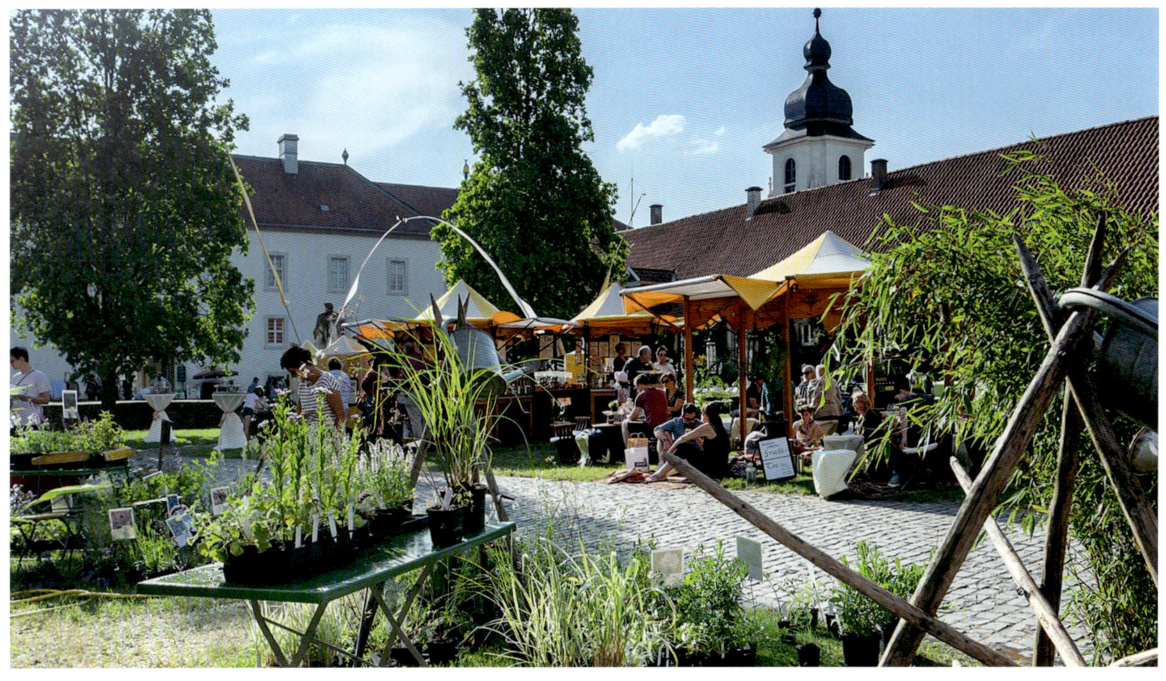

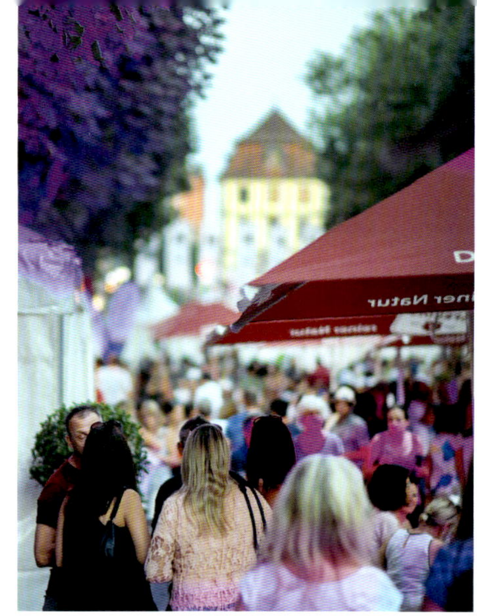

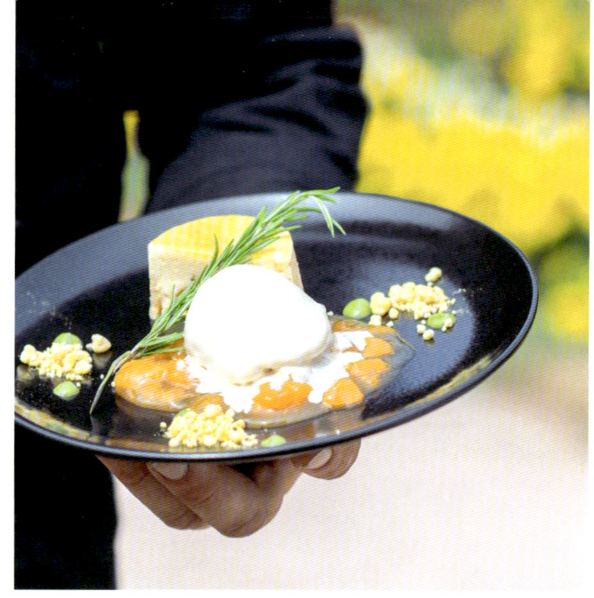

Genuss und barocke Lebensfreude: Das liegt in Fulda eng beieinander.

Culinary delights and baroque joie-de-vivre go hand-in-hand in Fulda.

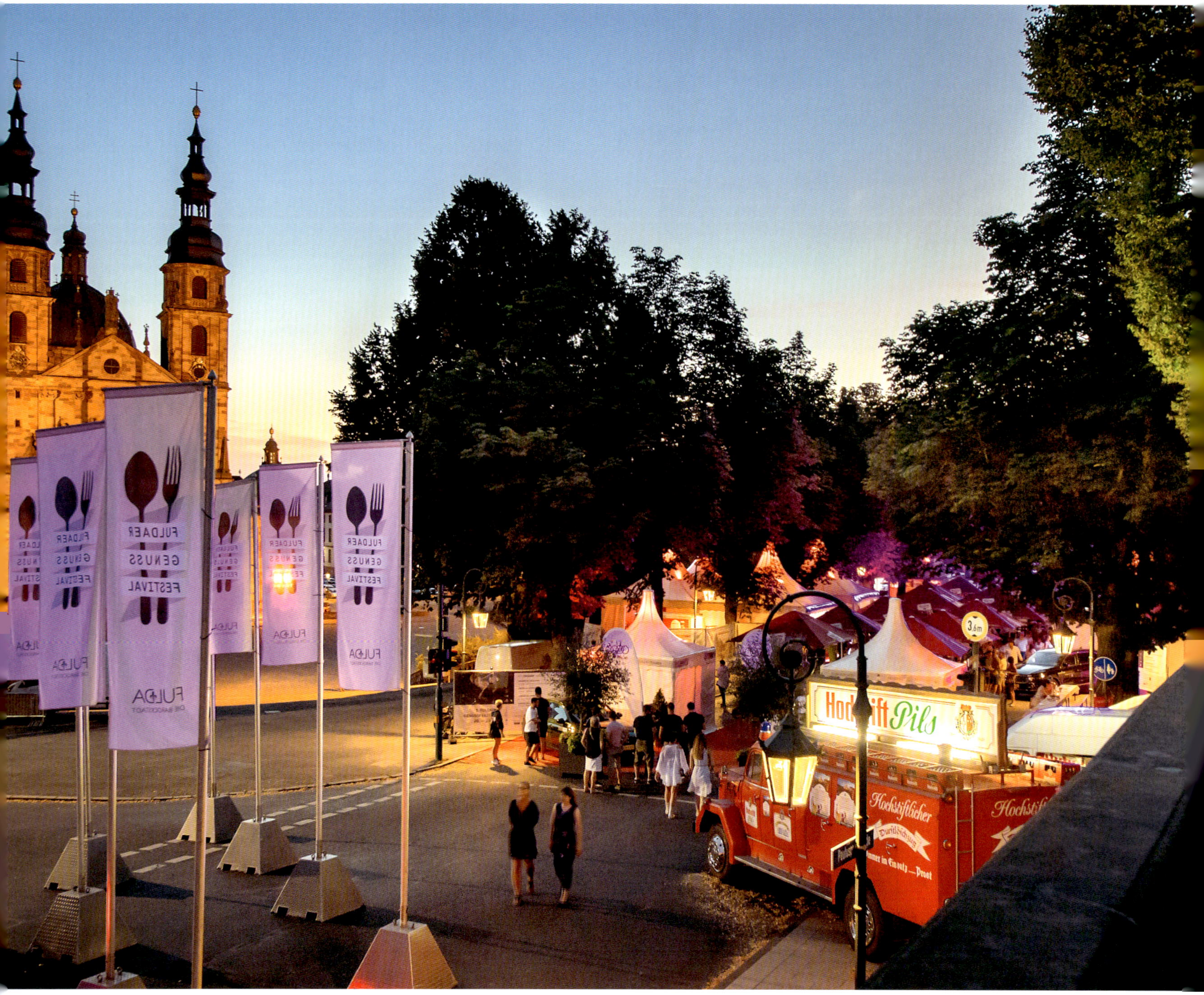

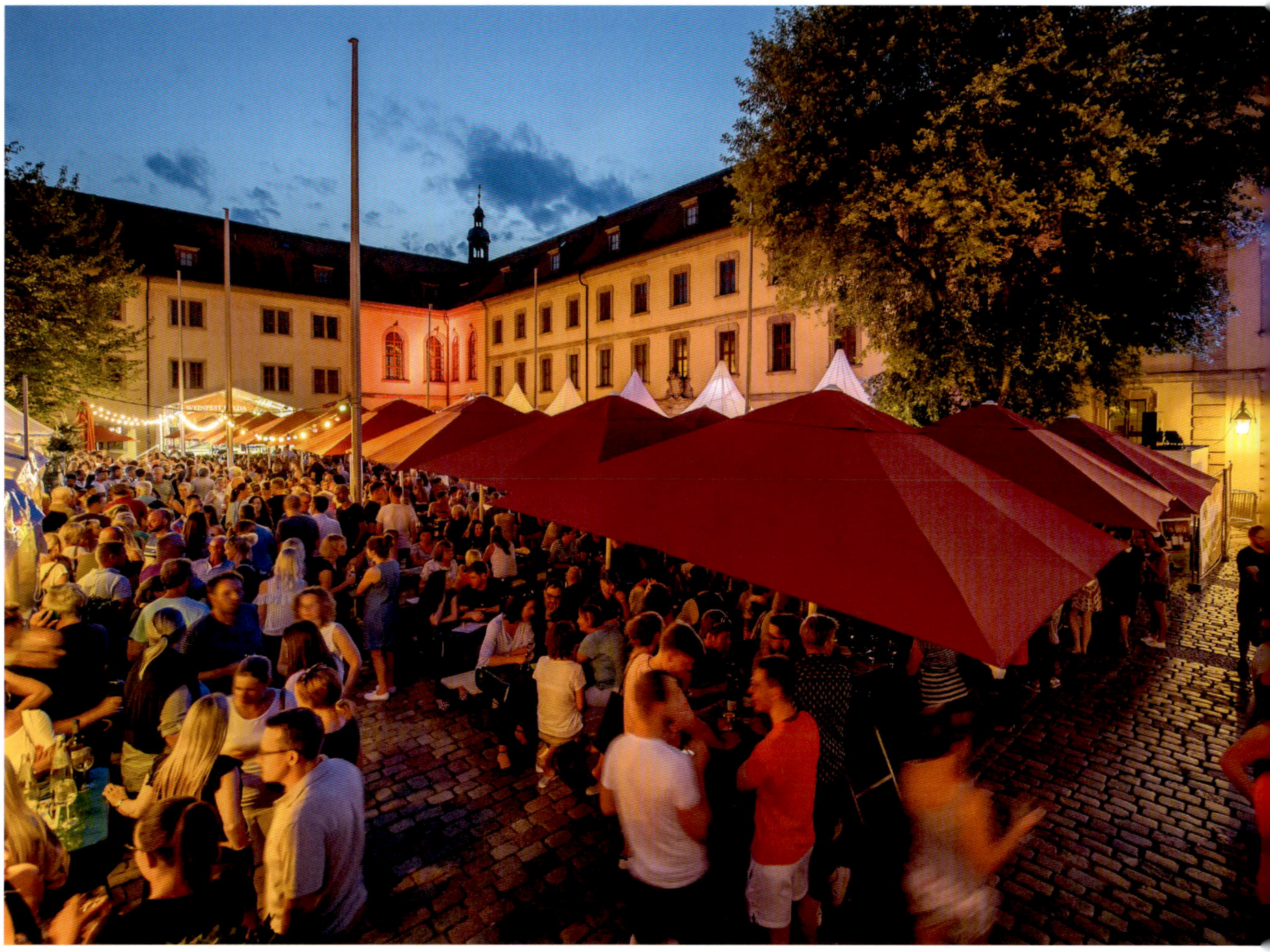

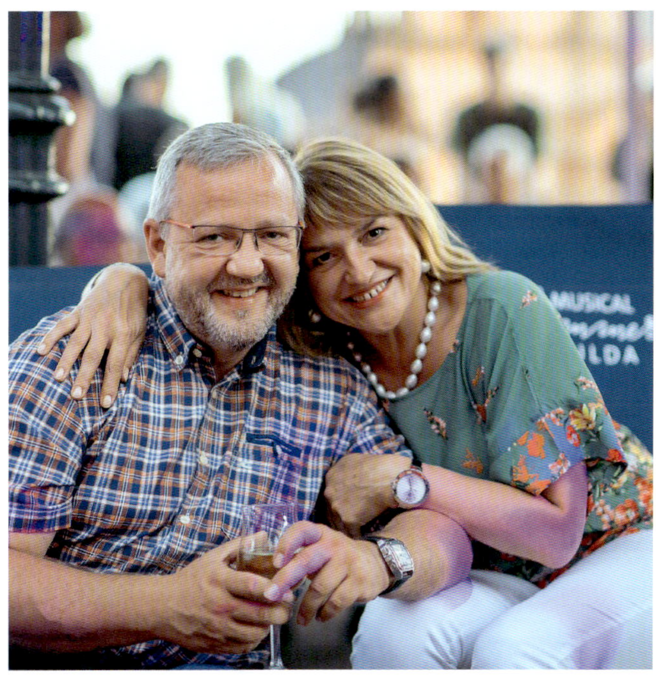

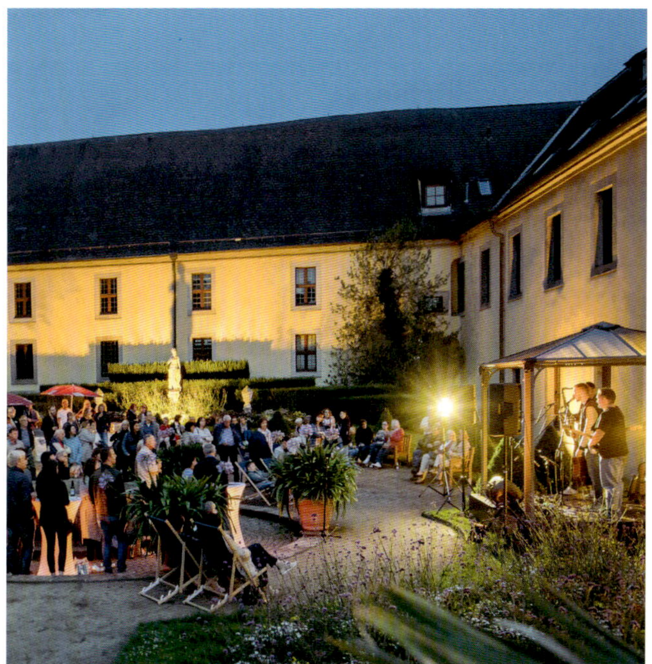

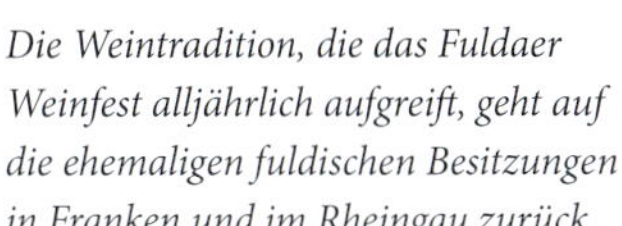

Die Weintradition, die das Fuldaer Weinfest alljährlich aufgreift, geht auf die ehemaligen fuldischen Besitzungen in Franken und im Rheingau zurück.

The Fulda wine tradition has its roots in the times when Fulda used to have vineyards in Franconia and on the Rhine.

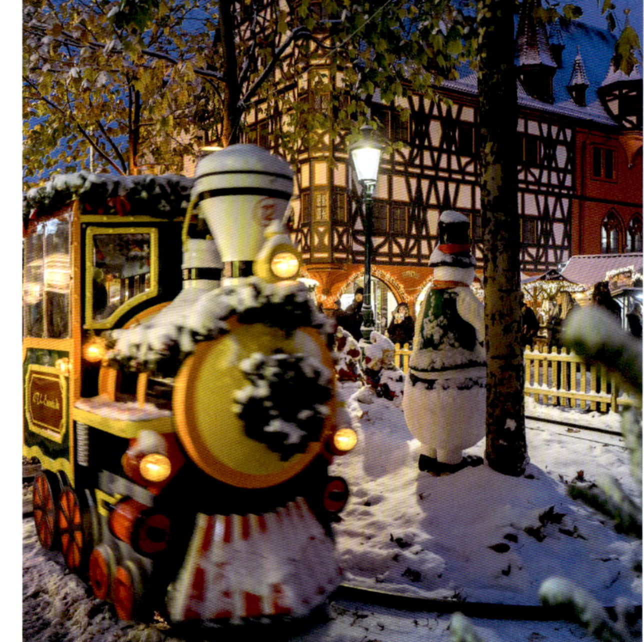

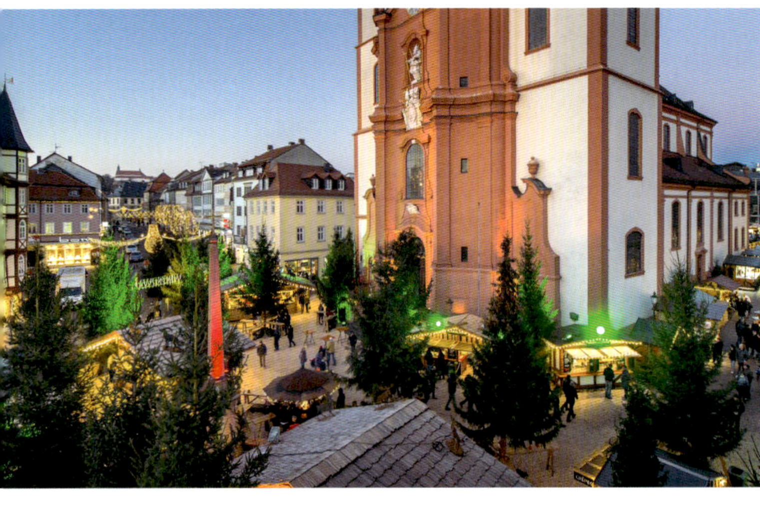

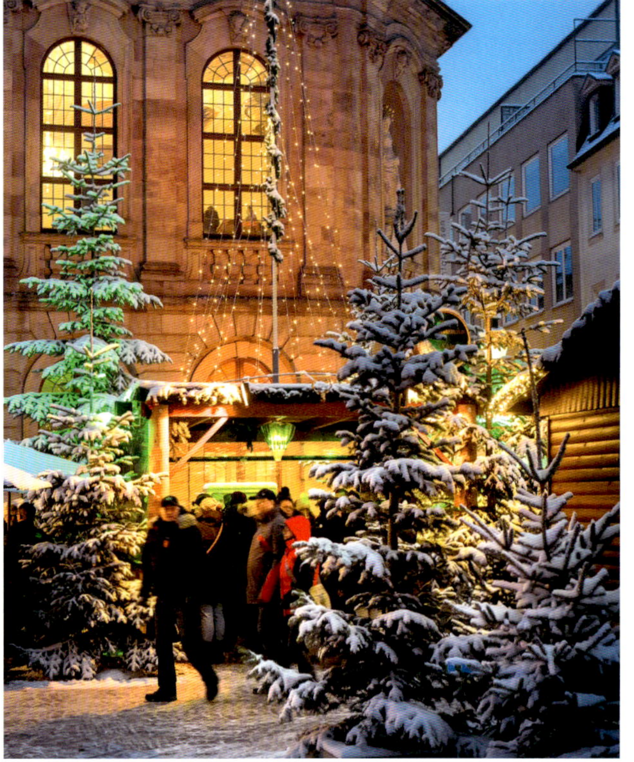

Das Areal des Fuldaer Weihnachtsmarkts erstreckt sich von der Bahnhofstraße über den Universitätsplatz und den Museumshof bis zur Stadtpfarrkirche und den Platz Unterm Heilig Kreuz.

The Christmas market stretches from the Bahnhofstrasse over the Universitätsplatz and Museumshof to the Stadtpfarrkirche and the Unterm Heilig Kreuz square.

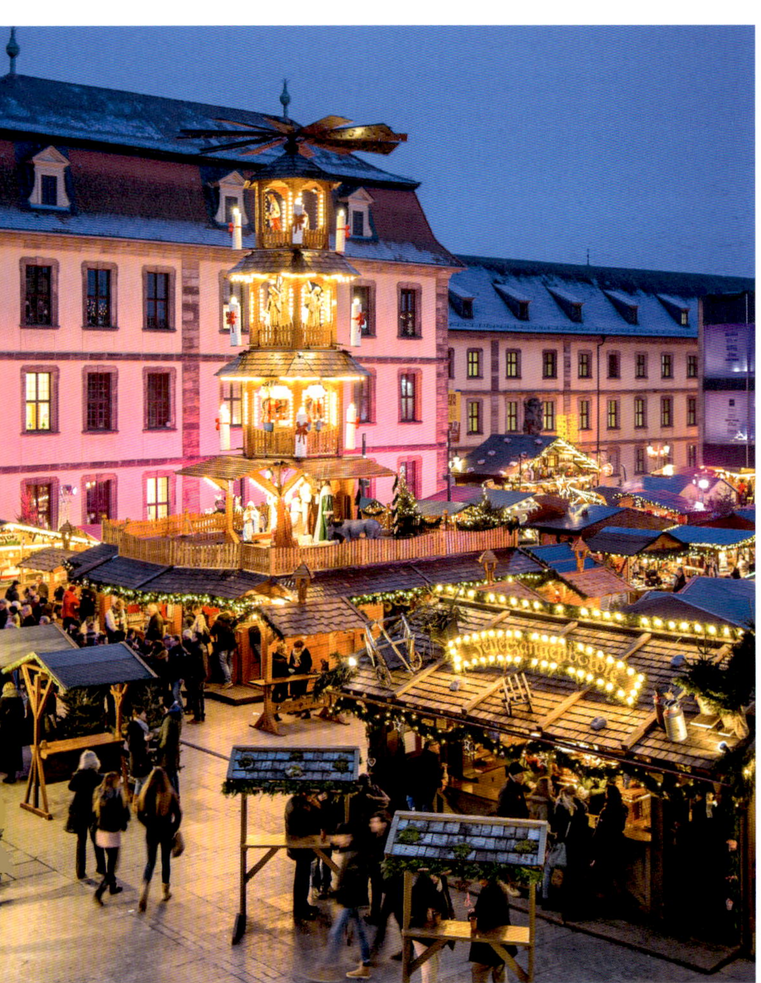

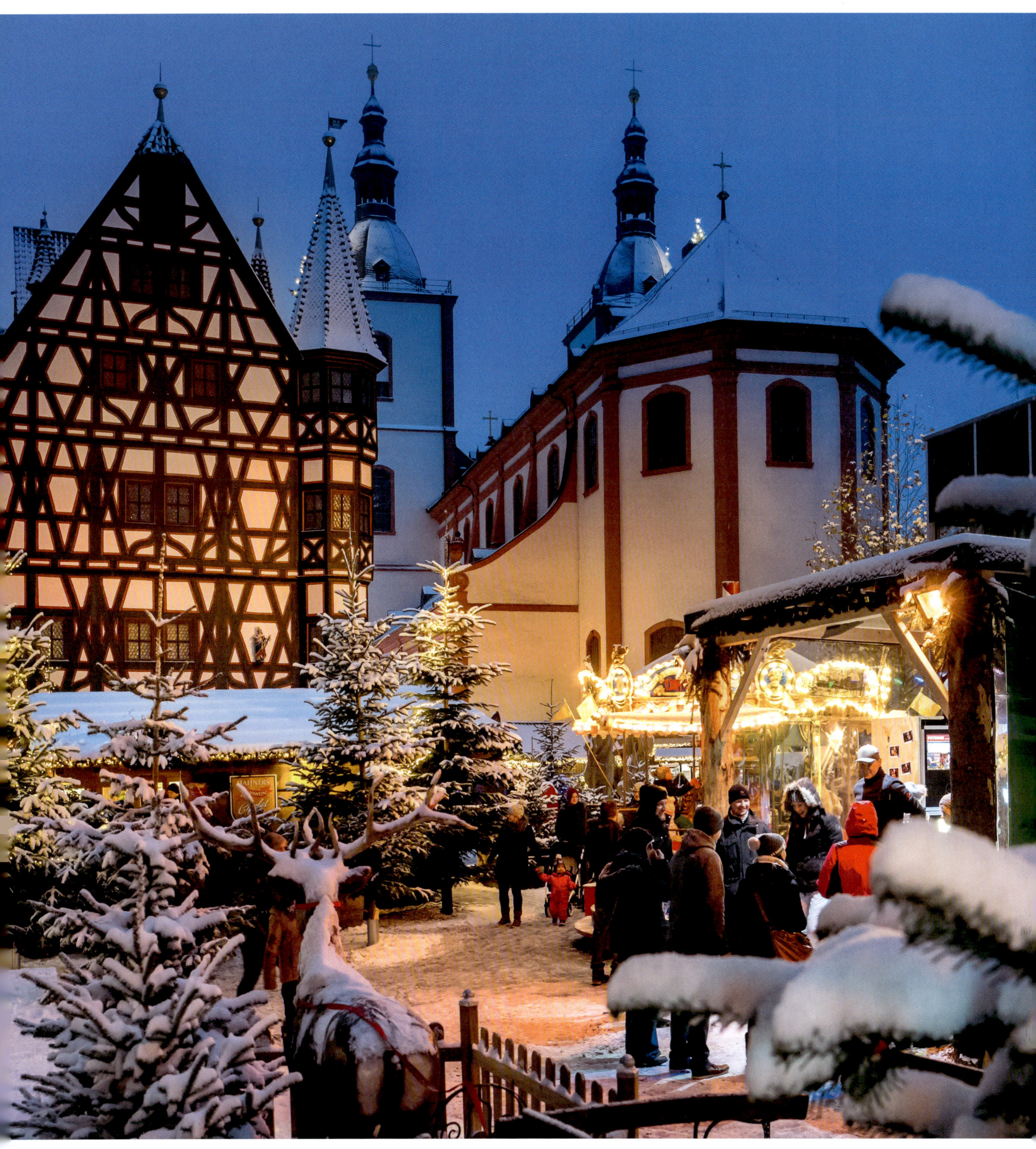

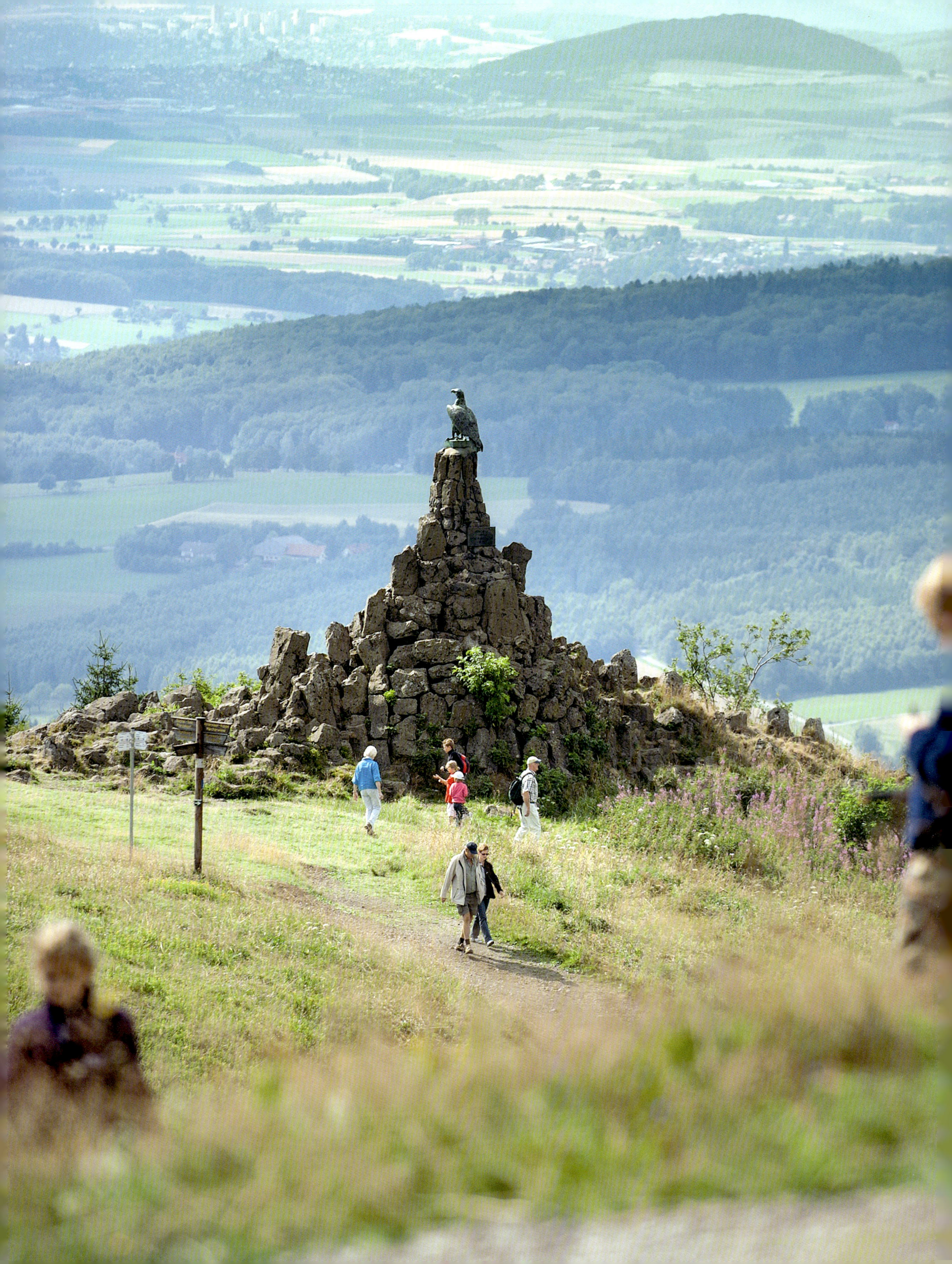

DIE RHÖN – URLAUBSZIEL DIREKT VOR DER HAUSTÜR

Die Fuldaer sind in ihre „Hausberge" regelrecht vernarrt und profitieren vom Biosphärenreservat

An der Entfernung liegt es nicht: Von Fulda aus betrachtet, sind Vogelsberg und Rhön ungefähr gleich weit weg. Doch während der Vogelsberg an Wochenenden meist nur wenige Besucher aus der nahen Domstadt zählt, so sind die Fuldaer in die Rhön geradezu vernarrt. Das besondere Liebesverhältnis hat wohl mehrere Ursachen: So gehörten weite Teile der Rhön einst zum Fürstbistum Fulda, auch sprachlich und konfessionell ist die größere Nähe mit Händen zu greifen. Hinzu kommt die markante Silhouette der Hauptkette der hessischen Rhön – von der Milseburg über Stellberg, Weiherberg, Wasserkuppe, Pferdskopf und Eube bis hin zu den Bergen der Dammersfeld-Rhön und der Mottener Haube –, welche von vielen Punkten der Stadt aus am östlichen Horizont präsent ist. Dabei bietet die Rhön die abwechslungsreichere Topografie als der flache Schildvulkan des Vogelsbergs, weshalb sie bei Wanderern, Spaziergängern, Radfahrern und Skiläufern die größeren Sympathien genießt.

Kurz gesagt: Die Rhön ist gewissermaßen das Urlaubsziel der Fuldaer direkt vor der Haustür. Und das mit langer Tradition: So hat beispielsweise auch der in drei Bundesländern aktive Rhönklub bereits seit der Gründung im Jahr 1876 seinen Hauptsitz in Fulda und hier auch eine große Mitgliederbasis. Seit 1991 ist die gesamte Rhön mit ihrem hessischen, thüringischen und bayerischen Anteil Unesco-Biosphärenreservat, was die überregionale Bekanntheit zusätzlich gesteigert hat.

The Rhön – A Holiday Destination on Your Doorstep

The attractiveness of Fulda and its high quality of life result from its proximity to forested hills

A common question: How come generally only very few people from Fulda set off to the Vogelsberg at the weekend, while they are crazy about the Rhön? It is not a question of distance as the two areas are just as far to travel. There are several reasons for this love affair: historically large areas of the Rhön belonged to the territories of the prince-bishops and both in language and denomination there is more of an affinity to the Rhön. In addition, there is the striking sky silhouette of the Rhön, which can be seen on the eastern horizon from many points in the city. The Rhön also offers a more varied landscape than the flatter Vogelsberg and therefore attracts more hikers, cyclists and skiers. To put it briefly, the Rhön is a holiday destination on your doorstep. This has been the case for many years now: the Rhön Club has had its headquarters in Fulda since its foundation in 1876 has a large membership base here. Since 1991 the entire Rhön area has been listed as UNESCO Biosphere Reserve, ensuring that the Rhön has become better known outside the region.

Das Fliegerdenkmal an der Wasserkuppe, 1923 zum Andenken an die im Ersten Weltkrieg getöteten Flieger geschaffen, ist eines der beliebtesten Fotomotive auf dem höchsten Berg der Rhön. Der Blick reicht von hier Richtung Westen bis ins Fuldaer Land und zum Vogelsberg, bei klarem Wetter sogar bis zum Taunus.

This monument on the Wasserkuppe, which was erected in 1923, is dedicated to the pilots who died in the WW I. It is one of the most popular photo motifs on the highest summit of the Rhön. From this point you have views to the west which reach over the Fulda area to the Vogelsberg mountains and, on clear days, all the way to the Taunus.

Der Basalt ist das prägende Gestein der Rhön – und war in früheren Zeiten ein regelrechter Exportschlager, etwa beim Bau von Hochwasserschutzanlagen an der Nordsee.

Basalt is the stone which is most associated with the Rhön. In the past, basalt was a real export hit and was, for example, used for the construction of sea walls along the North Sea coast.

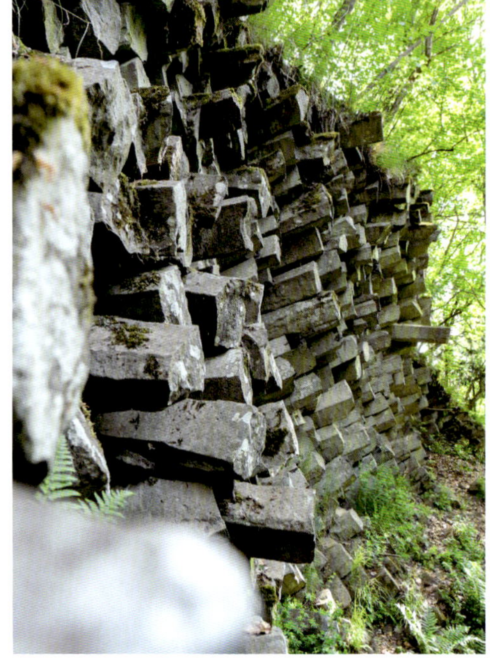

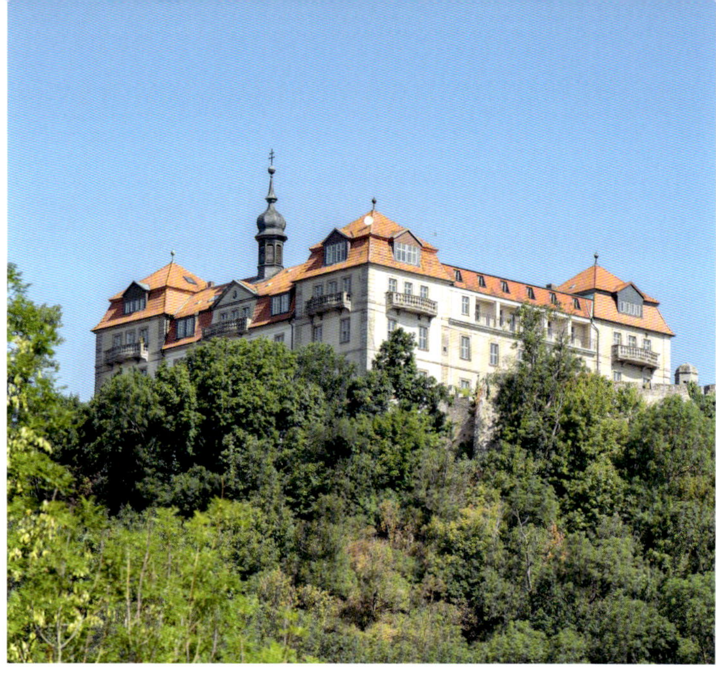

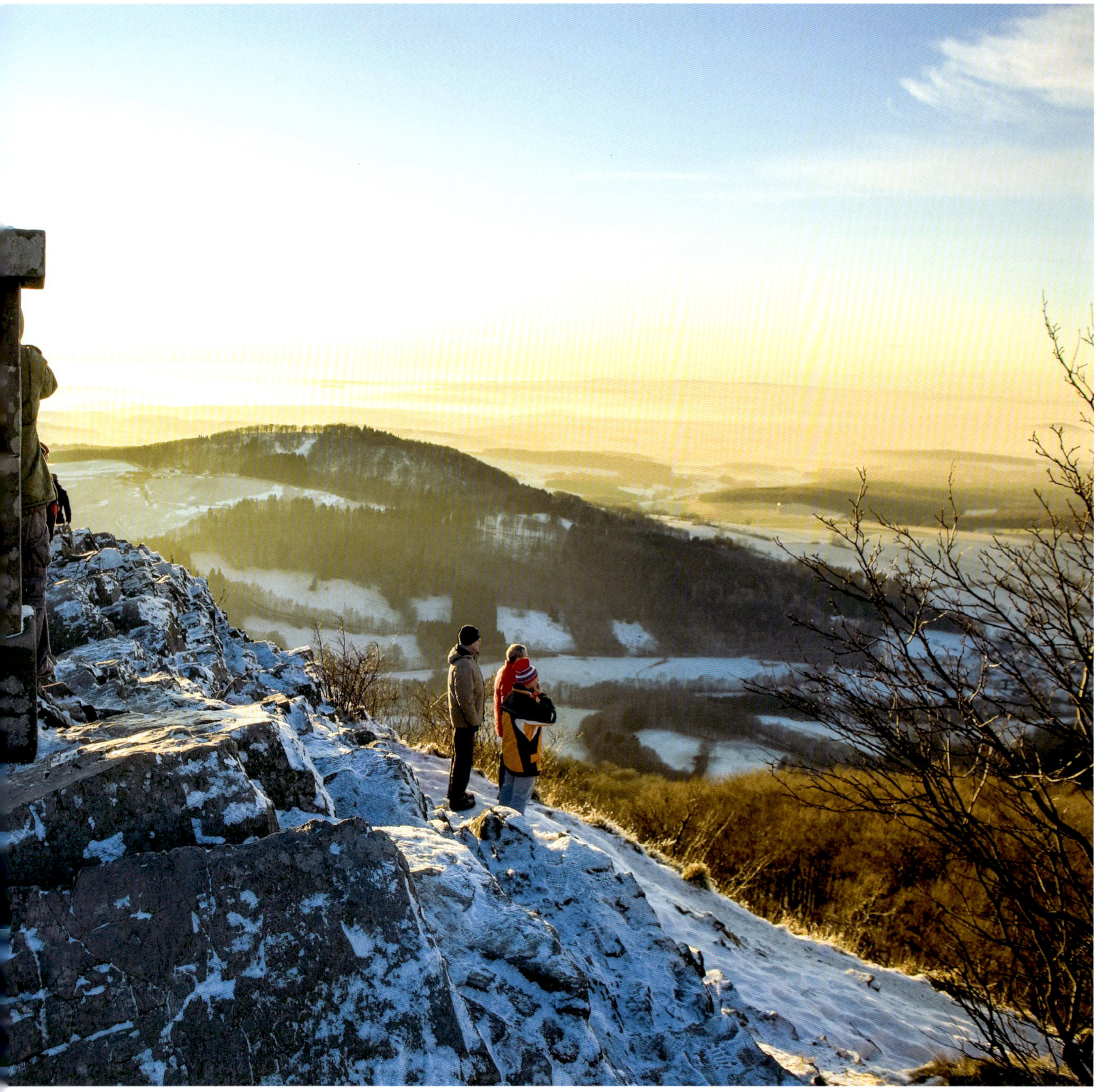

Zu allen Jahreszeiten hat die Rhön (links: der Gipfel der Milseburg) ihre Reize. Und architektonisch haben auch die Fuldaer Fürstäbte (wie hier auf Schloss Bieberstein, Foto oben) ihre Spuren hinterlassen.

In all seasons the Rhön has its attractions (here the peak of the Milseburg). Architecturally, the Fulda prince-abbots have also left their mark here (e.g. Schloss Bieberstein – top photo).

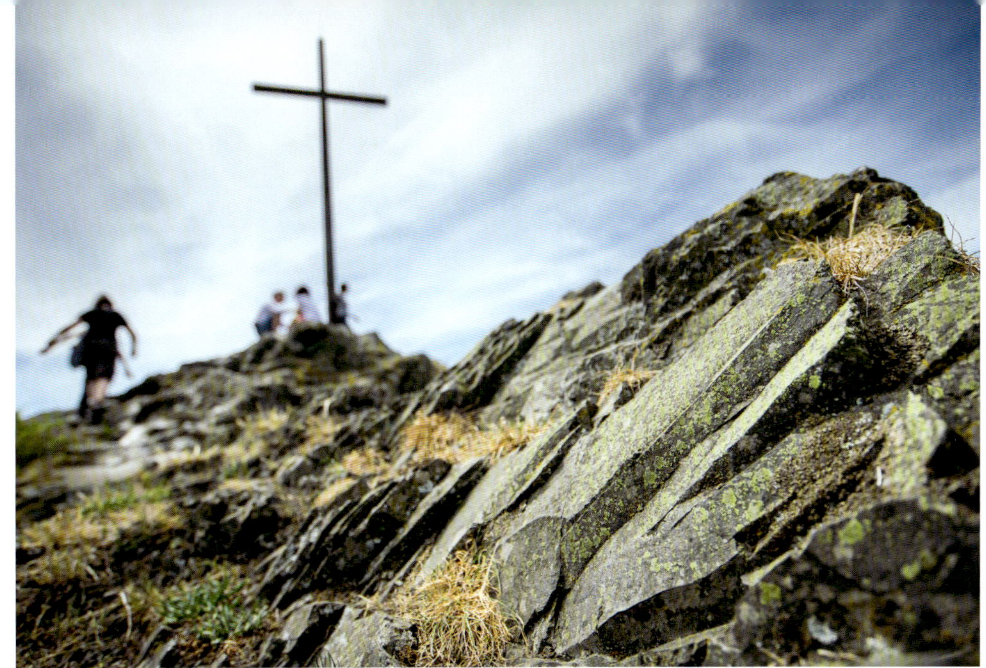

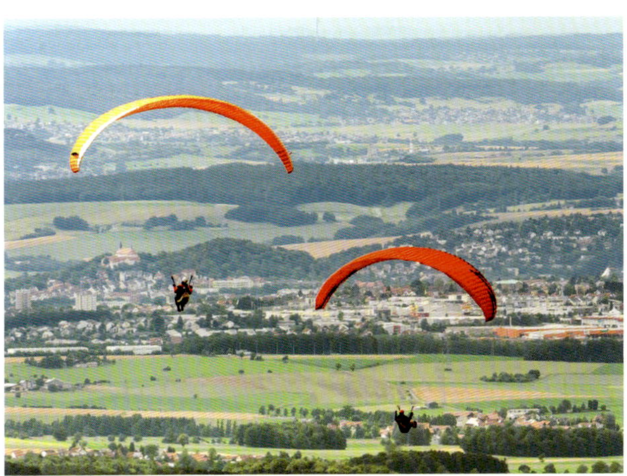

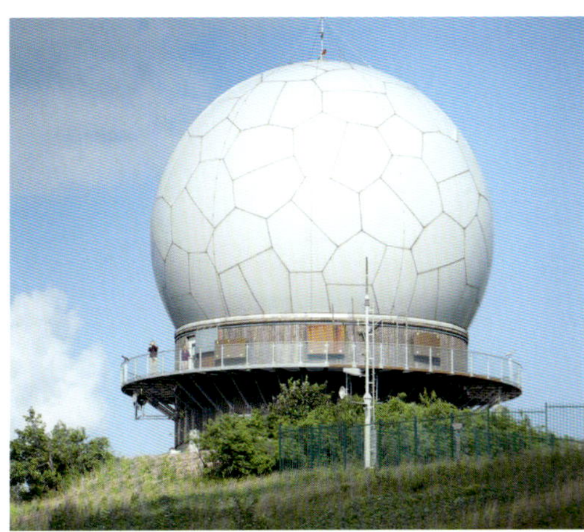

Die Wasserkuppe mit dem Radom als weithin sichtbare Landmarke gilt als Wiege des Segelflugs, noch heute ist sie ein Eldorado für Gleitschirmflieger, Drachenflieger, Segler – und im Winter auch der Snowkiter.

The Wasserkuppe, which is easily identified by its characteristic "radom", is regarded as the cradle of gliding. Still today, it is an eldorado for gliders, paragliders, hang gliders and, in winter, snowkiters.

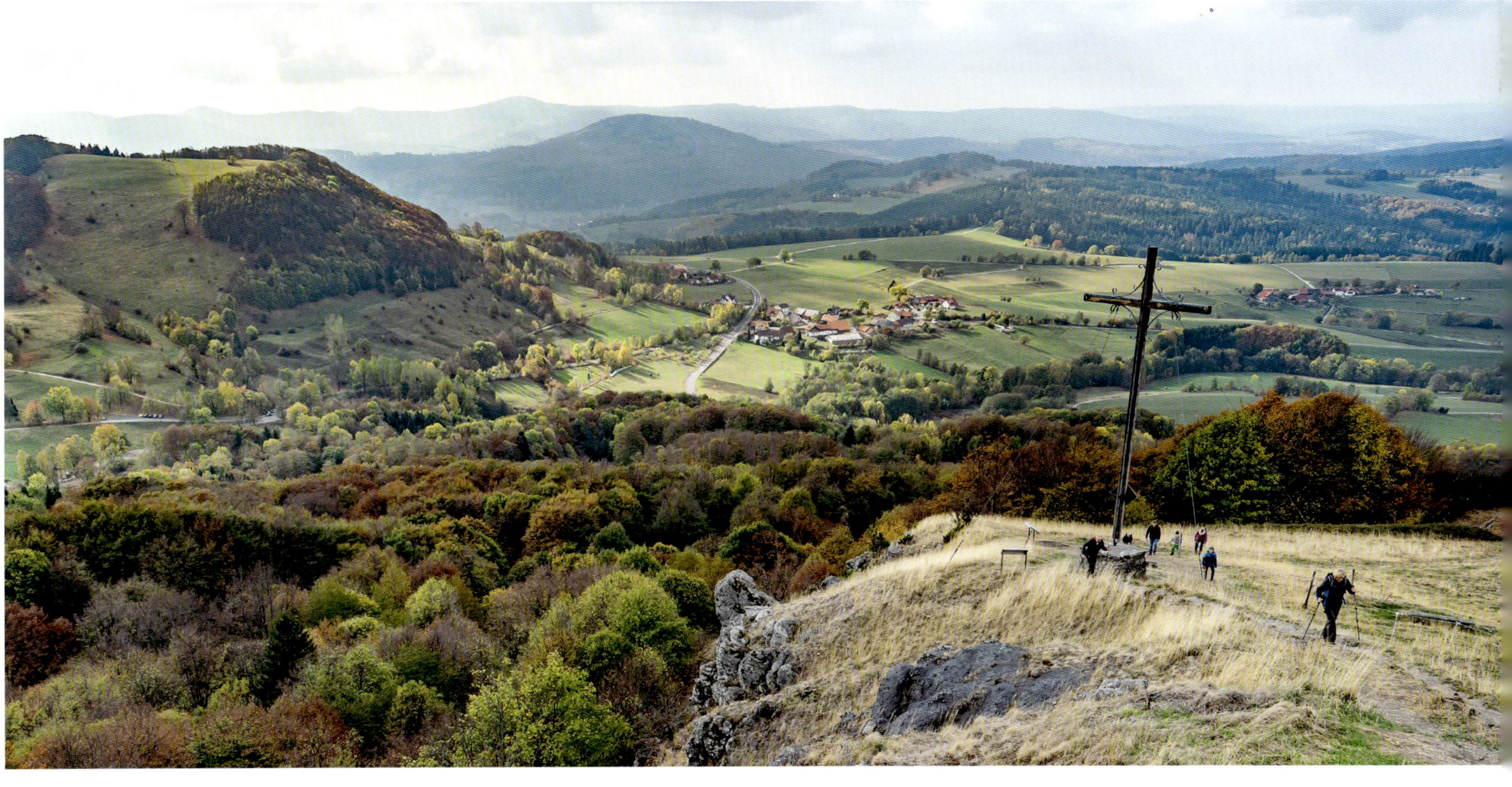

JOHANNES HELLER

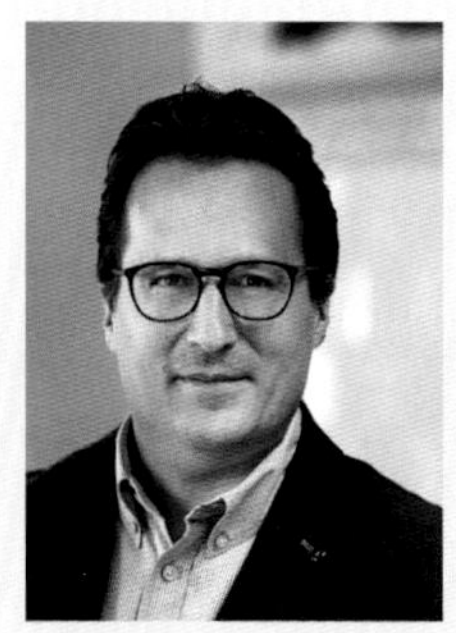

Johannes Heller (Jahrgang 1972) stammt aus Fulda und hat als Journalist 19 Jahre in seiner Heimatstadt gearbeitet, bevor er als Pressesprecher in die Magistratspressestelle der Stadt Fulda wechselte. Er möchte mit seinen Texten im Bildband Touristen und Einheimische gleichermaßen für die Schönheiten und Besonderheiten der Stadt sensibilisieren und sie gleichzeitig ermutigen, selbst auf Entdeckungsreise durch die Stadt zu gehen und dabei scheinbar Vertrautes aus neuen Perspektiven in den Blick zu nehmen.

CHRISTIAN TECH

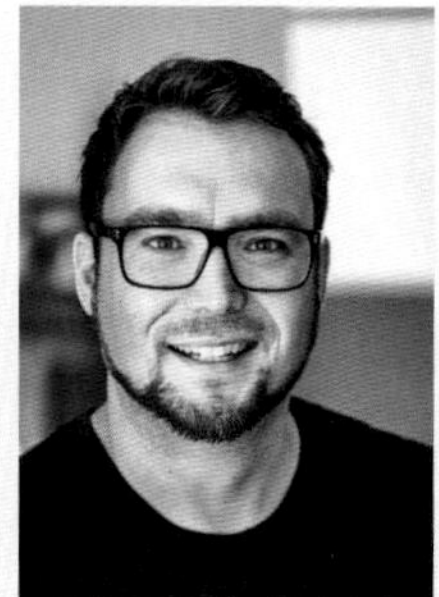

Christian Tech (Jahrgang 1980) ist selbstständiger Fotograf und Grafiker. Er lebt seit 15 Jahren in Fulda und schätzt die Barockstadt wegen ihres besonderen Flairs. Tech arbeitet nicht nur für Auftraggeber in der Region, sondern für Kunden in ganz Deutschland. Dazu zählen Unternehmen und Akteure aus vielen Branchen. Besonders wichtig ist ihm beim Fotografieren sauberes Handwerk, Hingabe und Beharrlichkeit für das perfekte Bild und Einfühlungsvermögen für Mensch und Motiv.

IMPRESSUM

EIN BILDERBOGEN AUS DER BAROCKSTADT FULDA
Von Johannes Heller und Christian Tech

Koordination
Elisabeth Schrimpf

Autor
Johannes Heller

Fotografie
Christian Tech

Gestaltung
Christian Tech, photoplusgraphic

Übersetzung
Rod Williams

Korrektorat
Dorotheé Baganz, Michael Imhof Verlag;
Michael Scuffil, Leverkusen (englisch)

Herstellung
Michael Imhof Verlag

1. Auflage 2019

Dank
Unser besonderer Dank gilt allen, die uns Türen geöffnet und damit ungewöhnliche Blickwinkel ermöglicht haben.

Stettiner Straße 25 | D-36100 Petersberg
Tel. 0661/2919166-0 | Fax 0661/2919166-9
info@imhof-verlag.de | www.imhof-verlag.com
Reproduktion: Michael Imhof Verlag
Druck: Druckerei Rindt GmbH & Co. KG, Fulda

ISBN 978-3-7319-0716-9
Printed in EU

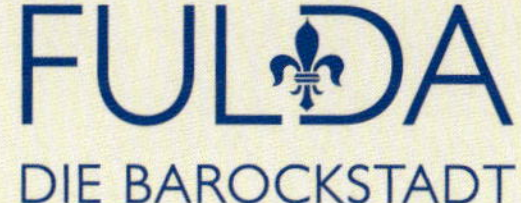

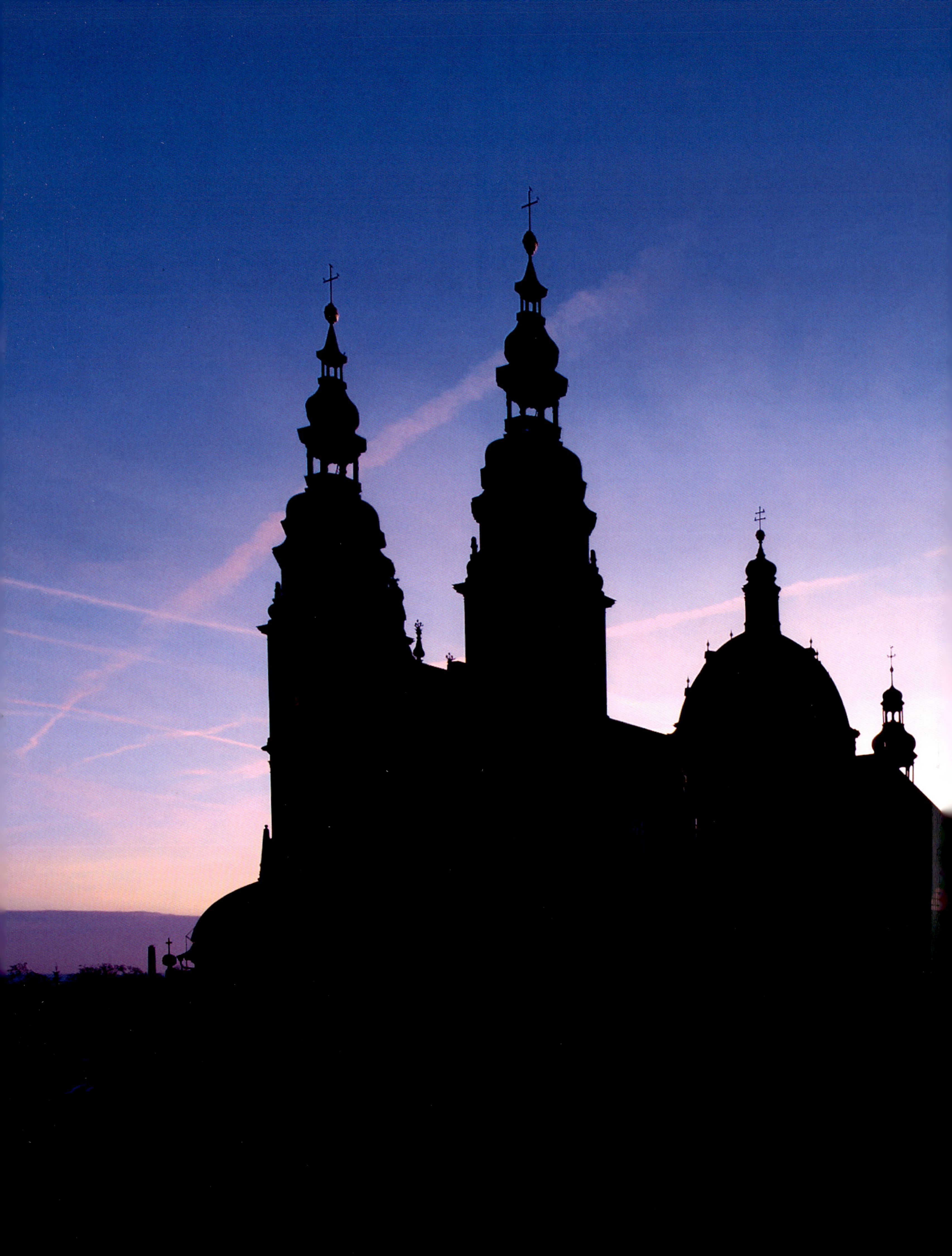